Advances in Spatial Science

The Regional Science Series

This series contains scientific studies focusing on spatial phenomena, utilising theoretical frameworks, analytical methods, and empirical procedures specifically designed for spatial analysis. Advances in Spatial Science brings together innovative spatial research utilising concepts, perspectives, and methods relevant to both basic science and policy making. The aim is to present advances in spatial science to an informed readership in universities, research organisations, and policy-making institutions throughout the world.

The type of material considered for publication in the series includes: Monographs of theoretical and applied research in spatial science; state-of-the-art volumes in areas of basic research; reports of innovative theories and methods in spatial science; tightly edited reports from specially organised research seminars. The series and the volumes published in it are indexed by Scopus.

More information about this series at http://www.springer.com/series/3302

Madalena Fonseca • Ugo Fratesi
Editors

Regional Upgrading in Southern Europe

Spatial Disparities and Human Capital

Springer

Editors
Madalena Fonseca
University of Porto
Lisboa, Portugal

Ugo Fratesi
Department ABC
Politecnico di Milano
Milano, Italy

ISSN 1430-9602 ISSN 2197-9375 (electronic)
Advances in Spatial Science
ISBN 978-3-319-49817-1 ISBN 978-3-319-49818-8 (eBook)
DOI 10.1007/978-3-319-49818-8

Library of Congress Control Number: 2017940044

Printed on acid-free paper

This Springer imprint is published by Springer Nature
The registered company is Springer International Publishing AG
The registered company address is: Gewerbestrasse 11, 6330 Cham, Switzerland

For my children Isabel and Alexandre, with love.

Madalena

Acknowledgement

This book is the result of a long, winding road. The initial idea was to bring together scholars from the four Southern European countries and different scientific areas related to regional development and European policies to discuss our common peripheral condition, but the project turned into a rather long process. Bringing together 30 people from different countries, regions and institutions, with their own commitments, engagements and everyday obligations was not easy. We are hence very grateful to our colleagues for their extraordinary contributions, critical and updated, and for sticking to the theme. We hope that this book will be a building block of a future relevant strand of research focused on Southern Europe.

We are confident that authors and readers alike will be happy with the result.

Madalena Fonseca
Ugo Fratesi

Contents

List of Contributors

Alberto Amaral holds a doctorate from Cambridge and is a professor at the University of Porto and a researcher at CIPES—Centre for Research on Higher Education Policies. He was the rector of Porto University from 1985 to 1998, former member of the Executive Board of the Conference of European Rectors, former chair of the Consortium of Higher Education Researchers, former member of IMHE (OECD) and life member of the International Association of University Presidents. At present, he is the chair of the administrative council of the Portuguese Agency for Assessment and Accreditation of Higher Education. Recent books include European Integration and Governance of Higher Education and Research (Springer), Higher Education in Portugal 1974–2009. A Nation, a Generation. (Springer), Quality Assurance in Higher Education. Contemporary Debates (Palgrave), Cross-Border Higher Education and Quality Assurance: Commerce, The Service Directive and Governing Higher Education (Palgrave) and Analysing European Policy Implementation: The Bologna Process (Palgrave).

Paul Benneworth is a senior researcher at the Center for Higher Education Policy Studies, University of Twente, the Netherlands, and Agderforskning, Kristiansand, Norway. Paul's research focuses on the dynamics of innovation and regional development and in particular the ways in which cooperations and coalitions function in supporting regional innovation processes. He has been chief scientist of projects for a range of research funders including the European Framework Programme/ERA-NET, research councils in the UK, the Netherlands and Norway as well as a wide range of government and not-for-profit funders. He is the editor of eight scientific works, including three in the RSA *Cities & Regions* series. He has published more than thirty peer-reviewed scientific articles in the last decade, serves as reviewer for a range of journals, research councils and funding agencies internationally and is currently acting as special scientific adviser to three research council funded projects in Norway, Italy and Belgium.

Ricardo Biscaia is an assistant professor at Universidade Portucalense Infante D. Henrique and an associate researcher at CIPES. He holds a PhD in Economics since January 2014, with a thesis on Location Theory. His main research interests are in the fields of Industrial Economics, Regional and Urban Economics and Higher Education Policies, the latter being focused on Higher Education funding and bibliometrics. Some of his work has been published in several Journals, such as Public Administration Review, Papers in Regional Science, Applied Economics, Higher Education, Studies in Higher Education or Cambridge Journal of Economics.

Roberta Capello is full professor of Regional Economics at Politecnico of Milan, former President of the Regional Science Association International (2009–2010), Treasurer of the European Regional Science Association (ERSA) (2000–2006) and National Secretary of the Italian Section of the International Regional Science Association (1995–1998). Editor in chief of Papers in Regional Science (Wiley Blackwell, Oxford) and of the Italian Journal of Regional Science (FrancoAngeli, Milan). Author of a textbook in Regional Economics, published in Italian (Il Mulino, 2004), in English (Routledge, 2007) and in Chinese (Economy and Management Publishing House, Beijin, China). Laurea Honoris Causa from the West University of Timisoara, Romania (October, 2012), and Fellow of the Regional Science Association International (since 2013).

Margarida F. Cardoso is Assistant Professor in the Biomedical School of University of Porto, Portugal: ICBAS—Instituto de Ciências Biomédicas Abel Salazar, in the scientific areas of biostatistics and epidemiology. Her research interests include Epidemiology, Public Health and Education. She is co-author of several publications in the area of higher education as a result of her collaboration with CIPES and has also publications in the biomedical area.

Nicola D. Coniglio obtained a PhD in Economics from the University of Glasgow (UK) and a doctorate at the University of Milan—Bicocca. Nicola is currently associate professor in Economics at the University of Bari (Italy). He is the Italian director of the Erasmus Mundus—Master in Economics of Globalisation and European Integration. His research interests include urban and regional economics, industrial policy, economics of migration, international trade and factor mobility and the economic consequences of climatic changes. He was awarded with the EPAINOS prize for the best research work presented by a young scholar at the European Regional Science Association meetings in 2003 and 2004.

Diogo de Abreu is a Full Professor in the Institute of Geography and Spatial Planning, Universidade de Lisboa, Portugal, and former Scientific Director of the Centre for Geographical Studies of the same university. Professor Abreu conducts research in demographic modelling, population forecasting, economic geography, transportation and urban and regional development. He was a team member of the FP7-funded project SECOA—Solutions for Environmental Contrasts in Coastal Areas.

Alina Esteves is Assistant Professor of Human Geography at IGOT, Universidade de Lisboa, Portugal, and a researcher at the unit MIGRARE—Migration, Spaces and Societies at the Centre for Geographical Studies. She has worked in the areas of migration studies and social and urban geography. She coordinated the project CRISIMI (2014–2015) on the impact of the economic crisis on the living conditions and labour market incorporation of immigrants in Portugal (funded by the High Commission for Migrations) and was part of the Portuguese teams of the projects GEITONIES (funded by EU FP7), THEMIS and Mobile Welfare (both funded by NORFACE).

Jose Andres Faiña is a Jean Monnet Professor of European Industrial Economics and Chairman of the Jean Monnet Research Group on Competition and Development (C+D) at the School of Business and Economics, University of A Coruña, Spain. He has a vast professional experience in European Affairs and in Regional Development Policy, as Director General of Economic Planning (Regional Government of Galicia (1998–2001) and Leader of the Phare Project Galicia-Opolskie (Poland, 2001–2002), as well as an independent expert evaluating the impact of ERDF programmes for the DG Regio (European Commission). His research and publications focus on constitutional political economy of the EU, regional economics and development policy, as well as industrial and competition economics and currently lean start-up and Business Management of Innovation.

Madalena Fonseca is a Geographer and Assistant Professor at the University of Porto, Department of Geography. She holds a PhD in Economic Geography. Currently, she is the General Secretary of the Portuguese Agency for Assessment and Accreditation of Higher Education—A3ES (Lisboa). Her main research topics are currently linked with higher education and human capital: offer and demand of higher education, access, the Portuguese higher education system, higher education and regional development and quality assurance. She is a member of the Board of the European Consortium for Accreditation—ECA (The Hague) and the international expert for international accreditations of the German agency ZEVA (Hannover). She takes part in two Erasmus+ research projects on strategic partnerships for higher education: EIQAS, Enhancing Internal Quality Assurance Systems (2014–2016), and MEHR, Migration, Education and Human Rights (2016–2019). She is the author and co-author of a large number of papers and chapters of books in the field of economic geography and regional development.

Maria Lucinda Fonseca is Full Professor of Human Geography and Migration Studies and the Dean of the Institute of Geography and Spatial Planning, Universidade de Lisboa, Portugal, and Director of the PhD Programme on Migration studies and Coordinator of the research unit MIGRARE. She has worked extensively in the areas of migration studies and social and urban geography. She was the principal investigator for the project GEITONIES—Generating interethnic tolerance and neighbourhood integration in European urban spaces (funded by EU FP7) and the coordinator of the Portuguese team of the projects THEMIS—Theorising the Evolution of the European Migration Systems and Mobile Welfare—European Welfare Systems in Times of Mobility (both funded by NORFACE).

Ugo Fratesi is Associate Professor of Regional Economics at Politecnico di Milano (since December 2010). He is Editor of main section papers and Book Review Editor of Regional Studies since 2013. Previously, he was member of the editorial board of the Italian Journal of Regional Science. He was member of the Council of the Italian Section of the Regional Science Association International (AISRe) for the period 2010–2016 and was its Treasurer for the period 2010–2013. He has been involved with various roles in a large number of research projects, especially at European level, financed by the Espon programme, the FP5, FP7, Horizon 2020 or the European Commission directly. He is co-author of several books and author of a large number of papers published in refereed journals in the field of regional economics, primarily on the themes of regional growth and development, the models for forecasting regional growth, regional policy, the theory and measurement of regional disparities and the territorial aspects of human capital and innovation.

Athanasios Kalogeresis is Assistant Professor at the School of Spatial Planning and Development, Faculty of Engineering, Aristotle University of Thessaloniki, where he teaches economic geography, urban and regional planning and globalisation. His research interests and recent work evolve around two main themes, namely, local and regional development and various aspects of the organisation of production (spatial, social, institutional and cultural). Within these broad themes, he has worked and published in a number of specific areas, such as the creative economy, the analysis of new forms of (multinational) organisation of economic activities, the role of multinational production and trade in knowledge spillovers, relations between international and local productive systems, the sources of regional disparities and the role of human capital and human capabilities.

Camilla Lenzi is associate professor of Regional Economics at Politecnico di Milano. She holds a PhD in Economics (2006, Università di Pavia) and an MSc in Industry and Innovation Analysis (2005, SPRU—University of Sussex). She is Jean Monnet module leader on EU Spatial Planning, Economics and Policies (2015–2018). From 2005 to 2008, Camilla stayed at the Department of Economics of Bocconi University and CESPRI (now ICRIOS) as a Postdoctoral Fellow. She participated with various roles in a large number of research projects, especially at European level, financed by the Espon programme, FP7 and FP6, and the European Commission directly. She is member of AISRe (Italian Regional Science Association) and ERSA (European Regional Science Association). She published on several international journals such as Journal of Urban Economics, Journal of Regional Science, Regional Studies, International Regional Science Review, Annals of Regional Science, Spatial Economic Analysis and Papers in Regional Science.

Enrique López-Bazo is full professor of applied economics at the University of Barcelona and member of the Regional Quantitative Analysis Research Institute (AQR). For more than 25 years, his research has been mainly in the area of regional and urban economics, having spawned numerous papers published in recognised journals and edited volumes. He serves on the editorial board of different international journals in the field of applied economics and spatial economics. He was a visiting research at the London School of Economics, the Free University of Amsterdam and the European Commission.

Jesús López-Rodriguez is Associate Professor of Economics at the University of A Coruña. He is also a senior research fellow at the Jean Monnet Research Group on Competition and Development (C+D) at the University of A Coruña where he served as director from 2013 to 2015. From 2013 to 2014, we worked at the Institute for Prospective Technological Studies-Joint Research Centre (IPTS-JRC) of the European Commission as senior research fellow. He has extensive track record of research in geographical economics, regional growth and disparities, EU regional policy, EU political economy and industrial economics and more recently in public economics. He has acted as consultant to several institutions including DG Regio, European Commission, European Parliament, Galician Court of Competition and Basque Court of Competition. He has also been visiting scholar at a number of universities including Harvard University, London School of Economics, Institute of Capital, Creativity and Innovation at the University of Texas and University of Exeter.

Vassilis Monastiriotis is Associate Professor of Political Economy at the European Institute, London School of Economics (UK). He is Director of the LSE Research Unit on Southeast Europe and holds affiliations with LSE's Department of Geography and Environment, the Hellenic Observatory and the ESRC Spatial Economics Research Centre. His main research interests are on regional and national labour markets, regional and local socioeconomic disparities, economic growth and macroeconomic policy, economic integration and the political economy of reforms. He has published numerous articles in economics and regional science journals and received various distinctions including the Moss Madden Medal in Regional Science (2008). He has a PhD in Economic Geography (LSE), an MSc in Economics (University of Macedonia) and a BSc in Economics (Aristotle University of Thessaloniki). He is Co-editor of Spatial Economic Analysis (Taylor & Francis) and Committee Member of the British and Irish Section of the Regional Science Association International.

Paulino Montes-Solla is Associate Researcher in Economics at the Jean Monnet Research Group on Competition and Development (C+D), Department of Economic Analysis and Business Administration, University of A Coruña, Spain. Has been a member of the expert group in Regional Policy and a regular contributor to the reports on ERDF funds for the European Commission since 2009 and acted as junior consultant to several institutions including the DG Regio, European Commission and

Basque Court of Competition. His research focuses on Regional Development, Business Management of Innovation, Renewable energy economy and Marketing and Consulting of European Community Funds. He has published its research outcomes in numerous international conferences and in scientific journals. He has also been visiting scholar at some universities including the European Policies Research Centre at the University of Strathclyde in Glasgow (UK) and Institute of Capital, Creativity and Innovation at the University of Texas at Austin (USA).

Elisabet Motellón is reader of economics at the Open University of Catalunya and member of the Regional Quantitative Analysis Research Institute (AQR) at the University of Barcelona. Her research focuses on the empirical analysis of labor economics combined with elements of spatial economics. She has published her work in this field in recognised journals.

Guido Pellegrini is Full Professor in Statistical Methods for Regional Policies and Statistics at the Department of Social Sciences and Economics, Sapienza, University of Rome (Italy). Previously, he was Economist at the Research Department of Bank of Italy, where he managed the Regional Analysis Unit. He participated in several projects and committees on European and national policy evaluation, in Italy and abroad. He was the Scientific Director of the evaluation of several national and regional programmes and policies. Recently, he collaborated in the definition of national and regional strategies for smart specialisation in Italy. He has published numerous papers in international journals and books on policy evaluation, industrial and regional policies, economic growth and convergence among regions, local development and economic statistics.

Rómulo Pinheiro is Professor of Public Policy and Administration at the University of Agder, Norway, where he heads the research group on Public Governance and Leadership. He is also a Senior Researcher at Agderforskning and the Centre for Advanced Studies in Regional Innovation Strategies (RIS), a Visiting Professor in Higher Education Policy & Management at the University of Tampere (Finland) and Affiliated Member of the ExCID (*Expert cultures and institutional dynamics: Studies in higher education and work)* research group based at the University of Oslo. Rómulo's research interests are located at the intersection of public policy and administration, organisational theory, economic geography, innovation and higher education studies. His work has been published in Public Administration Review, Science and Public Policy, Higher Education, Studies in Higher Education, European Journal of Higher Education, Cambridge Journal of Regions, Economy and Society, Tertiary Education and Management, City, Culture and Society, International Journal of Cultural Policy, etc.

Francesco Prota (PhD in Agricultural and Environmental Economics) is Lecturer in Economics at the University of Bari "Aldo Moro". His research interests include regional economics and international economic integration, development economics, public policy evaluation and innovation economics. Francesco is the author of several articles in economics journals. He has also written two books: *Senza cassa. Le politiche di sviluppo del Mezzogiorno dopo l'Intervento straordinario* (Il Mulino, 2012; coauthor G. Viesti) and *Le nuove politiche regionali dell'Unione Europea* (Il Mulino, 2008; coauthor G. Viesti). Besides serving as referee for international journals, he is Associate Editor for *Regional Studies, Regional Science*. Since 2011, Francesco has been acting as consultant to UNIDO (United Nations Industrial Development Organization) on cluster development and FDI in Africa. He has also a long track record of collaboration with different Italian government departments and agencies.

Yannis Psycharis is a Professor of Regional Economic Analysis at the Department Economic and Regional Development, Panteion University of Social and Political Sciences, Athens, Greece. He has also taught at the Department of Planning and Regional Development of the University of Thessaly in Volos (2000–2009). He had been Senior Research Fellow at the LSE (2007–2008). He is the former Director of the Greek National School of Public Administration and Local Government (2010–2012) and is currently President of the Greek section of the European Regional Science Association. His research interests include regional economic analysis, regional policy, regional public finance and public administration.

Laura Resmini is associate professor of Economic policy at the University of Milano-Bicocca and affiliated member of CERTeT, Center for Research on Regional Economics, Transport and Tourism at Bocconi University. She is the Treasurer of the European Regional Science Association (ERSA) and member of the Scientific Council of the Italian Section of the Regional Science Association International (AISRe). She is also co-editor of Scienze Regionali—Italian Journal of Regional Science and member of the Editorial Board of Papers in Regional Science. Throughout her professional life, she has been involved with various roles in several research projects, especially at European level. She is author of several papers published in refereed journals in the field of Foreign Direct Investment, Multinational corporations' location strategies and impact on local economic development.

Vera Rocha is a Postdoc in Economics of Entrepreneurship at Copenhagen Business School (Department of Innovation and Organizational Economics). Her main research interests are related to higher education (HE funding, competition and diversification), industrial organisation (firm and industry dynamics, new venture creation) and labour economics (wage differentials, human capital and occupational choice), with focus on entrepreneurial careers and entrepreneurship dynamics.

Isidoro Romero has a PhD in Economics and is an Associate Professor in the Department of Applied Economics at the University of Seville (Spain). He has been a visiting scholar at the University of Groningen (The Netherlands), the University of Illinois at Urbana-Champaign (USA) and the University of Reading (UK) and an invited lecturer in postgraduate programmes at the University of Palermo (Italy), the University of Aberystwyth (UK) and the Complutense University in Madrid, among other institutions. He is the Coordinator of PYMED—"SMEs and economic development" research group—at the University of Seville and a member of the European Union Regional Economic Applications Laboratory and the European Union Network for Input-Output Studies. He has served as Associate Dean for Research and Internationalization in the Faculty of Economics and Business Sciences at the University of Seville. His research lines are entrepreneurship, SMEs, regional development, innovation and enterprise policy.

Antonios Rovolis (economist, B.A. Athens, MA Sussex, PhD LSE) is associate professor of Spatial and Urban Economics at the Department of Economic and Regional Development, Panteion University of Athens. He has worked as a research fellow at the Queen Mary College, University of London, at the Institute of Regional Development and at the Institute of Urban Environment and Human Resources, Panteion University of Athens, and he has taught at Thessaly University and Harokopio University of Athens. He has been a visiting research fellow at Toronto University, McGill University, York University (Canada) and Concordia University.

Pedro Teixeira is Associate Professor in Economics and Vice Rector for Academic Affairs at the University of Porto and Director of CIPES—Centre of Research on Higher Education Policy. He is Secretary General of CHER—Consortium of Higher Education Researchers (since 2013) and member of the Scientific Board of RESUP. He is the Advisor on Higher Education and Science to the President of Portugal (since April 2016). He is a member of the Board of the Bial Foundation (since 2015) and a member of the Education Council of the Foundation Francisco Manuel dos Santos (since 2013). His research focuses on the economics of higher education and the history of economic thought, and his work has been published in leading scientific Journals including European Journal of History of Economic Thought, Higher Education, Higher Education Quarterly, Journal of Economic Methodology, Public Administration Review, Research Policy and Studies in Higher Education.

Vassilis Tselios is an Assistant Professor of Regional Economics at the Department of Planning and Regional Development of the University of Thessaly. He is an economic geographer (PhD, London School of Economics) and his research centres around the spatial analysis of socioeconomic phenomena. He was a Lecturer in Economic Geography at the University of Southampton, a Research Associate at the Department of Economic Geography of the University of Groningen and at the Spatial Economics Research Centre of the London School of Economics and a Lecturer in Economic Geography at Newcastle University. Vassilis has also worked for the World Bank as Consultant for the International Trade Department.

Laura Varela-Candamio is Assistant Professor in the Department of Economic Analysis and Business Administration since 2008 and a senior research fellow at the Jean Monnet Research Group on Competition and Development (C+D) at the University of Coruña. She is also a teacher-tutor at the National Distance Education University (UNED) in Lugo since 2011. She earned her doctorate in economics from the University of Coruna in 2011. Her research interests include public economics such as public finance, taxation and public policies, sustainable economic development and behavioural economics. She has published its research outcomes in numerous international conferences and in scientific journals such as Economics Letters, Applied Economics, Computers in Human Behavior, El Trimestre Económico, Sustainability, among others. She has been a visiting professor in American universities: Andrew Young School (Georgia State University) (2015), REAL (University of Illinois) (2013), Suffolk University (2012) and European universities: University of Porto (2014, 2011 and 2010).

Part I
Regional Upgrading in Southern Europe and its Regions: The Context

Chapter 1
Regional Upgrading in Southern Europe: A General Framework

Madalena Fonseca and Ugo Fratesi

1.1 The Context of the Book

More than 30 years of European Regional Policy have not enhanced convergence as hoped, especially in the four countries of Southern Europe (Portugal, Spain, Greece and Italy). In the large crisis which started in 2007–2008, the same regions which were more heavily assisted in the past because of their backwardness, appear to be among the most heavily hit (Fratesi and Rodríguez-Pose 2016).

Although a number of indicators have exhibited an overall improvement since the nineties, and some degree of convergence at the country level, economic convergence was in general not achieved and regional disparities at the sub-national level appeared to be in many cases even increasing. Regional inequalities remain in fact, and show a strong persistent character in Europe and convergence is far from being attained, apart from the progress of the new member countries (Camagni and Capello 2015; Petrakos et al. 2011). Some indicators even show more divergence than convergence, reinforcing the pattern of the *sticky places in slippery space* metaphor of Ann Markusen (Markusen 1996).

It is clear that the financial and banking crisis exacerbated some of the problems that Southern European countries and regions are facing, but is not the cause of them. For instance, the problems of balancing the growth and convergence

M. Fonseca (✉)
Faculty of Arts and Humanities, University of Porto, Porto, Portugal

Agency for Assessment and Accreditation of Higher Education—A3ES, Praça de Alvalade, nr 6, 5 Frente, 1700-036 Lisbon, Portugal
e-mail: madalena@letras.up.pt; madalena.fonseca@a3es.pt

U. Fratesi
Department of Architecture, Built Environment and Construction Engineering, Politecnico di Milano, Piazza Leonardo da Vinci, 32, 20133 Milan, Italy
e-mail: ugo.fratesi@polimi.it

M. Fonseca, U. Fratesi (eds.), *Regional Upgrading in Southern Europe*, Advances in Spatial Science, DOI 10.1007/978-3-319-49818-8_1

objectives, and in managing external assistance were already present well before (Mancha-Navarro and Garrido-Yserte 2008). Rodríguez-Pose and Fratesi have already identified, in 2004, the reinforcement of agglomeration of growth and concentration of high added value activities in the regions of the core of the European Union (Rodriguez-Pose and Fratesi 2004), and a growing specialisation of the periphery in labour intensive industries and non-market services (Rodriguez-Pose and Fratesi 2007). It is therefore necessary to look deeper inside the socio-economic structures and the economic base of Southern European countries in order to understand the persistent underdevelopment of many of their regions. Uneven patterns of development can lead not only to increasing polarisation and regional disparities, but give rise to a negative structural effect hindering the ability of lagging regions to "*engage in development*" (Farole et al. 2011, p. 1097). The question of *how lagging regions in advanced countries enhance and keep competitiveness* remains widely unanswered and this is the main reason for editing a book on *Regional Upgrading*. Without upgrading, in fact, lagging regions of advanced countries risk remaining squeezed between the richest regions and the competitors from countries with lower labour costs. As Camagni (2002) maintained, the principles of Ricardian comparative advantage don't hold at a local scale and regions whose economic structures are not competitive bear the risk of economic desertification with subsequent depopulation or persistent dependence on public assistance.

One important necessary condition of regional upgrading is the presence of human capital. There is substantial empirical evidence of the link between human capital and growth (Rodríguez-Pose and Vilalta-Bufí 2005), but still not a full theoretical understanding about the underlying causes of the relationship between human capital, local area employment (or population) and growth (Shapiro 2006). However, a highly educated population generates greater local productivity growth through different uses of knowledge (Becker 1993). Regional upgrading and economic performance of European regions is therefore strongly conditioned by human capital endowment and the subsequent potential for innovation and productivity enhancement, since "societies with a better endowment of human capital are considered to have a greater development potential than societies with scarce or inadequate human resources" (Rodríguez-Pose and Vilalta-Bufí 2005, p. 545). Considering the first two programming periods of European regional policy after the 1989 reform, Rodriguez-Pose and Fratesi (2004) concluded that the only axis with positive returns in the short and medium term was investment in human capital.

There is however an intrinsic difficulty in measuring the link between human capital and regional development. The assessment of human capital must be carried out through proxies. Proxies related to educational stock can be very poor and imperfect (Woessmann 2003), and to overcome data limitations, indicators of the labour market, employability, life-long-learning and other on-the-job training indicators, migration, etc. are usually developed.

A large number of the regions belonging to the Southern European countries which have been supported for about the last 30 years by European Structural Funds were also recipients of large foreign direct investment (FDI) since the 1980s. For those regions on the receiving end of new foreign direct investment, the location of new firms may induce new economic activities and the prospects of job growth. However, this does not always imply that it will be accompanied by a *functional or regional upgrading* in the medium to long term, which would imply a re-structuring of the economy towards sectors, functions, tasks and occupations with larger value added and commanding roles.

In fact, the most successful exit strategies of "vulnerable regions", defined in terms of specialisation in sectors more vulnerable to globalisation, have been identified in the reconversion of their economic base and movement a step ahead towards high value added sectors and activities (Affuso et al. 2011). On the contrary, in the last 30 years, many peripheral regions of Southern Europe have been attractive to foreign direct investments mostly because of their lower labour costs, public incentives or other facilities and new infrastructure, but those regions have not always been able to develop beyond the national and European support. After the European Eastern enlargement, and the integration of the new European member states, a relocation of firms from Southern peripheral regions to regions in these new member countries grew quickly, abandoning the former regions with unemployment and lower income (Capello et al. 2015; Marques 2015; Marques da Costa et al. 2015; Fonseca 2005).

Regional upgrading in the lagging regions of Southern European countries has hence been interrupted before being achieved, and a trend towards downgrading seems to be emerging, with the weakest regions risking being considered as liabilities to their own countries, especially following the major economic downturn, which forces the European Union and its countries to focus resources on other priorities such as recovering from the crisis, public debt and finances, and the banking system.

1.2 Contribution of the Book

The core of the book adopts a concept of *regional upgrading* under the argument that there is a critical link between regional disparities and human capital that has been shaping the regional map of growth and development in Southern Europe. In the main conceptualisation of the book, regional upgrading mostly originates from regional human capital and can be achieved through four main complementary drivers, each of them facilitated by the presence of adequate human capital or hindered by its absence (Fig. 1.1):

- Foreign direct investments (FDI) and national investments coming from outside the region, which, due to the scarcity of endogenous capital in lagging regions, can provide a spur to production and productivity in the economy (Beugelsdijk et al. 2008); human capital acts in this case as one important attracting factor and as a determinant of the impact (Borensztein et al. 1998);

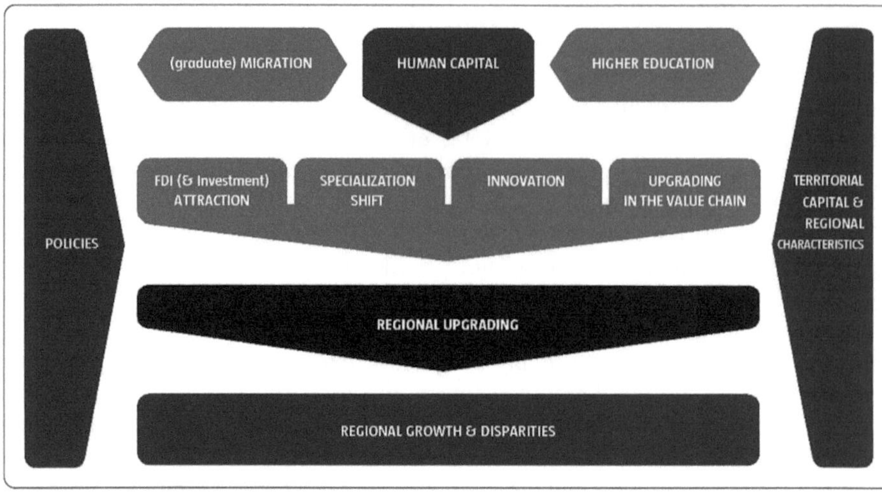

Fig. 1.1 Conceptual scheme of the book

- A specialisation shift, from sectors of lower value added to sectors with higher value added, productivity and therefore higher wages and salaries, which is not possible without adequate competences of the labour force, even if this is not a sufficient condition (Affuso et al. 2011);
- Product and process innovation, which allows the regional economy to shift towards better positions in the competitive scale, and needs qualified workforce, researchers and innovators, although some contributions in the book will show that innovation in lagging Southern European regions does not follow the same knowledge creating paradigm of the core regions in the centre of Europe (cfr. Chap. 4);
- Upgrading in the value chain (Storper 2010; Farole et al. 2011; Storper and Scott 2009; Coe and Yeung 2015; Glückler and Panitz 2016). Since the first three drivers should lead to an improvement along the value chain, the *upgrade in the value chain* can be considered a common feature more than an extra driver to regional upgrading.

Human capital supports and enhances the processes of upgrading along all four drivers. The main sources of human capital reinforcement and accumulation are education and particularly higher education, but the availability of human capital also depends heavily on migration processes, and in particular brain drain, which can be consistent from lagging regions and lead to the depletion of human resources despite policy efforts in the improvement of the education system (Ciriaci 2014; Coniglio and Prota 2008; Dotti et al. 2013; Faggian and McCann 2009; Fratesi and Percoco 2014; Garrido-Yserte and Gallo-Rivera 2010).

The complex network of interdependencies and links that accommodates regional upgrading is dependent on regional characteristics, including social and territorial capital, and thus should be tackled by strong, efficient and adaptive policies, whose role is pervasively investigated throughout the book.

The results of the process of regional upgrading, when significant, are enhanced growth in lagging regions and the consequent reduction of regional disparities. When, as in the case of many Southern European regions, regional upgrading is weak, the results are the presence of permanently lagging regions, often needing assistance, and persistent regional disparities at national and European levels.

The issue of regional upgrading will be addressed in the book through two main approaches:

- On the one hand, studies addressing the different facets of the process of structural upgrading and the endogenous factors of development, affecting the ability of regions to upgrade by taking advantage of the opportunities, including support policies, FDI, education system, etc.;
- On the other hand, papers addressing the structural upgrading, or the inability to upgrade, of specific groups of regions and/or specialisation areas in the Southern periphery of Europe, aiming for an *ex-post* assessment into the reasons of policy success or failure.

1.3 Originality and Approach

The book gathers contributions from different scientific areas, with a focus on the spatial effect of development processes. As the chapter authors—and the two editors—are from two different scientific disciplines, namely economics and geography, one of the originalities of the book lies in the multidisciplinary approach given to the same set of problems, in a kind of stereo vision. The editors live and work in Southern European countries but other contributions are included by scholars living and working outside the four target countries, which provides a mix of evidence from the internal and the external.

The diversity of the authors and their approaches or schools of thought enriches the book even when the approaches are very different. As editors, we have decided to respect the original texts and revisions of the authors to give voice to the different scientific perspectives, but we also managed to have an internal blind review by the authors of other chapters which, together with our own comments, allowed the authors of chapters to improve their work and make it more consistent with the general purpose of the book.

Apart from the confrontation between geographers and economists, the book includes scientific approaches from frontier or cross-cutting areas that reflect the development of intermediate and evolutionists theoretical proposals. Thus, some authors position themselves between geography and economy, coming from one or the other and with an evolving path towards each other—geographers who approached the economy and economists who approached the geography—but others developed throughout their education and research in less traditionally related areas, such as planning, regional development, sociology or public policies.

It is not easy to find a real intercultural and multidisciplinary language. It is easier to desire it than to achieve it. This book intends however, to be a small building block in this sense, an unpretentious contribution to an intercultural and interdisciplinary communication between a family of areas running from geography, to economy, sociology and crossing through planning, regional development, public policies, etc.

Some texts or chapters might provide controversial messages, especially for those readers who position themselves in more traditional areas and lines of thought, but the decision of us as editors has been to keep the original texts and especially ideas without "normalising" them, with the aim of enriching the debate on the development of Southern Europe.

1.4 The Structure of the Book

The book is articulated in three main parts. The first part is an introductory one, where the framework for the analysis and a presentation of the specific issues characterizing Southern European regions are presented. The second part investigates the main elements of regional structural upgrading in Southern European regions, in the perspective of Fig. 1.1. The third part focuses on human capital, its presence, use, accumulation and depletion in Southern European regions.

After this introductory chapter, the first part of the book, which presents a general framework for regional upgrading in Southern Europe, includes two chapters. The first one (Chap. 2) by Madalena Fonseca corresponds to a short version of an atlas of regional disparities of Southern Europe with the aim of building a meaning for the concept of regional upgrading. With the application of an analytical tool already developed by others—the social filter—Fonseca tries to summarise the present situation using indicators and variables of three domains: population, education (human capital) and economy. A principal component analysis was used to identify the main factors that can summarise a larger database of indicators collected in Eurostat for the most updated year available. This chapter launches the issue of the (rigidity) of unemployment and the historical persistence of the disparities. Unemployment is perhaps the most visible face of the backwardness of Southern European economic structures.

The chapter by Ugo Fratesi (Chap. 3) investigates the growth patterns of Southern European regions, in particular by evidencing to what extent there has been a productivity issue. This is put in relation to the issue of upgrading, and in particular to the fact that these regions tend to specialize in relatively low level functions which makes them less productive and more vulnerable to external decisions. Functions are measured through the professions of workers according to ISCO codes and Southern European regions, those belonging to former Objective 1 in particular, are particularly weak in functions related to command and control, innovation and technology, and creativity, This is also shown to be related to lower growth rates, as Southern European regions with lower levels of functions have been growing, ceteris paribus, less than the others. The chapter is also an opportunity to detect to what extent the regions of the four countries are a homogeneous group in terms of economic patterns, which is verified especially concerning growth which has been either stagnant or mostly reliant on employment creation with low improvements in productivity (see also Chap. 5).

Part II of the book centres on issues and aspects of regional upgrading and their manifestation in Southern European regions. In particular, the various chapters of this part are expected to analyse the various aspects depicted in Fig. 1.1 with the exception of human capital, which is left to Part III and territorial capital and other regional characteristics which are analysed in Chap. 2.

Roberta Capello and Camilla Lenzi (Chap. 4) study innovation in Southern European countries by applying the concept of territorial patterns of innovation and discuss the Southern European model of development, under the question, *Do Southern European regions really lag behind in their innovation trends?* They find that, despite investing less than the EU average in R&D and formal knowledge creation activities, these countries demonstrate substantial innovative activities, especially in the form of process innovation and that their dominant innovation pattern is based on the exploitation of informal knowledge rather than in formal knowledge produced through research activities. This innovation mode allows them to take advantage of their innovative patterns much more than is generally thought. Their main argument lies at the policy level. Policies to foster upgrading must be tailored according to each type of territorial pattern of innovation and the corresponding features of the regions covered. The "one size fits all" policies risk unsuccessful outcomes and inefficiency. There is a link between the proposals of these two authors and other contributions that explore alternative tools, like the "social filter" (Chap. 2). Besides, their results and conclusions meet a somehow common output and anticipate similar future scenarios with those from different approaches in the other chapters. We can even ask if the analysis of Roberta Capello and Camilla Lenzi can contribute to an answer to the "Spanish productivity paradox" described and discussed by Faiña, Lopez-Rodriguez, Montes-Solla, Romero and Varela-Candamio in their chapter (Chap. 5).

In Chap. 5, J. Andres Faiña, Jesus Lopez-Rodriguez, Paulino Montes-Solla, Isidoro Romero and Laura Varela-Candamio present a description of the spatial structure of the Spanish economy and its recent evolution in the framework of the European integration, putting the focus on what they call the "productivity paradox" in Spain. The paradox lies in the contrast between a strong GDP per capita growth and productivity stagnation. This antagonistic trends occurred in the context of investment-based regional development policy undertaken in the country. The Spanish economy featured a trade-off between the growth of employment and productivity, the authors argue. Unemployment and regional disparities are again in the core of this analysis, as was the case in other contributions. In fact, Faiña and his colleagues conclude in their chapter, the worst effect of the crisis has been the increase in job losses. The crisis has exposed the weaknesses of the economic base and the vulnerability of the reforms undertaken in the framework of the European integration, in Southern European countries. To Faiña and his colleagues, the

Spanish growth model was based on the increase in wages without a corresponding increase in productivity which led to the country's loss of competitiveness. The question is whether in the other Southern European countries the same occurred or not. We have to go back to Capello and Lenzi's contribution (Chap. 4) and review their taxonomy under the proposal of Faiña and colleagues as well as to López-Bazo and colleagues' one (Chap. 10). The "Spanish paradox" applies to Portugal, Greece and for part of Italy at least, and even through different approaches and with different tools of analysis, the results converge. The irregular rising and falling of immigration and outmigration in Portugal described by Lucinda Fonseca and her colleagues in Chap. 12 is but an example of similar processes in one of the other three countries.

Laura Resmini's chapter (Chap. 6) analyses the main features of Foreign Direct Investment (FDI) in Southern Europe, using data for the period between 2005 and 2007 in order to isolate the structural factors that affect regions' attractiveness without the impact of the recent economic crisis. Resmini's focus is to understand regional factors of attractiveness. The author argues that there is a poor attractiveness of Southern European countries for FDI. In this context, the least attractive regions are those belonging to Greece and Portugal, while Spanish regions are, generally speaking, perceived to be as attractive as other EU regions and the perceived unattractiveness of Italian regions seems to be limited to services FDI and intra-EU foreign investors. The chapter is not only descriptive but its main aim is to investigate the determinants of this unattractiveness and whether these are characteristics common to the Southern European periphery or rather to country specific peculiarities, pointing in particular to poor local government and poor national institutions in the four countries. Resmini's chapter brings another piece of the puzzle of the "Spanish paradox" of Faiña and colleagues, focusing on the weaknesses of the prevailing economic development model of Southern Europe.

Vassilis Tselios, Antonis Rovolis and Yannis Psycharis's chapter (Chap. 7) focuses on Greece with the aim of understanding the relationship between regional economic development, human capital and transport infrastructure, under the framework of what the authors call the role of geography. Their aim is also to trample down some mainstream theoretical models. This is a living snapshot of Greece from planning and regional development scholars who have a look at the Greek case from the inside but also from the outside. The main argument is to discuss the impact of human capital endowment and transport infrastructure on regional economic development and growth in Greece, with a special focus on the role of geography, because this relationship is complex. In particular, the chapter argues that geography plays an important role in the functioning and performance of regional economies in general and the Greek economy in particular. Both first nature of geography factors (i.e., physical geography of regions) and second nature of geography factors (i.e., geography of distance between economic agents) are argued to moderate this relationship.

Athanasios Kalogeresis's chapter (Chap. 8) focuses on Southern European production systems under the stress brought by the crisis and with a special focus on delocalisation and foreign direct investment (FDI). The chapter has a strong theoretical component with a discussion on the concepts of relocation, delocalisation and the impact of the different understandings of the concepts for the international division of labour. The author takes data from UNCTAD on FDI and other trade indicators including import and export for total trade in goods and services and sets up long time series in order to capture trends and the effects of the crisis on the four countries. The results of the chapter highlight (again) the weakness of the economic base of Portugal and Greece in relation to the two other countries of Southern Europe. Italy stands out with a better performance. Again, these results are not surprising when we consider the other studies even with a different focus and approaches. Besides, Kalogeresis brings back to our minds Alain Lipietz and his idea of *Peripheral Fordism in Southern Europe* (Lipietz 1987), which was perhaps the first book which focused specifically on the condition of Southern Europe.

The chapter of Guido Pellegrini (Chap. 9) focuses on policies and is, most of all, a critical thought based on the extensive empirical research already existing in the literature and referred to by the author. Pellegrini writes on Italy but his arguments serve the other countries of Southern Europe as well. Pellegrini analyses the Italian regional divide beyond the "golden age of convergence" of the South, which took place in the 1950s and 1960s. In the period between more or less 1952 and 1971, the south of Italy actually over performed. The Southern Italy Development Fund was a major player and large investments in social infrastructures and other support industries raised productivity and wellbeing in the South. Pellegrini argues that it was after the beginning of the 1970s that things changed due to policy changes. The main message of the chapter is that policies, as expected by us (Fig. 1.1), are very important but good regional policies alone cannot be successful in bringing regions out of backwardness. There are in fact a large number of policies which are mostly under control from the state like justice, education and human capital and crime, where the Italian government has not been able to bring the Mezzogiorno to levels similar to those of the rest of the country. This also reinforces the message by Resmini (Chap. 6) on the importance of good local and national institutions.

Following the general framework of Part I and the analysis of the various aspects of regional upgrading in Southern Europe developed in Part II, Part III of the book includes five chapters and focuses on human capital and its facets as condition and determinant. This part includes discussions on the role of human capital, education and over-education, migration and labour markets.

Enrique López-Bazo, Vassilis Monastiriotis and Elisabet Motellón (Chap. 10) analyse the relationship between wages and unemployment and how these two variables respond, both at the aggregate and the individual level, to the human capital endowments of regions and individuals and especially how this response varies across space (for different regions) in any particular point in time and over the business cycle. The analysis refers to Spain and Greece but the authors recognize that the conclusions should also be verifiable for Portugal and Italy. Beyond the descriptive detailed analysis of the three main indicators (unemployment, wages and returns to schooling), the main contribution of the chapter is to bring some insights into the mismatch between the qualification level and the demand from labour market in Spain and Greece at the country level and by regions at NUTS2 level that can be transferred to other countries and fundamental for future policies. The results are very interesting because they point to the fact that, in order to address the issue of unemployment, policies targeting the functioning of the labour market are more important than policies which focus on the endowment of human capital per se, since under-endowment is not always a characteristics of Southern European regions. This is a most important contribution to the development of the concept of regional upgrading. In this as in other chapters, unemployment expresses its presence as the elephant in the living room of Europe. The chapter explores the mismatch between supply and demand in labour market in what concerns qualifications or human capital. Again it is possible to take the arguments and evidences of these authors as contributions to explain problems and to answer some questions raised by others in their own chapters, as is the case of Andres Faiña and his colleagues in Chap. 5 with the "Spanish productivity paradox" or Lucinda Fonseca and her colleagues in Chap. 12, where the vulnerability of the Portuguese golden age of growth is explored.

Closely related to the issue shown in Chap. 10, i.e., the fact that Southern European regions are somehow under-endowed of human capital but, especially, are unable to use it effectively within their labour market, Nicola Coniglio and Francesco Prota write a chapter (Chap. 11), on the complex relation between human capital and the labour market with the aim of answering the question on its structural mismatch: "Why does the supply of human capital (in peripheral regions) not create its own demand?" The authors argue that it is necessary to take into account both offer and supply of human capital in the designed policies and measures for regional upgrading. Acting only on the offer side, enhancing the qualifications of the population, risks a "leakage", as the authors name it, of human capital through out-migration (brain drain). It is thus important to understand the processes of "absorption" of human capital by the labour markets. The authors have no hesitation about the absence of a clear correlation between the economic performance of regions and their human capital endowment. One of the examples that can be picked out is the North-South divide in Italy that has reduced strongly in human capital endowment but not in economic growth and development balance. The general message that the chapter provides is that promoting more (high-quality) local opportunities for human capital accumulation and boosting ties with local potential employment might translate into a reduced skilled out-migration from peripheral areas. At the same time, policies reinforcing human capital accumulation are also necessary, for example through investment attraction and start-up promotion policies which leverage the local supply of skilled and qualified individuals. The message for policymakers is hence to move qualified job opportunities to the periphery and develop measures to attract new and innovative entrepreneurs.

The Portuguese geographers group consisting of Lucinda Fonseca, Diogo Abreu and Alina Esteves (Chap. 12) write on two intertwined hot topics of the regional development status in Southern Europe: population ageing and migration. Although their analysis focuses on Portugal, most of the underlying processes are similar to the other Southern European countries. The Portuguese population is ageing. At present Portugal has the lowest total fertility rate in Europe and the current rate is also the lowest historical rate of the country. Immigration brought some dynamic to the national population during the period of economic growth of the 1990s and 2000s, but the economic and financial crisis had a deep effect on the recent evolution of migration flows to and from Portugal. The rising unemployment led to a reduction of labour inflows, expansion of return flows to the origin countries and even re-emigration to other countries. On the outflows side, there has been a growing emigration of Portuguese workers, similar to what happened in the 1960s. The chapter includes a model of population projections and the discussion of future scenarios. The authors leave some messages for policymakers; it is important to be aware of the relationship between population ageing, and labour market, and immigration policies should be based in consistent prospective scenarios.

Rómulo Pinheiro, a Portuguese living and working in Norway for more than 20 years and the British Paul Benneworth, now at the University of Twente in the Netherlands (Chap. 13), well aware of the risks of giving prescriptions for policymakers based on successful stories from other regions, describe two case studies that can work as examples of good practices on the effects of universities in regional development of the regions where they are located. This makes a contribution from the outside of the core of the book, both in terms of scientific areas and location, the consequences of which can however be highly relevant to the case of Southern European regions. The two cases refer to the University of Tromso in Norway and to the University of Twente in the Netherlands. Both cases have special attributes and are unrepeatable but can nevertheless be used as a reference. More specifically, these case studies show how academic groups associated with the field of medicine took pro-active steps to establish and further develop regional coalitions which, over time, have resulted in situated learning. The focus on processes of university-regional engagement and mutual satisfaction in a context where universities are pressured to be globally excellent allow lessons to be drawn for regions in Southern Europe. Subtle transfer is nevertheless required to account for universities' autonomies and organisational capacity to embed engagement at the institutional level. This reinforces the idea that just providing human capital through education is not going to solve the problems of Southern European regions and that, for universities to be agents of regional upgrading, university-regional engagement is fundamental. This is also proof that the outcomes of any policies cannot be taken as guaranteed just based on the assumption that the same measures were applied with success somewhere else.

Ricardo Biscaia, Pedro Teixeira, Vera Rocha and Maria Cardoso (Chap. 14), a Portuguese group of researcher from CIPES—The Centre of Research on Higher Education Policies develop an out of the "theoretical" box critical analysis of Southern European regional development patterns, focusing on human capital and higher education. They critically review the literature on migration and regional convergence, on the effects of higher educational institutions (HEI) on regional development and on the role of human capital in regional convergence. Besides a critical review of theory, the authors include an empirical essay for modelling the relationship between higher education institutions and economic growth at the regional level.

Chapter 15 is a critical postscript. Being directly involved in the book and its realization, as editors we thought it would be helpful to have an external view of the various materials and arguments put forward in the book. A *postface* by an author who was not directly involved with the research but who has a long direct experience with the issues of human capital and policies in Southern European regions. Alberto Amaral accepted this challenge and had the opportunity to read the various draft chapters before publication. The result is a chapter in itself which discusses the implications for European economic integration after Brexit.

1.5 The Findings: Is There a Different Geography in Southern Europe?

Reading the different chapters, it seems that all the authors face this challenge with the corresponding nuances of their own focus. A certain need for explaining a cruel reality seems to emerge from the texts; it is as if we feel bound to "save" our countries from drifting away or if we want to find a rescue strategy.

A common ground emerges from the different chapters: there is a widespread sense of failure, of misfortune, even if only in our collective subconscious. Maybe, this frustration arises from the great expectations that Southern Europe placed on European integration and on the strengthening of the education and qualification systems. As Coniglio and Prota say in their Chap. 11, Southern Europe expected a growth path (automatically) associated with investment in human capital.

What emerges, at the end, is a picture in which the four countries of Southern Europe, and especially their poorest regions, share a number of similarities. These similarities are related to the inability to significantly upgrade their economic structure, and this inability depends on a number of factors, including the relatively scarce ability to move to higher level functions, to increase productivity, to attract FDI. This is partly related to the fact that poorer local and national institutions don't facilitate the attraction of external assets and the full exploitation of internal ones, partly related to economic and geographical factors. Southern European regions also seem to be unable to move to advanced patterns of innovation, although this is not necessarily detrimental to their growth.

The key role of human capital, which was assumed in the general framework (Fig. 1.1) is confirmed in the book, but the results of the chapters point out that the main issue for Southern European regions is not the endowment of human capital per se, but is rather the inability to exploit this human capital in an effective labour market. The existence of mismatches characterizes Southern European regions, which are therefore plagued by brain drain and population aging. The educational system, different from what happened in other European countries, did not intertwine enough with the local productive structure and as such was not a determinant of upgrading.

What also emerges is that regional development policies, in the way in which they have been implemented so far, by the countries or the European Union, have not necessarily been ineffective but have certainly been insufficient to curb the relative decline of these regions, which suffered the processes of globalization, European unification and the economic and financial crisis significantly more than the rest of the EU.

The picture, however, is not all dark. Some positive aspects emerge, such as the ability to implement process innovations, to educate a labour force which could potentially be used locally, and to implement processes of employment creation, albeit in low-productivity jobs. Moreover, there are regions in the four countries whose success is stronger than what one could expect from the context in which they are inserted.

The book doesn't push itself so far as to provide policy prescriptions, and mostly remains at a positive level. This because of the complexity of the issues at stake, with four countries with different histories and economies, and very different regions inside. This does not imply that providing policy prescriptions is impossible, or that Southern European regions are "lost cases". On the contrary, we only believe that a fully-fledged normative framework will require a full book in itself, so that the different nuances of complex policy prescriptions can be discussed without making them simplistic.

Our next objective is hence to produce another book which, starting from all the positive evidence provided in this one, will go straight to the normative.

References

Affuso A, Capello R, Fratesi U (2011) Globalisation and competitive strategies in European vulnerable regions. Reg Stud 45(5):657–675

Becker GS (1993) Human capital. A theorethical and empirical analysis with special reference to education, 3rd edn. The University of Chicago Press, London

Beugelsdijk S, Smeets R, Zwinkels R (2008) The impact of horizontal and vertical FDI on host's country economic growth. Int Bus Rev 17(4):452–472

Borensztein E, De Gregorio J, Lee J-W (1998) How does foreign direct investment affect economic growth. J Int Econ 45(1):115–135

Camagni R (2002) On the concept of territorial competitiveness: sound or misleading? Urban Stud 39(13):2395–2411

Camagni R, Capello R (2015) Rationale and design of EU cohesion policies in a period of crisis. Reg Sci Policy Pract 7(1):25–47

Capello R, Caragliu A, Fratesi U (2015) Global trends and the economic crisis: future alternative European growth strategies. Technol Forecast Soc Chang 98:120–136

Ciriaci D (2014) Does university quality influence the interregional mobility of students and graduates? The case of Italy. Reg Stud 48:1592–1608

Coe NM, Yeung HW-C (2015) Global production networks: theorizing economic development in an interconnected world. Oxford University Press, Oxford

Coniglio ND, Prota F (2008) Human capital accumulation and migration in a peripheral EU region: the case of Basilicata. Pap Reg Sci 87(1):77–95
Dotti NF, Fratesi U, Lenzi C, Percoco M (2013) Local labour markets and the interregional mobility of Italian university students. Spat Econ Anal 8(4):443–468
Faggian A, McCann P (2009) Human capital, graduate migration and innovation in British regions. Camb J Econ 33(2):317–333
Farole T, Rodriguez-Pose A, Storper M (2011) Cohesion policy in the European Union: growth, geography, institutions. J Common Mark Stud:1089–1111
Fonseca M (2005) A Centralidade do Porto perante o Alargamento a Leste. In: Porto Cidade Região. Encontro de Reflexão Prospectiva. Comunicações. Universidade do Porto, Porto, pp 290–325
Fratesi U, Percoco M (2014) Selective migration, regional growth and convergence: evidence from Italy. Reg Stud 48(10):1650–1668
Fratesi U, Rodríguez-Pose A (2016) The crisis and regional employment in Europe: what role for sheltered economies? Camb J Reg Econ Soc 9(1):33–57
Garrido-Yserte R, Gallo-Rivera MT (2010) The impact of the university upon local economy: three methods to estimate demand-side effects. Ann Reg Sci 44:39–67
Glückler J, Panitz R (2016) Relational upgrading in global value networks. J Econ Geogr 16 (2016):1161–1185
Lipietz A (1987) Mirages and miracles: the crises of global fordism. Verso, London
Mancha-Navarro T, Garrido-Yserte R (2008) Regional policy in the European Union: the cohesion-competitiveness dilemma. Reg Sci Policy Pract 1(1):47–66
Markusen A (1996) Sticky places in slippery space: a typology of industrial districts. Econ Geogr 72(3):293–313
Marques da Costa E, Palma P, Marques da Costa N (2015) Regional disparities of SGI provision. In: Fassmann H, Rauhut D, da Costa EM, Humer A (eds) Services of general interest and territorial cohesion. V&R Unipress, Vienna University Press, Viena, pp 91–121
Marques P (2015) Why did the Portuguese economy stop converging with the OECD? Institutions, politics and innovation. J Econ Geogr 15(2015):1009–1031
Petrakos G, Kallioras D, Anagnostou A (2011) Regional convergence and growth in Europe: understanding patterns and determinants. Eur Urban Reg Stud 18:375–391
Rodriguez-Pose A, Fratesi U (2004) Between development and social policies: the impact of European structural funds in objective 1 regions. Reg Stud 38(1):97–113
Rodríguez-Pose A, Fratesi U (2007) Regional business cycles and the emergence of sheltered economies in the southern periphery of Europe. Growth Chang 38(4):621–648
Rodríguez-Pose A, Vilalta-Bufí M (2005) Education, migration, and job satisfaction: the regional returns of human capital in the EU. J Econ Geogr 5:545–566
Shapiro JM (2006) Smart cities: quality of life, productivity, and the growth effects of human capital. Rev Econ Stat:324–335
Storper M (2010) Why do regions develop and change? The challenge for geography and economics. J Econ Geogr:1–14
Storper M, Scott AJ (2009) Rethinking human capital, creativity and urban growth. JEG 9:147–167
Woessmann L (2003) Specifying Human Capital. J Econ Surv 17(3):239–270

Madalena Fonseca is a Geographer and Assistant Professor at the University of Porto, Department of Geography. She holds a PhD in Economic Geography. Currently, she is the General Secretary of the Portuguese Agency for Assessment and Accreditation of Higher Education—A3ES (Lisboa). Her main research topics are currently linked with higher education and human capital: offer and demand of higher education, access, the Portuguese higher education system, higher education and regional development and quality assurance. She is a member of the Board of the European Consortium for Accreditation—ECA (The Hague) and the international expert for international accreditations of the German agency ZEVA (Hannover). She takes part in two

Erasmus+ research projects on strategic partnerships for higher education: EIQAS, Enhancing Internal Quality Assurance Systems (2014–2016), and MEHR, Migration, Education and Human Rights (2016–2019). She is the author and co-author of a large number of papers and chapters of books in the field of economic geography and regional development.

Ugo Fratesi is Associate Professor of Regional Economics at Politecnico di Milano (since December 2010). He is Editor of main section papers and Book Review Editor of Regional Studies since 2013. Previously, he was member of the editorial board of the Italian Journal of Regional Science. He was member of the Council of the Italian Section of the Regional Science Association International (AISRe) for the period 2010–2016 and was its Treasurer for the period 2010–2013. He has been involved with various roles in a large number of research projects, especially at European level, financed by the Espon programme, the FP5, FP7, Horizon 2020 or the European Commission directly. He is co-author of several books and author of a large number of papers published in refereed journals in the field of regional economics, primarily on the themes of regional growth and development, the models for forecasting regional growth, regional policy, the theory and measurement of regional disparities and the territorial aspects of human capital and innovation.

Chapter 2
Southern Europe at a Glance: Regional Disparities and Human Capital

Madalena Fonseca

JEL Classification J24 • I25 • O47 • O57

2.1 Introduction

Looking at Southern Europe—Portugal, Spain, Italy and Greece—as a unique group of countries or a homogeneous area may not have an immediate justification. Maybe there are more things that keep us apart than common features that bind us together. Beyond its relative location as a large southern periphery of the European Union, there are however, some common trends and some indicators performing similarly. It is already commonplace that Southern Europe has been particularly hit by the present crisis (see also Chap. 3 in this volume), that it has an ageing population, and large regional disparities, as it is itself, as a block, a large peripheral region!

Although Greece, Portugal and Spain joined the European Union in the 1980s, creating the first great divide inside the community, Italy being one of the initial members had revealed the north-south contrast long before. In spite of this and the previous initiatives and projects for the development of Southern Italian *Mezzogiorno*, the addition of three new countries from Southern Europe led to structural changes in the community policies with a general aim of convergence. Ever since, convergence, or rather the lack of it, has dominated the European Agenda in different areas[1]. In the first years following the Southern enlargement the main focus of the European policies was convergence at the country level, and some goals have been achieved. However the strong wish for regional equilibrium has remained unattained. New policies have been designed and assessed and different

[1]Examples of some important milestones are the reform of the Structural Funds in 1989, the Sapir Report in 2004, the Lisbon Strategy for 2010 and more recently the Europe 2020 Agenda (Gardiner et al. 2005; EC 2010, 2016).

M. Fonseca (✉)
Faculty of Arts and Humanities, University of Porto, Porto, Portugal

A3ES—Agency for Assessment and Accreditation of Higher Education, Praça de Alvalade, nr. 6, 5. Frente, 1700-036 Lisbon, Portugal
e-mail: madalena@letras.up.pt; madalena.fonseca@a3es.pt

M. Fonseca, U. Fratesi (eds.), *Regional Upgrading in Southern Europe*, Advances in Spatial Science, DOI 10.1007/978-3-319-49818-8_2

approaches have been experimented with, but without the expected results. Research continues to focus on the underlying causes that keep regions lagging behind without upgrading, and continues to work on new ways of intervention, or, as Storper says, "change and causality" (2011, p. 334).

Studying Southern Europe is not only about analysing and testing regional development models or putting into question the regional policy of the European Union; it also allows us to question the theoretical proposals for addressing the condition of the intermediate and peripheral regions. This chapter is a presentation of Southern Europe, in a broad and comprehensive characterisation, with quite large-scale data and the most up-to-date information and attempts to bring an additional building block to the understanding of the persistence of *peripheralism*.

Why are there regions with no capacity for flourishing? Is there really an inability to upgrade?

This is a descriptive and analytical text, seeking to highlight the characteristics and profiles of the regions of the four countries in Southern Europe, keeping in mind a structural methodological doubt: are we studying the regional differences or are we analysing the available data, by the available levels of territorial breakdown? How much can our basic information influence our analysis and conclusions? This problem is out of the focus of the book and is not going to be discussed although we have to keep it in mind at every step of our work.

Both theories of endogenous growth and neoclassic with different variations have not yet definitively clarified the mechanisms that keep lagging regions from growing and upgrading (Storper 2011; Rodríguez-Pose and Fratesi 2007; Rodríguez-Pose and Fitjar 2013). Backward economic structures, poor infrastructure, R&D investment deficit, lower skills, lower labour productivity, lack of scale economies, no access to markets and inefficient policies are some of the most repeatedly charged problems in Southern European cases, even when the effects of dependencies and external control are considered (Rodríguez-Pose 2001; Balchin et al. 1999; Jarocinski 2003; Capello and Lenzi 2013).

On one topic all theories agree, innovation is a critical driver for economic growth (Simmie 2001; Meusburguer 2013). The knowledge-innovation-technology-economic growth and progress path, although intensively researched and developed at the theoretical level, is subject to many different nuances when it comes to the real regions and at present has some critical views (Capello and Lenzi 2013). The geography of agglomeration and polarisation is quite complex. Economic geography approaches are various and incorporate contributions and inputs from several scientific neighbours (Storper 2011; Scott 1988, Storper and Scott 2009; Bathelt and Glückler 2011). In the current exercise, we want to understand the spatial divisions of labour in Southern Europe and identify the main types of regional behaviour, using a multivariate analysis as a basic tool, complemented with other quantitative and qualitative data.

Regional upgrading understood as a development process, a learning and evolutionary path of economic growth and socio improvement does not occur in a social, cultural, political or economic vacuum (Meusburger 2013, p. 26). It is context sensitive and depends on local (regional) constraints, opportunities, knowledge contexts and other socio-economic and institutional frames. In fact, some policies have failed because they followed *one size fits all* schemes, overlooking regional specificities.[2]

Bearing in mind this framework, this analysis focuses on the identification of the features of the regions of the four countries of Southern Europe, using as a main methodological tool the concept of "social filter", introduced initially by Andrés Rodríguez-Pose—also a geographer and economist from Southern Europe (Rodríguez-Pose 1999; Crescenzi and Rodríguez-Pose 2013). We adapted the concept with some subsequent developments for the specific objectives of this study, in the selection of indicators and in the analysis.

This introductory chapter presents a tentative interpretation of the current map of Southern Europe and the regional disparities of the four selected countries with a special focus on the link between human capital, space and economy.

2.2 Regional Disparities

Regional disparities are not an innocuous and objective concept nor do they correspond to an image or snapshot of an enlarged spatial reality made up of multiple smaller territorial units. They are the outcome of many factors, and need a multidisciplinary approach to be understood. They assume different shapes according to the field of analysis and the corresponding selection of variables or indicators with which they are assessed. They are scale sensitive and politically biased. In fact, there is no global theory on regional disparities (Gyuris 2014) and "a decent theoretical understanding of uneven geographical development still remains to be written" (Harvey 2004). Even the wording is not consistent: geographical, spatial or regional disparities or inequalities. Beyond the wording there are implicit judgements, like unevenness or inequity, injustice or unfairness and an idea of differentiation, "quasi as things that are 'just out there'" (Gyuris 2014, p. 2). Gyuris gathered various approaches to spatial disparities, identifying the background of the main theoreticians, the analytical focus and scale of preference of theories, the political ideologies and systems they were aimed to legitimize, and the use of science as a source of legitimacy in a comprehensive exercise that included natural sciences, philosophy, political science, economics, sociology, history and geography (2014, p. 332) under the argument that there is a political component of the concept. Gyuris selects the term "spatial disparities" and describes them as "forms of unevenness in space that can be traced back to human agency" (2014, p. 13). Venables goes further and states that "spatial inequalities in economic activity and income arise endogenously and persistently, not just as transient phenomena" (2011, p. 1). On the other hand, evolutionary economic geography—or, as Martin

[2]The metaphors of RegioTopia, RegioCopia and RegioNova, used in a little story of Harald Bathelt and Johannes Glueckler (2002, p. 14) are particularly expressive.

and Sunley defend, development evolutionary geography—offers "a more systemic and holistic understanding of spatial economic evolution, one that considers not just industrial evolutionary dynamics but also the wider economic, institutional, and socio-political structures produced by and constitutive of uneven geographical development" (Martin and Sunley 2015, p. 720). Evolutionary economic geography is focused on economic development systems and is building up a framework that includes the perspectives of other theoretical models from the institutional economic geography and the geographical political economy in a synthesis important to the understanding of regional development landscapes (Martin and Sunley 2015). However, the complexity of the regional mosaics—*the geographical world is a messy one, it does not cohere* (Thrift 2005, p. 51)—cannot be approached by methods that include the recording of every aspect of the regions or a *backward gaze* (Thrift 2005, p. 2) that aims at understanding the future as a simple projection of past trends. Regional disparities are the outcome of polarised economic growth processes, i.e., the visible outlook of the geography of agglomeration or of geographically uneven development. They are the visible face of dependencies and changes in the international division of labour and the organisation of global values chains, migrations and other flows of people, information, commodities and power, changing constantly.

Agglomeration and polarisation or regional divides are at the core of economic geography, and innovation, knowledge (and technology) and human capital became the pillars of growth and development.

The first models in economic geography were based on the explanation of production processes based on the balance between capital and labour in an aggregate way. Labour corresponded to the sum of workers. With the development of human capital theory[3] there was a shift in the former, more traditional approaches and labour started to be considered in its different components and characteristics from quality, skills and other elements (Woessmann 2003). Postfordist division of labour made human capital more relevant (Storper and Scott 2009, p. 163) and led to a broader stratification. The qualification of labour with the acquisition of knowledge, skills, competences and life-long learning generates and brings up human capital.

Knowledge is immediately related to human capital, since human capital corresponds to a complex set of personal characteristics and components that differ from individual to individual and include knowledge, skills and various competences. The growing importance of knowledge in processes of producing and servicing goods and distributing them to markets developed in economic geography research

[3]The concept of human capital first appeared in the works developed by Adam Smith (1723–1790) and Marshall (1842–1924). However, this concept was misunderstood because there was no sense in qualifying *"labor as a type of capital"* (Teixeira 2007). By the late sixties of the twentieth century, the research on human capital took off. T. W. Schultz, Jacob Mincer and Gary S. Becker developed the main contributions on human capital theory and its different approaches. Human capital has been understood differently in other contexts and scientific areas. We will focus on economic geography approaches and uses of the concept of human capital.

as well as in other fields, from economy to sociology and cultural sciences. Modern economic growth and development theories assume that "economic growth is, at least partly, a function of stocks of knowledge in the form of human capital or the outcomes of research and development (R&D) activities" (Huggins and Thompson 2014, p. 1).

Knowledge however, has several particularities that make it a special "good" or commodity and constrain the development of a knowledge economy. First of all, it is not an homogeneous "good"; there are different types of knowledge from everyday knowledge to theoretical knowledge and action knowledge or explicit and implicit (tacit) knowledge and knowledge related to skills and competences or abilities (Glückler et al. 2013). Parallel to this, there are also different levels of quality in knowledge, and prior knowledge is critical for knowledge improvement (Rodríguez-Pose 2001, p. 281). Besides, offer and demand of knowledge are uncertain and it is difficult to anticipate the price or the value of knowledge as a commodity or good, not to mention the quasi-impossibility of measuring knowledge (Thönnessen and Gundlach 2013). Knowledge can grow infinitely since it can be endlessly re-used, can be combined and recombined (Storper and Scott 2009, p. 148); it can make people more productive (Shapiro 2006). In fact, it is only possessed by people and does not exist outside people. Knowledge flows involve people flows (Fratesi 2014). Human capital corresponds to knowledgeable people and is not a fixed asset of a region, since migrations can modify the map of human capital (Shapiro 2006). Knowledge cannot be produced in isolation nor entirely transferred, since part of it is inherent to the individual (Bathelt and Glückler 2011). Knowledge is highly localised and new knowledge is always local and scarce for a certain period of time, before it spreads and gives way to new knowledge divides and new regional disparities (Meusburger 2013, p. 19). That is also why a spatial perspective is needed to capture the functioning of the knowledge economy and that is how knowledge is, in our time, the critical driver of economic change (Bathelt and Glückler 2011; Simmie 2001).

In this context, human capital turns out to be the focus of what we can consider a modern approach in the geography of agglomeration. Human capital is unquestioned as the main factor for innovation in the strategic documents for the European Union's regional development, as is the case of the Lisbon Strategy for 2010 or the Europe 2020 strategy.

The link between human capital, innovation, economic growth and regional development is usually analysed through indicators of economic performance and of the educational stock of a region (Woessmann 2003; Crescenzi et al. 2013; Thönnessen and Gundlach 2013). There are however limitations and the real effect of education institutions on the economic growth and regional development of the regions where they are located remains a statement taken for granted more than an argument empirically and theoretically demonstrated. There is some empirical evidence but almost nothing about the underlying causes of this relationship (Shapiro 2006). The mismatch between educational stock and labour market demand, over-education and brain-drain are some of the evidences of the shortfalls of the methodologies used in most of the recent studies. Human capital is relevant but not only for the location where it is generated. Human capital stock of neighbouring regions can be used by a region, and regions with high human capital potential can underperform despite their assets. Migration and economic base and production structure or specialisation of a region as well as the polarization pattern of the main urban areas are also relevant (Storper and Scott 2009; Simmie and Martin 2010). Recently, for instance, more attention has been paid to the mismatch between higher education and the labour market at the level of the perceptions of the graduates who get frustrated and even regret having entered the university (Kucel and Vilalta-Bufí 2013a, b).

Knowledge and innovation have to be produced or generated, distributed, spread or diffused and absorbed and used by people and regions in order to enhance human capital and economic growth; it is not an automatic process. Investment or expenses in research and development are usually taken as the best proxy to assess the regional growth or upgrade potential of a region. The effects of the investment in research and development on the innovative potential of a region however, are conditioned by several factors including a minimum threshold of prior knowledge or human capital (Meusburger 2013, p. 19; Rodríguez-Pose 2001; Charlot et al. 2015). In fact, the richer regions in Europe benefit from their previous assets in terms of knowledge production and innovation while the poor regions do not have the same ability to innovate or catch up.

> For these regions [poor regions with low levels of R&D and human capital], investing marginally in such inputs [R&D] would be wasting money. In particular, the return to R&D expenditure is maximized between 2% and 3% of regional GDP, whereas HK [human capital] has a positive effect when at least 20% of the regional population has completed tertiary education (Charlot et al. 2015, p. 1250).

In spite of the lack of a strong theoretical framework, several criticisms have been made about the different strategic decisions on physical versus human capital investments, as is the case, for instance, for Southern European countries; some studies argue that policy measures have concentrated less on human capital enhancement than would be desirable:

> [Third], the Mediterranean countries do not invest enough in intangible capital. This will pose a serious threat to the economies of Italy and Spain in the coming decades (Gros and Roth 2012, p. 30).

And this remains an issue quite difficult to understand and assess.

2.3 The Social Filter Concept or the Absorptive Capacity of the Regions

The concept of social filter in the context of the geography of economic growth and regional development has been improved on by several authors in order to capture the structural preconditions of the regions that play a critical role in their successful development and has a special focus on the regional innovation systems

(Rodríguez-Pose 1999; Crescenzi et al. 2007, 2013; Crescenzi and Rodríguez-Pose 2013). The social filter corresponds to the social and institutional characteristics of a given region and the local systems of innovation that enable this region to produce and use or apply innovation and knowledge, as well as being able to learn from it and from others, and using knowledge flows from other regions (Crescenzi et al. 2013, p. 294). The social filter corresponds to a mix of characteristics that create the distinctiveness of a region (a "profile") and has to be proxied by indicators from education, economic base and demography (Crescenzi et al. 2013, p. 295). Each region has its unique Social Filter (Rodríguez-Pose 1999, p. 81).

This concept can be taken in association with the concept of absorptive capacity of the regions, i. e. "the importance of internal knowledge absorption capacity on external knowledge network development." (Storper and Scott 2009, p. 21; Meusburger 2013; Rodríguez-Pose and Fitjar 2013; Huggins and Thompson 2014). Both concepts recognize the importance of intangibles like the social or relational capital as a set of values of individuals operating within a particular local or regional milieu, to explain contributions to innovation and production through social investments in trust and reciprocity within this milieu (Storper and Scott 2009, p. 10). This social capital gradually builds up a network capital, both local and global or non-local, as Barthelt and Glücker name this relational regional asset (2011). Social and network capital are concepts associated with the institutional framework of a region, taken as broad as possible. Regional growth greatly depends on those network capital stocks that include knowledge access and calculative relations (Huggins and Thompson 2014).

Rodríguez-Pose speaks about institutional thickness and territorial capital, taking the latter as a mix of human or intellectual capital, social capital and political capital (2013). In a broader framework, empirical evidence has proved that the combination of a high human capital endowment with well-functioning institutions may lead to the formation of efficient regional systems of innovation (Rodríguez-Pose and Fitjar 2013).

"It is not a single socio-economic factor in isolation that matters for innovation: it is the combination of a set of local features—human capital, young people, favourable sector structure—that facilitates the genesis of local innovation. The relevance of these factors emerges only when they are assessed in an integrated framework able to capture their synergies and interactions." (Crescenzi and Rodríguez-Pose 2013, p. 289). The different concepts or formulations—social filter, absorptive capacity of the regions or innovation systems—converge in the importance of the institutional framework of the regions as the building blocks of growth and development.

In order to operationalise the concept of social filter and apply it to analyse the regional disparities in Southern European countries, a set of indicators from education, economic base and demography were selected, taking into account other studies and possible comparative models and situations. The most commonly used variables and indicators related to education focusing on human capital were selected; they are related to human capital theories and based on the rationale that there is a link between human capital, innovation, and economic growth (Bathelt and Glückler 2011; Glaeser 1994; Rodriguez-Pose and Fratesi 2004; Cowan and Zinovyeva 2007).

Although the social and economic returns on investment in education have been estimated in different methods (Patrinos and Psacharopoulos 2011), there are still some limitations to applying the concept in all contexts and in an aggregate way. Among other limitations, returns to schooling decrease along the levels of the education system and it is difficult to assess accumulated cognitive skills (Woessmann 2003). It is also necessary to distinguish between individual and collective returns (De La Fuente 2003).

Human capital endowment embodies educational stock and therefore higher education and qualification at higher levels of the school system are the most relevant components of human capital. Tertiary education enrolments and indicators from human resources in science and technology as well as investments in research and development have been considered as proxies for human capital in the present study. Keeping in mind all the limitations of the different approaches already developed, it is more or less generally accepted that higher education indicators proxy for human capital. Formal education, family background, lifelong learning and other factors can, however, change human capital. We tried to take this into consideration by including indicators on population and employment by the highest level of education attained. In fact, higher education indicators show a high relevance in most of the approaches based on the analysis of educational stock related to economic growth (Rodríguez-Pose and Vilalta-Bufí 2005; Goldstein and Renault 2004; Marginson 2007).

Gross Domestic Product (GDP), employment and unemployment rates, and the qualification of the employees, by sectors of activity and gender, among other demographics, are the main indicators used in the study to characterise the economic base of the four Southern European countries at the NUTS 2 level. It is somehow less controversial to select indicators on the basis of economics than on human capital endowments. Employment in agriculture and in industry, and in the technology and knowledge-intensive sectors of these two sectors are relevant (Crescenzi and Rodríguez-Pose 2013); population and employment by the highest level of education attained was also considered; research and development (R&D) expenditure and human resources were also included although we are aware of the limitations of this indicator. Alone, R&D expenditure is not enough to capture the spatial variation of knowledge production (Crescenzi and Rodríguez-Pose 2013, p. 290) but it has been used to assess the economic effort in innovation production.

As for the demographic context, a set of general variables and indicators of the ageing process as well as the flows of immigrants from outside the region were included. Special attention was paid to the age structure and fertility rates. Population density was not considered although we were aware that it has been included in most of the studies on the social filter (Crescenzi and Rodríguez-Pose 2013, p. 297); the option was based on the argument that agglomeration should emerge as a result (output) and not as an input.

2.4 Point of Departure: Southern Europe Map of Prosperity

Gross domestic product (GDP) at current market prices—Purchasing Power Standard per inhabitant in percentage of the EU average, at country level (EU28 = 100) is the most common indicator to assess the global health of the economy of the European countries.

The four countries in Southern Europe registered a very turbulent evolution from 2001 to 2014, the last year for which there are available data both for country and NUTS2 levèls (Fig. 2.1 and Annex 2.3). Italy, in 2001, almost reached 120% of EU 28 average but ever since there has been a continuous decline and recently (2014), the indicator was below 100%. Spain has been near the EU 28 average almost every year of this time period, surpassing the 100% limit between 2004 and 2009, although in 2014 it was only at 91%. Portugal presents the lowest values of the four countries throughout the time period, with 78% in 2014. Greece shows the most turbulent evolution with growth and decline since 2001; in 2009, Greece almost met the EU 28 average with 94%; by 2014, however, Greece's GDP was only 72% of that of EU 28. This value is even lower than in Portugal.

When looking at the GDP at a NUTS 2 level map for Southern Europe, we immediately tend to identify the rich and poor regions (Fig. 2.2). There are two main types of countries: Spain and Italy display a north south divide with a group of "richer" regions in the North and a vast "poor" space in the South. For instance, Italy has the highest number of regions above the EU average—11 regions, most of them located in the North of the country as is the case of Bolzano (144%) and Valle d'Aosta (133%). Those two regions in Italy presented the highest values of all four countries in 2014. Spain, like Italy, presents a North-South divide and some NUTS 2 regions like Pais Vasco (119%), Navarra (113%) or Cataluña (108%) largely surpass the EU 28 average. The capital regions of Madrid and Rome belong to the first type, the "richer". In both countries, the North corresponds to the most dynamic industrial areas.

Greece and Portugal, in turn, show different patterns, but similar to each other: the capital NUTS 2 regions of Lisboa and Athens are the richest regions opposed to the rest of their countries. This is a polarised richness pattern and is founded on a service and administrative or governance control economic model.

On the lower end of the GDP scale in Southern Europe between 2001 and 2014, are the regions that have often had the ten lowest scores: Anatoliki Makedonia, Thraki, Ipeiros, Calabria, Dytiki Ellada, Extremadura, Norte, Thessalia, Centro (PT), Voreio Aigaio and Campania. From 2011 onwards there was a downgrading of the Greek regions and in 2014, seven Greek regions registered the lowest values, all below 60% of EU 28 average: Anatoliki Makedonia, Thraki, with 50%, Ipeiros, with 51%, Dytiki Ellada, with 54%, Thessalia, with 55%, Kentriki Makedonia, with 56%, Voreio Aigaio, with 57%, and Peloponnisos with 58%.

No Greek region surpasses the 100% value. In Portugal, only Lisboa has a value over 100%.

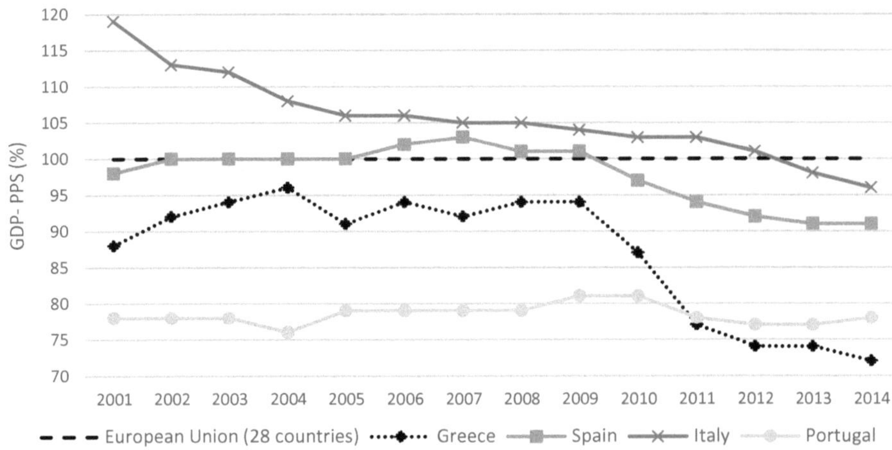

Fig. 2.1 Gross Domestic Product (GDP)—PPS per inhabitants % (EU28 = 100%). Source: Eurostat

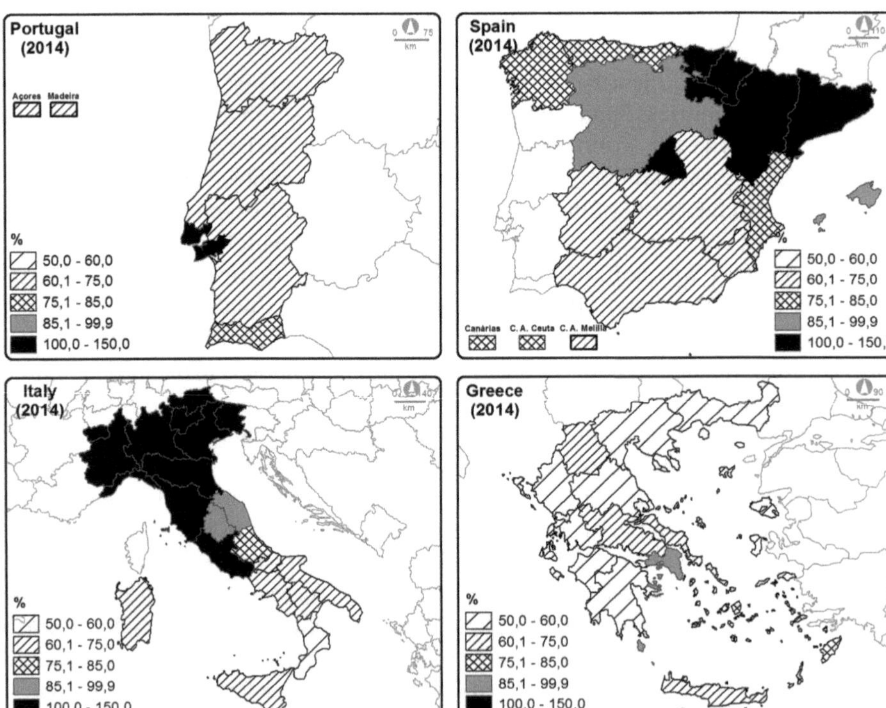

Fig. 2.2 GDP at current market prices—PPS per inhabitants % (EU28 = 100) 2014. Source: Eurostat

This is the map of regional development and prosperity in Southern Europe. The mismatch between the configurations of the disparities for different indicators, including the educational stock or other proxies for human capital, led us to the multivariate analysis that follows.

2.5 Regional Disparities Through the Lenses of the Social Filter Paradigm

The empirical exercise of analysing the regional disparities in Southern Europe with the "Social Filter" tool is based on data from Eurostat at the NUTS 2 level (or NUTS 3, in some cases), for 2014 or the most recent date for which there is data available.

The initial database included nearly 80 variables[4]. After running several rounds of an exploratory principal component analysis (PCA), we came out with a set of 31 variables[5], excluding all the absolute values and considering only percentages and ratios or indexes and covering the three main areas of the social filter, education, economic base and demography (Crescenzi et al. 2013). A principal component analysis (PCA) was again used to identify clusters of variables corresponding to the main axes of the regional "social filter" in Southern Europe. The results for the first five factors are included in Table 2.1, and Fig. 2.3. The factor loadings are presented in the Annex 2.1 for reasons of space.

Factor 1, named as *The Unemployment Rigidity Factor,* evidences how unemployment—specifically long term unemployment or structural unemployment, unemployment of females and total unemployment rates—shapes the face of Southern Europe and its regional disparities, and especially how it punishes the peripheral regions. Factor 1 gathers together nine variables with a positive loading or a positive correlation between the variables and the factor: five unemployment indicators for the year 2014, starting with the long-term unemployment rate; young people neither in employment nor in education and training; employment rate in agriculture, both total and in technology and knowledge-intensive sectors of agriculture, for the year 2013; population from 0 to 19 years as a percentage of NUTS' total population with a very weak weight. Six variables related to wealth and employment have a high negative loading or negative correlation with factor 1, including GDP per capita as a percentage of EU average (Annex 2.1) and R&D expenditure as a percentage of GDP.

This unemployment factor, the most relevant, explains nearly 30% of the variability and has an eigenvalue of 9.27.

---

[4]The datasets used in this chapter were all taken from Eurostat and are available in the corresponding website or delivered the author, by request.

[5]The list of those 31 variables is at the Annex 2.2.

Table 2.1 Results of the PCA analysis: Eigenvalues and variability

	F1	F2	F3	F4	F5
Eigenvalue	9.270	5.544	4.830	2.787	2.019
Variability (%)	29.902	17.885	15.581	8.990	6.513
Cumulative (%)	29.902	47.786	63.367	72.357	78.870

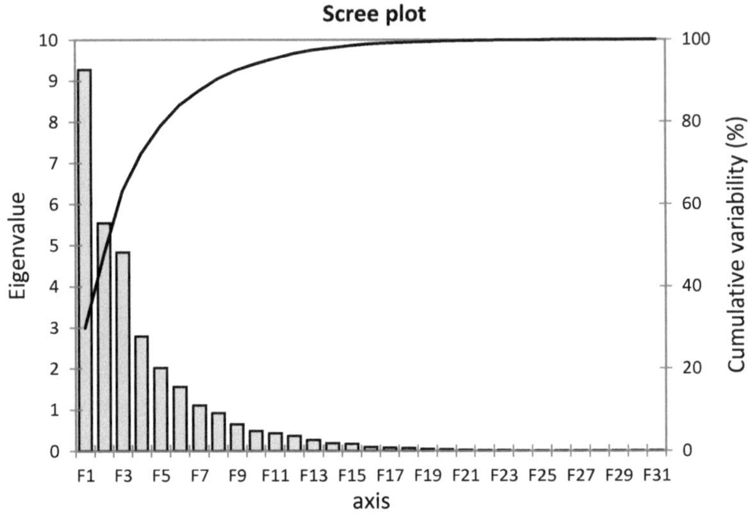

Fig. 2.3 Scree plot for PCA analysis

Factor 1 evidences the major divides in regional development of the four countries. Most of the regions in Southern Spain (Andalucia and Murcia) and in Southern Italy and almost all regions in Greece are the hardest hit regions by the negative components of Factor 1 (Fig. 2.4). These three countries present a highly contrasting pattern, with a sharp north-south divide in Spain and Italy. Continental Portugal, on the contrary, presents a smoother pattern.

The more dynamic regions (the richer regions?) with the best performance in Factor 1 correspond to the NUTS 2 regions with the lower unemployment rates and higher GDP and include almost all regions in continental Italy north of Molise; Pais Vasco and Navarra in the North of Spain; and at a slightly lower level, the three capitals, Madrid, Lisboa and Lazio where Roma is located. Attiki, the region where Athens is located is the better performing region in Greece although with a positive score in Factor 1 (0.791). All other Greek regions fall into very high scores of Factor 1 (higher than 4.31). Ceuta and Melilla however, register the highest scores.

It is however necessary to bear in mind that economic restructuring, in particular industrial evolution towards new production paradigms, always carries unemployment with it. Thus, unemployment rate can be a signal of innovation potential and on-going restructuring processes. Only the follow up of the evolution of the indicator will allow a more accurate analysis of this changing process.

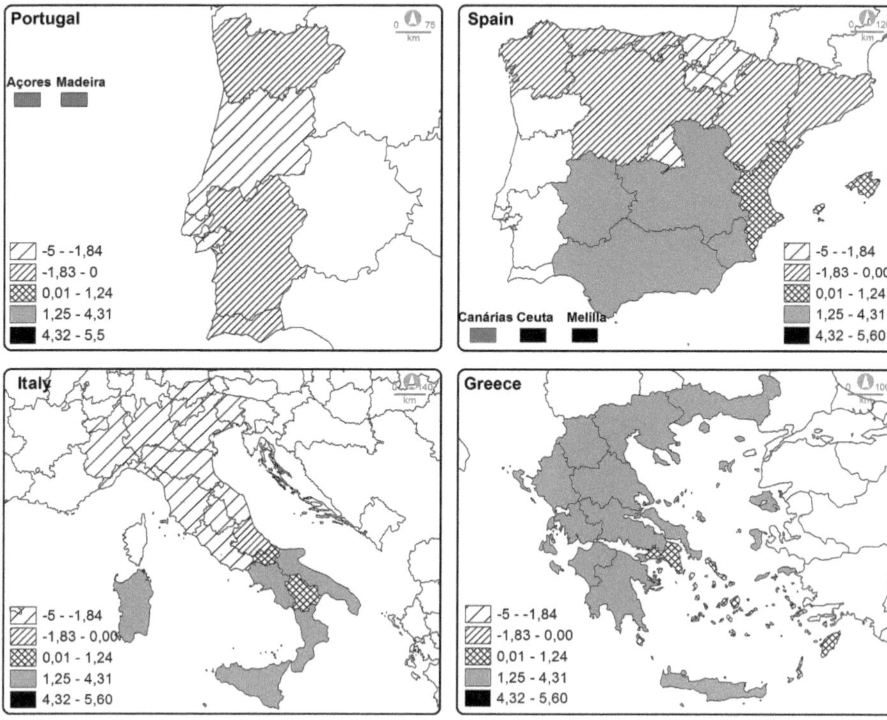

Fig. 2.4 Factor 1—The unemployment rigidity factor (Eigenvalue 9.270, variability 29.902%)

Factor 2, named as *The Human Capital and Innovation Factor* corresponds to a mix of variables. Factor 2 gathers together five variables with a positive loading or a positive correlation between the variables and the factor linked with higher education qualification population and human resources or active population and population variation. Factor 2 includes a variable with a negative loading or negative correlation corresponding to the population with a lower level of qualification: persons aged 25–64 with upper secondary education attainment, by sex and NUTS 2 regions (%).

This human capital and innovation factor explains nearly 18% of the variability and has an eigenvalue of 5.54.

Factor 2 is a complement of Factor 1 for building up the Social Filter concept; the regional disparity patterns of Factor 2 do not overlap with the former patterns of Factor 1 (Fig. 2.5).

Spain is the country that performs better; Madrid is the region with the highest score in all the four countries. Pais Vasco, Navarra and Cataluña also register high values, although lower than the value of Madrid; all the other regions in mainland Spain fall in the immediately lower values, still quite high. Opposite to this pattern, Portugal and Greece display quite contrasting situations. Both countries register high disparities with the corresponding capital regions presenting the best score, in

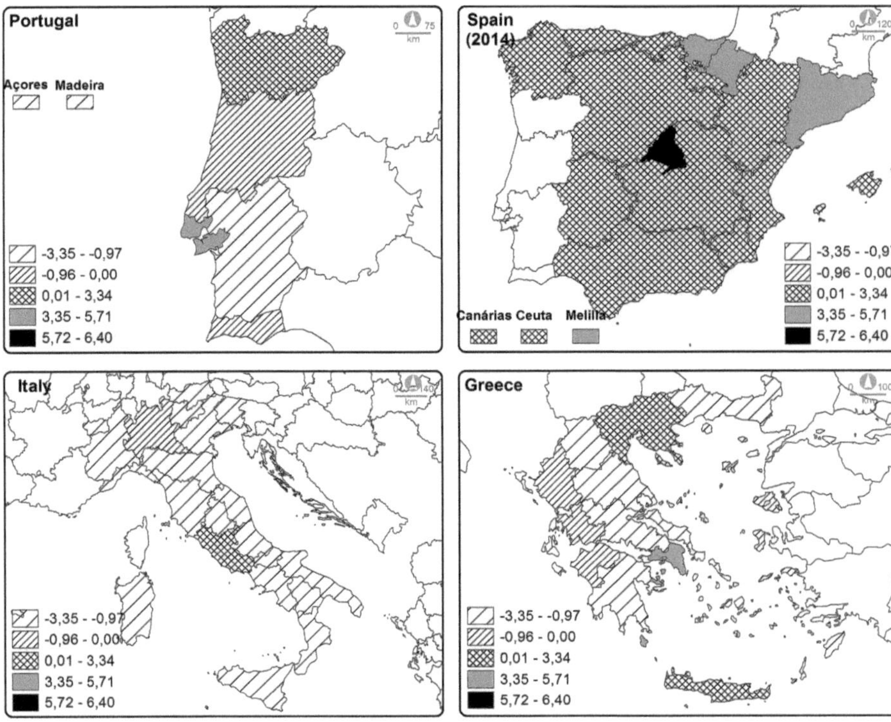

Fig. 2.5 Factor 2—The Human Capital and Innovation Factor (Eigenvalue 5.544, variability 17.885%)

both cases lower than Madrid. Italy does not display relevant disparities and presents a quite unexpected performance with low scores all over the country. Most of Italian NUTS 2 regions fall in the lower values of Factor 2. Exceptions are Lombardia with a higher score and Lazio, the region where Roma is located, with an even higher score. Lazio's score however is lower than that of Lisbon or Attiki and still lower than Madrid's. The pattern displayed by Italy in Factor 2 suggests that it is not relevant for explaining the Italian model of development.

The regional performance of Factor 2 supports the argument that human capital endowment of a region does not lead immediately to growth; it is necessary but not sufficient. Further, it is possible that Spain has implemented a formal higher education expansion policy that is already delivering results in terms of graduates but this is not a guarantee of economic growth and regional development, not to mention reduction in the regional disparities.

Factor 3, named as *The Educational Potential Factor*, is positively correlated with three variables, two of them related to higher education enrolments and students at the age of 17; the third variable positively correlated is the old age dependency. Factor 3 is negatively correlated with two variables from the education set: lower qualifications and school dropouts.

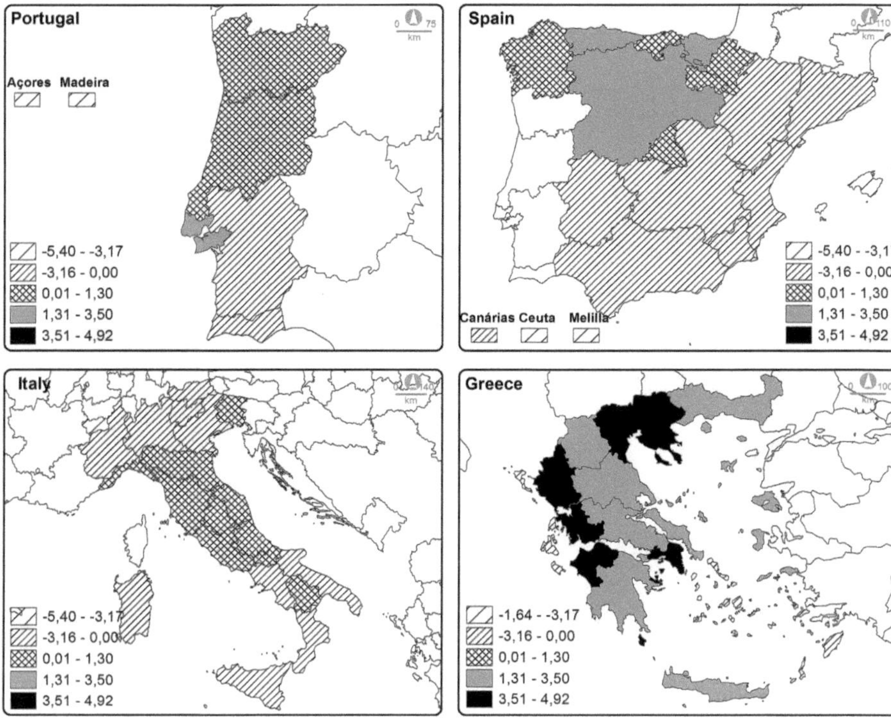

Fig. 2.6 Factor 3—Educational potential factor (Eigenvalue 4.830, variability 15.581%)

Factor 3 is much less relevant than the former two factors and accounts for explaining nearly 16% of the variability with an eigenvalue of 4.830.

The spatial pattern of the factor loadings of Factor 3 by NUTS 2 regions results in a complex landscape (Fig. 2.6). Regions with the higher scores correspond to regions with a potential growth of their human capital assets; at least apparently, those regions are benefiting from, for instance, education policies with the aim of broadening access to higher levels of the education system.

Factor 4, named as *The Population Potential Factor*, is positively correlated with two demographic variables: fertility rates and population density, and negatively correlated with school dropouts, for females.

Factor 4 is much less relevant than the former three factors and accounts for explaining nearly 9% of the variability with an eigenvalue of 2.787.

Related to this, and bearing in mind the critical level of the population ageing that Southern Europe is facing, it is understandable that this Factor only assumes real relevance in certain regions. Factor 4 reflects how quickly the population in vast hinterlands in the several countries is ageing. Noteworthy are the younger population bastions. In Portugal and Spain, Lisbon, Madrid, Pais Vasco and Navarra stand out as demographic dynamic poles. Greece has not such a contrasted pattern as the former countries but, the country still displays strong regional

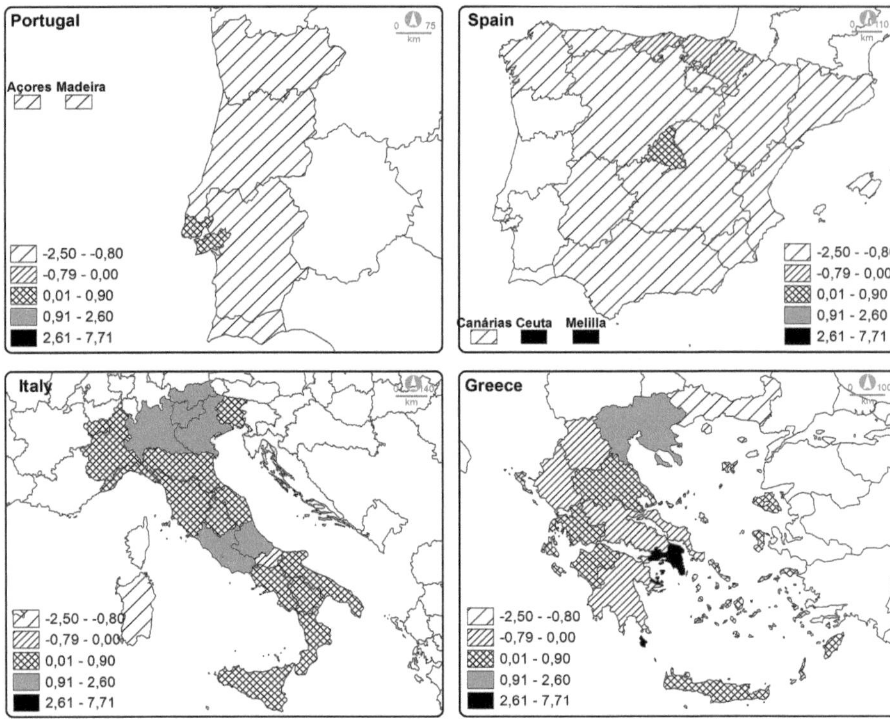

Fig. 2.7 Factor 4—Population potential factor (Eigenvalue 2.878, variability 8.990%)

contrasts. Italy is certainly the exception in the four countries. The country does not have as great contrasts as the others and most of the regions perform better, with higher scores. The spatial pattern of the factor loadings of Factor 4 by NUTS 2 regions results in a rural-urban landscape for Portugal, Spain and Greece and a more balanced scenario in Italy (Fig. 2.7). Italy has a less ageing population and a stronger and more dynamic economic base, in addition to the massive influx of immigrants from outside Europe.

Factor 5, named as *Human Capital II*, is residual; it is positively correlated with two educational variables: student distribution by region and students at the second stage of tertiary education leading to an advanced research qualification (level 6).

Factor 5 is less relevant when compared to the former four factors, explaining nearly 7% of the variability with an eigenvalue of 2.019. Still it is important to highlight the relevance in certain regions as is the case of Norte (PT) and Centro (PT) and some Italian regions spread all over the country as well as some Spanish regions in the industrial areas in the North of the country (Fig. 2.8). Factor 5 reflects both some residual demographic potential and educational policies of bringing young generations to the school and to research and development. Regions with the highest scores are those that strongly support research and development.

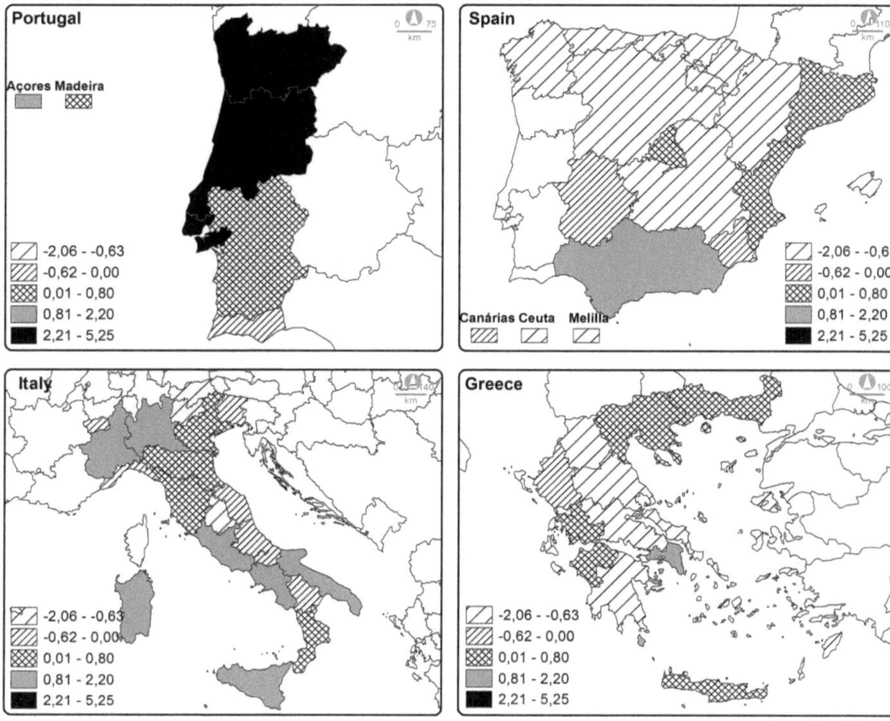

Fig. 2.8 Factor 5—Human capital II factor (Eigenvalue 2.019, variability 6.513%)

Considering the squared cosines of the observations, i.e. the NUTS 2 and for each region the factor for which the squared cosine is the highest, it is possible to infer the relevance of each factor for each region. The output can be considered a synthesis of the social filter application in the four Southern Europe countries by NUTS 2 (Fig. 2.9).

Factor 1 is again the most relevant for the major number of regions and more adequate for explaining the regional patchwork in Spain and Italy—the most economically robust countries. It is also adequate for certain Greek regions in the central part of the country. Factor 2 is particularly relevant for some of the more dynamic Spanish regions, old industrial areas, like Pais Vasco, Navarra and Cataluña as well as for Madrid and other regions; it is also important for Alentejo (PT) and some regions in Italy, but there is no clear relationship between the economic base of those regions and the scores of factor 2.

Some features must be highlighted, however. Besides the impact of factor 1, strongly conditioned by unemployment and to a lesser degree, factor 2 and the human capital and innovation potential, there are no overlapping patterns for the different maps separately. We already knew that there are larger inequalities within countries than between countries and that the national policies are not playing the main role any longer (Puga 2002). Still, there are national institutional constraints.

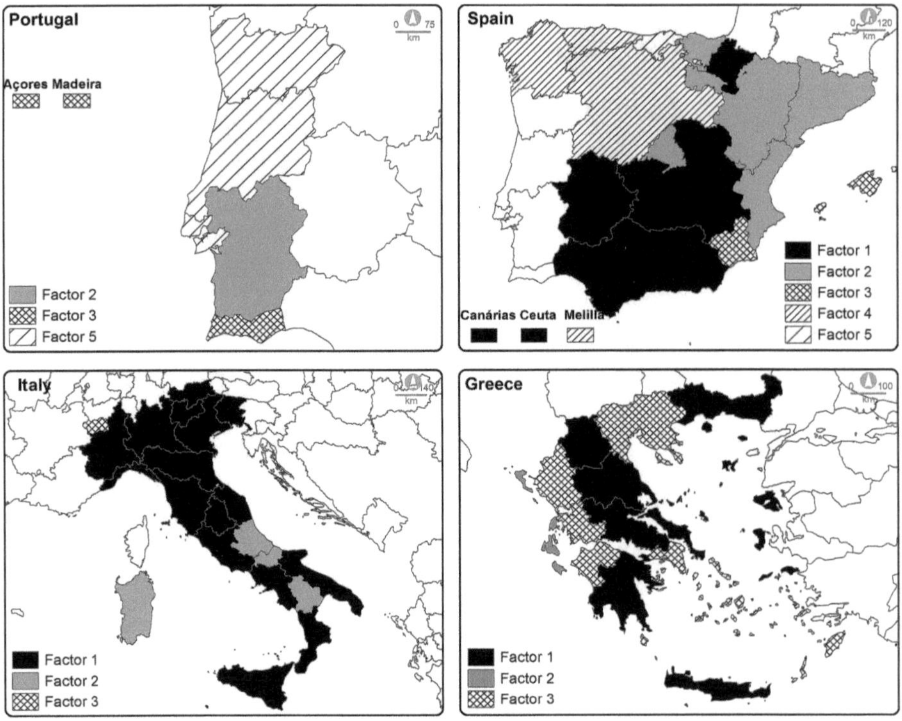

Fig. 2.9 Largest squared cosines of the NUTS 2 for the five factors (PCA)

For instance in some countries including Italy, Spain and Portugal, salaries are defined at the national level.

2.6 A Short Complementary Exercise

In order to answer the question, "Is R&D investment in lagging areas of Europe worthwhile?" Rodríguez-Pose tested the link between investment in R&D and economic growth in the European regions at the NUTS 2 level, based on the evolution of GDP per capita measured in PPS and the evolution of R&D expenditure as a percentage of GDP between 1986 and 1996 (2001). Skipping the theoretical and empirical analysis of that study at the risk of too much simplification, in short, the author concluded that "it is difficult to definitively prove that the increase in growth may be the direct result of the expansion in R&D investments." (Rodríguez-Pose 2001, p. 292). Making a comparative exercise with the same indicators, from the same source (Eurostat), for the four Southern European countries at the NUTS 2 level, for 2003 and 2013, it is again not possible to state unequivocally that investments in R&D in the peripheral regions ensure economic growth.

Between 2003 and 2013, two NUTS 2 regions maintained the same value for the GDP per capita (PPS), while three other regions registered a positive variation. Galicia in Spain and Centro in Portugal maintained the same value of GDP per capita in 2003 and in 2013. The north of Portugal, the Azores, and Bolzano in Italy, were the three NUTS 2 regions of Southern Europe with positive changes. All other NUTS 2 regions of the four countries of Southern Europe registered a negative variation of its GDP per capita in PPS as a percentage of the UE28 average between 2003 and 2013. In contrast with this performance, only five NUTS 2 regions of the four countries recorded a negative change in R&D expenditure as a percentage of GDP. Three of these regions are special cases; Ceuta and the Canary Islands in Spain and the Azores in Portugal. Abruzzo and Lazio in Italy are the other two regions with negative variations; all the other regions registered a positive variation, ten of which were higher than 100%. Sterea Ellada, in Greece, registered an increase of 500%; Ionia Nisia and Peloponnisos, an increase of 237.5 and 225.0% respectively.

Between 2003 and 2013, only two NUTS 2 regions in Southern Europe registered an increase, both in GDP per capita (PPS) and in R&D expenditure as a percentage of GDP. Those were the regions of Norte in Portugal and Bolzano in Italy. We cannot identify a clear pattern; no correlation exists between the two variables to be possible to sustain an argument of causality, nor is there a linear direct path between innovation and economic growth, as measured by these indicators.

The regions with the higher scores of GDP per capita in PPS in 2003 are represented in Fig. 2.10. and the regions from the bottom of the same ranking, for 2003, are plotted in Fig. 2.11. Figure 2.12 is a kind of legend for the two previous figures. The intermediate regions were not represented for clearness of the graphics.

As already mentioned, only Bolzano registered an increase in GDP per capita; all other NUTS 2 regions declined in average in the 10 year time span. Nevertheless all regions registered an increase of R&D expenditure as a percentage of the GDP.

Lagging regions registered a similar performance: decrease of GDP in spite of increases in R&D expenditure. These "poorer" regions even registered the higher increase in R&D expenditure, as could be anticipated, taking into account other studies (Charlot et al. 2015, p. 1229). Nevertheless the "richer" regions have much higher values of GDP per capita than the former. Norte Portugal stands out as the exception. The region had a very small increase in its GDP and an increase in R&D. Norte Portugal was the region with the lowest score of GDP per capita, from all the four countries in Southern Europe, in 2013.

Even without clear patterns, there is however, some similarity in both graphs (Fig. 2.10. and 2.11) and it is possible to identify two main groups of regions outside the exceptions of regions that registered a growth in one or two indicators: those whose arrows are longer but with a slight slope (W–E) and those with a shorter but sharper slope (NW–SE). It is possible to include two or three NUTS 2 regions in the first group from both "richer" and "poorer" regions. Those are regions with a higher

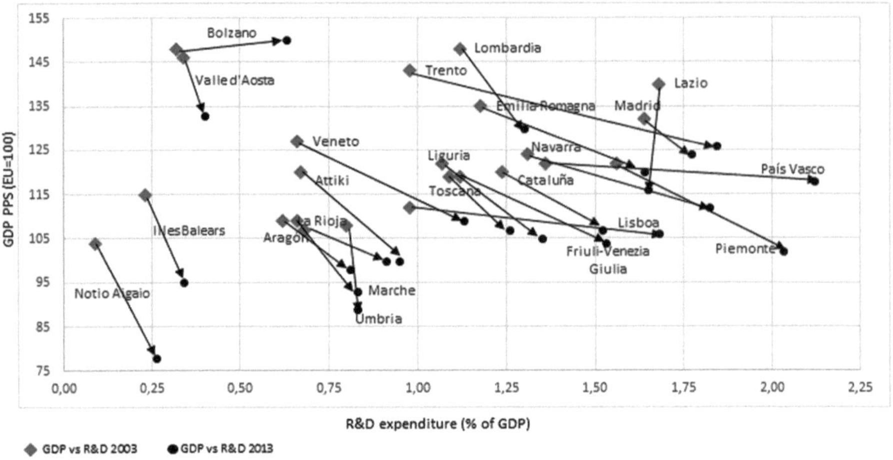

Fig. 2.10 Evolution of GDP vs R&D (2003–2013) in richer regions

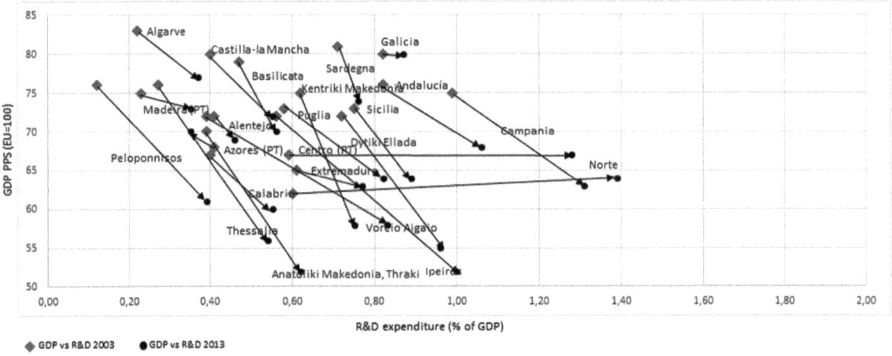

Fig. 2.11 Evolution of GDP vs R&D (2003–2013) in lagging regions

increase in R&D expenditure that lost less ground than the others in what concerns GDP per capita. We can find them in the capital regions, in industrial areas or in the most remote parts of Southern Europe, suggesting that this can be the result of localised plans or projects more than larger policies.

Once again it is not possible to infer from this data that the R&D investment (knowledge and innovation) does not lead to economic growth. Considering the above results, one reason for the underperformance of Southern European regions in the time span analysed, could be that the investment levels in R&D are not high enough; they are still far below the 3% target of the Europe 2020 strategy. Another limitation can be found on the specialisation at the regional level that has to be taken into account, as has been highlighted by the Smart Specialisation Strategy (SSS) developed by the EC.

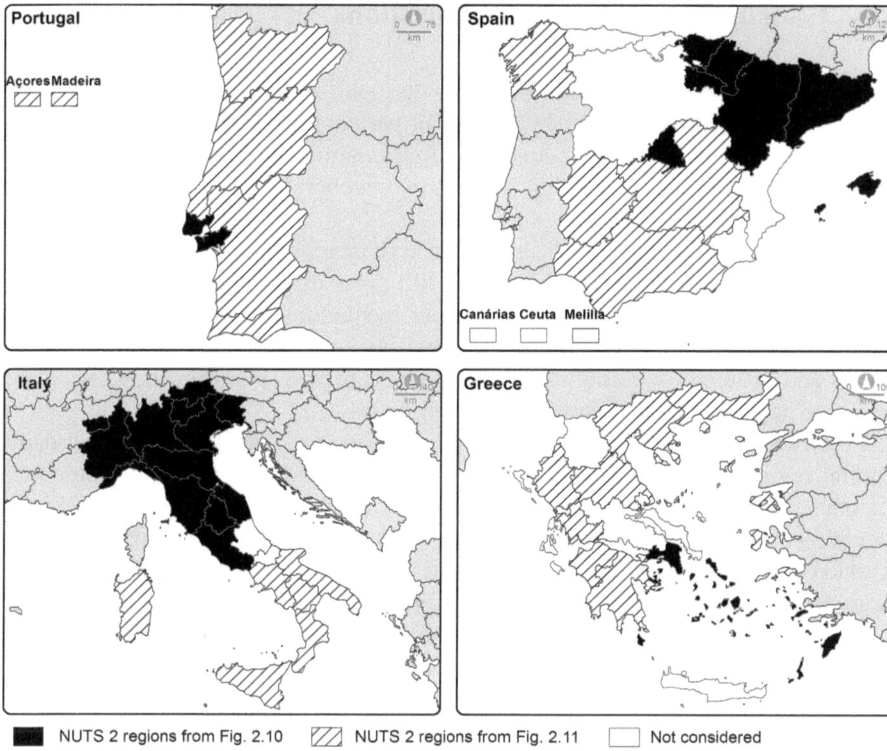

Fig. 2.12 Top and bottom regions NUTS2 (by GDP 2003) covered by Figs. 2.10 and 2.11

In fact, R&D's effects on growth and development have always been an important issue in Europe and for the European Commission. By the implementation of the Lisbon Strategy in 2005, the EC established the group of experts on Knowledge for Growth (K4G) in order to provide high-level advice on the research and innovation policy. The idea of a persistent deficit in R&D expenditures in comparison with the USA has always played an important role in the design of a European innovation policy. However, the K4G group developed a new concept, the Smart Specialisation Strategy, that should support countries and regions in identifying what they can do best in terms of science and technology and the research and innovation domains in which they can hope to be excellent. R&D expenditure should concentrate in those domains, 'the "right" S&T specialisations', in order to be efficient (Foray 2006).

The implementation of the SSS and the results of the K4G group have however, until now, been not quite disseminated.

2.7 Conclusions and Further Questions

The four countries in Southern Europe—Portugal, Spain, Italy and Greece—in 2014, displayed, at the country level, a GDP per capita below the EU 28 average. Parallel to this, at the NUTS 2 level, the four countries present huge contrasts in different configurations according to the socio-economic variables and indicators under consideration.

Regional disparities are persistent and tend to increase. A discussion on the final targets of the European Regional Policy is still open: do European regional policies aim to reduce personal rather than regional inequalities (Puga 2002)? Whatever arguments can be gathered for the possible answers, there are major structural causes and different working mechanisms across regions that prevent balance and reinforce agglomeration even with changing poles.

Polarisation shapes the face of Southern Europe's development landscape. Capital regions and old industrial regions in Spain and Italy perform better than the others. The Northern half of Italy, including Lazio; Northeast regions of Spain, including Pais Vasco, Navarra La Rioja, Aragon, Cataluña and Madrid; Lisboa and Attikki constitute the first *league* of regional performance in Southern Europe. "The large urban areas attract ever greater capital and human resources often at the expenses of intermediate and peripheral city and regions" (Rodríguez-Pose and Fitjar 2013, p. 369) and the expected spreading effects from the core areas to the peripheral ones did not occur.

Some of the regions of the four countries in Southern Europe even display similar development status and patterns of other regions in the core of the European Union and are integrated in supra national networks of knowledge, people and commodity flows. Other regions, vast areas of the four countries, are getting ever distant from the core, ageing, losing their jobs although keeping the education system working and expanding. Those regions may even keep on feeding core regions with high qualified young workers (Fratesi and Percoco 2014). Broadening access to education and particularly to higher education may be a political option in order to give some extra-support to regions lagging behind. Actually, peripheral regions can be penalised in various ways; remoteness forces higher transport costs and by consequence leaves fewer resources for the education and qualification of workers. In order to be able to compete in the global markets those regions structure their strategies in cost reduction wherever they can, suffering what Redding and Schott called the "additional penalty of remoteness" (Redding and Schott 2003, p. 516). Central governments take the initiative of offsetting such trends.

Rodrígues-Pose and Fratesi identified what they called the *sheltered economies or regions* in Southern Europe (Rodríguez-Pose and Fratesi 2007). Those are remote assisted regions, encapsulated in themselves, suffering from isolation, with low levels of employment, high unemployment, or dependence on nonmarket oriented sectors, underperforming economically and depending on transfers from the central governments and public policies. It is easier to identify some of those situations in Southern Italy and Greece in our analysis at the NUTS 2 level. In Portugal, due to the dimension of NUTS 2, those regions do not emerge so clearly but the results of the PCA for the Norte region suggest this kind of structural problem.

Education is important but not enough, even if differences in human capital endowment have been identified as barriers to convergence in the European Union (Rodríguez-Pose and Vilalta-Bufí 2005). In fact, the link between research and development, innovation and economic growth is not always an easy path; some areas are more successful than others (Rodríguez-Pose 1999). In the present case, regions outside the main poles display high scores for education indicators; they have, however, not been able to catch up in what concerns economic growth. Those regions face the risks of turning themselves into tanks or reserves of qualified (educated) young people that will be ready to migrate to the core regions feeding the already strong brain-drain flows.

The regional disparities in Southern Europe evidence the limits of the European Regional Policy that has the explicit aim of reducing them. Again the balance between physical and human capital investments has to be reworked. Ann Markusen defends a stereo vision for regional planning, arguing that a balanced mix should be carefully structured in regional policies and policy measures since prioritising physical capital investments (transport infrastructures, among others) has led to very unexpected results of new polarisations and regional disparities (Markusen 2008).

Is there inescapable path dependence for Southern Europe or do we need new policies and measures?

Annex

Annex 2.1

	Factor loadings	Correlations between variables and factors	Squared cosines of the variables	Contribution of the variables (%)	Description of the variables
Factor 1: The unemployment rigidity (Eigenvalue 9270, Variability 29,902%)					
V39_2014	0.889	0.889	**0.790**	8.528	Long-term unemployment (12 months and more) by NUTS 2 regions: Long-term unemployment rate
V38_2014	0.878	0.878	**0.772**	8.325	Unemployment rates by sex, age and NUTS 2 regions (%): Females 20–64 years
V36_2014	0.864	0.864	**0.746**	8.052	Unemployment rates by sex, age and NUTS 2 regions (%): Total, 20–64 years
V37_2014	0.821	0.821	**0.673**	7.264	Unemployment rates by sex, age and NUTS 2 regions (%): Males, 20–64 years
V102_2014	0.659	0.659	**0.434**	4.679	Young people neither in employment nor in education and training by sex and NUTS 2 regions (NEET rates)
V40_2014	0.639	0.639	**0.409**	4.407	Long-term unemployment (12 months and more) by NUTS 2 regions: Long-term unemployment as a percentage of the total unemployment
V305A_2014	0.590	0.590	**0.349**	3.761	Employment by age, economic activity and NUTS 2 regions (NACE Rev. 2) – 1000 (age 15–64). Agriculture, Forestry and Fishing

V309AB_2013	0.573	0.573	**0.328**	3.540	Employment in technology and knowledge-intensive sectors by NUTS 2 regions and sex (from 2008 onwards, NACE Rev. 2). Agriculture, Foretry, Fishing; Mining and Quarrying
V12_2014	0.478	0.478	**0.229**	2.467	Population from 0 to 19 years as a percentage of NUT's total population
V26_2012	−0.670	−0.670	**0.449**	4.842	Total intramural R&D expenditure (GERD) by sectors of performance – All sectors (Euro per inhabitant; Percentage of GDP)
V305BE_2014	−0.695	−0.695	**0.482**	5.204	Employment by age, economic activity and NUTS 2 regions (NACE Rev. 2) – 1000 (age 15–64): Industry (except construction)
V309C_2013	−0.714	−0.714	**0.510**	5.502	Employment in technology and knowledge-intensive sectors by NUTS 2 regions and sex (from 2008 onwards, NACE Rev. 2) Manufactury
V306F_2014	−0.809	−0.809	**0.654**	7.053	Employment rates by sex, age and NUTS 2 regions (%) FEMALES
V19_2013	−0.843	−0.843	**0.710**	7.663	Gross domestic product (GDP) at current market prices – Purchasing Power Standard per inhabitant in percentage of the EU average
V306_2014	−0.865	−0.865	**0.748**	8.068	Employment rates by sex, age and NUTS 2 regions (15–64 years) (%)
Factor 2: Human capital and innovation (Eigenvalue 5544, Variability 17,885%)					
V10_2014	0.868	0.868	**0.754**	13.595	Persons aged 25–64 with tertiary education attainment by sex and NUTS 2 regions (%)
V22Pc_2014	0.867	0.867	**0.751**	13.542	Economically active population by sex, age, highest level of education attained – First and second stage of tertiary education (levels 5–6)

(continued)

Annex 2.1 (continued)

	Factor loadings	Correlations between variables and factors	Squared cosines of the variables	Contribution of the variables (%)	Description of the variables
					(25–64 years) (Total), as % of economically active population (25–64) (Total)
V308_2013	0.676	0.676	**0.457**	8.250	HRST by category and NUTS 2 regions – Persons with tertiary education (ISCED) and/or employed in science and technology – Percentage of active population
V11Txv2001_2011	0.624	0.624	**0.389**	7.016	Population variation rate 2001–2014
V31_2012	0.576	0.576	**0.332**	5.987	Total R&D personnel and researchers by sectors of performance, sex – (Total R&D personnel; Researchers) (Total(M + F)) (All sectors) (Percentage of active population – numerator in head count; Percentage of total employment – numerator in head count; Head count)
V9_2014	−0.624	−0.624	**0.389**	7.024	Persons aged 25–64 with upper secondary education attainment, by sex and NUTS 2 regions (%)
Factor 3: Educational potential (Eigenvalue 4830, Variability 15,581%)					
V1_2012	0.748	0.748	**0.560**	11.591	Students in tertiary education (ISCED 5–6) – as % of the population aged 20–24 years at regional level
V4_2012	0.659	0.659	**0.434**	8.978	Students (all ISCED levels) aged 17 at regional level – as % of corresponding age population
V202_2013	0.590	0.590	**0.348**	7.210	Old age dependency ratio (Population 65+/ Population 15–64)

V8_2014	−0.552	−0.552	**0.305**	6.309	Persons aged 25–64 with lower secondary education attainment, by sex and NUTS 2 regions (%)
V101_2014	−0.733	−0.733	**0.538**	11.139	Early leavers from education and training by sex and labour status
Factor 4: Population potential (Eigenvalue 2787, Variability 8990%)					
V17_2013	0.806	0.806	**0.649**	23.292	Fertility rates by age and NUTS 2 regions
V200_2013	0.719	0.719	**0.517**	18.559	Population density
V101F_2014	−0.585	−0.585	**0.342**	12.262	Early leavers from education and training by sex and labour status (Females)
Factor 5: Human capital II (Eigenvalue 2019, Variability 6513%)					
V3_2012	0.785	0.785	**0.617**	30.552	Students (ISCED 5–6) at regional level – as % of total country level students
V7P_2012	0.710	0.710	**0.504**	24.974	No. of students – Second stage of tertiary education leading to an advanced research qualification (level 6)

Annex 2.2

	Description	Unit	Year used in PCA	Eurostat Table
Education				
V1	Students in tertiary education (ISCED 5–6) – as % of the population aged 20–24 years at regional level	% of total 20–24 population on the same region	2012	educ_regind
V3	Students (ISCED 5–6) at regional level – as % of total country level students (ISCED 5–6)	% of country level students	2012	educ_regind
V4	Students (all ISCED levels) aged 17 at regional level – as % of corresponding age population	%	2012	educ_regind
V7P	No. of students – Second stage of tertiary education leading to an advanced research qualification (level 6)	%	2012	educ_renrlrg1
V8	Persons aged 25–64 with lower secondary education attainment, by sex and NUTS 2 regions (%)	% of poopulation 25–64	2014	No longer available on Eurostat
V9	Persons aged 25–64 with upper secondary education attainment, by sex and NUTS 2 regions (%)	% of poopulation 25–64	2014	No longer available on Eurostat
V10	Persons aged 25–64 with tertiary education attainment by sex and NUTS 2 regions (%)	% of poopulation 25–64	2014	No longer available on Eurostat
V101	Early leavers from education and training by sex and labour status	% population age 18–24	2014	edat_lfse_16
V101F	Early leavers from education and training by sex and labour status FEMALES	% population age 18–24	2014	edat_lfse_16
V102	Young people neither in employment nor in education and training by sex and NUTS 2 regions (NEET rates)	% population age 15–24	2014	edat_lfse_22
Demographics				
V11Txv	Population Variation rate 2001–2014 (%)	TxVar	Var-2001–2011	demo_r_d2jan
V12	% Population from 0 to 19 years over NUT total	%	2014	demo_r_pjangroup
V17	Fertility rates by age and NUTS 2 regions	Births per woman	2013	demo_r_frate2
V200	Population density	Habitants per km^2	2013	demo_r_d3dens

V202	Old age dependency ratio (Population 65+/Population 15–64)	%	2013	demo_r_pjangroup
Economics and employment				
V19	Gross domestic product (GDP) at current market prices – Purchasing power standard per inhabitant in percentage of the EU average	%	2013	nama_10r_2gdp
V305A	Employment by age, economic activity and NUTS 2 regions (NACE Rev. 2) – 1000 (age 15–64). Agriculture, Forestry and Fishing	% of country total for each category	2014	lfst_r_lfe2en2
V305BE	Employment by age, economic activity and NUTS 2 regions (NACE Rev. 2) – 1000 (age 15–64): Industry (except construction)	% of country total for each category	2014	lfst_r_lfe2en2
V309AB	Employment in technology and knowledge-intensive sectors by NUTS 2 regions and sex (from 2008 onwards, NACE Rev. 2). Agriculture, Forestry, Fishing; Mining and Quarrying	% of country total for each category	2013	htec_emp_reg2
V309C	Employment in technology and knowledge-intensive sectors by NUTS 2 regions and sex (from 2008 onwards, NACE Rev. 2) Manufacturing	% of country total for each category	2013	htec_emp_reg2
V22Pc	Economically active population by sex, age, highest level of education attained – First and second stage of tertiary education (levels 5–6) (25–64 years) (Total), as % of Economically active population (25–64) (Total)	% active population 25–64	2014	lfst_r_lfp2acedu
V26	Total intramural R&D expenditure (GERD) by sectors of performance – All sectors (Euro per inhabitant; Percentage of GDP)	% of GDP	2012	rd_e_gerdreg
V31	Total R&D personnel and researchers by sectors of performance, sex – (Total R&D personnel; Researchers) (Total(M+F)) (All sectors) (Percentage of active population – numerator in head count; Percentage of total employment – numerator in head count; Head count)	% of employment	2013	rd_p_persreg
V36	Unemployment rates by sex, age and NUTS 2 regions (%): Total, 20–64 years	% of population 20–64	2014	lfst_r_lfu3rt
V37	Unemployment rates by sex, age and NUTS 2 regions (%): Males, 20–64 years	% of population 20–64	2014	lfst_r_lfu3rt
V38		% of population 20–64	2014	lfst_r_lfu3rt

(continued)

Annex 2.2 (continued)

	Description	Unit	Year used in PCA	Eurostat Table
	Unemployment rates by sex, age and NUTS 2 regions (%): Females 20-64 years			
V39	Long-term unemployment (12 months and more) by NUTS 2 regions: Long-term unemployment rate	% of active population	2014	lfst_r_lfu2ltu
V40	Long-term unemployment (12 months and more) by NUTS 2 regions: Long-term unemployment as a percentage of the total unemployment	% of total unemployment	2014	lfst_r_lfu2ltu
V306	Employment rates by sex, age and NUTS 2 regions (15–64) (%)	% of population 15–64	2014	lfst_r_lfe2emprt
V306F	Employment rates by sex, age and NUTS 2 regions (%) FEMALES	% of population 15–64	2014	lfst_r_lfe2emprt
V308	HRST by category and NUTS 2 regions – Persons with tertiary education (ISCED) and/or employed in science and technology – Percentage of active population	% of active population	2013	hrst_st_rcat

Annex 2.3 GDP per capita pps (EU28 = 100%) Source: Eurostat (06.04.2016)

GEO	Name	2001	2002	2003	2004	2005	2006	2007	2008	2009	2010	2011	2012	2013	2014
EJ28	European Union (28 countries)	100	100	100	100	100	100	100	100	100	100	100	100	100	100
EL	Greece	88	92	94	96	91	94	92	94	94	87	77	74	74	72
EL11	Anatoliki Makedonia, Thraki	67	69	70	69	66	64	64	67	67	64	55	53	52	50
EL12	Kentriki Makedonia	73	75	75	77	72	74	73	75	75	68	60	58	58	56
EL13	Dytiki Makedonia	77	83	86	86	83	81	76	72	78	75	70	71	70	66
EL21	Ipeiros	67	71	72	70	66	66	64	64	64	61	55	52	52	51
EL14	Tnessalia	68	71	76	76	69	72	69	70	70	62	55	55	56	55
EL22	Ionia Nisia	89	88	94	94	92	92	90	93	89	82	69	67	66	67
EL23	Dytiki Ellada	66	70	72	73	70	73	71	70	69	66	58	56	55	54
EL24	Sterea Ellada	93	93	94	91	88	87	83	84	82	76	68	66	67	61
EL25	Peloponnisos	73	75	76	75	72	74	73	74	74	69	62	60	61	58
EL30	Attiki	111	118	120	125	120	124	122	125	128	118	105	101	100	99
EL41	Voreio Aigaio	64	65	72	72	71	73	73	76	75	68	61	57	58	57
EL42	Notio Aigaio	101	100	104	106	104	104	102	106	101	93	81	78	78	80
EL43	Kriti	81	84	85	87	82	84	80	82	82	74	64	60	63	63
ES	Spain	98	100	100	100	100	102	103	101	101	97	94	92	91	91
ES11	Galicia	76	79	80	81	83	86	88	89	89	86	83	80	80	80
ES12	Principado de Asturias	82	85	85	86	88	92	94	93	92	89	86	82	80	80
ES13	Cantabria	91	94	93	93	94	96	96	95	95	91	87	84	82	82
ES21	País Vasco	119	122	122	123	125	129	130	131	130	126	122	120	118	119
ES22	Comunidad Foral de Navarra	122	125	124	124	125	127	127	126	125	120	117	113	112	113
ES23	La Rioja	107	108	109	107	107	110	110	109	108	105	101	98	98	100
ES24	Aragón	102	106	107	107	108	110	112	111	110	107	104	100	100	100
ES30	Comunidad de Madrid	131	132	132	131	132	136	136	134	136	130	127	126	124	125
ES41	Castilla y León	88	91	91	92	92	94	95	94	95	91	89	87	85	86

(continued)

Annex 2.3 (continued)

ES42	Castilla-la Mancha	76	79	80	79	81	82	83	82	82	79	76	74	72	72
ES43	Extremadura	62	64	65	65	67	68	69	70	70	69	65	63	63	63
ES51	Cataluña	119	121	120	119	118	121	121	118	118	114	109	108	107	108
ES52	Comunidad Valenciana	94	95	94	92	92	94	93	91	90	86	83	80	79	80
ES53	Illes Balears	121	120	115	113	111	112	110	107	105	101	98	96	95	96
ES61	Andalucía	72	75	76	77	78	79	79	78	77	74	71	69	68	67
ES62	Región de Murcia	81	84	84	83	84	86	86	85	83	80	77	75	75	74
ES63	Ciudad Autónoma de Ceuta (ES)	84	86	87	87	87	88	88	87	87	83	78	76	76	76
ES64	Ciudad Autónoma de Melilla (ES)	82	84	86	87	86	86	84	82	82	77	73	69	69	68
ES70	Canarias (ES)	95	96	96	93	92	92	91	89	87	84	81	79	78	78
IT	Italy	119	113	112	108	106	106	105	105	104	103	103	101	98	96
ITC1	Piemonte	129	123	122	118	116	115	114	113	109	110	109	106	102	100
ITC2	Valle d'Aosta/Vallée d'Aoste	150	142	146	139	137	135	133	136	134	136	135	136	133	133
ITC3	Liguria	130	122	122	118	116	115	117	118	117	113	113	111	105	104
ITC4	Lombardia	156	149	148	141	138	136	135	138	136	137	136	133	130	126
ITH1	Provincia Autonoma di Bokano/Bozen	160	149	148	145	141	142	141	143	146	146	146	152	150	144
ITH2	Provincia Autonoma di Trento	154	145	143	136	132	130	130	130	131	130	128	128	126	123
ITH3	Veneto	135	126	127	123	120	119	118	116	116	114	115	113	109	108
ITH4	Friuli-Venezia Giulia	130	123	119	115	115	115	115	112	110	111	110	107	104	101
ITH5	Emilia-Romagna	146	137	135	130	127	128	128	127	124	123	124	122	120	117
ITI1	Toscana	126	120	119	114	112	111	111	110	111	109	109	108	107	104
ITI2	Umbria	117	110	108	104	101	102	101	100	97	95	93	91	89	87
ITI3	Marche	115	111	109	105	103	104	104	102	102	99	98	96	93	92
ITI4	Lazio	146	141	140	138	135	133	132	130	132	128	126	121	116	114
ITF1	Abruzzo	104	97	95	88	89	89	88	89	89	89	90	90	88	84
ITF2	Molise	91	86	85	82	81	83	83	81	82	80	78	77	75	75
ITF3	Campania	79	76	75	72	70	70	70	70	70	67	65	65	63	61

ITF4	Puglia	78	73	73	70	68	68	67	66	67	66	65	66	64	63
ITF5	Basilicata	86	81	79	76	74	75	76	75	74	72	72	72	70	69
ITF6	Calabria	72	68	67	66	66	65	65	65	66	64	64	63	60	59
ITG1	Sicilia	77	73	73	70	70	70	69	69	69	68	66	66	64	62
ITG2	Sardegna	85	80	81	79	78	78	77	78	79	77	76	76	74	72
PT	Portugal	78	78	78	76	79	79	79	79	81	81	78	77	77	78
FT11	Norte	63	63	62	60	62	62	63	63	65	65	63	64	64	65
PT15	Algarve	81	82	83	80	84	84	84	83	82	80	76	77	77	78
FT16	Centro (PT)	67	66	67	66	68	68	67	66	69	69	66	67	67	67
PT17	Área Metropolitana de Lisboa	112	112	112	110	114	113	113	112	115	114	109	106	106	106
PT18	Alentejo	71	71	72	71	73	74	73	71	72	74	71	70	69	70
PT20	Região Autónoma dos Açores (FT)	66	67	68	67	70	70	70	71	74	74	71	70	70	71
PT30	Região Autónoma da Madeira (FT)	68	74	75	76	79	79	78	78	79	78	77	73	73	73

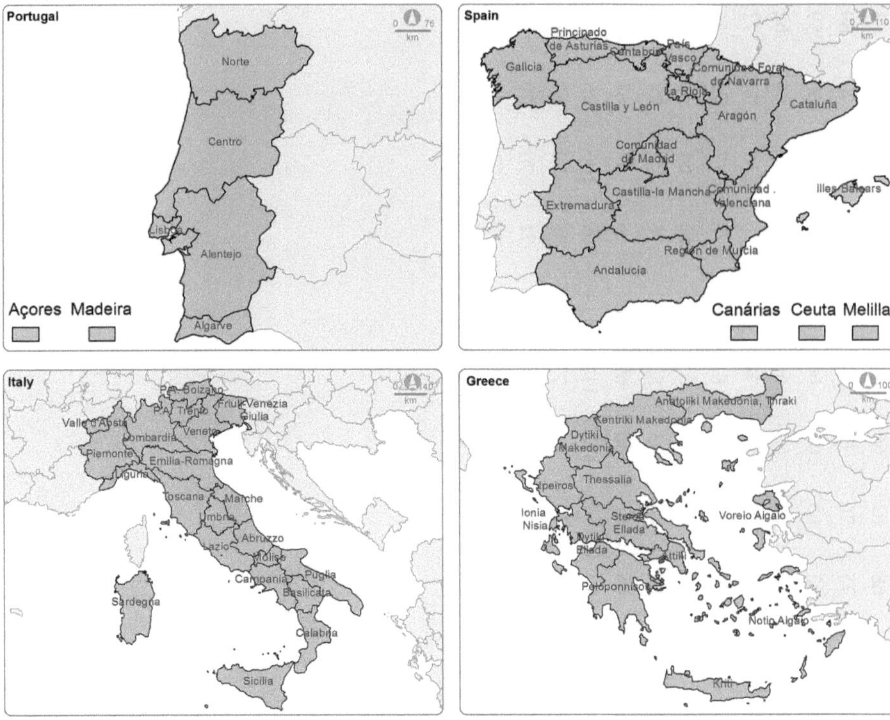

Annex 2.4 The four countries in Southern Europe

References

Balchin P, Sýkora L, Bull G (1999) Regional policy and planning in Europe. Routledge, London

Bathelt H, Glückler J (2002) Wirtschaftsgeographie, 2. Auflage edn. Ulmer, Stuttgart

Bathelt H, Glückler J (2011) The relational economy. Geographies of knowing and learning. Oxford University Press, Oxford

Capello R, Lenzi C (2013) Territorial patterns of innovation and economic growth in European regions. Growth Chang 44:195–227. doi:10.1111/grow.12009

Charlot S, Crescenzi R, Musolesi A (2015) Econometric modelling of the regional knowledge production function in Europe. J Econ Geogr 15:1227–1259

Cowan R, Zinovyeva N (2007) Short-term effects of new universities on regional innovation. Working paper series. United Nations University UNU-MERIT, Maastricht

Crescenzi R, Rodríguez-Pose A (2013) R&D, socio-economic conditions, and regional innovation in the U.S. Growth Chang 44(2):287–320

Crescenzi R, Rodríguez-Pose A, Storper M (2007) The geographical processes behind innovation: a Europe—United States comparative analysis. WP 2007–2013. Instituto Madrileño de Estudios Avanzados (IMDEA) Ciencias Sociales, Madrid

Crescenzi R, Pietrobelli C, Rabelotti R (2013) Innovation drivers, value chains and the geography of multinational corporations in Europe. J Econ Geogr:1–34
De La Fuente A (2003) Human capital in a global and knowledge-based economy. European Commission (Employment and Social Affairs), Brussels
EC (2010) Europe 2020. A strategy for smart, sustainable and inclusive growth. COM (2010) 2020. EC, Brussels
EC (2016) Europe 2020, 16 Feb. Retrieved from http://ec.europa.eu/europe2020/index_en.htm
Foray D (Rapporteur) (2006) Globalization of R&D: linking better the European economy to "foreign" sources of knowledge and making EU a more attractive place for R&D investment. Expert group "knowledge for growth", 4 Apr 2006. http://ec.europa.eu/invest-in-research/pdf/download_en/foray_report.pdf
Fratesi U (2014) Editorial: the mobility of high-skilled workers—causes and consequences. Reg Stud 48:1587–1591. doi:10.1080/00343404.2014.955689
Fratesi U, Percoco M (2014) Selective migration, regional growth and convergence: evidence from Italy. Reg Stud 48(10):1650–1668
Gardiner B, Martin R, Tyler P (2005) Regional dimensions of Europe's growth problem: some brief reflections on the sapir report. Reg Stud 39(7):979–986
Glaeser EL (1994) Why does schooling generate economic growth? Econ Lett 44:333–337
Goldstein HA, Renault CS (2004) Contributions of universities to regional economic development: a quasi-experimental approach. Reg Stud 38:733–746
Glückler J, Meusburger P, Meskioui ME (2013) Introduction: knowledge and the geography of the economy. In: Meusburger P, Glueckler J, Meskioui ME (eds) Knowledge and the economy. Springer Science+Business Media, Dordrecht, pp 3–14
Gros D, Roth F (2012) The Europe 2020 strategy. Can it maintain the EU's competitiveness in the world? Brussels: Centre for Education Policy Studies (CEPS)
Gyuris F (2014) The political discourse of spatial disparities: geographical inequalities between science and propaganda. Springer, Cham
Harvey D (2004) Retrospect on the limits to capital. Antipode:543–549
Huggins R, Thompson P (2014) A network-based view of regional growth. J Econ Geogr 14:511–545. doi:10.1093/jeg/lbt012
Jarocinski M (2003) Nominal and real convergence in Spain, Portugal and Greece during their accession to the EMU. No 0256, Case network studies and analyses. CASE-Center for Social and Economic Research, Warsaw. http://EconPapers.repec.org/RePEc:sec:cnstan:0256
Kucel A, Vilalta-Bufí M (2013a) Job satisfaction of University Graduates. Rev de Econ Apl 61:29–55
Kucel A, Vilalta-Bufí M (2013b) Why do tertiary education graduates regret their study program? A comparison between Spain and the Netherlands. High Educ 65:565–579
Marginson S (2007) The public/private divide in higher education: a global revision. High Educ 53 (3):307–333
Markusen A (2008) Human capital versus physical capital. Government's role in regional development. In: Martinez-Vazquez J, Vaillancourt F (eds) Public policy for regional development. Routledge, Oxford, pp 47–65
Martin R, Sunley P (2015) Towards a developmental turn in evolutionary economic geography? Reg Stud 49(5):712–732
Meusburger P (2013) Relations between knowledge and economic development: some methodological considerations. In: Meusburger P, Glueckler J, el Meskioui M (eds) Knowledge and the economy. Springer, Dordrecht, pp 15–42
Patrinos HA, Psacharopoulos G (2011) Education. Past, present and future global challenges. The World Bank, Human Development Network
Puga D (2002) European regional policies in light of recent location theories. J Econ Geogr 2 (4):373–406
Redding S, Schott PK (2003) Distance, skill deepening and development: will peripheral countries ever get rich? J Dev Econ 72:515–541

Rodríguez-Pose A (1999) Innovation prone and innovation adverse societies: economic performance in Europe. Growth Chang 30(Winter 1999):75–105
Rodríguez-Pose A (2001) Is R&D investment in lagging areas of Europe worthwhile? Theory and empirical evidence. Pap Reg Sci 80:275–295. doi:10.1007/PL00013631
Rodríguez-Pose A (2013) Do institutions matter for regional development? Reg Stud 47 (7):1034–1047
Rodríguez-Pose A, Fitjar RD (2013) Buzz, archipelago economies and the future of intermediate and peripheral areas in a spiky world. Eur Plan Stud 21(3):355–372
Rodriguez-Pose A, Fratesi U (2004) Between development and social policies: the impact of European structural funds in objective 1 regions. Reg Stud 38(1):97–113
Rodríguez-Pose A, Fratesi U (2007) Regional business cycles and the emergence of sheltered economies in the southern periphery of Europe. Growth Chang 38(4):621–648
Rodríguez-Pose A, Vilalta-Bufí M (2005) Education, migration, and job satisfaction: the regional returns of human capital in the EU. J Econ Geogr:545–566
Scott A (1988) Metropolis: from the division of labor to urban form. University of California Press, Berkeley
Shapiro JM (2006) Smart cities: quality of life, productivity, and the growth effects of human capital. Rev Econ Stat 88(2):324–335
Simmie J (ed) (2001) Innovative cities. Spon Press, London
Simmie J, Martin RL (2010) The economic resilience of regions: towards an evolutionary approach. Camb J Reg Econ Soc 3(1):27–43
Storper M (2011) Why do regions develop and change? The challenge for geography and economics. J Econ Geogr 11(2):333–346
Storper M, Scott AJ (2009) Rethinking human capital, creativity and urban growth. J Econ Geogr 9:147–167. doi:10.1093/jeg/lbn052
Teixeira PN (2007) Jacob Mincer, a founding father of modern labor economics. Oxford University Press, Oxford
Thönnessen R, Gundlach E (2013) The size of human capital externalities: cross-country evidence. Public Choice 157(3):671–689
Thrift N (2005) Knowing capitalism. Sage, London
Venables AJ (2011) Productivity in cities: self-selection and sorting. J Econ Geogr 11(2):241–251
Woessmann L (2003) Specifying human capital. J Econ Surv 17(3):239–270

Madalena Fonseca is a Geographer and Assistant Professor at the University of Porto, Department of Geography. She holds a PhD in Economic Geography. Currently, she is the General Secretary of the Portuguese Agency for Assessment and Accreditation of Higher Education—A3ES (Lisboa). Her main research topics are currently linked with higher education and human capital: offer and demand of higher education, access, the Portuguese higher education system, higher education and regional development and quality assurance. She is a member of the Board of the European Consortium for Accreditation—ECA (The Hague) and the international expert for international accreditations of the German agency ZEVA (Hannover). She takes part in two Erasmus+ research projects on strategic partnerships for higher education: EIQAS, Enhancing Internal Quality Assurance Systems (2014–2016), and MEHR, Migration, Education and Human Rights (2016–2019). She is the author and co-author of a large number of papers and chapters of books in the field of economic geography and regional development.

Chapter 3
The Role of Functions in Economic Underperformance of Southern European Regions

Ugo Fratesi

JEL Classification R11 • R12 • O47

3.1 Introduction: Greece, Italy, Portugal and Spain before and after the crisis

Structural upgrading has been considered in the literature as fundamental for the possibility of middle and high income regions and countries to thrive in the global economy. In fact globalization has been proceeding very fast, and significantly affecting the European regions, providing them with important challenges (Capello et al. 2011).

To remain competitive is an imperative for regions in a globalized economy, despite an important and still on-going debate as to what the meaning of regional competitiveness is, since short and long run aspect merge and it is not easy to transfer concepts developed at a firm level to a territorial level (Bristow 2005; Camagni 2002; Gardiner et al. 2004). The issue of territorial competitiveness, however, is very important not only theoretically, but practically and for the policy makers, as shown by the recent attention and the different attempts to assess it (Huggins et al. 2014; Huggins 2013).

The competitiveness of regions is strictly linked to their role in the global value chain. Recently Coe and Yeung (2015) pointed out that the existence of networks which are increasingly fragmented and dispersed is one main reason for uneven development levels. Regions inserted in global networks can play different roles: they can be frontrunners, specialized in high-level phases for which innovativeness and managerial capabilities are important factors, or they can be specialized in production phases, for which they need low production costs with adequate quality levels. In this context, the intermediate regions which are present in the peripheries of developed countries can be

U. Fratesi (✉)
Department of Architecture, Built Environment and Construction Engineering, Politecnico di Milano, Piazza Leonardo da Vinci, 32, 20133 Milan, Italy
e-mail: ugo.fratesi@polimi.it

M. Fonseca, U. Fratesi (eds.), *Regional Upgrading in Southern Europe*, Advances in Spatial Science, DOI 10.1007/978-3-319-49818-8_3

squeezed in the middle, as many multinationals which de-locate production from core areas do it directly towards areas in emerging countries where greenfield investments are easier and possible on a larger scale. Also, once-successful production models such as the Italian industrial districts need to comply with the challenges coming from the upgrading of international competitors and remain successful insofar as they are no longer isolated but play the global game by delocalising activities with low value-added, and concentrate on higher level functions related to creativity, technology, innovation and retail. However, this also comes with a difficult equilibrium to be found between the local and the global (Chiarvesio et al. 2010; Dunford 2006).

For peripheral regions of European countries, upgrading towards higher level phases is therefore no longer needed for the purpose of converging towards the richest regions, but rather avoiding the decline which comes as a consequence if they don't do it. Three possible successful strategies for regions affected by the globalization processes are possible (Affuso et al. 2011): increasing productivity through innovation, reconverting to higher phases of the production process, and reconverting the regional sectoral structure. According to Ezcurra et al. (2007) the latter is probably less important, as the industry mix contributed only in minor part to the dispersion of productivity among European regions over the period 1977–1999, while national and spatial, region-specific, effects were more relevant. However, there is still disagreement on that and the relative importance of intra-sectoral and inter-sectoral structural change is still a matter of debate and investigation (O'Leary and Webber 2015).

Spain, Portugal Italy and Greece share a geographical location at the southern fringe of the European Union and, with some notable exceptions (such as Madrid, Catalonia or Lombardy which are often considered to be among the European motors) their regions are in this uncomfortable intermediate situation with respect to global value chains. The purpose of this chapter is to analyse the economic patterns of southern European countries and their regions, detecting to what extent they are coherent with the rest of the EU or different, and then to show that they have lags in GDP growth due to low productivity growth and finally show that this depends at least in part on inability to rise to higher functions.

The starting point of the analysis is the observation that the four countries relatively underperformed in the past 20 years with respect to the EU average, despite initial levels of GDP per person below those of the old 15 members of the union. As can be observed from Fig. 3.1, in 2012, among the four countries only Italy was marginally above the average of the then EU 27 in terms of GDP per person in PPS, while Spain was slightly below. Greece and Portugal, on the other hand, had values which placed them in the middle of the group of the 13 new member states which entered the EU on 1st January 2004 or afterwards, and this despite being members of the EU since respectively 1981 and 1986. On the contrary, Petrakos et al. (2012) evidence an adverse impact of integration for Greek regions over the period after accession, 1981–2005.

Before the crisis, indeed, some level of convergence between these four countries and the rest of the old members of the EU was taking place. Figure 3.2 plots their level of GDP and the GDP of the rest of the EU countries, plotting the figures

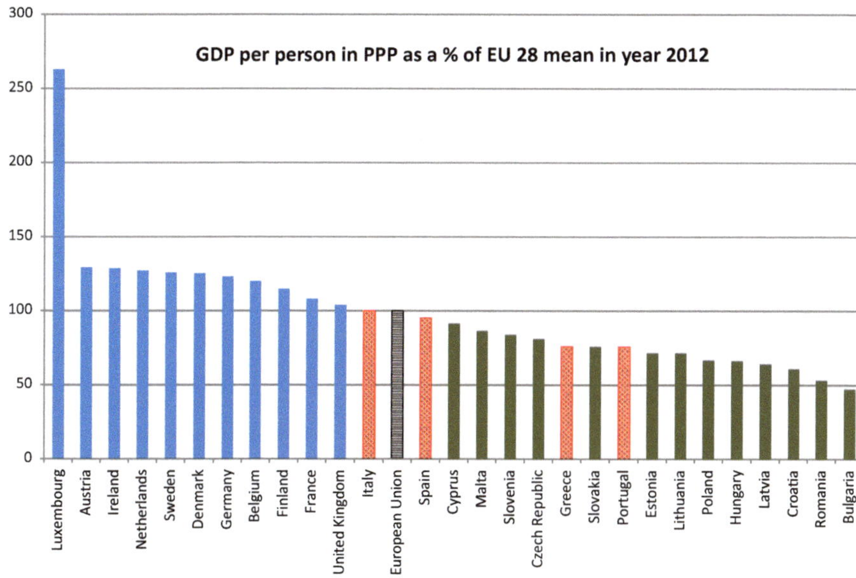

Fig. 3.1 Income per capita in PPS in 2012 as a percentage of the EU27mean. Italy, Spain, Portugal and Greece in *red*; other old members of the EU in *blue*, new members of the EU in *green*. Source: Elaborations on Eurostat data

as an index which uses 2008 as the basis year as this was the one with highest total GDP in Europe before the decrease with the crisis.

Before the crisis, Greece and Spain were growing less than the new member states of the EU, but they also were outperforming the old member states. Portugal was growing more than the EU average in the 1990s but less than the average in the 2000s, so that its performance in the total 13 year period is the same of the rest of the old member states. Italy, finally, which was the richest of the four countries in 1995 (and still is, even if to a lower extent) has been growing significantly less than the new and the old member states, as well as Greece, Portugal and Spain.

Then the crisis hit, starting in 2007–2008, and the four southern European countries, confirming their weakness, were again more affected than the rest of the Union. The right part of Fig. 3.2 shows this very clearly. The 13 new member states went down by less than 3.6% in 2009, then rebounded and in 2013 were already at 103.5% of the values of 2008. The other 11 old EU member states went down by 4.5% in 2009 and then—slowly—recovered, until slightly surpassing the pre-crisis values.

The four countries were all more affected than the European average. Greece is the most notable case which, due to a large number of financial and structural issues, went steadily down until reaching 76.5% of 2008 GDP in 2013; i.e., almost one quarter of total GDP was lost in just 5 years. The other countries were not hit so hard, but still had a pattern which is very different from the rest of the EU, due to the

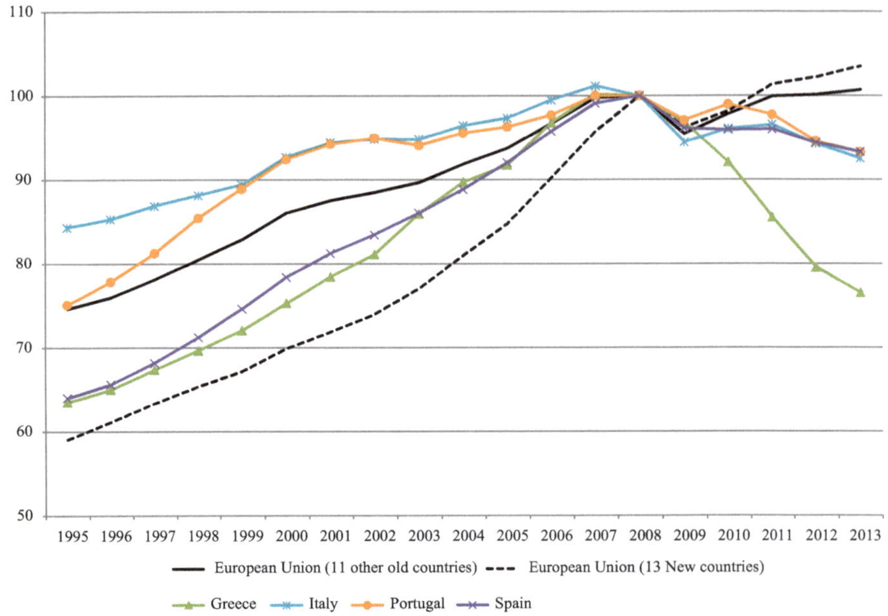

Fig. 3.2 Growth of total GDP of European Union countries 1995–2013 (index with 2008 = 100). Source: Elaborations on Eurostat data

fact that after the hit of 2009 and the recovery of 2010, Italy Portugal and Spain were again decreasing their total GDP. This is most notable in Portugal, which survived the first 2 years of crisis better than the average, but then rapidly lost ground, while Italy and Spain, larger countries, had smoother paths. The result, however, is strikingly similar, with Spain and Portugal being at about 93.3% of 2008 GDP in 2013, and Italy at 92.5%.

In a big crisis, which was originated in the financial sector (and only trigged by the real estate sector), and was later nourished by important difficulties in public finances and in the banking sector, the explanations at the/a national level are certainly of paramount importance, as all these processes take place at the country macro level. For example, Moro and Beker (2016) provide an interesting history of how the crisis extended from the international banking system to a European sovereign debt crisis, hitting countries with high levels of public debt particularly hard.

However, there are also issues linked to the regions, since some of them have weaker economic structures and hence experience more difficulties remaining competitive in the real economy. Using the theory of territorial capital, it is possible to say that some regional structures are less endowed with material, immaterial, public and private assets of growth, which makes them weaker in the long run (Camagni 2009).

It is possible to look at the same period of time and the same indicator of Fig. 3.2 (the variation of total GDP as a percentage of the 2008 value) at the regional level, in a map (Fig. 3.3). The map clearly shows national effects. All Polish and Swedish regions have a positive increment of GDP, and the same holds true for a large majority of German and British regions. The four southern European countries which are the object of this book are all composed by regions with negative GDP growth, so that the strong impact of the crisis which was detected at the national level in Fig. 3.2 has no exception at the regional level.

However, the map also shows that there also are important differentiations in the way the crisis hit the regions, within the same countries. For many countries, the capital areas, or the areas with the most dynamic large cities are above the national average; this applies, for example, to London, Stockholm, Munich, Berlin, Paris, Warsaw, Bratislava, Sofia.

In the four southern European countries, significant differentiations also exist. While Greece is relatively homogeneous, in Portugal there is a clear north-south differentiation, with the south more strongly hit by the crisis. In Spain the differentiation is along the traditional division between more developed and less developed regions, since the crisis hit less hard in Madrid, Catalonia and the Basque Country. In Italy there is a more nuanced pattern: while the Mezzogiorno performed badly, also some areas in the north, such as Piedmont, and in the Centre, such as Umbria, went worse than the average.

The evidence shown in Figs. 3.2 and 3.3 points to the weakness of southern European countries and their regions. Beyond the financial and macroeconomic issues, which are out of the scope of this book, this is also due to structural issues in the real economy of the regions of these countries.

One major issue which has been pointed out is the one of productivity: regions of these countries experienced lower productivity growth for a long time before the crisis, which also made them more vulnerable to the crisis.

The aim of this second introductory chapter is hence to show the low level of functional upgrading in southern European regions, which contributes to explain their low productivity levels and their relative low growth. In this chapter upgrading will be measured through the functions performed in the economy. The logical progression of the chapter is hence to analyse the economic patterns of southern European countries, showing to what extent they are coherent with rest of the EU or different, then show that they have lags in GDP due to productivity and that these depend at least in part on the inability of their regions to rise to higher functions.

Accordingly, the next section will present the macroeconomic patterns of southern European countries. In the following sections the functions performed in these countries will be assessed and, after having shown their specialization in low-level functions, this will be related to the levels of regional growth.

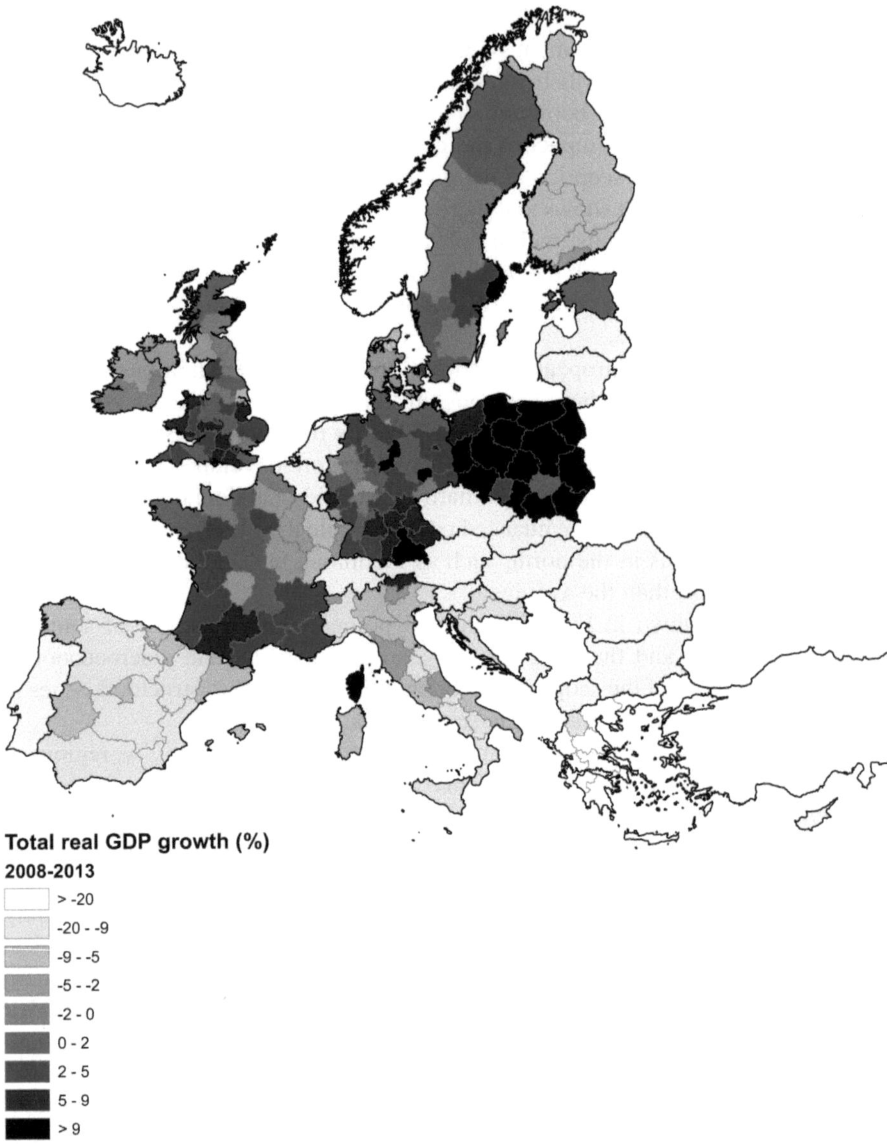

Fig. 3.3 Growth of total GDP of European Union regions 2008–2013 (with respect to 2008 = 100)

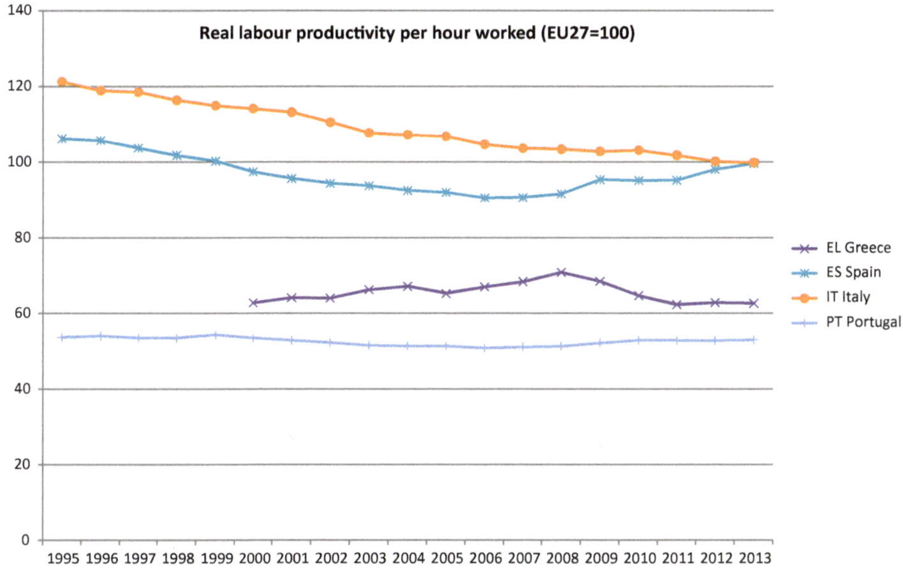

Fig. 3.4 Real labour productivity per hour worked (EU27 = 100). Source: Eurostat

3.2 Macroeconomic Patterns of Southern European Countries and Their Regions

The issue of productivity is an important and long standing one, contributing to the explanation of the economic troubles of southern European countries. As evidenced in Fig. 3.4, real productivity has historically been very low with respect to the rest of Europe in Portugal, and has also been low in Greece, with some small increments in the years prior to the crisis which were compensated by decrements in the years of crisis.

Italy, the only one of the four countries with significantly higher labour productivity in 1995 (more than 120% of the EU average) also decreased in this measure significantly and steadily over the following 18 years, with the same speed of decline in the years before and during the crisis.

Finally, the Spanish case is peculiar. Starting from slightly higher than average productivity levels in 1995, these declined steadily until the beginning of the crisis, and then recovered during the crisis due to strong restructuring and layoffs in the Spanish economy in these years.

Adopting a rougher measure of productivity, the gross value added per employee, it is possible to get a more disaggregated picture of the patterns of productivity in southern European countries with respect to the EU. This is presented in Table 3.1, where the values of GVA per person[1], employment and

[1]In order to disaggregate between types of regions, these data come from regional level statistics, which provide GVA rather than GDP.

Table 3.1 GVA, employment and productivity trends in southern European countries and the rest of the EU (EU27 = 100)

GVA per person as a % of EU27			
	1995	2001	2006
Old North	135.3	134.5	133.5
Old South non obj1	122.9	120.3	111.5
Old South obj1	66.4	67.3	67.5
EU27[a]	100.0	100.0	100.0
Employment rate as a % of EU27			
	1995	2001	2006
Old North	101.9	104.3	102.8
Old South non obj1	100.3	104.9	107.3
Old South obj1	81.9	84.3	87.6
EU27[a]	100.0	100.0	100.0
GVA per employee as a % of EU27			
	1995	2001	2006
Old North	132.8	128.9	129.9
Old South non obj1	122.6	114.7	103.9
Old South obj1	81.1	79.8	77.1
EU27[a]	100.0	100.0	100.0

[a]Excluding Finland, countries with only one region and the French overseas departments

productivity are presented for the long period before the economic crisis. This table allows for a dynamic comparison of the trends in Southern European countries to the rest of the EU, separating old western members and new eastern members, and disaggregating between poorer and richer regions, i.e., regions which belonged to objective 1 in the 2007–2013 EU cohesion policy programming period, to be eligible for which, a GVA per person in pps lower than 75% of the EU average was needed.

The first to be observed is the trend of GVA per person. While in the 11 years before the crisis the eastern countries showed important degrees of convergence, the lagging regions of southern European countries did not significantly converge, remaining at about 67% of the EU average. At the same time, the richest regions of these countries, which were at more than 122% of the EU average in 1995, slowly lost ground, reaching 111% in 2006; this path is very different from the one of the other rich regions, as the regions of the northern old members of the EU did not lose ground, if only marginally.

This general trend is the result of two concurring trends going in opposite directions. In terms of employment rate, in fact, the southern European countries increased with respect to the EU average, both in lagging and in rich regions. The first ones, starting from lower than average levels improved towards the mean, while the latter, starting around the mean, significantly improved until reaching levels higher than the ones of northern old members of the EU.

The trend of productivity, however, goes in the opposite direction. The richest regions of southern European countries started from levels well above the EU mean, at 122%, and lost ground very quickly, going to 103% before the start of the crisis. The poorest regions of southern European countries started at levels significantly lower than the average and still decreased to 77% of the EU average. This decrease is less marked than the one of richer regions but is still important, considering that the starting point was much lower.

It has to be observed that this trend is not due to the well-known productivity increases of new member states, as the northern old members of the EU did not experience the same important relative decline despite starting from very high levels.

It is therefore clear that the regions of southern European countries, in the years before the crisis, were quite good at creating jobs but much less at creating new output, and this implied an important decrease of average productivity.

To consider both indicators at the same time, it is possible to represent the patterns of employment and productivity growth in a single graph, in a way first introduced by Camagni (1991) for manufacturing and extended to the whole regional economy by Affuso et al. (2011).

Departing from Camagni (1991), the indicators are not calculated here relative to the national average, but to the European average, in order to show where the regions of southern European countries stand with respect to the other regions of Europe.

On the horizontal axis, there will therefore be the relative growth of employment in a certain programming period, calculated as:

$$RelativeEmploymentGrowth_r = \left(\frac{Emp_r^{2006}}{Emp_r^{1995}}\right)^{1/11} - \left(\frac{Emp_{EU}^{2006}}{Emp_{EU}^{1995}}\right)^{1/11}, \tag{3.1}$$

where *Emp* is total employment, *r* is the subscript for the regional value and *N* is the subscript for the national value.

On the vertical axis, there is the relative growth of productivity in the programming period, calculated as:

$$Relative\mathrm{P}roductivityGrowth_r = \left(\frac{\mathrm{Prod}_r^{2006}}{\mathrm{Prod}_r^{1995}}\right)^{1/11} - \left(\frac{\mathrm{Prod}_{EU}^{2006}}{\mathrm{Prod}_{EU}^{1995}}\right)^{1/11}, \tag{3.2}$$

where *Prod* is productivity calculated as GVA per employee and *r* is again the subscript for the regional value.

Putting these two indicators in the same graph brings an interesting property: a 135°, negatively sloped line passing through the origin evidences a condition of regional GVA growth equal to the European average. In fact, a region may develop at the same rate as the European GVA either if both productivity and employment grow at the same rate as the average or if productivity increases at a lower rate but employment does so at a proportionally higher-than-average rate, and vice-versa. If

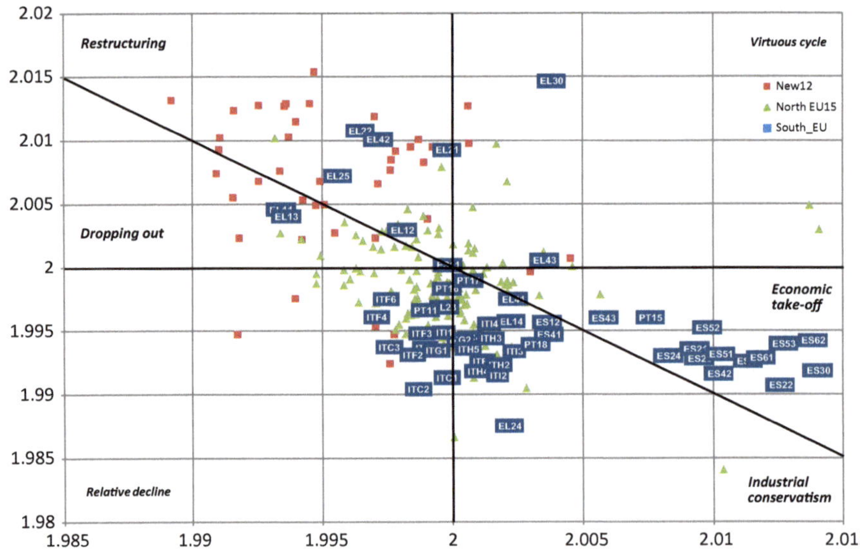

Fig. 3.5 Growth patterns of European regions 1995–2006 (EU27 = 100) (logarithmic scale used to improve readability)

a region is above this line, it increases its total GVA more than the average of the EU; if it is below it, the GVA growth rate is below average.

For this reason, the graph can be divided into six sectors rather than the usual four quadrants, each of them representing a specific possible pattern of regional economic development. Following Affuso et al. (2011) these patterns can be defined as follows (Fig. 3.5):

1. Virtuous cycle, when the regional economy is able to grow more than the average in terms of output thanks to both higher-than-average productivity growth and employment growth;
2. Restructuring, when higher-than-average productivity growth is achieved through employment cuts, leading nevertheless to good GVA performance due to the increases of productivity;
3. Dropping-out, when productivity growth is achieved by dropping inefficient production units, therefore generating not only lower than average employment growth, but also lower-than-average GVA growth;
4. Relative decline[2], defined as a vicious cycle in which employment cuts are unable to restore competitiveness, a condition in which there is therefore very low job and output growth;

[2]In this context and for this quadrant it is preferable to detach from the definition used in Affuso et al. who called this quadrant de-industrialization.

5. Industrial conservatism, when poor productivity growth is accompanied (and sometimes explained) by better-than-average employment growth; this pattern is more likely to take place in the presence of public assistance and industrial rescues;
6. Economic take-off, when lower-than-average productivity performance occurs together with very good employment performance, so that the effect on total value added is positive.

From Fig. 3.5 some very strong evidence emerges: even in the years before the all the turmoil due to the financial and the public finance crisis (Moro and Beker 2016), the regions of southern European countries were following specific growth patterns which would be the only ones compatible with a specialization in lower level production phases.

In particular, only one region, Attiki, clearly qualified as a *virtuous cycle* region, with positive growth of both employment and productivity. Two others, Ipeiros and Kriti are only marginally in the same sector. Other Greek regions are in the *restructuring* and *dropping out* quadrants, i.e., they were losing employment and increasing productivity, but only in some cases was this increase of productivity sizeable enough to compensate for employment losses. Apart from these Greek regions, no other region of southern European countries experienced a higher than average productivity growth.

The Spanish regions, in fact, are for the most part in the *economic take-off quadrant*, i.e., with respect to the EU mean, they were growing more than the average thanks to a very strong employment performance, coupled however with a relative decline of productivity. It is interesting to note that the region where this patters is more marked is Comunidad de Madrid. In other words, the capital in this case is the most representative region in the trend of the whole country.

Finally, Italian and Portuguese regions are all clustered in two sectors, *relative decline* and *industrial conservatism*. These are quadrants with lower than average GVA growth and lower than average productivity growth. In some cases, especially for some central and northern Italian regions[3] such as Veneto, Tuscany, and Emilia Romagna, employment growth has been higher than average. This is also the case of the last two Greek regions, Thessalia and Sterea Ellada, and, in the case of Portugal, of Lisbon.

The last group of regions is in the weakest *relative decline* quadrant, with lower than average growth in all three variables. It is possible to find there many regions belonging to the Italian Mezzogiorno, such as Apulia, Calabria, Sicily, as well as some weak regions in the north of the country, notably Liguria. In this quadrant we also find the Portuguese North and Centro.

[3]Due to the long standing and well-known dualism in this country, northern regions are also normally richer (Dunford 2002; Trigilia 2012).

3.3 The Functions Performed in Southern European Countries and Their Regions

The previous sections have illustrated the homogeneity and the weakness in economic terms of southern European regions with respect to the rest of the EU, in particular for what concerns productivity growth. Consistent with the main purpose of the book, this section analyses the issue with respect to the inability of these regions to restructure their economy.

The most common indicator could be one of sectoral change, but the presence of a certain sector does not give significant enough information on the role a region plays in the international division of labour. In fact, intra-sectoral trade has been growing very fast in the last decades, and international trade has been unbundled into smaller and smaller tasks (Grossman and Rossi-Hansberg 2008; Baldwin 2006).

From the European Labour Force data, however, it is also possible to know what type of occupation is performed by the worker, according to a classification which is called ISCO (International Standard Classification of Occupations). The jobs described in this classification are not always and necessarily linked with higher or lower functions, for instance there is no way to understand whether a clerk performs higher or lower functions than a plant operator. There are other occupations, however, which are clearly linked to high level functions performed in the economy. For example, a person employed as physicist in a region implies that there are activities with high technology level and, most likely, innovative ones.

Among all the professions of the ISCO classification, the following ones are theoretically expected to be related to the presence of high level functions in the economy of a region: Legislators and senior officials (ISCO11); Corporate managers (ISCO12); Managers of small enterprises (ISCO13); Physical, mathematical and engineering science professionals (ISCO21); College, university and higher education teaching professionals (ISCO231); Business professionals (ISCO241). To these professions, Writers and creative or performing artists (ISCO245) were also added because of the literature which points out creativity as one aspect which allows places to be competitive by performing creative, innovative and high value added activities (Lee et al. 2004; Lorenz and Lundvall 2010; Marrocu and Paci 2012).

The limitation with the use of these data is that the sample of the Labour Force survey is large but not huge, so that in order to analyse the professions at the regional level, 3 year averages are more reliable; in this case, the most recent period which avoids any bias introduced by the crisis is the one just before it, i.e. 2005–2007.

Table 3.2 presents the presence of high level ISCO occupations in southern European countries and the rest of the EU as a percentage of the total labour force. Again, a distinction was made between poorer and richer regions in these countries, by using the eligibility for Objective 1 cohesion policy support in 2000–2006.

Table 3.2 High level ISCO occupations in southern European countries and the rest of the EU (% of the total). Average over 2005–2007

		ISCO denominations	Legislators and senior officials	Corporate managers	Managers of small enterprises	Physical, mathematical and engineering science professionals	College, university and higher education teaching professionals	Business professionals	Writers and creative or performing artists
		ISCO codes	11	12	13	21	231	241	245
Group of regions	Number of regions								
Old North	142		0.51	5.77	3.31	3.37	0.52	1.40	0.63
Old South non obj1	22		0.69	2.50	3.58	1.65	0.39	0.66	0.61
Old South obj1	33		0.46	1.44	7.47	1.27	0.34	0.60	0.27
New 12	51		0.47	3.32	2.98	1.94	0.36	1.59	0.41
EU mean	248		0.51	4.42	3.86	2.66	0.45	1.25	0.54
Sig			***	***	***	***	***	***	***
F			25.1625	188.5864	75.5542	39.1205	32.5722	64.3482	49.9712

Source of data: elaborations on Labour Force Survey microdata
***,**,*Significant respectively at the 99%, 95%, and 90% confidence level

According to the data, the regions of southern European countries are characterized by a larger share of *Legislators and senior officials* (ISCO11). These are significantly above the levels of the EU mean in the richest non-objective 1 regions, while they are below the mean in the poorer objective 1 regions. This is likely due to a larger overall presence of the public sector in the four countries, with a concentration of the highest levels of these functions in the richest regions of the countries, which are also those with the most important administrative cities. Poorer regions of southern European countries, in fact, are poorly endowed of these professions, meaning that they tend to be dependent on the richer regions of their countries for strategic decision making in the public sector.

Going to the private sector, the share of *Corporate managers* (ISCO12) in southern European countries is significantly lower than the average of northern old members of the EU, and also of new member states. This holds true for both poorer and richer regions, especially for the former as expected. This seems to confirm that the four countries are less reliant on large businesses, less likely to host the headquarters of large firms, including multinationals which tend to follow determinants which are less present there (Basile et al. 2008). It is certainly a problem if a region is in this situation, as the most important economic decisions of the private sector are taken elsewhere and the region is likely dependent on other regions, with all consequences of a relationship in which there is a dominant external operator.

The private sector appears to be stronger concerning the *Managers of small enterprises* (ISCO13), which are slightly over-represented in the richest regions of southern European countries, while in the poorest ones the concentration is so high that it more than doubles the EU15 mean. This is a signal of the presence of a large number of entrepreneurial initiatives; however it is also likely that this very high value is a signal of a weak private sector economy in which small businesses are set-up by the individuals to compensate for the lack of job opportunities, while small initiatives are unable to grow due to the lack of support by a weak socio-economic fabric.

This interpretation is confirmed by the evidence provided in the various categories of professionals. In all of them, the share of persons with these occupations in southern European countries is lower than the northern old members of the EU. *Physical, mathematical and engineering science professionals* (ISCO21) are clearly under-represented in these regions, which hence more rarely perform advanced production activities or research and development functions. *College, university and higher education teaching professionals* (ISCO231) are also significantly under-represented, even if to a less evident extent than the previous case. The literature is well aware of the importance of the interactions between academia, the private and the public sectors, and of the fact that universities can have many functions in the economy, including providing knowledge through research, forming human capital by teaching and also nurturing potential new ventures (Gunasekara 2006; Leydesdorff and Etzkowitz 1998). Having less of these professions means being, ceteris paribus, weaker in these functions, with significant disadvantages in terms of dynamic regional economic performance.

The occupation of *Business professionals* is also significantly under-represented, and this is also a bad signal, as these professionals tend to be service workers whose presence is needed in advanced economic activities, included innovative manufacturing because they are increasingly important inputs in the production function (Cuadrado-Roura 2013). It has been estimated that the services make a relatively small share of global exports in gross terms but a much larger one in terms of value added (Low 2013).

Finally, also the creative class appears to be little represented in southern European countries, even if this is mostly due to their poorer regions, which lack employment opportunities for *Writers and creative or performing artists* (ISCO245), while the richest regions are almost at the same levels of the rest of the old member countries.

3.4 Functional Upgrading and Regional Growth in Southern European Countries

At this point it is important to consider whether, as could be assumed by the empirical evidence illustrated so far, the issue of low level functions is related to regional growth. For this reason a first econometric analysis is present henceforth. This analysis follows the same conceptual scheme of the book, presented in the introduction to the volume, and asks itself whether those regions in southern European countries which remain specialized in low-level functions are growing less than the others which were able to improve their role by moving towards upper level functions.

In order to analyse/test/explore this, a panel database with 3 year averages of data has been built for the same 12-year period which was the object of the descriptive analysis. The dependent variable is the growth of total regional real GDP, an indicator consistent with regional competitiveness, and the explanatory variable of interest is the level of high-value functions. Consistent with the previous section of this chapter, the level of functions is proxied through the percentage of workers who report as occupation to be working as Physical, mathematical and engineering science professionals (ISCO21); the results with other proxies are generally similar.

A number of controls are added to the regression in order to avoid an omitted variable bias as much as possible. First of all, in order to account for national and time effects, a set of time-country dummies is added. These account for a region being in a specific country in a specific 3 year period. Moreover, other control variables are added: the percentage of workers in science and technology, and the level of education of the labour force, measured with the percentage of people holding at least a degree. Finally, the level of income per capita is also added to the regressions in order to account for additional socio-economic heterogeneity in the regional structure.

The sample uses regional averages over 3 years for 5 periods (1996–1998, 1999–2001, 2002–2004, 2005–2007, 2008–2010) and adopts the level of Nuts2 as classification. The main source of data is Eurostat and the regressions are run with fixed effects and report robust standard errors (Table 3.3).

Table 3.3 Panel regression results

Dependent variable	(1)	(2)	(3)	(4)	(5)	(6)
Regional real GDP growth						
Income per capita	−345.5***	−344.8***		−365.2***	−606.3***	−593.8***
	(99.22)	(94.28)		(117.1)	(119.6)	(122.9)
High value functions		61.55***	61.87**	47.65**	48.43**	
		(20.23)	(23.35)	(20.10)	(19.81)	
Human resources in science and technology (core definition)				0.248*	0.339**	0.332**
				(0.148)	(0.153)	(0.165)
Education					0.108*	0.0971
					(0.0609)	(0.0620)
Constant	9.134***	8.025***	1.224***	5.716***	6.188**	7.295**
	(1.911)	(1.773)	(0.413)	(2.072)	(2.733)	(2.760)
Time and country dummies	Significant	Significant	Significant	Significant	Significant	Significant
Observations	290	290	290	277	199	199
R-squared	0.682	0.691	0.664	0.700	0.810	0.805
Number of groups	58	58	58	58	58	58

Robust standard errors in parentheses, *** $p < 0.01$, ** $p < 0.05$, * $p < 0.1$

In order to verify whether the result for the main explanatory variable is due to the presence on the absence of controls, the regressions are run with different combinations of controls and also with no control at all. Additionally, to control for the coefficients of regressors, regressions with only the controls and without the target explanatory variable are also run.

The results of the regressions are presented in Table 3.3. All the coefficients are significant and have the expected sign. The target explanatory variable, i.e., the level of high level functions in the region, is always positively and significantly related to regional growth, independently from whether the controls are included and which set of controls are included. This provides preliminary support to the intuition, coming from the descriptive analysis, that low levels of upgrading in southern European regions are detrimental to growth.

The control variables also have the expected sign: there is, ceteris paribus, some degree of internal convergence, as the initial level of GDP per person has negative sign, as is common in the literature. Moreover, the levels of human resources in science and technology and the levels of education are positively and significantly related to growth. As they maintain the same sign and almost the same coefficient in all the regressions which are presented, these results prove to be robust to different specifications. Also in the last case, without high level functions, in which the education levels are no longer significant, they are only very marginally so, as the coefficient is basically the same and so is the standard error.

These regressions could be further reinforced by having other controls which are not available as a panel over the same time span, such as FDI data (see the chapter by Resmini in this volume) or the level of institutions in the regions, which was shown to contribute to explain the lack of transition towards higher level functions in Portugal (Marques 2015). They are however clearly supportive of the idea that the reduced productivity growth in the regions of Southern European countries is correlated with their low level of functions and their inability to rise towards higher level functions.

3.5 Conclusions

This second introductory chapter looked at some important economic problems of southern European countries. In fact, despite starting at levels of income per capita around or below the average of the EU, these countries did not catch up and, especially in the years of the crisis, significantly lost ground with respect to their northern partners.

There are certainly very important national aspects to explain that. For example, problems related to the presence of a currency union, the Eurozone, with different inflation rates, which made the real effective exchange rates of these countries deteriorate significantly. Other important aspects at the national level include the problems of public finances, which has been so important for these countries as to be the main determinant of the second hit of the big crisis. Having a very large standing debt in an unstable global financial situation is a big problem, since this raises selectively the interest rates for these countries and puts additional strain on the public finances than in a "normal" period of recession, when increased welfare and public investment expenditure is needed.

However, as this chapter pointed out, there is an issue coming from the real supply-side economy in these four countries, which was present well before the crisis, namely the inability to increase productivity at the same rate of other comparable countries. This is an aspect of a weak economic structure, which is more vulnerable to crisis and to new international competition which first generally arise in traditional low-value-added productions.

The chapter showed that the four southern European countries were able to create jobs in the years before the crisis but not to increase their level of production by raising productivity. This problem was common at the national level, but more concentrated in the weakest regions of these countries, those eligible for Objective 1 support by the EU structural funds. In this chapter, this was shown to be due to a problem of functions performed in the various regions of these countries: by looking at the professions performed by workers in the regions of these countries, it clearly emerges that they are specialized in low level functions, apart from public sector command functions in the richest southern European regions (which, however, are normally more related to internal domination) and apart from small and medium enterprise managers, which are, however, more linked to the creation of self-employment and the inability of small firms to grow, than to strong entrepreneurship. The regions of southern European countries lack in functions related to research, to engineering and innovation, in professional support functions and, finally, also in creative ones. And in this aspect there is a significant level of homogeneity between these countries, confirming the evidence provided in the previous chapter by Fonseca (2017).

This inability to upgrade their structure and move towards higher value added functions has been detrimental to growth. As shown by an empirical analysis, those regions which had higher functions were, ceteris paribus, outperforming the others. There is hence an important contribution of regional functions to growth, especially in southern European countries. In general, therefore, southern European peripheral regions specialize in lower-level functions and have not upgraded them, and this can hinder growth and helps explain their difficulties in catching-up.

This evidence raises a large number of questions. First of all, why were these regions unable to upgrade their functions and improve their productive structure? This is not due to a single explanation, but to a number of concurrent causes. This explanation has to be looked for in low level infrastructure, inability to attract FDI, difficult innovative patterns, politics and institutions, and to a large extent to weak human capital and especially to the inability to use it, all coupled with ineffective public policies. The following chapters will cover these aspects in detail.

Finally, the evidence provided in this chapter also raises questions for policies. It appears that, with some localized exceptions, policies have largely been ineffective in bringing development to these places. Normally, these policies were not directly targeting the upgrading of the economic structure, but rather the basic infrastructure upon which the economy is built, or the set-up of new businesses. Helping firms to rise to an upper level of functions is not an easy task, as this requires them to move from production to ideation, or from local do-it-all-in-house production to growing by keeping only the highest value added phases and relocating those of lower levels. These are processes which are not incremental growth, but involve destructive organizational growth. These are also processes which cannot take place in the short run. However, they will be necessary if the regions of southern European countries want to avoid being squeezed between the advanced and innovative core regions of northern European countries and the cost-effective regions of emerging countries.

References

Affuso A, Capello R, Fratesi U (2011) Globalization and competitive strategies in European vulnerable regions. Reg Stud 45(5):657–675

Baldwin R (2006) Globalisation: the great unbundling (s). Economic Council of Finland, 20 Sept, p 51

Basile R, Castellani D, Zanfei A (2008) Location choices of multinational firms in Europe: the role of EU cohesion policy. J Int Econ 74:328–340

Bristow G (2005) Everyone's a "winner": problematising the discourse of regional competitiveness. J Econ Geogr 5(3):285–304

Camagni R (1991) Regional deindustrialization and revitalization processes in Italy. In: Rodwin R, Sazanami H (eds) Industrial change and regional economic transformation. Harper Collins, London, pp 137–167

Camagni R (2002) On the concept of territorial competitiveness: sound or misleading? Urban Stud 39(13):2395–2411

Camagni R (2009) Territorial capital and regional development. In: Capello R, Nijkamp P (eds) Handbook of regional growth and development theories. Edward Elgar, Cheltenham, pp 118–132

Capello R, Fratesi U, Resmini L (2011) Globalization and regional growth in Europe: past trends and future scenarios. Advances in spatial science. Springer, Berlin

Chiarvesio M, Di Maria E, Micelli S (2010) Global value chains and open networks: the case of Italian industrial districts. European Planning Studies

Coe NM, Yeung HW (2015) Global production networks: theorizing economic development in an interconnected world

Cuadrado-Roura JR (2013) Towards increasingly "tertiarised" economies: facts, factors and prospects. In: Cuadrado-Roura JR (ed) Service industries and regions: growth, location and regional effects. Springer, Berlin, pp 21–42

Dunford M (2002) Italian regional evolutions. Environ Plan A 34(4):657–694

Dunford M (2006) Industrial districts, magic circles and the restructuring of the Italian textiles and clothing chain. Econ Geogr 82(1):27–59

Ezcurra R, Pascual P, Rapun M (2007) Spatial inequality in productivity in the European Union: sectoral and regional factors. Int Reg Sci Rev 30(4):384–407

Fonseca M (2017) Southern Europe at a glance: regional disparities and human capital. In: Fonseca M, Fratesi U (eds) Regional upgrading in southern Europe. Springer, Berlin

Gardiner B, Martin R, Tyler P (2004) Competitiveness, productivity and economic growth across the European regions. Reg Stud 38:1045–1067

Grossman GM, Rossi-Hansberg E (2008) Trading tasks: a simple theory of offshoring. Am Econ Assoc 98:1978–1997

Gunasekara C (2006) Reframing the role of Universities in the development of regional innovation systems. J Technol Transfer 31(1):101–113
Huggins R (2013) Regional competitiveness: theories and methodologies for empirical analysis. J Cent Cath 6(2):155–172
Huggins R, Izushi H, Prokop D, Thompson P (2014) The global competitiveness of regions. Routledge, London
Lee SY, Florida R, Acs ZJ (2004) Creativity and entrepreneurship: a regional analysis of new firm formation. Reg Stud 38:879–891
Leydesdorff L, Etzkowitz H (1998) The triple helix as a model for innovation studies. Sci Public Policy 25(3):195–203
Lorenz E, Lundvall B (2010) Accounting for creativity in the European Union: a multi-level analysis of individual competence, labour market structure, and systems of education and training. Camb J Econ 35(2):269–294
Low P (2013) The role of services. In: Elms DK, Low P (eds) Global value chains in a changing world. WTO, Geneva, pp 61–81
Marques P (2015) Why did the Portuguese economy stop converging with the OECD? Institutions, politics and innovation. J Econ Geogr 15(March):1009–1031
Marrocu E, Paci R (2012) Regional development and creativity. Int Reg Sci Rev 36(3):354–391
Moro B, Beker VA (2016) Modern financial crises: Argentina, United States and Europe. Springer, Berlin
O'Leary E, Webber DJ (2015) The role of structural change in European regional productivity growth. Reg Stud 49(9):1548–1560
Petrakos G, Fotopoulos G, Kallioras D (2012) Peripherality and integration: industrial growth and decline in the Greek regions. Environ Plann C Gov Policy 30(2):347–361
Trigilia C (2012) Why the Italian Mezzogiorno did not achieve a sustainable growth: social capital and political constraints. Cambio 2(4):138–148

Ugo Fratesi is Associate Professor of Regional Economics at Politecnico di Milano (since December 2010). He is Editor of main section papers and Book Review Editor of Regional Studies since 2013. Previously, he was member of the editorial board of the Italian Journal of Regional Science. He was member of the Council of the Italian Section of the Regional Science Association International (AISRe) for the period 2010–2016 and was its Treasurer for the period 2010–2013. He has been involved with various roles in a large number of research projects, especially at European level, financed by the Espon programme, the FP5, FP7, Horizon 2020 or the European Commission directly. He is co-author of several books and author of a large number of papers published in refereed journals in the field of regional economics, primarily on the themes of regional growth and development, the models for forecasting regional growth, regional policy, the theory and measurement of regional disparities and the territorial aspects of human capital and innovation.

Part II
Regional Upgrading I: Innovation, Productivity, FDI, Infrastructure and Policies

Chapter 4
Do Southern European Regions Really Lag Behind in Their Innovation Trends?

Roberta Capello and Camilla Lenzi

JEL Classification R11 • O31

4.1 Introduction

Southern European countries, and in particular Spain, Italy, Greece and Portugal, show a lower R&D over GDP level with respect to the European average. In the period 2000–2002, these countries achieved 0.73% of R&D/GDP, against an EU average of 1.37%. Recent data further confirm this situation; in 2006–2007, the R&D/GDP ratio in the four Southern countries reached a level of 0.87% against an EU average of 1.44%.

It is common belief that their poorer GDP growth with respect to the EU average (e.g., 3% against 3.6% in the period 2005–2007, the pre-crisis period) is attributed to their scant investments in R&D, and therefore their limited capacity to generate new knowledge and transform this knowledge into higher economic efficiency and growth. The aim of the present chapter is to show that this common belief is true up to a certain level. If it is certainly undeniable that these countries invest relatively less than the EU average in R&D, it is also true that they show specific patterns of innovation that are not necessarily based on formal knowledge to achieve innovation, and to translate innovation into economic efficiency.

In order to prove such a statement, the framework applied is that of territorial patterns of innovation, defined as spatial breakdowns of variants of the knowledge—invention—innovation logical path according to the presence/absence of territorial preconditions for knowledge and innovation creation and attraction (Capello 2013). This chapter provides an empirical application of this concept to European regions, while highlighting the specificities of Southern ones. Once their specific patterns are outlined, the chapter demonstrates that Southern European regions are able to take advantage of their innovation patterns in terms of total factor productivity and economic efficiency in general.

R. Capello • C. Lenzi (✉)
Department of Architecture, Built Environment and Construction Engineering, Politecnico di Milano, Piazza Leonardo da Vinci 32, 20133 Milan, Italy
e-mail: camilla.lenzi@polimi.it

M. Fonseca, U. Fratesi (eds.), *Regional Upgrading in Southern Europe*, Advances in Spatial Science, DOI 10.1007/978-3-319-49818-8_4

The results of this study have important policy implications. The 'one size fits all' policy suggested in the Europe 2020 agenda to increase R&D investments over GDP to improve European competitiveness can be misleading if translated from the national to the regional level without acknowledging the heterogeneity and specificities of regional innovation modes. Southern European regions, in fact, require specific policies that reinforce their own pattern of innovation and make the best out of their innovative assets and activities.

The following section describes innovation trends and patterns in Southern European regions, with a comparison with general trends and patterns in Europe, and links their innovative performance to efficiency and growth performance. The result of this empirical analysis shows that R&D-driven innovation mode is not the one applied in these countries; these countries are in fact particularly strong in process innovation (Sect. 4.2). For this reason, a territorial pattern of innovation approach is presented and applied to interpret the innovation mode of Southern countries and regions (Sects. 4.3 and 4.4). The conclusions propose specific normative strategies helpful for the re-launch of economic growth through innovation in these regions.

4.2 Knowledge and Innovation Trends in Southern Europe

This section contains a descriptive analysis of the knowledge and innovation trends in Southern Europe.[1] Generally, Southern countries considerably underperform the other European countries with respect to several indicators, especially the most traditional ones such as R&D expenditures as a percentage of GDP, patent intensity and the share of highly educated human capital (Table 4.1). Interestingly, all Southern countries lag behind the EU far more in patent intensity than in general R&D expenditures. On the one hand, our measure of R&D includes both public and private expenditures; on the other, especially in the European context, patenting is primarily the output of private research activities. Hence, this result may indicate a relatively more important share of public expenditures over private ones, which reflects also in a lower patent intensity in these countries.

Also, Southern countries lag behind in most innovation indicators. As to product innovation, this result is highly consistent with the general underperformance in terms of R&D expenditures and patent intensity, usually at the basis of the capacity to develop new products. As to marketing and/or organizational innovation, which is diffused especially in advanced services, this figure may relate to some delay experienced by Southern countries in the tertiarisation trends nowadays affecting most European economies moving from traditional manufacturing towards knowledge-intensive services and/or a lower pervasiveness of advanced services in these countries.

---

[1]The data applied are presented in details in Appendix 1.

Table 4.1 Knowledge and innovation trends in Southern European countries and in the rest of Europe—mean differences t-tests

Variable	Southern EU regions (55)	Rest of Europe (207)	T-test
R&D/GDP % (2000–2002)	0.73	1.54	<***
Patent per capita (1999–2001)	0.02	0.11	<***
Human capital % (1999–2001)	6.53	9.86	<***
Knowledge embedded in capabilities (1997–2001)	***0.52***	0.37	>***
Product innovation % (2002–2004)	4.40	12.00	<***
Process innovation % (2002–2004)	***12.81***	10.58	>***
Product and process innovation % (2002–2004)	12.56	15.61	<***
Product and/or process innovation % (2002–2004)	29.74	37.08	<***
Marketing and/or organizational innovation % (2002–2004)	22.64	26.88	<**

Note: number of regions in parentheses. *** $p < 0.01$; ** $p < 0.05$; * $p < 0.10$

However, it is worth also noting some important exceptions to this general trend. Importantly, Southern countries outperform the EU in two main dimensions: informal knowledge embedded in professional capabilities on the one hand, and process innovation on the other. These results are indeed highly consistent. In fact, innovative activities aimed at introducing new processes are on average less research-intensive than activities aimed at introducing new products. For process innovation, craft, tacit and knowledge embedded in professional capabilities can be an important source and repository of embodied knowledge and absorptive capacity necessary to identify possibilities, to develop and to implement solutions, as to increase efficiency in production processes. Therefore, a description of knowledge creation and innovation activities based only on R&D expenditures and patent intensity provides quite an unbalanced description of the actual innovation intensity and patterns in Southern European regions.

Still, the good performance in terms of process innovation in Southern countries does not offset the negative performance in terms of product innovation; both product and process innovation as well as product and/or process innovation are considerably lower in Southern countries than in the rest of Europe. All the differences are indeed highly significant at conventional levels as t-tests reported in Table 4.1 confirm.

At the country level, some interesting national specificities emerge. Concerning R&D expenditures and patent activities, Italy performs better than the other Southern countries (although still below the rest of the EU), especially in terms of patenting, suggesting a more balanced engagement and contribution of public and private funding and actors in the creation of new knowledge with respect to the other three countries. On the contrary, Italy significantly underperforms the other Southern countries in terms of human capital and knowledge embedded in capabilities, showing a three times lower share of highly educated population than the EU. In contrast, Spain departs from the average Southern countries profile in terms

Table 4.2 Knowledge and innovation trends by Southern Europe countries (average values)

Variable	EU (262)	Spain (16)	Greece (13)	Italy (21)	Portugal (5)
R&D/GDP % (2000–2002)	1.37	0.75	0.43	0.91	0.76
Patent per capita (1999–2001)	0.09	0.02	0.002	0.05	0.001
Human capital % (1999–2001)	9.16	11.77	6.47	3.07	4.53
Knowledge embedded in capabilities (1997–2001)	0.41	0.65	0.76	0.25	0.62
Product innovation % (2002–2004)	10.40	4.78	2.26	5.29	4.78
Process innovation % (2002–2004)	11.05	12.71	9.34	14.27	15.99
Product and process innovation % (2002–2004)	14.97	12.83	18.12	8.03	16.28
Product and/or process innovation % (2002–2004)	35.53	30.32	29.72	27.59	37.05
Marketing and/or organizational innovation % (2002–2004)	25.99	20.77	24.76	20.13	33.67

Note: number of regions in parentheses

of highly educated human capital; this indicator is in fact greater than the EU average and suggests that Spain has considerably caught the EU frontier in this regard. Nevertheless, Italy is able to make a very efficient use of local intellectual skills to achieve innovation, especially product innovation that, within the Southern block, is the highest precisely in Italy (Table 4.2).

Concerning innovative activities, the aggregate share of firms introducing product and/or process innovation is mostly driven by process innovation in the case of Italy, suggesting a stronger specialization in this type of innovative activities. In the Iberian countries on the other hand, product and/or process innovation is equally based on process innovation and on process and product innovation, indicating that in this case firms that introduce process innovation frequently accompany the development and adoption of new processes with the introduction of new products. In Greece, however, firms seem to pursue a joint strategy of product and process innovation, which is in fact the largest category of innovators contributing to the overall innovative performance (i.e., in terms of product and/or process innovation).

Overall, these results show that the innovation mode of these countries is based neither on R&D nor on product innovation only but rather on a mix of product and mostly process innovation, mainly driven by informal rather than formal knowledge. This result opens the way to a reflection on the fact that countries and regions can have different innovation modes that depart from an R&D-driven innovation mode. The next section presents a conceptual and empirical framework with which to interpret alternative innovation modes.

4.3 Territorial Patterns of Innovation

4.3.1 The Conceptual Approach

A conceptual framework with which to interpret alternative innovation modes has recently been suggested in the literature (Capello and Lenzi 2013), based on the large body of theoretical and empirical studies that, over time, have considerably expanded and enriched the scientific understanding of knowledge and innovation processes in space, as confirmed by the multiple approaches and paradigms on which they draw. For example, economic geography, the evolutionary theory of innovation (Dosi 1982; Nelson and Winter 1977), neo-Schumpeterian theories on local development (Aydalot 1986; Camagni 1991; Calafati 2009), and evolutionary geography (Boschma and Frenken 2006; Neffke et al. 2011). The capacity of generating local knowledge, and of turning it into innovation and growth, has long been related to the presence of specific territorial conditions (Camagni 1991; Capello 1999; Lundvall and Johnson 1994; Trippl 2010). Interestingly, most contributions emphasise the crucial role of knowledge in regional innovation and growth and share the idea that the higher the local (formal) knowledge endowment the better the local innovative and economic performance. Consistently with the Schumpeterian tradition, innovation is viewed as the outcome of investments in very costly and risky research activities. Accordingly, the empirical tests are mostly based on the use of R&D statistics (or patent counts) as proxies for innovation outcomes, returning a highly concentrated picture of knowledge creation (and thus innovation) activities in space (see among the many others Rodríguez-Pose and Crescenzi 2008; Sterlacchini 2008; Anselin et al. 2000).

If the relationship among knowledge, innovation, productivity increases and economic growth is largely undisputable, it is nevertheless true that some regions may be more able than others to grasp the advantages stemming from knowledge and innovation. From an evolutionary perspective in fact, knowledge creation and innovation are highly cumulative processes leading to a markedly differentiated cognitive base, absorptive capacity and potential for learning across actors and regions (Iammarino and McCann 2006). Therefore, the capacity to exploit knowledge and innovation for strategic purposes is not equally distributed among firms, institutions and, in general, regions (Capello 1994). Consequently, the link between formal knowledge and innovation, and their impacts on economic growth, may be very complex and heterogeneous at the regional level and regions may succeed in innovating and growing although they lack strong local (formal) knowledge creation capabilities (Capello and Lenzi 2014). In fact, the literature implicitly provides explanations for situations in which the knowledge-innovation nexus does not hold at the local level, and innovation takes place without a strong formal local knowledge base; these explanations rest in: (i) the existence in some areas of informal knowledge; and/or (ii) knowledge spillover processes from knowledge-intensive regions.

R&D investments are indicators of what can be termed 'analytical' and 'formal' knowledge (Asheim and Coenen 2005), and thus provide a highly selective, if not unbalanced, description of the knowledge creation efforts. Innovation processes increasingly rely upon a mix of differentiated knowledge types and sources that tend to vary with specific characteristics of innovative agents. Specifically, the importance of formal knowledge tends to decrease for smaller firms and more traditional sectors, which instead rely more on technologies embodied in machinery and equipment and on informal knowledge embedded in professionals rather than on formal knowledge (Conte and Vivarelli 2005; Piergiovanni et al. 1997). Moreover, R&D and patent indicators neglect all innovative efforts that can be developed either in the form of process, marketing and organizational innovations or in the form of product innovation not necessary obtained via research and patenting activities, as highlighted in the debate on development and catching-up achieved through social capabilities (Abramowitz 1986; Archibugi and Coco 2005; Fagerberg and Shrolec 2008).

In addition, regions can innovate based on external knowledge, acquired through networking with leading regions, and of specific know-how in local application sectors (Licht 2009). More in general, there may be regions with weak internal formal knowledge creation capacity but which are able to leverage on external knowledge sources to innovate and develop. These considerations become more compelling when one moves from the national to the regional level of analysis, because of the highly concentrated spatial profile of research activities (e.g., Rodríguez-Pose and Crescenzi (2008) for Europe and Feldman (1994) for the US) and the paramount importance of knowledge spillovers selectively diffusing across geographical (Jaffe et al. 1993; Moreno et al. 2005) and cognitive spaces (Boschma 2005; Capello and Caragliu 2012; Caragliu 2015).

The literature therefore suggests that not only knowledge and innovation shall be distinguished as two different (and subsequent) stages of the innovation process, but also that they can mix in space in a variety of ways. As a consequence, it supports the need of a conceptual framework interpreting not only a single phase of the innovation process, but the different modes of performing the different phases of the innovation process, leading to the identification of different *territorial patterns of innovation* (Capello 2013).

The novelty of this approach rests on the idea that knowledge and innovation are not necessarily overlapping processes in space nor necessarily sequential at the local level, and that different types of knowledge (e.g., formal vs. informal, internal vs. external) may be needed to innovate in different contexts. In particular, *territorial patterns of innovation* can be conceived as spatial breakdowns of variants of the knowledge—invention—innovation logical path according to the presence/absence of territorial preconditions for knowledge creation, knowledge attraction, and innovation.

Accordingly, alternative situations can be envisaged and the well-established literature on knowledge and innovation at the regional level helps in choosing the most interesting combinations between innovation phases and territorial elements. In particular, three main 'archetypal' innovation modes, each of them reflecting a specific body of literature on knowledge and innovation in space, may be identified (Capello 2013):

(a) *A science-based pattern*, where highly innovative firms belonging to high added value and technology-intensive sectors are expected to cluster because they seek and require those local conditions—like the presence of universities, research centers, highly advanced human capital—that fully support the creation of knowledge. Moreover, in this group of regions the preconditions for turning knowledge into innovation, like the presence of entrepreneurial spirit and creativity, guarantee the transformation of knowledge into innovation. Given the complex nature of knowledge creation today, tight interrelations among regions in the form of international scientific networks characterize this pattern. From the conceptual point of view, this advanced pattern is the one considered by most of the literature dealing with knowledge and innovation creation and diffusion (Audretsch and Feldman 1996; Mack 2014);
(b) *A creative application pattern* characterized by the presence of (small and medium) enterprises belonging to traditional or medium-tech sectors, curious enough to look for knowledge outside the region—given the scarcity of local knowledge—and creative enough to apply external knowledge to local innovation needs (Foray 2009; EC 2010c; Licht 2009). Knowledge providers supporting the innovative activities of local firms are mostly located outside the region, and knowledge exchanges are nourished more by cognitive and sectoral proximity (i.e., shared cognitive maps) than by belonging to the same local community;
(c) *An imitative innovation pattern*, where firms in traditional sectors, or branches of multinational enterprises in different sectors, seeking low labor-cost areas to locate their lower value-added functions, base their innovation capacity on imitation of already existing innovations, albeit with different degrees of adaptation. In several cases, regions in this pattern are likely to be characterized by a higher presence of firms with few learning and innovative activities. This pattern is based on the literature dealing with innovation diffusion (Hägerstrand 1952; Pavlínek 2002; Varga and Schalk 2004).

Conceptually speaking, these three patterns represent by-and-large the different ways in which knowledge and innovation can take place in a regional economy. Each of them represents a different way of innovating; the importance of highlighting which innovation pattern is present in the countries of our analyses lies in the fact that their differences call for different policy styles to support each of them. In order to suggest the right innovation policy goals and tools in the countries of our analyses (Sect. 4.7), it is therefore vital to highlight which innovation pattern characterizes the different regions of the countries (Sects. 4.4 and 4.5) and the economic performance these innovation patterns have (Sect. 4.6).

4.4 A Taxonomy of European Innovative Regions

Territorial patterns of innovation have been empirically detected in a recent study by means of a cluster analysis based on a series of indicators capturing the different knowledge and innovation attitudes across European regions (Capello and Lenzi 2013).[2] The empirical results highlight that there exists a variety even more fragmented than conceptually envisaged. Two clusters have emerged that can be associated with our conceptual "Science-based pattern" described above (i.e., endogenous innovation pattern), whose difference resides in the intensity of knowledge creation, but especially in the type of knowledge created. Moreover, two patterns can be associated with a "Creative application Pattern" described above (i.e., creative application pattern) whose difference lies in the type of knowledge that they acquire from outside the region: one mainly looks for formal knowledge (in the form of patents in specific technologies) outside the region and the other acquires tacit knowledge, embedded in capabilities.

Interestingly, the five groups exhibit sizeable differences in the variables considered in the clustering exercise. Figure 4.1 shows the five patterns, which are briefly described below.

The **European science-based area (ESBA)** is composed of strong knowledge and innovation producing regions, specialized in general purpose technologies, with the highest generality and originality of the science-based local knowledge, and the highest degree of knowledge acquisition from other regions. R&D expenditures, too, are the highest in these regions.

The **Applied science area (ASA)** is similarly made up of strong knowledge producing regions, albeit characterized by a local knowledge base of an applied nature, and by a high degree of knowledge acquisition from other regions. R&D activity is high in this group of regions as well.

The **Smart technological application area (STAA)** exhibits a high product innovation rate, a more limited degree of local basic science, but a high level of creativity, which enables the translation of external basic and applied scientific knowledge into innovation with respect to the other four clusters. The knowledge intensity is lower than in the previous two cases, although not negligible.

The **Smart and creative diversification area (SCDA)** exhibits a low degree of local formal knowledge in the form of patents and R&D; a non-negligible internal innovation capacity; a high degree of local informal and tacit knowledge embedded in specialized human capital, creativity and entrepreneurship; and a high degree of acquisition of external knowledge embedded in technical and organizational capabilities, with respect to the other four clusters.

[2]The indicators used were the regional EU share of total patents, the regional share of firms introducing product and/or process innovation, and the regional share of firms introducing marketing and/or organizational innovation. For further details on the variables used in the cluster analysis and the variables representing the key territorial distinctive traits of the different groups of regions see Capello and Lenzi (2013).

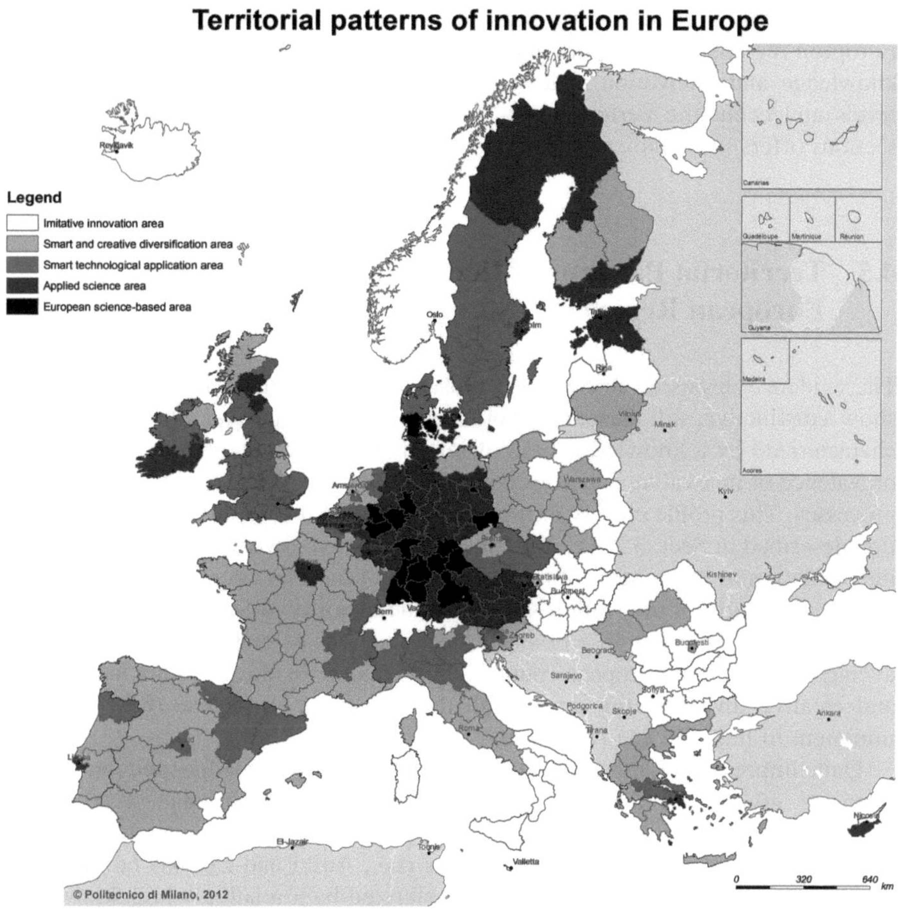

Fig. 4.1 Territorial patterns of innovation in Europe. Source: Capello and Lenzi (2013)

Lastly, the **Imitative innovation area (IIA)** displays a low knowledge and innovation intensity but high entrepreneurship, creativity, attractiveness and innovation potentials, with respect to the European Science Based area and the Applied science area.

The five groups therefore differ not only in terms of their knowledge and innovation endowments, but, interestingly, also in the type and nature of the knowledge used in innovative activities and in the enabling territorial factors supporting the creation and acquisition of different types of knowledge and its successful conversion into innovation. Whereas scientific and formal (being either generic or specific) knowledge, as captured by patents and R&D expenditures is prominent in the first three groups, in the last two, the relevant knowledge is more of the informal type, i.e., embedded in the human capital of specialized workers (i.e., capabilities).

The identification of such a large heterogeneity in innovation modes across European regions raises important questions about their relative capacity to exploit knowledge and innovation endowments in order to achieve higher productivity levels and economic performances. The empirical work developed in the next sections offers some indications in this direction.

4.5 Territorial Patterns of Innovation in Southern European Regions

The evidence discussed in Sect. 4.2 illustrates that Southern European countries show a distinctive, still reasonably homogenous, knowledge and innovation profile, characterized by a knowledge base of informal and tacit nature, and a consistent prevalence of innovative activities dedicated to the introduction of new production processes. This profile closely mirrors one of the five territorial patterns of innovation described in Sect. 3.2, i.e., the Smart and creative diversification area. In fact, the tabulation of the number of regions in each of the four countries across the five territorial patterns of innovation shows that the majority of Southern regions fall in this group and represent 40% of all European regions belonging to this cluster. On average, in Southern European countries more than 63% of regions are in the Smart and creative diversification area, with the maximum in Greece (85%) and the minimum in Italy (52%) (Table 4.3).

Quite impressively, there are no regions in the most knowledge- and innovation-intensive group specialized in general-purpose technologies and with a more original and general knowledge base (i.e., the European science-based area). There are instead only two capital regions (i.e., Attiki and Lisboa) falling in the Applied science area (which is also characterized by a relatively high knowledge and innovation intensity but with a more applied and specific knowledge base). This (somewhat unexpected) result is possibly related to the mono-centric structure of

Table 4.3 Share (%) of regions by territorial patterns of innovation in EU and Southern European countries

	Spain	Greece	Italy	Portugal	Total Southern EU	Rest of EU	EU
European science-based area	–	–	–	–	–	100	20
Applied science area	–	1.96	–	1.96	3.92	96.08	51
Smart technological application area	7.46	1.49	3.45	1.46	16.42	83.58	67
Smart and creative diversification area	11.49	12.64	12.64	3.45	40.23	59.77	87
Imitative innovation area	2.70	–	16.22	–	18.92	81.08	37
Number of regions	16	13	21	5	55	207	262

both Greece and Portugal, which may lead to a very high concentration of knowledge and innovation activities in the capital regions.

A relatively larger number of regions (11 regions) can be classified in the Smart technological application area; however they represent, only 16% of all European regions belonging to this cluster. They are mostly Italian and Spanish regions located in the northern part of the two countries (Piemonte, Lombardia, Veneto and Emilia Romagna in Italy, and Madrid, Cataluña, País Vasco, Navarra and Aragón in Spain), one Portuguese region (Norte) and one Greek (Sterea Ellada). All these regions were indeed characterized by a well-established manufacturing sector, relatively specialized in traditional and medium-tech productions, nowadays being affected by important tertiarization trends. The dualistic structure of both Spain and Italy can possibly explain their more heterogeneous innovation patterns.

In Italy, there are also six regions (i.e., 28.6% of Italian regions) in the Imitative innovation area (i.e., the least knowledge- and innovation-intensive group), signaling that Italy is the most diverse country in terms of variety of innovation patterns. Imitative regions are located in the South of the country and the islands (with the exception of Abruzzo, Molise and Campania) and make up 20% of the European imitative group. In addition, Spain has one region (Murcia) in this cluster.

Overall, it is possible to conclude that the most diffused pattern of innovation in Southern regions is characterized by an informal knowledge base embedded in professionals coupled with a higher propensity to develop process innovations. Interestingly, there is very little variance across and, to some extent, within countries in terms of patterns of innovation as most regions fall in the Smart and creative diversification group. Remarkably, Southern regions are almost totally absent in the most knowledge- and innovation-intensive clusters, with just a minority of regions able to enter the Smart technological application area which is however paralleled by a group of regions, of quite a comparable size, lagging behind in the Imitative innovation area.

This evidence therefore brings to the forefront the question of how this relatively lower performance in terms of formal knowledge creation and innovation can hinder the growth and efficiency potentials of Southern regions. The next section describes the way the different Southern European regional patterns of innovation perform in economic terms and the association between the innovation and economic performance at the regional level.

4.6 Efficiency and Growth of Southern European Regional Patterns of Innovation

By looking at the data on economic performance, the comparison between the Southern block and the rest of Europe does not seem to suggest major differences in terms of Total Factor Productivity (TFP) and employment growth, but a significant underperformance in terms of GDP growth rate (Table 4.4). This result is actually

Table 4.4 Differences in economic performance average values between Southern European regions and the rest of Europe

	TFP (2005–2007)	Employment growth rate % (2005–2007)	GDP growth rate % (2005–2007)
Southern European regions (55)	0.084	3.893	3.055
Rest of Europe (207)	−0.022	3.747	3.801
T-test mean difference	Not significant	Not significant	<***
Southern European regions (55)	0.084	3.893	3.055
Rest of EU15 (151)	0.204	3.220	3.111
T-test mean difference	<**	>*	Not significant

Note: number of regions in parentheses. *** $p < 0.01$; ** $p < 0.05$; * $p < 0.10$

due to the dramatic growth in Eastern European countries, which experienced a rapid catch-up trajectory in the past decade. In fact, the comparison of the Southern block and the rest of old European countries (EU15) indicate that their performance in terms of GDP growth is not statistically different, although driven by different strategies: employment growth in Southern Europe and efficiency increases achieved through higher TFP levels in the rest of EU15. More in detail, Spain and Greece outperform the EU average in all respects; Italy is more similar to the average EU behavior in terms of employment growth, but with a much lower TFP level (the lowest of the Southern countries group) and a lower GDP growth rate (which is almost half of that of the EU). On the other hand, Portugal underperforms the EU according to all dimensions, with the lowest employment and GDP growth rates in the southern countries group (Table 4.8 in Appendix 2).

The differences across territorial patterns of innovation explain to a certain extent the differences in national performances (Table 4.5). In fact, an ANOVA test, comparing the average value of TFP, employment growth rate and GDP growth rate across the five territorial patterns and in the EU, indicates that there seem to be quite large differences, especially with regard to TFP. TFP is considerably lower in the Imitative innovation area with respect to the other clusters, and employment growth is substantially lower in the Smart technological application area. On the other hand, the differences in terms of GDP growth rate are less substantial and significant only at the 10% level.

More in detail, the results of pair-wise t-tests on the mean values of TFP across the five territorial patterns of innovation indicate that the Imitative innovation group is significantly lagging behind the others. On the other hand, the other four groups seem able to achieve statistically similar efficiency levels. This result can explain the unsatisfactory TFP performance in Italy, in which 28% of regions fall in this group. In terms of employment growth, and to a large extent also GDP growth, pair-wise t-tests on the mean values of this indicator point out that the Smart technological application group is the one experiencing the lowest performance, whereas

Table 4.5 Economic performance across territorial patterns of innovation in European regions—ANOVA test

	TFP (2005–2007)	Employment growth rate % (2005–2007)	GDP growth rate % (2005–2007)
EU average (262)	0	3.778	3.644
European science-based area (20)	0.154	4.115	3.286
Applied science area (51)	0.075	4.353	3.649
Smart technological application area (67)	0.119	2.664	3.171
Smart and creative diversification area (87)	0.099	3.995	3.854
Imitative innovation area (37)	−0.634	4.322	4.197
ANOVA p-value	$p < 0.01$	$p < 0.01$	$p < 0.10$

Note: number of regions in parentheses

the other four clusters do not show statistically significant differences. Again, this result may help to explain the lower performance of Italy according to this dimension, as about 20% of Italian regions are in this cluster. More interestingly, regions in the Smart and creative diversification area, which attracts the largest majority of Southern European regions, do not underperform the other more knowledge- and innovation-intensive clusters. Rather, they do even better than regions in the Smart technological application area in terms of employment and GDP growth (Table 4.9 in Appendix 2).

Different from the European average trends, the performance of the Smart and creative diversification area stands out in Southern countries. Interestingly enough, within the Southern block, this group shows the highest value of all economic performance indicators with respect to the Smart technological application area and the Imitative innovation area and, more generally, the average performance in the Southern group (Fig. 4.2). It seems therefore that regions in the Smart and creative diversification area largely drive the performance of Southern regions.

In addition, Southern regions in the Smart technological application group underperform the European average behavior of the Smart technological application area in terms of TFP and GDP growth, despite a higher increase in employment (Fig. 4.3). This is actually consistent with evidence from Table 4.5, which shows that growth in Southern Europe has been mostly driven by employment growth rather than by efficiency (i.e., TFP) increases. On the other hand, Southern regions in the Smart and creative diversification area considerably outperform the European average behavior of the Smart and creative diversification in terms of TFP and employment growth, despite a somewhat lower GDP growth rate. Finally, Southern regions in the Imitative innovation area underperform the European average behavior of the Imitative innovation group in terms of employment and GDP growth, despite a higher TFP level. As this group is made up mostly of Eastern European regions, possibly many of these differences can be related to the different economic

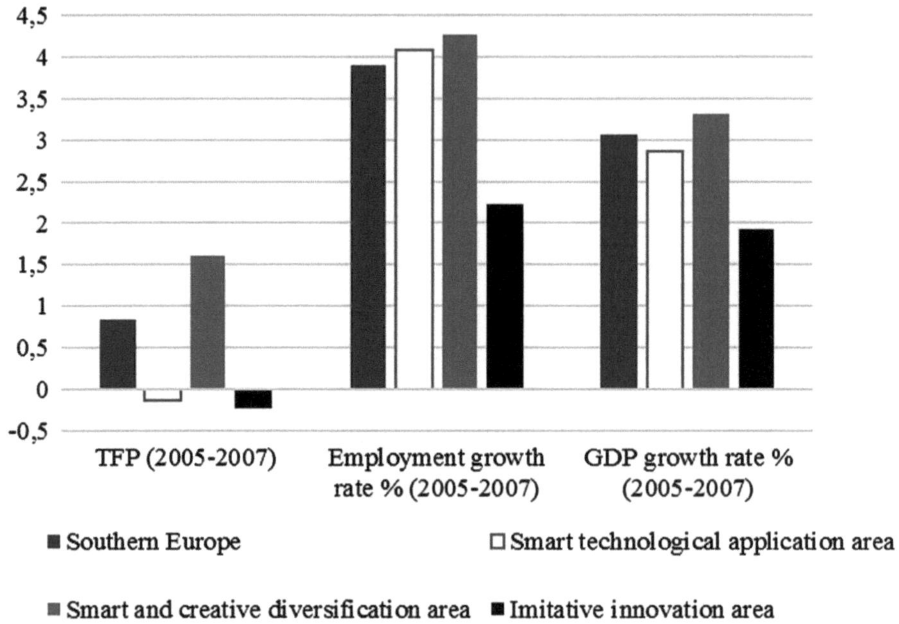

Fig. 4.2 Economic performance across territorial patterns of innovation in Southern Europe. Note: The European science based area was excluded because no Southern regions fall in this group; similarly, the Applied science area was excluded from these comparisons because only two regions fall in this group making the average value highly erratic and of little significance. ANOVA test significant at 1% for TFP, 10% for GDP growth rate, not significant for employment growth rate. TFP values are multiplied by 10 to improve the visual representation

trends in the EU15 and EU12 blocks, as discussed in Table 4.5 above. In general, these differences are also statistically significant as shown by pair-wise t-tests (implemented within the Southern block; Table 4.10 in Appendix 2). In particular, the tests confirm the significant underperformance in terms of TFP of the regions in the Smart technological application area with respect to regions in the Smart and creative diversification area, as well as the significant underperformance in terms of employment and GDP growth of the Imitative innovation group with respect to the Smart and creative diversification group.

Finally, also within the same innovation pattern, countries may show some specificities and heterogeneous behavior (Table 4.6). For example, the comparison of the performance of Spanish and Italian regions within the Smart technological application group show that Italian regions significantly underperform Spanish ones in GDP growth because of a lower employment growth.[3] On the other hand, the comparison of the performance of the four countries in the Smart and creative

[3]Comparisons were implemented only for the Smart technological application group (only between Spain and Italy) and the Smart and creative diversification group (among all countries) because of the very low number of regions in the other patterns.

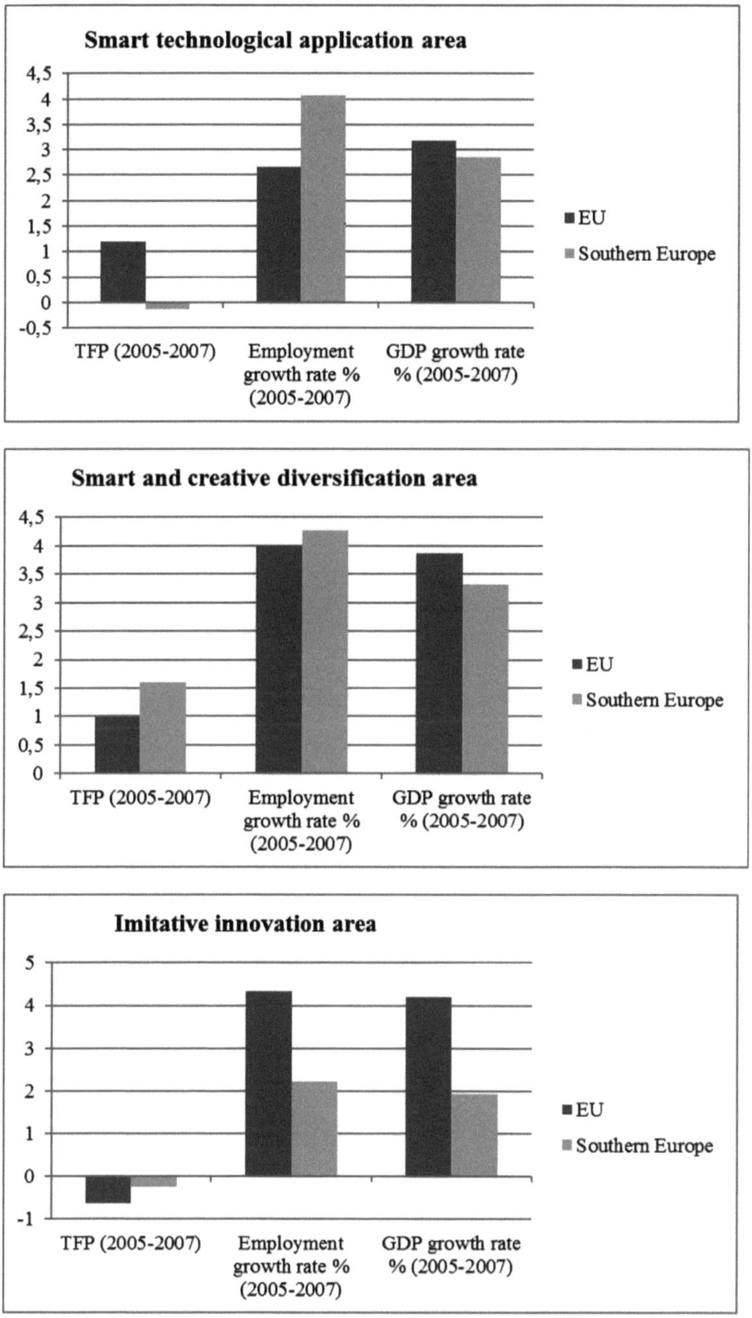

Fig. 4.3 Economic performance across territorial patterns of innovation in Southern Europe. Note: The European science based area was excluded because no Southern regions fall in this group; similarly, the Applied science area was excluded from these comparison because only two regions fall in this group making the average value highly erratic and of little significance

Table 4.6 Differences in economic performance across territorial patterns of innovation in Southern Europe—pairwise t-tests

Smart technological application area	TFP (2005–2007)	Employment growth rate % (2005–2007)	GDP growth rate % (2005–2007)
Spain (5)	0.019	5.977	3.862
Italy (4)	−0.184	2.879	1.898
T-test	ns	$p < 0.01$	$p < 0.01$
Smart and creative diversification area	TFP (2005–2007)	Employment growth rate % (2005–2007)	GDP growth rate % (2005–2007)
Spain (10)	0.190	7.191	3.745
Greece (11)	0.0395	2.921	4.438
Italy (11)	−0.045	3.597	2.187
Portugal (3)	−0.052	1.874	1.853
ANOVA p-value	$p < 0.05$	$p < 0.01$	$p < 0.01$

Note: number of regions in parentheses

diversification group indicate that Spanish regions significantly outperform Italian regions in all respects and they outperform Greek and Portuguese regions in terms of GDP growth because of a greater employment growth. In turn, Greek regions outperform Italian and Portuguese regions in terms of GDP growth because of higher efficiency levels in terms of TFP.[4] Lastly, Portuguese and Italian regions do not differ in any respect.

From this evidence, therefore, we can conclude that countries and regions characterized by an innovation mode based on informal and tacit knowledge embedded in professional capabilities and driven by process innovation do not necessarily underperform and do not necessarily show lower static (i.e., TFP level) and dynamic efficiency (i.e., employment and GDP growth). For these regions, thus, appropriate knowledge and innovation policies, not exclusively based on neutral and generic R&D incentives and targets, should be conceived and devised to make them fully contributing to the achievement of the smart growth goal set at the European level, as it will be discussed in the next section.

4.7 Conclusions: Which Innovation Policies for Regions with Low R&D Intensity?

This chapter studied innovation patterns in Southern European countries and highlighted the commonalities and specificities in the four countries. On the one hand, all countries share an innovation profile characterized by low R&D and patent

[4]Differences are statistically significant at conventional levels. T-tests are available upon request.

intensity and somewhat lag behind the European average in terms of more traditional indicators of knowledge creation and innovation. On the other hand, the four countries are ahead of the European average in terms of intensity of informal knowledge and process innovation. The results discussed in this chapter also confirm that Southern countries implement a different mode of combining knowledge to achieve innovation with respect to other countries in Europe. Innovation patterns based on new formal knowledge developed through R&D activities and translated into the introduction of new products are only one of the possible innovation modes in which regions develop innovation. Importantly, the evidence provided in this chapter shows that, despite a relatively lower endowment of traditional knowledge and innovative inputs, Southern regions are very efficient and smart in using knowledge and innovation for growing and achieving productive efficiency.

Still, some differences among the four countries can be noticed both in the within-country heterogeneity of innovation patterns and the overall innovative and economic performance, suggesting that also within the Southern block some regions are more able than others to combine and use knowledge inputs for innovation and growth, as for example in the case of Spain.

Hence, the results of this study have important policy implications. The 'one size fits all' policy suggested in the Europe 2020 agenda to increase R&D investments over GDP to improve European competitiveness can be misleading if translated from the national to the regional level without acknowledging the heterogeneity and specificities of regional innovation modes. Southern European regions, in fact, require specific policies that reinforce their own pattern of innovation and make the best out of their innovative assets and activities.

Therefore, a re-orientation of innovation strategies at the regional level seems particularly urgent, as to move away from a thematically/regionally neutral and generic innovation strategy towards a *thematically/regionally focused innovation policy* approach, as also proposed in the current debate on smart specialization (Coffano and Foray 2014; McCann and Ortega-Argilés 2014; Camagni and Capello 2013). The smart specialization debate in fact strongly emphasises the embeddedness of policies in the local context, in local assets and strategic design capabilities, possibly reinforced by the achievement of external knowledge through strong and virtuous linkages with the external world (McCann and Ortega-Argilés 2014).

In a similar vein, smart innovation policies have recently been proposed (Camagni and Capello 2013), defined as those policies able to increase the innovation capability of an area and to enhance local expertise in knowledge production and use. Such policies should act on specificities, characteristics, strengths and weaknesses of existing local innovation modes. An R&D support policy can be extremely useful for the first kind of innovation pattern. Incentives for co-invented applications, enhancing the ability of regions to change rapidly in response to external stimuli (such as the emergence of a new technology) and to promote upgrading of present specializations or shifting from old to new uses, is a good policy aim for the second pattern. The maximum return to imitation is the right policy aim of the third innovation pattern, and this aim is achieved through an adaptation of already existing innovations in order to reach particular market niches or specific territories.

In the context of Southern European regions, smart innovation policies will strengthen the prevailing regional innovation mode (i.e., the Smart and creative diversification mode) while sustaining the upgrading of most advanced regions and their move towards the Smart technological application area, if not their jump on the Applied science area. Sustaining a creative application means to put in place policies that help regions to shift existing technologies from old to new uses, with the aim of improving productivity in existing uses; in this way the right policy tool of these regional innovation patterns are achieved, i.e., that of maximising the return to co-inventing applications. In a word: support to 'D', and to co-operative 'D' rather than to 'R'. In the case of regions in the Smart technological application pattern, policy actions for the achievement of such goals can take into account incentives to technological projects that foresee new and creative use of existing scientific knowledge. In the case of regions in the Smart and creative diversification pattern, support and incentives to search in product/market diversification and to entrepreneurial creativity look more appropriate.

Policy tools for knowledge acquisition in these two patterns are incentives for creative applications. For such a purpose, cooperative research activities in related sectors in those regions where a minimal applied science base exists are an efficient policy tool for the Smart technological application area. On the one hand, participation of local actors in specialized international fairs, the attraction of star researchers even for short periods of time, or support for work experiences in best practice knowledge-creation firms in related sectors are right incentives to stimulate innovation in the Smart and creative diversification area whose innovation capacity lies in the brightness of local entrepreneurs to find the right applied knowledge outside the area on which to innovate and move towards a specialized diversification in related sectors.

Finally, in the Imitative innovation area, attention has to be devoted to the achievement of the maximum return to imitation, through fast diffusion of already existing innovation, strengthening of local receptivity to innovation (or reducing social or institutional barriers to change) and supporting favourable negotiations between local firms and MNCs on complementary projects and innovative, specialized subcontracting.

The previous policy suggestions are meant to increase the efficiency and effectiveness of innovation processes inside each single pattern. However, within each pattern, regions exist that are more advanced than others, and that potentially could move to a different pattern. For these regions, evolutionary policies can be foreseen, devoted to the achievement of an upgrading of innovation processes. As Camagni et al. (2014) highlighted, the most efficient regions in the Imitative innovation area could jump either into a Smart and creative diversification area or a Smart technological application area through the creation of new local competence and entrepreneurial spirit, adding local value to external knowledge. The most efficient regions in the pattern "Smart and creative diversification area" could be supported in order to move towards the Smart technological application pattern through the reinforcement of local applied science and development research.

Smart innovation policies designed according to these principles and guidelines could represent conceptually and operationally adequate new policy tools to attain the goals of smart growth and Innovation Union (EC 2010a, b, c), consistently with the smart specialization strategy proposed by DG Research and the necessary place-based reform of the EU regional policy advocated by the Barca Report and the recent documents of DG Regio.

Appendix 1: The NUTS2 Database for the Empirical Analysis

Table 4.7 Description of the variables[a]

Indicators	Measure	Computation	Year	Source
Knowledge				
R&D	R&D expenditures	Share of R&D expenditures on GDP	Average value 2000–2002	CRENoS database
Knowledge	Patent intensity	Patents on total population	Total patents in the period 1998–2001	Authors' calculation on CRENoS database
Highly educated human capital	Share of highly educated people	Share of people aged 15 and over with tertiary education on total population	Average value 1999–2001	CRENoS database
Capabilities[b] (knowledge embedded in human capital)	Share of managers and technicians	Factor analysis on the share of production and specialized service managers and engineering associate professionals (ISCO codes 13 and 31); factor score min-max normalized	Average value 1997–2001	Authors' calculation on European Labour Force Survey data
Innovation[c]				
Product and/or process innovation	Firms introducing a new product and/or a new process in the market	Share of firms introducing product and/or process innovations	One value for the period 2002–2004	Authors' estimation on CIS (Eurostat) data
Marketing and/or organizational innovation	Firms introducing a marketing and/or an organisational innovation	Share of firms introducing marketing and/or organizational innovations	One value for the period 2002–2004	Authors' estimation on CIS (Eurostat) data

(continued)

Table 4.7 (continued)

Indicators	Measure	Computation	Year	Source
Product innovation	Firms introducing a new product in the market	Share of firms introducing a product innovation	One value for the period 2002–2004	Authors' estimation on CIS (Eurostat) data
Process innovation	Firms introducing a new process in the market	Share of firms introducing a process innovation	One value for the period 2002–2004	Authors' estimation on CIS (Eurostat) data
Product and process innovation	Firms introducing both a new product and a new process in the market	Share of firms introducing both product and process innovations	One value for the period 2002–2004	Authors' estimation on CIS (Eurostat) data
Economic performance				
TFP[d]	Economic efficiency	Residuals	Average value 2005–2007	Authors' estimation on Eurostat data
Employment growth rate %	Employment dynamics	Average annual rate of growth	2005–2007	Authors' calculation on Eurostat data
GDP growth rate %	Economic growth	Average annual rate of growth	2005–2007	Authors' calculation on Eurostat data

[a]All variables, with the exception of the knowledge and innovation variables, are computed for the years 2005–2007, to avoid simultaneity with knowledge and innovation indicators

[b]This indicator was derived from a factor analysis synthesizing the information provided by two variables, i.e. the share of managers and technicians on total employment. In fact, skilled and specialized human capital is an important repository of embedded and tacit knowledge and can identify the pool of capabilities locally available

[c]To measure the regional innovative intensity, we developed a series of indicators based on data from the Community Innovation Survey (CIS) EUROSTAT database. In particular, innovation indicators were based on national CIS4 wave figures (covering the 2002–2004 period), next developed at the NUTS2 level. For an in-depth explanation of the estimation methodology of NUTS2 CIS data and the benchmark exercises implemented as consistency and robustness checks on our estimates, see Capello and Lenzi (2013). Previous exercises implemented for the DG Industry and DG Regio (Hollanders et al. 2009) elaborated and used as well a dedicated estimation strategy to derive regional innovation data. Notwithstanding the use of a different methodology, our results are reasonably consistent with previous estimates

[d]Regional TFP level was estimated in a traditional growth accounting approach to capital-labor multi-factor productivity as the residual of the log-linearized version of a standard Cobb-Douglas production function model where the regional GDP is regressed on the regional capital stock and the regional employment level. GDP, capital stock and labor were averaged over the years 2005–2007 to smooth possible effects related to specific years of estimation. For additional details, see Capello and Lenzi (2013)

Appendix 2: Selected Additional Results

Table 4.8 Economic performance in EU and in Southern Europe countries (average values)

Variable	EU (262)	Spain (16)	Greece (13)	Italy (21)	Portugal (5)
TFP (2005–2007)	0	0.139	0.332	–0.077	–0.055
Employment growth rate % (2005–2007)	3.778	6.535	2.980	3.041	1.393
GDP growth rate % (2005–2007)	3.644	3.795	4.376	1.962	1.846

Note: number of regions in parentheses

Table 4.9 Differences in economic performance across territorial patterns of innovation in European regions—pairwise t-tests

TFP (2005–2007)	ESBA	ASA	STAA	SCDA
European science-based area (ESBA)	–			
Applied science area (ASA)	ns	–		
Smart technological application area (STAA)	ns	ns	–	
Smart and creative diversification area (SCDA)	ns	ns	ns	–
Imitative innovation area (IIA)	< ***	< ***	< ***	< ***
Employment growth rate % (2005–2007)	ESBA	ASA	STAA	SCDA
European science-based area (ESBA)				
Applied science area (ASA)				
Smart technological application area (STAA)	< **	< ***	–	
Smart and creative diversification area (SCDA)	ns	ns	> ***	–
Imitative innovation area (IIA)	ns	ns	> ***	ns
GDP growth rate % (2005–2007)	ESBA	ASA	STAA	SCDA
European science-based area (ESBA)	–			
Applied science area (ASA)	ns			
Smart technological application area (STAA)	ns	< **	–	
Smart and creative diversification area (SCDA)	ns	ns	> **	–
Imitative innovation area (IIA)	ns	ns	> **	ns

Note: ns = not significant; * $p < 0.10$, ** $p < 0.05$, *** $p < 0.01$

Table 4.10 Differences in economic performance across territorial patterns of innovation in Southern Europe—pairwise t-tests

TFP (2005–2007)	STAA	SCDA
Smart and creative diversification area (SCDA)	> **	–
Imitative innovation area (IIA)	ns	ns
Employment growth rate % (2005–2007)	STAA	SCDA
Smart and creative diversification area (SCDA)	ns	–
Imitative innovation area (IIA)	< *	< *
GDP growth rate % (2005–2007)	STAA	SCDA
Smart and creative diversification area (SCDA)	ns	–
Imitative innovation area (IIA)	< *	< ***

Note: The European science based area was excluded because no Southern regions fall in this group; similarly, the Applied science area was excluded from these comparisons because only two regions fall in this group making comparison tests of little significance

References

Abramowitz M (1986) Catching up, forging ahead, and falling behind. J Econ Hist 46(2):386–406
Anselin L, Varga A, Acs ZJ (2000) Geographic and sectoral characteristics of academic knowledge externalities. Pap Reg Sci 74(4):435–443
Archibugi D, Coco A (2005) Measuring technological capabilities at the country level: a survey and a menu for choice. Res Policy 34(2):175–194
Asheim BT, Coenen L (2005) Knowledge bases and regional innovation systems: comparing Nordic clusters. Res Policy 34(8):1173–1190
Audretsch DB, Feldman MP (1996) R&D spillovers and the geography of innovation and production. Am Econ Rev 86(3):630–640
Aydalot P (1986) Milieux Innovateurs en Europe. GREMI editions, Paris
Boschma RA (2005) Proximity and innovation. A critical survey. Reg Stud 39(1):61–74
Boschma R, Frenken K (2006) Why is economic geography not an evolutionary science? Towards an evolutionary economic geography. J Econ Geogr 6(3):273–302
Calafati A (2009) Macro-regions, local systems and cities: conceptualization of territory in Italy since 1950s. Sci Reg Ital J Reg Sci 8(3):511–534
Camagni R (1991) Technological change, uncertainty and innovation networks: towards dynamic theory of economic space. In: Camagni R (ed) Innovation networks: spatial perspectives. Belhaven-Pinter, London, pp 121–144
Camagni R, Capello R (2013) Regional innovation strategies and the EU regional policy reform: towards smart innovation policies. Growth Chang 44(2):355–389
Camagni R, Capello R, Lenzi C (2014) A territorial taxonomy of innovative regions and the European regional policy reform: smart innovation policies. Sci Reg Ital J Reg Sci 13 (1):69–106
Capello R (1994) Spatial economic analysis of telecommunications network externalities. Ashgate, Aldershot
Capello R (1999) Spatial transfer of knowledge in high-technology milieux: learning vs. collective learning processes. Reg Stud 33(4):353–365
Capello R (2013) Territorial patterns of innovation. In: Capello R, Lenzi C (eds) Territorial patterns of innovation. An inquiry on the knowledge economy in European regions. Routledge, Oxford, pp 129–150
Capello R, Caragliu A (2012) Proximities and the intensity of scientific relations. Paper presented at the International Tinbergen Institute Workshop, 2012
Capello R, Lenzi C (2014) Spatial heterogeneity in the knowledge, innovation and economic growth nexus: conceptual reflections and empirical evidence. J Reg Sci 54(2):186–214
Capello R, Lenzi C (eds) (2013) Territorial patterns of innovation. An inquiry on the knowledge economy in European regions. Routledge, Oxford
Caragliu A (2015) The economics of proximity: regional growth beyond geographic proximity, PhD, Dissertation, Free University of Amsterdam, Amsterdam
Coffano M, Foray D (2014) The centrality of entrepreneurial discovery in building and implementing a smart specialization strategy. Sci Reg Ital J Reg Sci 13(1):33–50
Conte A, Vivarelli M (2005) One or many knowledge production functions? Mapping innovative activity using microdata. IZA discussion papers 1878
Dosi G (1982) Technological paradigms and technological trajectories: a suggested interpretation of the determinants and directions of technical change. Res Policy 2(3):147–162
European Commission (2010a) Europe 2020: a strategy for smart, sustainable and inclusive growth, COM(2010) 2020 final, Brussels, 3 Mar 2010
European Commission (2010b) Europe 2020 flagship initiative innovation union, Communication from the Commission to the European Parliament, the Council, the European Economic and Social Committee and the Committee of the Regions, SEC(2010) 1161, COM(2010) 546 final, 6 Oct 2010

European Commission (2010c) Regional policy contributing to smart growth in Europe, Communication from the Commission to the European Parliament, the Council, the European Economic and Social Committee and the Committee of the Regions, SEC(2010)1183, COM(2010) 553 final, Brussels, 6 Oct 2010
Fagerberg JE, Shrolec M (2008) National innovation systems: capabilities and economic development. Res Policy 37(9):1417–1435
Feldman MP (1994) The geography of innovation. Kluwer, Boston, MA
Foray D (2009) Understanding smart specialisation. In: Pontikakis D, Kyriakou D, van Bavel R (eds) The question of R&D specialisation, JRC, European Commission, Directoral General for Research, Brussels, pp 19–28
Hägerstrand T (1952) The propagation of innovation waves. Lund Stud Geogr Hum Geogr Ser B 4:3–19
Hollanders H, Tarantola S, Loschky A (2009) Regional Innovation Scoreboard (RIS) 2009, Pro Inno Europe Paper no 14, Entreprise and Industry Magazine, Brussels. Available at http://www.proinno-europe.eu/page/regional-innovation-scoreboard
Iammarino S, McCann P (2006) The structure and evolution of industrial clusters: transactions, technology and knowledge spillovers. Res Policy 35:1018–1036
Jaffe AB, Trajtenberg M, Henderson R (1993) Geographic localization of knowledge spillovers as evidenced by patent citations. Q J Econ 108(3):577–598
Licht G (2009) How to better diffuse technologies in Europe. Knowl Econ Policy Brief 7:1–5
Lundvall BA, Johnson B (1994) The learning economy. J Ind Stud 1(1):23–42
Mack E (2014) Broadband and knowledge intensive firm clusters: essential link or auxiliary connection? Pap Reg Sci 93(1):3–29
McCann P, Ortega-Argilés R (2014) The role of the smart specialisation agenda in a reformed EU cohesion policy. Sci Reg Ital J Reg Sci 13(1):15–32
Moreno R, Paci R, Usai S (2005) Spatial spillovers and innovation activity in European regions. Environ Plann A 37(10):1793–1812
Neffke F, Henning M, Boschma R (2011) How do regions diversify over time? Industry relatedness and the development of new growth paths in regions. Econ Geogr 87(3):237–265
Nelson R, Winter S (1977) In search of a useful theory of innovation. Res Policy 6(1):36–77
Pavlínek P (2002) Transformation of central and east European passenger car industry: selective peripheral integration through foreign direct investment. Environ Plann A 34:1685–1709
Piergiovanni R, Santarelli E, Vivarelli M (1997) From which source do small firm derive their innovative inputs? Some evidence from Italian provinces. Rev Ind Organ 12:243–258
Rodríguez-Pose A, Crescenzi R (2008) Research and development, spillovers, innovation systems, and the genesis of regional growth in Europe. Reg Stud 42(1):51–67
Sterlacchini A (2008) R&D, higher education and regional growth: uneven linkages among European regions. Res Policy 37:1096–1107
Trippl M (2010) Developing cross-border regional innovation systems: key factors and challenges. Tijdschr Econ Soc Geogr TESG 101(2):150–160
Varga A, Schalk H (2004) Knowledge spillovers, agglomeration and macroeconomic growth: an empirical approach. Reg Stud 38(8):977–989

Roberta Capello is full professor of Regional and Urban Economics at Politecnico of Milan, former President of the Regional Science Association International (2009–2010), Treasurer of the European Regional Science Association (ERSA) (2000–2006) and National Secretary of the Italian Section of the International Regional Science Association (1995–1998). Editor in chief of Papers in Regional Science (Wiley Blackwell, Oxford) and of the Italian Journal of Regional Science (FrancoAngeli, Milan). Author of a textbook in Regional Economics, published in Italian (Il Mulino, 2004), in English (Routledge, 2007) and in Chinese (Economy and Management Publishing House, Beijin, China). Laurea Honoris Causa from the West University of Timisoara, Romania (October, 2012), and Fellow of the Regional Science Association International (since 2013).

Camilla Lenzi is associate professor of Regional and Urban Economics at Politecnico di Milano. She holds a PhD in Economics (2006, Università di Pavia) and an MSc in Industry and Innovation Analysis (2005, SPRU—University of Sussex). She is Jean Monnet module leader on EU Spatial Planning, Economics and Policies (2015–2018). From 2005 to 2008, Camilla stayed at the Department of Economics of Bocconi University and CESPRI (now ICRIOS) as a Postdoctoral Fellow. She participated with various roles in a large number of research projects, especially at European level, financed by the Espon programme, FP7 and FP6, and the European Commission directly. She is member of AISRe (Italian Regional Science Association) and ERSA (European Regional Science Association). She published on several international journals such as Journal of Urban Economics, Journal of Regional Science, Regional Studies, International Regional Science Review, Annals of Regional Science, Spatial Economic Analysis and Papers in Regional Science.

Chapter 5
Regional Development and Structural Change: The Productivity Paradox of Spanish Peripheral Regions

J. Andres Faiña, Jesus Lopez-Rodriguez, Paulino Montes-Solla, Isidoro Romero, and Laura Varela-Candamio

JEL Classification O10 • O30 • O43 • R11 • R58

Over the last 20 years, Spain has stood out for rapid growth of per capita income, capital accumulation and creation of employment. However, the most important structural phenomenon of the strong growth of the Spanish economy, especially in the decade from 1998 to 2007, was the limited growth in terms of output per worker and total factor productivity (TFP), which in combination with wage increases has led to a loss of competitiveness for Spain both at the global level and within the European Union (EU).

Unlike most developed European countries, during the late 1990s and the beginning of the 2000s Spain experienced a process of intense economic growth and convergence with European per capita GDP levels that in a rather surprising manner was associated with a flat rate of capital deepening. This growth pattern can be called mere "capital widening", a process where the increase of capital stock is mainly absorbed by intense job creation and strong increases in employed population, while the capital/labour and the productivity per employee ratios remained almost constant (and productivity even shrank).

How that can happen is a challenging question for mainstream growth theory models. The full employment assumption clearly did not apply in the case of Spain, where usually very high unemployment rates (between 16.9 and 20.0% in 1989–1992) shrank with economic growth to almost full employment (8.6% in 2007) and then rose again (20.1% in 2010) with the impact of the economic crisis. Furthermore, the Spanish growth pattern from 1995 to 2007 featuring high growth rates of per capita GDP (GDPpc) with constant—or declining—ratios of

J. Andres Faiña (✉) • J. Lopez-Rodriguez • P. Montes-Solla • I. Romero • L. Varela-Candamio
Faculty of Economics, Jean Monnet Group on Competition and Development (C+D), University of A Coruña, Campus de Elviña, s/n, 15071 A Coruña, Spain

Department of Applied Economics, University of Seville, Seville, Spain
e-mail: fai@udc.es

M. Fonseca, U. Fratesi (eds.), *Regional Upgrading in Southern Europe*, Advances in Spatial Science, DOI 10.1007/978-3-319-49818-8_5

productivity (GDP per employee, Y/L) and capital per employee (K/L) can hardly be explained by Keynesian macroeconomics.[1]

The growth of an economy is determined by its ability to accumulate productive factors (capital and labour) and the productivity with which these factors are used. Specifically, the way in which productivity behaves is a key factor in the capacity for long-term growth potential of any economic space (Krugman 1990, 1991). In this case, it is convenient to have information on trends in terms of output per worker (apparent labour productivity) and the main variables that affect it. The apparent labour productivity measures the output obtained for each labour unit in the production process (the number of people employed in production),[2] thereby making it an indicator of productive efficiency. However, this is a partial indicator, as it can be directly influenced by the quantities used of other factors, specifically the capital-labour ratio, as well as human capital itself and the technological characteristics of the production processes of the economy.

The aim of this chapter is to analyse the main features which characterise the regional development in Spain since its accession to the EU (1986) and the effective launching of the European Cohesion Policy (1989[3]).

The chapter is organized in five sections. Section 5.1 briefly describes the spatial structure of the Spanish economy in the European context and the broad connections between remoteness and economic development levels. Section 5.2 focuses on the main features of the economic growth in Spain by considering the contrast between a strong GDPpc growth and productivity stagnation and the investment-based regional development policy undertaken in the country. Section 5.3 is devoted to an in depth analysis of the productivity drivers and the existence of a productivity paradox in Spain. Section 5.4 concentrates on the link between regional disparities and regional growth models, as well as on presenting the devastating impact of the financial crisis and the economic downturn on employment. Finally, Sect. 5.5 concludes by commenting on the main challenges of the Spanish regions in the forthcoming years.

[1]Keynesian macroeconomics highlighted insufficient capital formation as a cause of medium term unemployment influencing the Non-Accelerating Inflation Rate of Unemployment (NAIRU) and several studies found supporting evidence in OECD economies (Rowthorn 1999; Stockhammer and Klär 2011; Karanassou and Sala 2010; Arestis et al. 2007).

[2]Nevertheless, labour productivity is influenced by the technology that is available, the composition of the work and the amount of remaining production factors used.

[3]The new European Cohesion Policy (formally introduced by the Single European Act in 1987) was effectively started by the first 1989–1993 programming period.

5.1 Peripherality and Backwardness in the Spanish Regions

With regards to the dynamic forecasts of the spatial distribution of economic activities, geographical economics models (GEM) have not found much support in the empirical evidence (Head and Mayer 2004, 2006). Spatial concentration structures have demonstrated to be much more stable than the predictions resulting from simulations with GEM. However, as highlighted by Head and Mayer (2004, 2006), GEM predictions exhibit a marked asymmetry and they provide good explanations of the significant differences in wages and per capita income between peripheral and central areas, which are extensively supported by the empirical estimation of the so-called "nominal wage equation" in different settings (Lopez-Rodriguez and Faiña 2007; Lopez-Rodriguez et al. 2007b; Redding and Venables 2004; Hanson 2005; Mion 2004; Pires 2006).

The recent situation in Europe does not seem to indicate that there has been a rapid increase in the spatial concentration due to a reduction in transportation costs and economic concentration (Lopez-Rodriguez et al. 2007a). Since the 1980s, EU policies have generated an important convergence in the development levels of member countries. Nevertheless, regional disparities within each country tend to increase (Rodriguez-Pose 1999; Puga 2002; Farole et al. 2013) but the spatial structure of the regional differences in per capita income has clearly been maintained. In Europe as well as in the whole world, central cities and cities of the largest size tend to reach higher and more stable rates of growth compared to areas with lower agglomeration levels (Kanbur and Venables 2005).

The spatial structure of the European Union is depicted by means of a map of population potentials (see left side of Fig. 5.1) which was computed considering all of the countries belonging to the European economic space, including Norway and Switzerland. Europe's economic activities are concentrated in a large central area (London-Paris-Ruhr), with successive concentric lines of decreasing accessibility to the markets, in a sort of core-periphery pattern or centre-periphery gradient together with the areas of concentration in the north of Italy.

Redding and Schott (2003), using a geographical economics framework, developed a theoretical explanation for the difficulty that peripheral regions have to achieve high levels of income and wealth, showing that the most highly qualified types of work are typically concentrated in industrial and advance services sectors mostly localised in central areas. Peripheral regions compensate for their competitive disadvantages by paying lower salaries and specializing in low quality undifferentiated products. This effect reduces the benefits of salaries paid to highly qualified workers, and reduces any incentives towards investing in human capital. On the contrary, central regions further specialize in high quality differentiated products exhibiting increasing returns to scale, and are able to have a greater intensity in qualified work and therefore pay higher salaries.

The strategic complementarity between the accumulation of human capital and Research Development and Innovation (RDI) investments generates a low

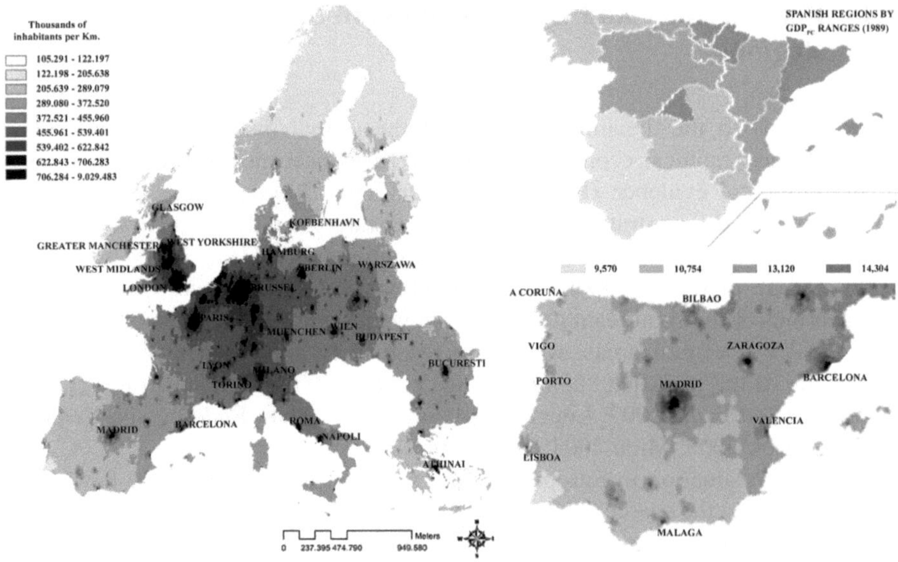

Fig. 5.1 Spain and the spatial structure of European Economic Space. Source: Faíña and López-Rodríguez (2006)

productivity trap where the economy is stuck in a low skills and low quality products equilibrium (Redding 1996). This is of increased importance in peripheral areas due on the one hand to the existence of synergies between the degree of regions' centrality and the hierarchy in the range-size of cities, and on the other to the levels of human capital and firms' investment in RDI and high quality products (Farole et al. 2011).

This structure of incentives is harmful for peripheral areas, where lower salaries and a lower demand for highly qualified labour make them prone to fall into a weak growth and competitiveness trap, getting stuck in low qualification/low quality equilibriums. As a result, peripheral locations with low access to the main markets and knowledge networks have to face an important penalty for their growth and convergence to the most centrally located and advanced locations.

The right-side map at the bottom of Fig. 5.1 describes the spatial structure of the Iberian Peninsula. In Spain, it can be seen that there is a clear difference in terms of accessibility to the markets between the North-East quadrant which takes in the Basque Country, Madrid and Catalonia and the rest of the peripheral areas in the centre of the peninsula (Castile and Extremadura), the South in Andalusia and Murcia, and in the Atlantic North-West, comprising Galicia and Asturias.

Traditionally, the areas in the North-East quadrant, closest to the rest of Europe and with the greatest market access are the most developed parts of the country, with a large percentage of population and economic activities, and generating the highest levels of growth and per capita income. These regional differences in the development of Spain can be seen in the top right side map of Fig. 5.1.

The traditional approach towards dealing with the adverse effects of remoteness focused on improving access and reducing distance costs by improving transport infrastructures (roads, railways, ports and airports). However, regional development policy measures have been extended to include human capital, emphasising the movement of the economy towards services, improving technologies and significantly reducing transport costs, as well as the development of ICTs, eliminating trade barriers and promoting greater European integration, to help soften the adverse effects of remoteness.

5.2 Economic Growth in Spain

The main initial constraints of the Spanish economy in the late 1980s were a large territory in the periphery of Europe with a disconnected spatial structure and low market access, suffering from development backwardness and poor endowments of public services (communication, transport, environmental and technological infrastructures) and private capital, as well as low human capital (knowledge, technological and educational attainments) and business and managerial capabilities.

The accession of Greece, Spain and Portugal to the EU was followed by a change in the Economic and Social Cohesion Policy (European Single Act, 1987), which from 1989 onwards dedicated a significant part of its resources to regions with structural development deficits (known as Objective 1 regions). Countries within the EU experienced a significant convergence in terms of per capita income, although at the regional level there are more doubts regarding convergence and the reduction of differences in terms of growth and per capita income.

In the case of Spain, its peripheral location and territorial size were combined with a major lack of capital provisions at the public and private level. The resources provided by the EU's regional policy allowed for an extensive investment programme focusing on territorial integration and providing access to the markets for Spanish regions (most of which were in peripheral regions), as well as improving environmental infrastructures, education and health (human capital) and the capital and business capacities of the productive system.

The result was an important process of economic development, with cumulative growth rates in per capita income well above the average for the former EU-15 in the period 1989–2010. In Spain, this convergence in per capita income also applies to all its regions, including the most peripheral and underdeveloped ones, which grew faster than the EU-15 average. However, this process was mainly based on a mere capital (and employment) widening process without substantial improvements in labour productivity (Myro 2011).

During the economic boom, from the late 1990s until the breakout of the crisis of 2008, a rapid growth of GDP and a large increase in production was associated with a strong job creation that absorbed a high level of structural unemployment and important immigration flows, while the capital/labour ratio remained almost constant and the productivity per employee slightly shrank.

The European Monetary Union (EMU) removed exchange market barriers and integrated Europe's financial markets (Fagan and Gaspar 2008), but regulatory and institutional settings were not adapted for the sound watching and risk assessments of private indebtedness and the overall system of financial markets (De Grauwe 1998). The EMU and the single currency brought with it an important drop in real interest rates in peripheral or lower-income countries whose risk premiums (mainly in private indebtedness) almost vanished[4] (EC 2008, pp. 109–110). The Euro brought a large positive interest shock to these countries by lowering rates and yield differentials (Lane 2010) reinforced by a credit expansion fed by foreign borrowing through national banks and savings institutions (Kelly 2010; Suarez 2010), whereas Foreign Direct Investment (FDI) was relatively small.

Lacking the exchange market and the current account constraint in foreign payments, real interest rate effects gave rise to adverse feed-back circles through the non-tradable sector and asset booms (EC 2008, p. 62). The demand shock induced by a reduction in the risk premium led to additional stimuli due to an increase in prices in the non-tradable sector affecting the effective Exchange rate (REER).[5] That can lead to serious problems in the case of large low-competitive services sectors (regulated, professionals, retail, transport, etc.), as well as real estate assets and residential building.

The most tangible achievement in the first 10 years of the Euro was a surge in jobs with a record of 16 million jobs created within the Euro area. Employment rose by almost 15% and unemployment fell to about 7% of the labour force in 2008, clearly outperforming the USA (EC 2008). However, the growth and convergence process was hampered by relevant asymmetries and imbalances in the basic variables related to the productivity of Euro area countries, especially the southern ones. The largest portion of the job creation in the Euro area took place during the growth boom in Spain (the so called "miracle") and it has already disappeared with the severe depression unleashed following the 2008 crisis.

The Euro area had poor productivity performance from 1999 to 2007 and the southern European countries suffered from severe productivity stagnation problems. The most serious cases were those of Italy and Spain with annual average growth rates in productivity of 0.03% and −0.16% (in terms of hours actually worked) respectively. Nevertheless, both countries were not outperformed in terms of development by the Euro area; Italy kept close to the average growth of GDPpc and Spain reached exceptional results (1.8% of GDP growth per capita). These results were attributable to the large employment impulse (increases in the employed population ratio), but finally both countries were to face serious problems

[4]To illustrate the magnitude of the risk premium shock associated to the vanishing of traditionally large and persistent inflation differentials.

[5]Consequently, investment and private consumption experienced a permanent increase fed by the booming in the non-tradable sector as well as in assets and real estate markets (Blanchard 2007a, 2007b; Fagan and Gaspar 2007; Giavazzi and Spaventa 2010). Selected data can illustrate the magnitude of the effects induced in these sectors (as discussed in European Commission 2006; Martinez-Mongay et al. 2007).

following the crisis (2008–2013) and the so called "Spanish miracle" would vanish with a dramatic adjustment in employment.

5.2.1 *The Contrast Between per Capita GDP and Productivity*

A characteristic and somewhat anomalous feature of Spain's growth is the fact that the convergence in terms of per capita income with regard to the EU-15 did not go hand-in-hand with convergence in terms of output per worker. This is also an important drawback for the global competitiveness of the Spanish economy which was affected by the productivity decline observed in the European countries with regard to productivity in the most dynamic world economies, especially the USA, since mid-1990s.[6]

Labour productivity only began to recover as a result of the tough readjustments that were made through the devastating effect on employment of the acute and prolonged recession that affected the Spanish economy since last quarter of 2007. The accumulative downturn in per capita income terms in Spain was 1.3%, meaning a major decrease with regard to the average for the EU-15 (−0.05%) and a major increase in unemployment, reaching 25% in 2012.

The increase in endowments of productive factors in the Spanish economy led to a significant process of development from 1989 until 2007. GDPpc in Spain grew at a cumulative rate greater than 2% and caught up with the EU-15 average; the GDPpc ratio increased from 62% in 1989 to 70% in 2007. However, productivity was a serious drawback in the Spanish development and convergence process. Labour productivity (GDP per employee) was not able to follow the path of GDPpc in Spain and the productivity gap between Spain and the EU-15 widened from 20 to 30 percentage points, the comparative level of Spain's productivity fell from 82% in 1989 to 70% of EU-15 average in 2007. Table 5.1 shows the reference values for Spain and the EU-15 at constant 2000 prices.

However, labour productivity (GDP per employee) in Spain evolved along different patterns in the 1989–1999 and 1999–2007 periods. During the first period, labour productivity (GDP per employee) grew at a 1% cumulative rate during the period 1989–1999, considerably less than GDPpc (2.1%) and well below the 15-member EU average (1.4%). Furthermore, during the growth boom of the period 1999–2007, labour productivity (GDP per employee) was stagnant in Spain with an average cumulative rate of growth of -0.36%. This pattern of evolution is robust with regard to changes in the average worked hours per employee. As shown in the

[6]This fact was broadly mentioned in examined literature; see among others European Commission (2007 not in the references), Timmer, O'Mahony and Van Ark (2007 not in the references) and Maroto y Rubalcaba (2008 not in the references).

Table 5.1 Productivity and GDP per capita in Spain vs. EU15 (Euro, constant value 2000)

	1989	1999	2007	2010	ρ 89-99	ρ 99-07	ρ 07-10
EU15							
GDP/per employee	44,331	51,588	55,678	55,590	1.38%	0.85%	−0.04%
GDP/per capita	19,207	22,492	25,573	24,557	1.44%	1.43%	−1.01%
Spain							
GDP/per employee	36,464	40,841	39,171	41,845	1.03%	−0.46%	1.65%
GDP/per capita	11,918	15,077	17,825	16,836	2.14%	1.86%	−1.43%
Worked hours/per employee[a]		1753	1703	1710		−0.36%	0.10%
GDP/per worked K-hs[a]		23,298	23,001	24,471		−0.16%	2.06%
% Spain/EU15							
GDP/per employee	82.25%	79.17%	70.35%	75.27%			
GDP/per capita	62.05%	67.03%	69.70%	68.56%			

ρ = average cumulative rate of growth, the coefficient of a time exponential growth function (log differences divided by the number of years)
Source: EU15 data from Cambridge Econometrics, Spain data from IVIE and INE
[a]Data in 1999 column correspond to year 2000.

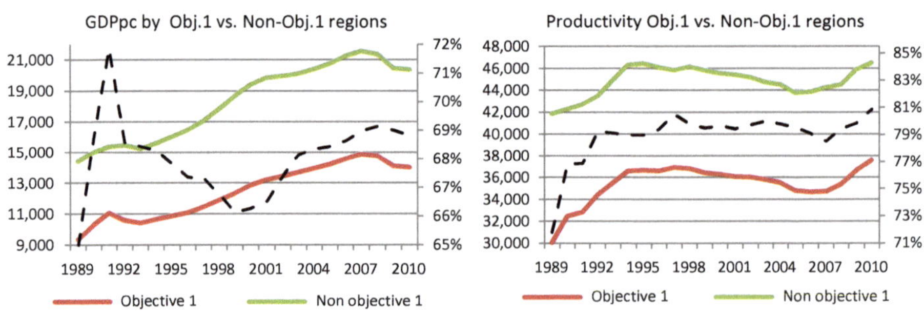

Fig. 5.2 GDPpc and Productivity by regions (1989–2010). Source: Own elaboration from IVIE dataset

corresponding row of Table 5.1, the average cumulative rate of growth of GDP per K-hours worked in the 1999–2007 period was −0.16%.

Growth was not uniform over the period, and the growth in per capita income was affected by the crisis of 1992, although from 1994 onwards there was a period of sustained growth until the outbreak of the current crisis in 2008. On the contrary, the growth of labour productivity (output per person in employment) followed a very different and contrary path. It grew significantly in the 1990s, growing rapidly from 1989, and then slowing down from 1995 onwards, and then following a downward trend from 1998 until the outbreak of the current economic crisis. Figure 5.2 illustrates these patterns.

The left side of Fig. 5.2 shows the trends for per capita income for the country as a whole, differentiating between the less developed Objective 1 regions and the others. During the first few years of the period, the Objective 1 regions converged in terms of per capita income then decreased quite significantly during the 1990s, to once again converge during the growth period in the 2000s.

The right side of Fig. 5.2 shows the trends in productivity of the Spanish regions at constant 2000 prices (euros). Here we can see that there was a significant growth in the first few years, a turning point around 1994, followed by a marked decrease from 1999 onwards, precisely during the process of significant economic growth from the end of the 1990s, accompanied by a major increase in the population (with high immigration rates) and employment rates that reduced the average labour productivity. This processes of economic boom and strong job creation was the result of a mere capital (and employment) widening process aggravated by the join effect of the real interest rate effect and unlimited foreign credit during the first 9 years of the last phase of the EMU and the creation of the Euro as a single currency.

The contrasting development of growth of per capita income and labour productivity, a feature of the Spanish growth process, can once again be seen in the growth rates of the Objective 1 regions in comparison to those of the more developed regions. Convergence in terms of productivity slowed down during the period of greatest growth, becoming more acute during the major downturn in employment as a result of the current economic crisis. This crisis and the recession from 2008 onwards have led to major adjustments with high job losses, focused on less productive jobs, resulting in a peak in terms of output per worker during the years of the crisis, at the expense of employment.

However, as we will see later on, the two groups of regions (the most developed and the Objective 1 regions) do not display common growth patterns at an internal level. In particular, during the growth boom from the end of the 1990s until 2007, the growth patterns in terms of increased employment and productivity crisscrossed between regions with very different levels of development.

5.2.2 A Growth Policy Heavily Based on Investment

One of the most relevant features of the growth process in Spain is that it was driven by a major process of investment and accumulation of capital.

The graphics on both sides of Fig. 5.3 show the evolution of the capital stock and the investment effort of the Spanish economy from 1989 onwards. The stock of real (net) capital more than doubled during the period 1989–2010. However, despite starting out with low capital stock volumes, the period with the highest investment effort in terms of the investment/capital stock ratio was not the initial period between the end of the 1980s and early 1990s, but instead the booming period of

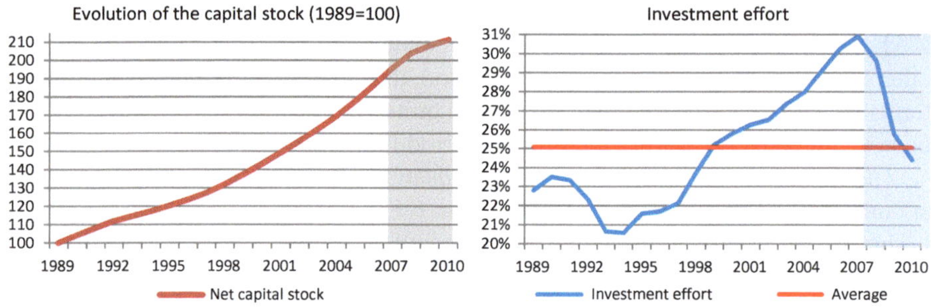

Fig. 5.3 Evolution of the capital stock and the investment effort of the Spanish economy (1989–2010). Source: Own elaboration from the database of FBBVA-IVIE, 2013

the Spanish economy was from 1998 until 2007. To a large extent, the investment boom in Spain was reinforced during the first 9 years of the Euro by the joint effect of low real interest and easy access to foreign credit. The investment effort in Spain, fuelled by high levels of private indebtedness, increased from 25% of GDP in 1999 to 31% 2007.

With the outbreak of the crisis, the economic downturn and subsequent recession, the investment effort dramatically decreased and the accumulation of capital in the Spanish economy fell (Mas et al. 2013). The drop-in income and adjustments to high unemployment rates hinder the sustainability of a model with large stocks of capital, as depreciation starts to represent a very significant proportion of reduced flows of investment (Mas et al. 2013). The consequences of the drop-in investment were dramatic, and capital depreciation rose to very significant percentages of the investment (more than 80% in 2010).

As a result of this major process of capital accumulation, the operating conditions of the Spanish economy changed dramatically with the 2008 crisis, and the depreciation of the capital stock began to absorb very significant parts of the total GDP (Fig. 5.4).

At the initial stages of growth in Spain (including the 1980s and 1990s), the lack of infrastructures and capital provisions were so significant that it was taken as read that the marginal productivity of investments in the renewal and extension of stocks (especially in cases of fixed capital with long useful lives) was very high. However, the situation changed dramatically in the 2000s. Investments with excessively high forecasts during the boom and the housing bubble aggravated the problem of the loose consideration of cost efficiency and sustainability of a substantial percentage of the major investments planned in an exponential stage of outlooks for growth in the GDP and the population (immigrants, residents from other countries, tourists, etc.).

The economic boom in Spain generated many jobs, leveraged productive inputs and took the economy to near full employment, but unfortunately was only a mere capital (and employment) widening process that did not involve a deepening of capital per worker or an increase in productivity.

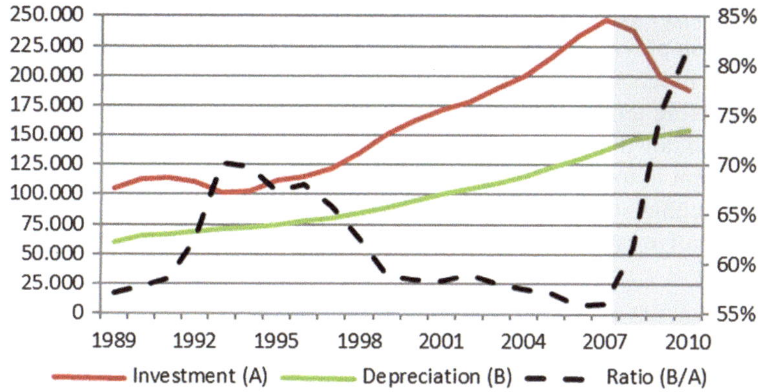

Fig. 5.4 Investment and depreciation in million constant 2000. Source: Own elaboration from the database of FBBVA-IVIE, 2013

5.3 Productivity Drivers in Spanish Economy

Growth accounting techniques (Aghion and Howitt 2007; Solow 1956) are commonly used to deconstruct growth rates into their different components as well as to explain long-term growth tendencies (Jorgenson 1995) by analysing total factor productivity (TFP) growth patterns. However, these techniques cannot explain the determinants of capital deepening (the ratio of capital stock to employed population). Capital deepening is "generally taken as input in economic growth" (Judzik 2014) and little effort has been devoted to disentangle the effect of endogenous changes in total factor productivity in growth accounting (Aghion and Howitt 2007). "A problem associated with the traditional growth accounting framework is that it does not give any information about factors that are responsible for capital deepening" (Madsen 2010, p. 641).

In recent decades, most advanced European countries experienced sustained economic growth based on processes of capital deepening. As many studies pointed out (Jorgenson and Stiroh 2000; Whelan 2000), these processes can generate increases in knowledge capital and technological improvements, as well as increases in productivity per employee. Some studies in recent decades have empirically shown large variations in the shares of labour in GDP and in the capital-labour ratios of OECD countries (Blanchard 1997; Bentolila and Saint-Paul 2003).

The contrast between high growth in terms of per capita income and stagnation in terms of labour productivity in the Spanish economy, together with the contrasting evolution of regional differences in terms of per capita income and output per worker (employee) is a surprising phenomenon which is more complex than it might initially appear. Much of this is because growth theory, long-term oriented, implicitly considers that the amount of work available in the economy (e.g., employment and/or hours worked) is a limiting factor for growth. All this changes dramatically when it is admitted that high structural unemployment can exist and that labour supply can be elastic along significant periods of time. Though it is hard to explain through the lens of usual growth theory, it is a plain reason behind a growth process based on mere capital (and employment) widening with constant ratio of capital per employee and any increase in labour productivity (GDP per employee).

In accounting terms, per capita income (as well as its cumulative growth rate) can be broken down into the product of the productivity per employee and the share of employment in total population (employment-to-population ratio, EPR). Consequently, the cumulative growth rate of GDPpc can be decomposed into the product of the cumulative rates of growth of productivity and EPR.

$$y_{pc} = \frac{Y}{pop_{tot}} = \frac{Y}{pop_{empl}} \cdot \frac{pop_{empl}}{pop_{tot}}$$

$$y_{pc} = Labour\ productivity \cdot Employment - to - Population - ratio$$

The simple breakdown of the per capita income into its two factors of output per worker and employment clearly shows that since entering the EU, Spain has developed significantly with a growth model mainly driven by the enlargement of productive endowments and employment. The growth of per capita income was mainly due to the increase in the employment ratio, and even more during the period of 1999–2007 employment increased so quickly that it easily compensated for the drop in productivity.

However, the growth process in Spain was associated with significant social and economic progress, seen in a wide variety of indicators ranging from an increase in female participation in the labour market and a rise in the educational level of the population, to the internationalisation and opening to foreign trade of the economy, and including major investments and high rates of growth for the capital and resources associated with ICT and RDI (Mas et al. 2009). On the other hand, human capital has played an important role in Spain's TFP, and efforts to improve the stock of human capital in Spain over the last few decades have made possible the approach to the average of the OECD countries. This improvement has also strengthened the ability of Spanish companies to learn and absorb new technologies, and has had a significantly beneficial impact on the improvements in productivity (Cubel et al. 2011).

Mas et al. (2009) studied the role of ICTs in the slowdown of Spanish productivity. By distinguishing between capital assets related (and not related) to ICTs (software, communication and hardware) in the FBBA-Ivie dataset, a growth accounting exercise was applied to the non-primary sectors of the Spanish market economy. The main findings showed that ICT capital growth rates (9.7% between 1995 and 2004) almost doubled those of total capital, while the ICT intensive cluster (the branches using ICTs most intensively, mainly business services and financial intermediation) experienced an important labour productivity (as well as TFP) growth contributing to partially attenuate the fall in the TFP of the Spanish Economy. However, the negative tendency of productivity remains a major issue in Spain, apart from some other lagging features in the economy (such as small share of ICTs in total investment, productive structure and the lack of technical training and qualifications) and some probable measurement problems. One of the main conclusions reached by Mas et al. (2009) is that "in Spain, the (presumably beneficial) full effects of ICT capital on total factor productivity growth are not observable as yet. A late start is probably one of the main reasons for not finding yet clear evidence of a productivity pick up induced by ICT technologies".

Martinez et al. (2008) studied the Spanish evidence on a productivity paradox of the new economy in the sense of the famous statement by Robert Solow (New York Times Book Review, July 12th 1987) that "the computer age [was seen] everywhere, except in the productivity statistics". A computable general equilibrium model (with labour and six types of capital assets for calibrating the cost shares of the productive factors) is used to identify the sources of productivity growth in Spain during the late 1990s and early 2000s, which are compared with the evidence available for the USA and other countries. A negative tendency in TFP is also found for Spain, although an interesting conclusion is reached on the transition process: "the relevant (but potential) benefits of ICT need time to come true [and spill over the whole economy]. Adjustment costs and inefficiencies derived from inappropriate qualifications in the labour force lead to transitional dynamics in which productivity suffers low and even negative growth rates" (Martinez et al. 2008).

An extended Solow growth model was estimated with panel data for 17 Spanish regions[7] to measure the contribution of different factors of production (with special interest in the stock of private and human capital, as well as the gap of transport infrastructure capital) to the productivity of labour and the temporal evolution of TFP over the period 1989–2010 (Montes-Solla et al. 2015).

Output per worker is explained by means of a Cobb-Douglas production function of the per worker stocks of private and human capital, as well as the transport infrastructure capital weighted by the inverse of a saturation index (the relative lack of capital to reach a convenient provision of transport infrastructure endowment per worker). The latter variable is intended to capture the conditional or moderating effect of infrastructure endowment saturation over the influence of transport infrastructure investments to increase the output per worker.[8] The model is linearized by

[7]The database consists of a strong balanced regional panel provided by FBBVA-IVIE with figures expressed in euros at constant 2000 values. This database satisfies usual reliability conditions and has been incorporated in other international databases of the OECD and the EU KLEMS project. For more details, see Montes-Solla (2015).

[8]For this purpose, an index of infrastructure provision is calculated by dividing the capital stock of infrastructure by the geometric mean of the population and the regional area (the square root of the product of the two) and then draws on the increased regional provision of infrastructure (in our database it corresponds to Madrid in 2010), to which the index value 1 terrestrial infrastructure endowment is allocated. For other regions and years, rates below saturation are constructed to capture the relative distance to the reference infrastructure:

$$satindex = \frac{\frac{k_{(i,t)}{}^{inf}}{\sqrt{pop_{(i,t)} \cdot area_{(i,t)}}}}{Max\left(\frac{k_{(i,t)}{}^{inf}}{\sqrt{pop_{(i,t)} \cdot area_{(i,t)}}}\right)} \Rightarrow satindex1 = (1 - satindex) \Rightarrow (1 - satindex_{i,t})lnk_{inf\,po_{(i,t)}}$$
$$= satindex1 \cdot lnk_{inf\,po_{(i,t)}}.$$

means of log transformation and the cumulative rate of growth of total factor productivity (TFP) is estimated by means of an exponential function of time (the variable year) jointly with the annual ratio of Research and Technological Development (RTD) intensity of the economy, measured as the share of RTD expenditure on regional GDP in each period of time.[9]

The results are significant and consistent with the evidence provided in the previous works. The Cobb-Douglas expanded production function provides a suitable tool to explain the output per worker in the Spanish economy and provides accurate estimates of its elasticity to the endowments of productive factors (the stocks of private and human capital and the stock of infrastructure weighted by regional relative distances to saturation along the period). Furthermore, the cumulative rate of growth of TFP is estimated by the coefficient of the year variable and the accelerating variable linked to the regional RTD shares on GDP.

Estimations show that the most influential variables on labour productivity are the stock of private capital per worker (elasticity of 0.51) and human capital per worker (elasticity of 0.46). This is in line with other studies' findings on human capital as one of the most important determining factors of per capita income, labour productivity and economic growth, as it has clearly direct and indirect effects on these areas. A higher level of education leads to increased labour productivity, and in an environment of market efficiency, greater business incentives to invest in physical and technological capital (Doménech 2008).

The capital stock per worker in transport infrastructure takes a small but significant positive value (elasticity of 0.02), which corresponds to a saturation index equal to 1 (the case of the best endowed region, Madrid in the year 2010). However, this elasticity increases for other regions and time periods due to the multiplier effect of saturation indexes lower than 1.[10] These results are in line with previous studies (De la Fuente 2010) providing evidence that public investment in infrastructure has had a positive impact on production and employment in Spain and promoted income convergence among regions, especially since the Spanish accession to the EU. However, turning to the regional redistribution of investments in infrastructures, it has probably had significant efficiency costs.

---

[9]The TFP trend is estimated by means of the expression: $Ln\left(A_0 \cdot e^{\lambda \cdot t + \mu \cdot \rho_t}\right) = LnA_0 + \lambda \cdot t + \mu \cdot \rho_t$, where λ denotes the cumulative rate of growth of TFP (total factor productivity along time), μ represents the cumulative rate of growth of TFP induced by the RTD intensity of the economy, ρ. The base line model for estimations is given by the following expression:

$$lny_{po(i,t)} = lnA_0 + \lambda \cdot t + \mu \cdot \rho_t + \delta_l \cdot \varphi(s)_{(i,t)} + \delta_k \cdot lnk_{priv_{po}(i,t)} + \delta_g \cdot satindex1_{i,t} lnk_{inf\,po_{(i,t)}}$$

where $\varphi(s)$ stands for Human Capital adjusted according to the length of each educational level, $Kpriv_{po}$ denotes the ratio of private capital stock per employee, $Kinf_{po}$ corresponds to the ratio of infrastructure capital per employee and finally satindex is a measure of regional infrastructure gaps measured as the comparative distance to the reference level of the best-endowed region at the end of the period.

[10]As, for example, in peripheral regions such as Andalusia and Galicia, where capital infrastructure elasticity values reached respectively 0.066 and 0.053 in 1989, 0.035 and 0.025 in 1999, and finally fell to 0.024 and 0.016 in 2010.

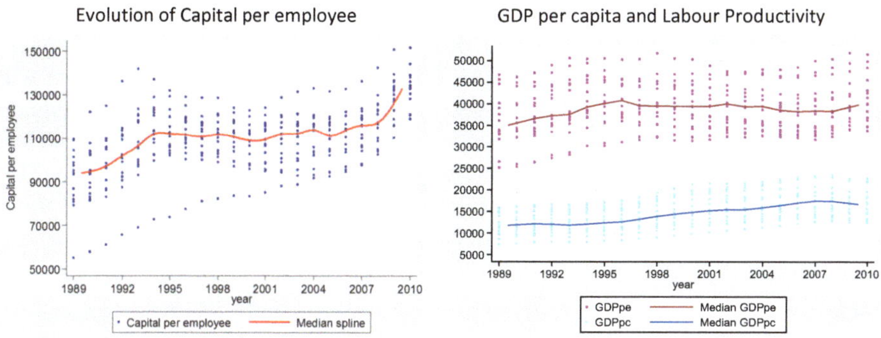

Fig. 5.5 Evolution of capital per employee and GDP per capita and labour productivity. Source: Elaborated from FBBVA-IVIE database

The time trend of TFP reached an average cumulative decreasing rate of −0.013%, whereas the share of RTD on GDP was a significant driver of total factor productivity (TFP) growth with an estimated coefficient of 0.031. However, the low levels of RTD shares in Spain, despite their rapid growth since the late 1990s, were insufficient to overcome the mere capital widening nature of the Spanish economic growth model. Overall, the results for the TFP rate of growth, as a result of both components (time trend and the RTD shares), show that output per worker was lower than their potentially expected values once the amounts of investment are taken into account. Total Factor Productivity (TFP) in Spain experienced a negative rate of growth of around −0.012% (cumulative annual average) confirming the mere capital widening nature of the growth process in Spain.[11]

The evolution of capital per employee in the Spanish regions (shown in the left side of Fig. 5.5) was relatively flat along the central part (1995–2005) of the period under study. In spite of large volume investments and increasing capital stocks, the ratio of capital per employee remained constant in most of the Spanish regions during the central part of period of study, a relatively long growth's period (1995–2005).

However, most of the Spanish regions achieved fast and important GDPpc growth during the period of 1999–2007 (It is clearly shown in the right side of Fig. 5.5). This intense development process was linked to large investments and rapid capital accumulation which gave rise to a strong expansion in employment (both employed and working population). GDPpc growth was mainly absorbed by a strong jobs creation process with almost no capital deepening and technological improvement in TFP. Consequently, as shown in the upper line of the right-side graph in Fig. 5.5, productivity per employee (GDP/employee) stagnated or even declined in Spain from the late 1990s until the outbreak of the 2008 crisis.

[11]Other estimates with different objectives have focused on the interregional variation of TFP with a panel of industry data (Escribá and Murgui 2011).

Both graphs of Fig. 5.5 together provide a visual image of the most prominent features of the regional development process in Spain: (1) Intense growth of per capita income driven both by extensive investment and capital accumulation with strong job creation and rapid increases in the working population, (2) Stagnant capital ratio per employee and absence of capital deepening, and finally (3) a serious stagnation problem in productivity per employee and a decline in TFP. These problems together with other imbalances (huge current account foreign payments deficit and high private indebtedness) made Spain highly vulnerable to the impact of the 2008 crisis.

5.4 Spanish Regional Puzzle: Growth and Regional Disparities in Productivity and GDPpc

5.4.1 Spanish Regional Puzzle

Regional disparities in Spain have experienced some paradoxical features that have been referred to as the "Spanish Regional Puzzle" (Garrido-Yserte and Mancha-Navarro 2010). Spain underwent an overall process of regional convergence in the levels of income per capita and productivity while experiencing increasing regional concentration in the aggregate values of production, employment and population (La Caixa 2007).

Spanish regional levels of income per capita and labour productivity evolved in opposite ways and so did regional disparities (in GDPpc and labour productivity), due to the prevailing effect of employment creation in a context of capital widening and labour productivity stagnation. Most regional disparities in GDPpc in Spain (almost 85% of the inequality) can be explained by differences in the employment-to-population ratio (EPR) (Garrido-Yserte and Mancha-Navarro 2010; Lopez-Rodriguez et al. 2011).

The Spanish economy featured a trade-off between the growth of employment and productivity. Broadly speaking, the greatest increases in GDPpc tend to occur in the regions with the greatest employment/population ratios, very often associated with decreasing or stagnant productivity (Cuadrado-Roura and Maroto-Sanchez 2010; Escribá and Murgui 2013). This fact fits in relatively well with the capital widening nature of the Spanish growth model, where productivity increases were linked to job destruction and vice versa.

A trade-off between employment and productivity has been at work in Spain in the last decades. This phenomenon is characterized by lower productivity growths in the regions with higher employment growth rates. Since the mid-1990s, changes in the employment rate have been as a rule higher than variations in the rate of productivity. To a large extent, this feature can be considered as a consequence of the "capital widening" nature of the Spanish growth model. It was mainly based on large investment efforts to increase capital endowments in public infrastructures, private companies and human capital, without substantial development in the overall performance of productive system. Total factor productivity (TFP) exhibited a decreasing trend over the period, whereas the rapid growth of investments in ICTs related assets and RTDI projects did not seem to deliver productivity improvements in the large majority of economic activities and was not enough to counteract the shrinking tendency of TPF growth. There is some evidence of a "productivity paradox" in Spain, despite the fact that GDPpc development in Spain was mainly driven by continuous increases in per worker capital endowments (both physical and human capital) and the employment-to-population ratio (EPR).

5.4.2 Regional Disparities

The average personal income in Spain grew more rapidly than the EU-15 average, if calculated at constant prices (base year 2000). This convergence process of the Spanish regions along with the EU-15 was much higher in terms of Purchasing Power Standards (PPS), unity measure used by the Cohesion Policy, which triggered the exit of the majority of the Spanish regions from the Convergence Objective (known before as Objective 1).

In this context, regional disparities in GDPpc in Spain experienced an increase between 1989 and 1999, followed by an also important decrease during the period 1999–2007. The outbreak of the current economic crisis in Europe has again increased the economic divergence among the Spanish regions.[12]

Regional disparities in terms of GDPpc as a rule widened during the periods with productivity increases and narrowed in those with productivity shrinkages. As can be seen in Table 5.2, regional GDPpc disparities experienced a relatively important increase between 1989 and 1999 when GDP per employee grew at an average cumulative rate of 1% a year. Next they were reduced to a comparable extent along the growth boom from 1999 to 2007 in a context of productivity decline (average rate of −0.46% and −0.16% in GDP per employee and hours of work, respectively) and finally they increased again in the years of the economic crisis with productivity gains of 2% a year (average rate for 2007–2010).

[12]The process of convergence (measured in constant euro, taking 2000 as the year base) is considerably larger in terms of Purchasing Power Standards (PPS), the metric (unity measure) used in the Cohesion Policy. In the programming period 2007–2013, the Canary Islands, Castile & Leon, and Valencia left the convergence objective as they surpassed 75% of the EU-15 GDP per capità (phasing-in regions). On the other hand, Asturias and Murcia left the same objective, surpassing the 75% threshold of the EU-27 GDP per capita, as a result of the statistical effect linked to the decrease of the EU average after the accession of the Eastern Countries. In the new programming period 2014–2020, only Extremadura will continue to be eligible as a convergence region, though Andalusia, Castile-La Mancha and Galicia will still be aided by a privileged transitory regime.

Table 5.2 GDP per capita in Spain (1000 €, constant value 2000)

GDP/POP	1989	1999	2007	2010	ρ 89-99	ρ 99-07	ρ 07-10
NUTs 2 regions							
Range	5.982	10.878	8.841	9.444			
Mean	11.937	14.910	17.671	16.819	2.2%	2.1%	−1.6%
Std. Dev.	2.367	3.167	3.323	3.255	2.9%	0.6%	−0.7%
Variation	19.8%	21.2%	18.8%	19.3%			

Source: Own elaboration from IVIE dataset

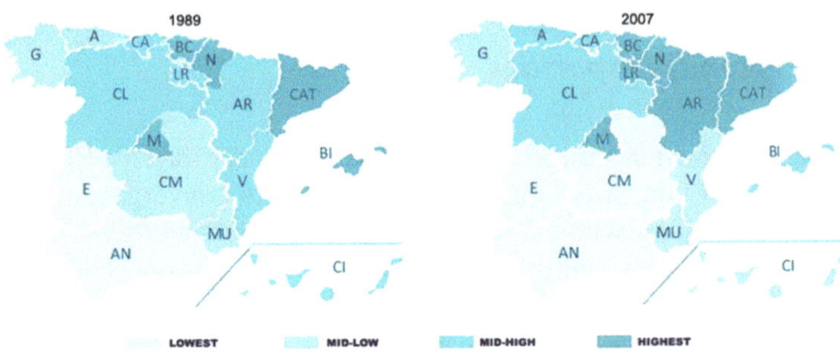

AN: Andalusia AR: Aragon A: Asturias BI: Balearic Islands CI: Canary Islands
CA: Cantabria CM: Castile-La Mancha CL: Castile-Leon CAT: Catatonia V: Valencia
E: Extremadura G: Galicia M: Madrid MU: Murcia N: Navarra
BC: Basque Country LR: La Rioja

Fig. 5.6 Map of GDPpc in Spanish regions throughout the period 1989–2010. Source: Own elaboration from data base IVIE (2013)

Nevertheless, relative development ranges in the distribution of Spanish regions did not experience many changes throughout the period 1989–2007. Spanish regions were classified in four ranges according to their position with regard to the whole country average (x) plus or minus one half of the standard deviation (δ). These four ranges are correlatively highest (above $x+0.5\delta$), mid-high (x, $x+0.5\delta$) mid-low ($x-0.5\delta$, x) and lowest (below $x-0.5\delta$). Their map plots for the years 1989 and 2007 (2010 map did not differ from 2007) are offered in Fig. 5.6.

Regional disparities in terms of productivity (GDP per employee) evolved in a different way from the pattern for differences in GDPpc, exhibiting a relative convergence. Throughout the whole of the period, a gradual reduction can be seen in the distance between the highest and lowest regional productivity levels. In turn, the relative coefficient of variation decreases in the first stage from 1989 to 1999, then increases slightly during the period 1999–2007 and then finally decreases once again due to job destruction caused by the economic downturn.

Table 5.3 shows the growth in regional differences in output per worker.

Nevertheless, the regional structure by productivity ranges has not experienced any spectacular changes and the central core of the most developed regions coincides with those which have the highest productivity (the Basque Country,

Table 5.3 Productivity in Spain (1000 €, constant value 2000)

GDP/EMPL	1989	1999	2007	2010	ρ 89-99	ρ 99-07	ρ 07-10
NUTs 2 regions							
Range	21.518	19.044	18.300	17.703			
Mean	36.060	40.071	38.815	41.138	1.1%	−0.4%	1.9%
Std. Dev.	5.882	5.061	5.372	5.202	−1.5%	0.7%	−1.1%
Variation	16.3%	12.6%	13.8%	12.6%			

Source: Own elaboration from IVIE dataset

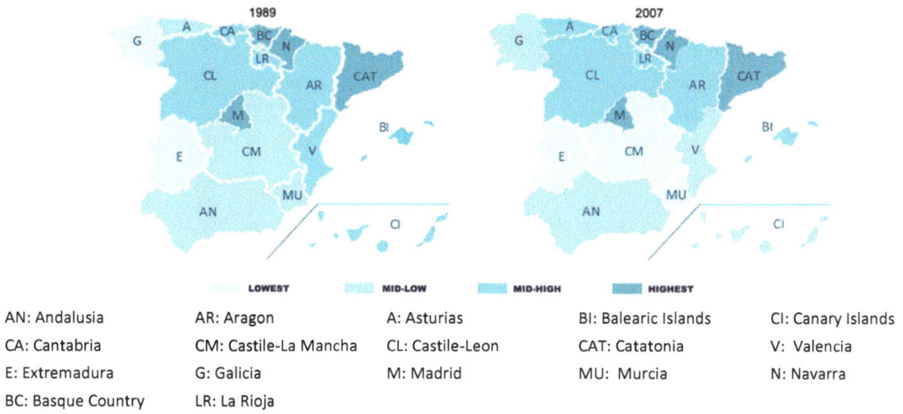

Fig. 5.7 Map of productivity in Spanish regions throughout the period 1989–2010. Source: Own elaboration from data base IVIE (2013)

Navarra, Madrid and Catalonia). As can be seen in Fig. 5.7, the medium-high level is also characterised by relative stability, comprising Aragón, Cantabria and Castile-Leon. Other regions such as Asturias and La Rioja could also be included in this level, while other major tourism areas such as the Balearic and Canary Islands have descended to the medium-low level.

There is greater movement in the lowest productivity ranges. The lowest position was initially occupied by Extremadura and Galicia, followed by another two convergence regions, Castile-La Mancha and Murcia, which eventually fell to the lowest range, while Galicia managed to climb up to the medium-low level. Figure 5.7 shows the growth in labour productivity in the Spanish region, classified according to a ranking.

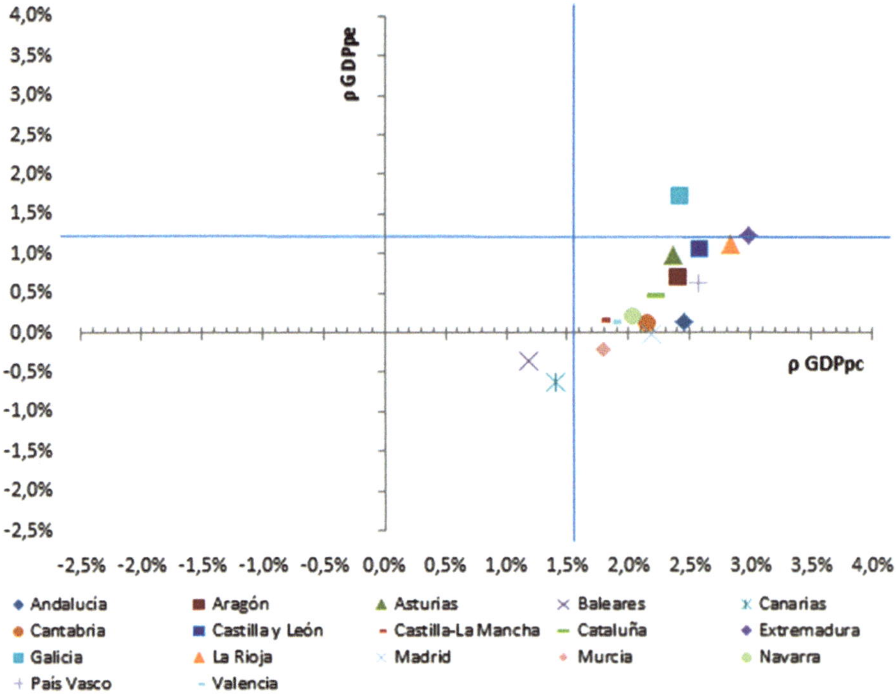

Fig. 5.8 GDPpe and GDPpc regional growth rate (1989-2007). Note: *Blue axis* in the first quadrant represent the corresponding average rates of growth in EU 15. Source: Own elaboration from FBBVA-Ivie database 2013

5.4.3 Regional Growth Patterns and the Impact of the Crisis of 2008

Overall, the main patterns of growth of Spanish regions fit quite well with the evolution of the country as a whole, and the main patterns of the growth models of Spanish regions do not significantly differ between convergence regions and the most developed regions. However, there are some specific features in the regional growth patterns that can be commented on.

Figure 5.8 shows the patterns of evolution of GDPpc and labour productivity in Spanish regions during the period 1989–2007. The vertical axis shows the accumulative productivity growth rates, while the horizontal axis shows the rates of growth for per capita income. The straight solid lines in the first quadrant indicate the average values for the EU-15 for the whole of the period 1989–2007.

Again, a very different development model to that of the EU-15 is shown. Practically all regions grew at high per capita income rates with zero or negative growth in labour productivity.

There is a slight positive association between the growth in productivity and per capita income, although it is of little significance. Specifically, convergence regions such as Extremadura and Galicia have grown with productivity increases close to those of the EU, while others such as Andalusia (in convergence objective) and Madrid (in the core of the most developed region) have achieved very significant increases in per capita income without any increase in productivity whatsoever. They share this situation with other more developed regions such as Catalonia, the Basque Country and Navarra.

The main feature of an intense and widespread development boom with stagnation (and even a reduction) in productivity in the vast majority of Spanish regions can be seen in a clearer way when the period 1999–2007 is considered separately.

After the crisis and the economic downturn, the evolution of the Spanish regions' GDP in 2012 was characterised by a widespread recession. Spanish Regional Accounts reported the regional distribution of the real growth rate of the Spanish economy estimated at −1.4% for 2012.[13] In line with the deep and widespread recession of 2012, employment problems were exacerbated all across Spanish regions and the unemployment rate rose to 26.02% in the whole country.[14] The most significant feature of the economic development in the Spanish regions in 2012 is the deep and widespread recession of GDP and the rise in unemployment rates.

The recession had a profound impact on the Spanish labour market (an average unemployment rate of 21.7%). The more technologically advanced regions (competitiveness regions, such as the Basque Country, Navarra, Madrid and Catalonia) found it easier to deal with the crisis, while some of the convergence, phasing-out and phasing-in regions were facing serious problems with unemployment and economic stagnation. Beyond these broad features, it is hard to find a general and systematic pattern.

However, the spatial distribution of the regional rates of unemployment for 2012, are shown in Fig. 5.9.

Unemployment rates were high (in the range of 15.9%, 19.2%), but well below the Spanish average, in the best performing regions (the Basque Country, Navarra, La Rioja and Cantabria), whereas a group of regions (Valencia, Murcia and Castile-La Mancha) placed above the Spanish average (in the range of 28.1%, 30.0%) and finally the worst-performing regions (the Canary Islands, Extremadura and Andalusia) reached unemployment rates well above 30% (in the range of 32.9%, 35.9%).

Regarding the main changes in regional disparities, the ranking of Spanish regions by GDPpc has not changed significantly over the last few years. On average, the GDP per head in current euros shrank by around 1.6% between 2010 and 2012, although the per capita GDP of the poorest region (Extremadura) remained approximately equal to half of the richest (Basque Country). In a similar

[13]INE, Quarterly National Accounting of Spain, 28th of February 2013 and INE, Gross Domestic Product by Region, Year 2012 (Spanish Regional Accounts. Base 2008), 21 March 2013.

[14]INE, Economically Active Population Survey (EAPS), 4th Quarter 2012, 24 January 2013.

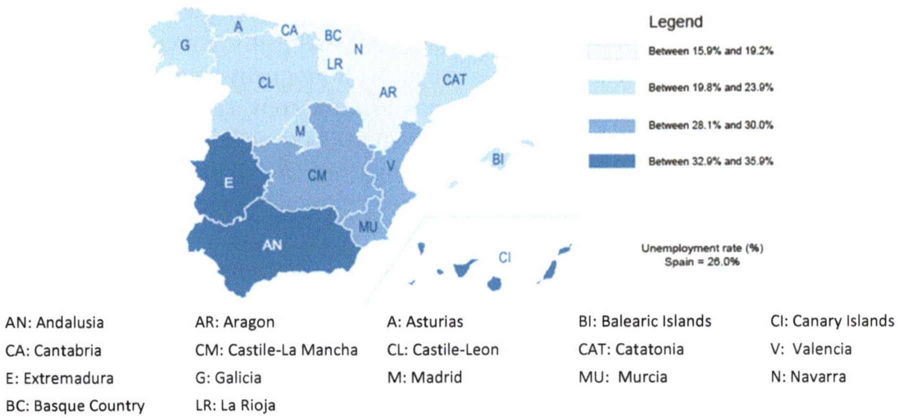

Fig. 5.9 Unemployment rate (%) for Spanish regions in 2012. Source: Own elaboration based on Spanish Statistical Institute (INE) data

vein, the unemployment rate in Spain increased considerably (by 40%) between 2009 and 2012, but the relative distance between the worst and the best performing regions (Andalusia and the Basque Country, respectively) also remained at around 1/2.[15]

In general, the more technologically advanced regions (competitiveness regions, such as the Basque Country, Navarra, Madrid and Catalonia) have not been affected by the crisis as seriously as some convergence, phasing-out and phasing-in Southern and Mediterranean regions, which are facing dramatic problems in terms of unemployment and economic stagnation. Overall, regional disparities have remained constant, but unemployment and economic stagnation are widespread and dramatic.

The sovereign debt crisis, the credit crunch and credit spreads, as well as public expenditure cuts and tax increases have given rise to an additional depressive impact in the short run. This process has been carried out within the EMU system and the single currency. However, currently it seems that the contraction hits bottom at the end of summer 2013. The austerity measures and structural reforms undertaken by the central government have had a bigger impact on those regions whose regional governments have the highest debt and public deficit. These regions

[15]The evidence of the crisis' impact on regional differences is unclear. On the one hand, the coefficient of variation in the GDPpc of the Spanish regions has shown a certain upward trend, from 18.6% in 2008 to 19.8% in 2012 (with the estimated data from the National Statistics Institute). However, the most outstanding feature is the general downturn in all of the regions and in the average of the country (from 23.8 thousand euros to 22.7 between both dates, minus 4.6%). This said, the worst effect of the crisis has been the increase in job losses, with the unemployment rate soaring from 8.6% in 2007 to 26% in 2012 (in the last quarter), rising to more than 30% in Andalusia, the Canary Islands and Extremadura. However, the overall increase in all of the regions meant that the coefficient of variation in the unemployment rates fell from 34.6% to 31.3% during this period.

have had to make the most severe adjustments, which has naturally affected their situation in the short term. These adjustments have been especially severe in Castile-La Mancha (which reduced its public deficit from 9% GDP in 2011 to 1.5% in 2012), while some others are still facing fiscal adjustment problems (1.96% for Catalonia, 2.02% for Andalusia, and 3.02% for the Region of Murcia).

5.5 Conclusions

The Spanish growth model, based on a process of significant investment and a considerable increase in the capital stock can be classified as a capital widening growth model, in which the capital growth leads more to an increase in production and employment than to increases in productivity, both in terms of output per worker and Total Factor Productivity (TFP).

However, the potential benefits of ICT and RTD investments need time to spill over the whole economy to significantly improve productivity statistics.[16] Increased productivity derived from ICTs and technological change calls for new types of business organisation, education and professional training in order to spread new technical and economic opportunities. The experience of the USA and other countries reveals the importance of bringing flexibility and competitiveness to the markets in order to facilitate the diffusion and beneficial use of ICTs and reduce the time needed for their benefits to spill over the general productivity of the country.

This transitional problem was aggravated in Spain by the boom that occurred after the introduction of the Euro (1999–2008), when low interest rates and widespread access to credit resulted in a housing bubble with extraordinary growth in the construction sector, and an overall rise in salaries that negatively affected the country's productivity and competitiveness. These unbalancing impacts have been an effect of a low real interest rate with the EMU.

Since entering the EU, the Spanish economy has achieved GDP growth rates higher than the European average, together with significant increases in population and high job creation, which has made it possible to substantially reduce the unemployment rate and converge towards the higher levels of per capita income of the EU-15, which includes its most developed members. However, this process had a negative side in terms of productivity. Labour productivity has been growing very slowly in Spain since 1995, and TFP is negative. Furthermore, the downturn in productivity and the increase in salaries during the boom period of the 2000s led the country to suffer from a loss of competitiveness with regard to EU and non-EU countries (FBBVA 2006).

The accumulation of capital and the creation of employment were important factors, yet the improvements in productivity were scarce in nearly all sectors. The specialisation of production has not strengthened the presence of innovative

[16]This possibility for Spain was pointed out by Mas et al. (2009) and Martinez et al. (2008).

activities and those with a high technological content as would be expected from an advanced economy, but instead in traditional and highly cyclical sectors such as construction. Low productivity levels have affected nearly all of the country's activities, despite an increase in capital assets per worker during this period. However, these were much more serious in the construction sector, as during the housing boom a large number of investment projects based their short-term profitability on expectations for the revaluing of the assets and not on productivity.

The pattern of growth of the Spanish economy in the 2000s was fragile and unsustainable in the long term. On the one hand, "the competitiveness of Spain at a global level has placed too much trust in the short-term benefits derived from the arrival of the Euro" (Pérez et al. 2011), while on the other, the risks and imbalances accumulated during the period of expansion and housing boom (a high current account deficit and heavy debt burden) led the Spanish economy to be highly vulnerable to the impact of the international crisis.

An overview of Spain's economic policy in the last few decades would highlight excessive trust in economic integration in the EU, as today it is clear that integration in European markets and the short-term financial benefits of the Euro are not sufficient in order to face up to the challenges of the new economy and intensified competition on a global scale.

The outbreak of the crisis caught the Spanish economy in a vulnerable situation, and the need for adjustments in productivity led to a significant and generalised increase in unemployment in all of the country's regions.

One lesson that has been learned is that in the future, it will be necessary to insist on greater rigour in the selection of investments, in order to guarantee a cost effectiveness and productivity in line with the capital resources.

The major challenges facing Spanish regions are recovery from economic depression and a need to reinforce their supply capabilities to successfully face increased competition resulting from globalization. The recent FBBVA-IVIE (Fernández de Guevara 2011) report clearly highlights the main productivity problems that need to be tackled by the Spanish economy: (1) Internal company changes: new growth requires better, bigger and more productive companies, capable of competing in larger markets with higher quality services and products, greater dynamism and internationalization. (2) Redirecting productive specialization: enhancing the largest added-value activities in the service sector, reinforcing productivity in the manufacturing sector and fomenting the production and intensive use of ICT. (3) Promoting the productive use of knowledge: fostering technological or process innovation and business RTDI projects, intensifying the use of human capital, and enhancing the use and exploitation of ICT as the basis for competitiveness (Faiña et al. 2013).

Acknowledgement The authors would like to acknowledge the help of IVIE and Prof. Matilde Mas, as well as the specific effort of the third author (Paulino Montes-Solla) in Sects. 5.3 and 5.4 which are parts of his research in the PhD programme of the School of Economics, University of Coruña.

The second author thanks the financial support from Xunta de Galicia Grant EM2014/051.

References

Aghion P, Howitt P (2007) Capital, Innovation and Growth accounting. Oxf Rev Econ Policy 23 (1):79–93

Arestis P, Baddeley M, Sawyer M (2007) The relationship between capital stock, unemployment and wages in nine EMU countries. Bull Econ Res 59(2):125–148

Bentolila S, Saint-Paul G (2003) Explaining movements in the labor share. Contrib Macroecon 3 (1): Article 9

Blanchard O (1997) The medium run. Brook Pap Econ Act 28(2):89–158

Blanchard O (2007a) Adjustment within the Euro. The difficult case of Portugal. Port Econ J 6 (1):1–21

Blanchard O (2007b) Current account deficits in rich countries. MIT Department Economics Working Paper No. 07-06

La Caixa (2007) Diagnóstico estratégico. Colección Comunidades Autónomas.

Cuadrado-Roura JR, Maroto-Sanchez A (2010) Regional productivity convergence and changes in the productive structure. In: Juan R. Cuadrado (ed) Regional policy, economic growth and convergence: lessons from the Spanish case. Springer, pp 149–170, Chapter 7

Cubel A, Esteve V, Sanchis J, Sanchis MT (2011) Innovación y crecimiento de la productividad en España durante la segunda mitad del siglo XX. Econ Ind 382:101–108

De Grauwe P (1998) The Euro and the financial crises. Financial Times

De la Fuente A (2010) Infrastructure investment, growth, and regional convergence in Spain. In Juan R. Cuadrado (ed) Regional policy, economic growth and convergence: lessons from the Spanish case. Springer, pp 171–185, Chapter 8

Doménech R (2008) La evolución de la productividad en España y el capital humano. Documento de trabajo 141/2008, Fundación Alternativas

EC (2006) The EU economy: 2006 review – adjustment dynamics in the euro area. Eur Econ 6

EC (2008) EMU@10: successes and challenges after 10 years of Economic and Monetary Union. Eur Econ 2

Escribá FJ, Murgui MJ (2011) Determinantes regionales de la PTF en la economía española 1995-2008. Documentos de Trabajo de la Dirección General de Presupuestos

Escribá FJ, Murgui MJ (2013) Productividad y Empleo Regional en España: Un enfoque dinámico. Invest Reg 27:65–89

Fagan G, Gaspar V (2007) Adjusting to the Euro. ECB Working Paper 716

Fagan G, Gaspar V (2008) Macroeconomic adjustment to Monetary Union. ECB Working Paper 946

Faiña A, López-Rodríguez J, (2006) European Union enlargement, European spatial development perspective and regional policy: lessons from population potentials. Investigaciones Regionales 9:3–21

Faiña A, Lopez-Rodriguez J, Montes-Solla P (2013) Expert evaluation network delivering policy analysis on the performance of Cohesion policy 2007-2013, Year 3 – Task 2: Country report on achievements of cohesion policy. INFO-REGIO

Farole T, Rodriguez-Pose A, Storper M (2011) Cohesion policy in the European union: growth, geography, institutions. J Common Mark Stud 49(5):1089–1111

Farole T, Rodríguez-Pose A, Tselios V, Winkler D (2013) Geography and the determinants of firm exports in Indonesia. CEPR Discussion Papers 9342

FBBVA (2006) Las fuentes del crecimiento económico español: cambios recientes. Cuadernos de divulgación del proyecto Capital y crecimiento

Fernández de Guevara J (2011) La productividad sectorial en España. Una perspectiva micro. Economía y Sociedad, FBBVA-IVIE

Garrido-Yserte R, Mancha-Navarro T (2010) The Spanish regional puzzle: convergence, divergence and structural change. In: Cuadrado JR (ed) Regional policy, economic growth and convergence: lessons from the Spanish case. Springer, Berlin, pp 103–124. Chapter 5

Giavazzi F, Spaventa L (2010) Why the current account may matter in a monetary union: lessons from the financial crisis in the Euro area. CEPR Discussion Papers 8008
Hanson G (2005) Market potential, increasing returns and geographic concentration. J Int Econ 67 (1):1–24
Head K, Mayer T (2004) The empirics of agglomeration and trade. In: Henderson V, Thisse JF (eds) Handbook of urban and regional economics, vol 4, Chapter 59, Elsevier
Head K, Mayer T (2006) Regional wage and employment responses to market potential in the EU. Reg Sci Urban Econ 36:573–594
Jorgenson DW (1995) Productivity. MIT Press, Cambridge
Jorgenson DW, Stiroh KJ (2000) Raising the speed limit: U.S. economic growth in the information age. Brook Pap Econ Act 1:125–211
Judzik D (2014) The determinants of capital deepening: evidence for the U.S., Japan, Spain and Canada. Encuentros Asociacion Libre de Economia. http://encuentros.alde.es/anteriores/xvieea/trabajos/j/pdf/180.pdf
Kanbur R, Venables AJ (2005) Spatial inequality and development. Spec Issue J Econ Geogr 5(1), Oxford University Press
Karanassou M, Sala H (2010) Labour market dynamics in Australia: what drives unemployment? Econ Rec 86(273):185–209
Kelly M (2010) Whatever happened to Ireland? CEPR Discussion Paper 7811
Krugman P (1990) Increasing returns and economic geography. NBER Working Papers 3275, National Bureau of Economic Research, Inc.
Krugman P (1991) Geography and trade. Leuven University Press, Leuven
Lane PR (2010) A European perspective on external imbalances. SIEPS Report 5
Lopez-Rodriguez J, Faiña A (2007) Regional wage disparities in Europe: what role for market access?", Investigaciones Regionales, pp 3–21
Lopez-Rodriguez J, Faiña A, Garcia-Lorenzo A (2007a) The geographic concentration of population and income in Europe: results for the period 1984-1999. Econ Bull 18(7):1–7
Lopez-Rodriguez J, Faiña Medin A, Lopez Rodriguez J (2007b) Human capital accumulation and geography: empirical evidence in the European Union. Reg Stud J Reg Stud Assoc 4 (2):217–234
Lopez-Rodriguez J, Márquez MA, Faiña A (2011) asta qué punto la perificidad económica es responsable de las diferencias en el PIB per cápita entre las provincias españolas? El Trimestre Económico 0(311):583–611
Madsen JB (2010) Growth and capital deepening since 1870: Is it all technological progress? J Macroecon 32(2):641–656
Martinez D, Rodriguez J, Torres JL (2008) The productivity paradox and the new economy: the case of Spain. J Macroecon 30:1569–1586
Martinez-Mongay C, Maza-Lasierra L, Yaniz-Igal J (2007) Asset booms and tax receipts: the case of Spain, 1995-2006. Eur Econ, Economic Papers 293
Mas M, Pérez F, Quesada J (2009) The sources of Spanish regional growth. In: Cuadrado JR (ed) Regional policy, economic growth and convergence: lessons from the Spanish case. Springer, New York, pp 125–148. Chapter 6
Mas M, Pérez F, Uriel E (eds) (2013) Inversión y stock de capital en España (1964-2011): evolución y perspectivas del patrón de acumulación. Reports, Fundación BBVA, 2013147
Mion G (2004) Spatial externalities and empirical analysis: the case of Italy. J Urban Econ 56:97–118
Montes-Solla P (2015) Three essays on peripherality and economic development. PhD Dissertation, University of Coruña (Spain). http://ruc.udc.es/handle/2183/15511
Montes-Solla P, Faiña JA, Lopez-Rodriguez J (2015) Regional development in Spain 1989-2010: capital widening and productivity stagnation. MPRA Paper No. 73566
Myro R (2011) Crecimiento económico y cambio estructural. in Garcia-Delgado JL (coord) Lecciones de economía española, pp 37–62

Pérez F (dir), Mas M, Maudos J, Quesada J, Serrano L, Chorén P, Cucarella V, Hernández L, Robledo JC, Solaz M, Soler A (2011) Crecimiento y competitividad. Trayectoria y perspectivas de la economía española, Fundación BBVA
Pires GAJ (2006) Estimating Krugman's economic geography model for the Spanish regions. Span Econ Rev 8:83–112
Puga D (2002) European regional policies in light of recent location theories. J Econ Geogr 2 (4):373–406
Redding S (1996) The low-skill, low-quality trap. Econ J 106:458–470
Redding S, Schott P (2003) Distance, skill deepening and development: will peripheral country clubs ever get rich? J Dev Econ 72:515–541
Redding S, Venables AJ (2004) Economic geography and international inequality. J Int Econ 62 (1):53–82
Rodriguez-Pose A (1999) Convergente or divergence? Types of regional response to socioeconomic change. Tridschrift voor Economische en Sociale Geografie 90:363–378
Rowthorn R (1999) Unemployment, wage bargaining and capital-labour substitution. Camb J Econ 23:413–425
Solow RM (1956) A contribution to the theory of economic growth. Q J Econ 70(1):65–94
Stockhammer E, Klär E (2011) Capital accumulation, labour market institutions and unemployment in the medium run. Camb J Econ 35:437–457
Suarez J (2010) The Spanish crisis: background and policy challenges. CEPR Discussion Paper DP7909
Whelan K (2000) Computers, obsolescence, and productivity. Board of Governors of the Federal Reserve System Finance and Economics Discussion Series, 6

Jose Andres Faiña is a Jean Monnet Professor of European Industrial Economics and Chairman of the Jean Monnet Research Group on Competition and Development (C+D) at the School of Business and Economics, University of A Coruña, Spain. He has a vast professional experience in European Affairs and in Regional Development Policy, as Director General of Economic Planning (Regional Government of Galicia (1998–2001) and Leader of the Phare Project Galicia-Opolskie (Poland, 2001–2002), as well as an independent expert evaluating the impact of ERDF programmes for the DG Regio (European Commission). His research and publications focus on constitutional political economy of the EU, regional economics and development policy, as well as industrial and competition economics and currently lean start-up and Business Management of Innovation.

Jesus Lopez-Rodriguez is Associate Professor of Economics at the University of A Coruña. He is also a senior research fellow at the Jean Monnet Research Group on Competition and Development (C+D) at the University of A Coruña where he served as director from 2013 to 2015. From 2013 to 2014, he worked at the Institute for Prospective Technological Studies-Joint Research Centre (IPTS-JRC) of the European Commission as senior research fellow. He has extensive track record of research in geographical economics, regional growth and disparities, EU regional policy, EU political economy and industrial economics and more recently in public economics. He has acted as consultant to several institutions including DG Regio, European Commission, European Parliament, Galician Court of Competition and Basque Court of Competition. He has also been visiting scholar at a number of universities including Harvard University, London School of Economics, Institute of Capital, Creativity and Innovation at the University of Texas and University of Exeter.

Paulino Montes-Solla is Associate Researcher in Economics at the Jean Monnet Research Group on Competition and Development (C+D), Department of Economic Analysis and Business Administration, University of A Coruña, Spain. He has been a member of the expert group in Regional Policy and a regular contributor to the reports on ERDF funds for the European Commission since 2009 and acted as junior consultant to several institutions including the DG Regio, European Commission and Basque Court of Competition. His research focuses on Regional

Development, Business Management of Innovation, Renewable energy economy and Marketing and Consulting of European Community Funds. He has also been visiting scholar at the European Policies Research Centre (University of Strathclyde, UK) and at the Institute of Capital, Creativity and Innovation (University of Texas at Austin, USA).

Isidoro Romero has a PhD in Economics and is an Associate Professor in the Department of Applied Economics at the University of Seville (Spain). He has been a visiting scholar at the University of Groningen (The Netherlands), the University of Illinois at Urbana-Champaign (USA) and the University of Reading (UK) and an invited lecturer in postgraduate programmes at the University of Palermo (Italy), the University of Aberystwyth (UK) and the Complutense University in Madrid, among other institutions. He is the Coordinator of PYMED—"SMEs and economic development" research group—at the University of Seville and a member of the European Union Regional Economic Applications Laboratory and the European Union Network for Input-Output Studies. He has served as Associate Dean for Research and Internationalization in the Faculty of Economics and Business Sciences at the University of Seville. His research lines are entrepreneurship, SMEs, regional development, innovation and enterprise policy.

Laura Varela-Candamio is Assistant Professor in the Department of Economic Analysis and Business Administration since 2008 and a senior research fellow at the Jean Monnet Research Group on Competition and Development (C+D) at the University of Coruña. She is also a teacher-tutor at the National Distance Education University (UNED) in Lugo since 2011. She earned her doctorate in economics from the University of Coruna in 2011. Her research interests include public economics such as public finance, taxation and public policies, sustainable economic development and behavioural economics. She has published its research outcomes in scientific journals such as Economics Letters, Applied Economics, Computers in Human Behavior, El Trimestre Económico and Sustainability, among others. She has been a visiting scholar in a number of universities, Andrew Young School (Georgia State University) (2015), REAL (University of Illinois) (2013), Suffolk University (2012) and University of Porto (2014, 2011 and 2010).

Chapter 6
Patterns of Foreign Direct Investment in Southern European Periphery

Laura Resmini

JEL Classification F23 • R12 • C21

6.1 Introduction

The potentials of the single market, as well as the ability of European firms to compete successfully in foreign markets, both within and outside the European Union (EU) boundaries, have made the EU one of the major players in global Foreign Direct Investment (FDI). Generally speaking the EU is considered an attractive location by foreign investors because of its liberal FDI regulation, a highly educated and productive labour force, as well as a large and integrated market for both final goods and services and intermediates. The consistency of FDI stocks, whose amount has reached impressive figures in the last decades, is a proof of the EU attractiveness (Eurostat 2013).

Despite that, the distribution of FDI across the EU is quite uneven, with some regions attracting more FDI than others both within and across countries. Southern European (SE) regions are at the margin of the FDI attraction game accounting for a very small share of total inward FDI in the EU.

This fact raises two questions: first, why did these regions attract such a low number of foreign investors? And second, does it depend on regional characteristics or on country characteristics?

One explanation for this fact is that SE regions have a low potential to attract FDI, since their characteristics are not those that foreign firms are looking for. This implies that the observed FDI inflows just reflect the scarcity of location advantages of those regions. A second explanation is that the capacity of SE regions to attract FDI is conditioned by their respective countries' performances, characterized with respect to other EU countries by poor market regulations and legal enforcement, as well as low quality and inefficient administrative systems; in a few words, Southern

L. Resmini (✉)
Department of Sociology and Social Research, University of Milano-Bicocca, Via Bicocca degli Arcimboldi, 8, 20136 Milano, Italy

CERTeT—Università Commerciale "L. Bocconi", Via Roentgen, 1, 20136 Milano, Italy
e-mail: laura.resmini@unimib.it

M. Fonseca, U. Fratesi (eds.), *Regional Upgrading in Southern Europe*, Advances in Spatial Science, DOI 10.1007/978-3-319-49818-8_6

Europe seems to suffer from the lack of a business environment conducive for foreign investments (Golub et al. 2003; Committeri 2004).

In order to better understand the determinants of inward FDI flows in the EU and potential differences between Southern regions and other EU regions, this contribution provides the following analysis:

- an overall picture of the main characteristics of patterns of inward FDI in SE regions at geographical and sectoral levels and their potential differences with patterns of FDI in other EU regions;
- the factors that drive FDI inflows to EU regions;
- an assessment of the potential attractiveness of SE regions, both in absolute terms and with respect to other EU regions.

The degree of attractiveness of FDI of SE regions and potential differences with respect to other EU regions are analysed by using the number of newly created foreign firms—disaggregated by 252 NUTS2 EU regions, the most important sectors of economic activity, and the origin of foreign firms within or outside the EU—as a proxy for inward FDI in the period from 2005 to 2007.[1] Figures reflect averages over the period instead of annual flows in order to minimize excessive fluctuations in the FDI variable and avoid single counting.[2] Moreover, the period ends in 2007 since this work aims to isolate the structural factors that affect regions' attractiveness rather than to understand the impact of the recent economic downturn on regions' capacity to attract FDI.

This paper is not the only one dealing with location choices of multinational firms in Europe, but it is the first focusing on Southern European regions in a comparative perspective. Some previous works have addressed the question of why some regions attract more or less FDI than other regions within specific Southern European countries.[3] However, a single country perspective does not allow for considering either the potential effects on regions' competitiveness of national factors—an issue particularly relevant for targeting appropriate FDI promotion policies—or the potential effects of inter-country competition, which arises in integrated spaces like the EU where competition to attract FDI may occur not

[1]These figures come from FDIRegio database. See Capello et al. (2011) for a comprehensive description of the database and further information on its reliability in describing patterns of FDI in the EU.

[2]Although the evaluation of several consecutive periods of time would have allowed a more in depth and exhaustive study, it should be born in mind that the availability of data is a major constraint in the analysis of factors driving FDI at regional level.

[3]Basile et al. (2005), Bronzini (2004), Mariotti and Piscitello (1995) analyzed the distribution of foreign firms across Italian regions, while Mota and Brandao (2001), Barbosa et al. (2004) and Guimarães et al. (2000) focused on patterns of FDI across Portuguese regions. The distribution of FDI across Spanish regions has been investigated by Egea and Lopez (1991), Villaverde and Maza (2012) and Rodrıguez and Pallas (2008), while Jordaan and Monastiriotis (2011) and Petrakou (2013) deals with the attractiveness of Greek regions.

only within but also across countries (Basile et al. 2009; Crozet et al. 2004; Pusterla and Resmini 2007).

This contribution is organized in five sections. The second section provides some evidence on patterns of intra- and extra-EU foreign investments in SE regions. Factors driving regions attractiveness are investigated from a theoretical and an empirical perspective in the following two sections. In the last section some preliminary conclusions are drawn.

6.2 Patterns of FDI in Southern Europe

Focusing on SE regions, the aim of this section is to illustrate the main cross-country and cross-industry features of patterns of FDI and highlight some of the questions that need to be addressed to understand the economic factors that underlie this phenomenon as well as the role that policy can play in promoting inflows of FDI into these regions.

The data presented in Table 6.1 shows that Southern Europe attracted very few foreign companies: only 33 per million of inhabitants.[4] This number is below the EU average (225 foreign firms per million of inhabitants) and very far from the average of Central and Eastern European regions, which have attracted a lot of foreign companies since the beginning of their transition towards market economy and the EU. If one considers extra-EU foreign firms only, SE regions are even more unattractive, with only 6 firms per million of inhabitants. Table 6.1 also indicates that Southern Europe is not a homogenous area and that the capacity to attract FDI varies considerably across countries. Spain is the best performer, with about 40 foreign firms per million of inhabitants, followed by Italy and Portugal. Greece ranks last, with only 15 foreign firms per million of inhabitants.

Table 6.1 FDI in Southern Europe (number of foreign firms per million of inhabitants)

	FDI	Intra EU	Extra EU
EU26	224.83	149.40	75.43
Eastern Europe	402.81	276.52	126.29
Southern Europe	33.72	28.07	5.65
Greece	14.83	13.21	1.62
Italy	30.94	25.38	5.56
Portugal	20.54	19.97	0.57
Spain	45.43	37.41	8.02

Source: FDIRegio database

[4]Numbers of newly created foreign firms have been normalized by population in order to eliminate the size effect, according to which larger countries are able to attract more firms than smaller ones. In so doing, figures showed in Table 6.1 are directly comparable.

Table 6.2 FDI in Southern Europe by sector (percentages)

	Southern Europe			All EU 26		
Sectors	All	Intra-EU	Extra-EU	All	Intra-EU	Extra EU
Primary	1.12	1.23	0.57	1.06	1.08	1.01
Manufacturing	33.52	33.18	35.19	18.63	20.69	14.56
Energy and construction	5.23	5.65	3.13	4.15	5.10	2.28
Services	60.13	0.60	0.61	76.16	73.13	82.15
Total	100.00	100.00	100.00	100.00	100.00	100.00

Source: FDIRegio database

At the sectoral level, further heterogeneity emerges. Generally speaking, 60% of foreign affiliates in Southern Europe operate in the services sectors; another 34% in the manufacturing sectors and the remaining share in primary and energy and construction sectors (Table 6.2). This distribution only partially reflects patterns of FDI into the EU26. As indicated by the last three columns of Table 6.2, the share of FDI projects in the services sectors is now larger (about 76%), while that of FDI projects in manufacturing is smaller (below 20%). Two other interesting features are worth mentioning: First, the share of extra-EU FDI projects in service sectors reached 82%. Secondly, extra-EU FDI in manufacturing represents about 35% of total FDI projects in Southern Europe but only 14% in the EU26. As for intra-EU foreign firms, these shares amount to 33% and 21% respectively. Overall, these patterns suggest that SE regions are, on the one hand, more attractive for manufacturing rather than services FDI; on the other hand, extra- and intra-EU foreign investors may have different motivations for investing in the EU and mainly in Southern European regions. The lesser attractiveness of SE regions for foreign services providers may be due to their peripheral position within the EU, while the preference granted to them by foreign manufacturer may reflect cost-advantages, which are at the core of location decisions of vertically integrated foreign firms.[5]

By crossing the geographical and sectoral dimensions other interesting features emerge. Table 6.3 reports the Index of Specialization (SPI) of inward FDI in primary, manufacturing, services activities, and energy and construction. The SPI of FDI is given by:

[5]The theory of FDI usually distinguishes four types of FDI: (i) horizontal FDI, which occurs when a firm is interested in exploiting foreign markets; (ii) vertical FDI, which occurs when firms fragment different stages of the production process in one or more locations in order to exploit international differences in input prices; (iii) resource seeking FDI which occurs when firms are searching for affordable provision of natural resources; and (iv) strategic asset seeking FDI, which occurs when firms aim to gain access to advanced technologies, skills and other production capabilities in foreign locations. See Barba Navaretti and Venables (2004) and Iammarino and McCann (2013) for a thorough discussion of these and other theoretical issues related to multinational enterprises.

Table 6.3 Index of FDI penetration in Southern Europe

	Spain	Greece	Italy	Portugal	SE
Primary	1.43	1.15	0.73	0.44	1.06
Manufacturing	1.27	0.91	2.53	1.24	1.80
Services	0.90	1.03	0.64	0.82	0.79
Energy and construction	1.46	0.73	0.82	3.44	1.26
(Southern Europe only)					
Primary	1.34	1.08	0.69	0.41	–
Manufacturing	0.70	0.51	1.41	0.69	–
Services	1.14	1.31	0.81	1.03	–
Energy and construction	1.16	0.58	0.65	2.73	–

Source: Own calculation from FDIRegio database

$$SPI_{sc} = (FDI_{sc}/\Sigma_s FDI_{sc})/(\Sigma_c FDI_{sc}/\Sigma_s \Sigma_c FDI_{sc}) \quad (6.1)$$

where *FDI* is the number of foreign firms, and *s* and *c* refer to sectors and countries, respectively. The index is built relative to both the EU average (upper panel of Table 6.3) and Southern Europe average (bottom panel of Table 6.3) and shows the extent to which each of the four countries under consideration and the Southern European area taken as a whole receive more or fewer foreign firms than the EU—or Southern Europe as whole—in each of the reported sectors. By definition, the average value of the index for a particular sector in the EU (Southern Europe) is 1; therefore, values greater (or lower) than 1 indicate that country *c* shows a concentration of FDI in sector *s* above (or below) the EU (or Southern Europe) average.

Table 6.3 confirms that Southern European countries attract relatively more FDI in production rather than in services activities. Only Spain and Greece show an SPI of inward FDI above the EU average in the primary sector, while Italy seems to be more attractive than other EU countries in manufacturing rather than in services, as indicated by the respective SPIs.

Overall, these results confirm the idea that patterns of FDI in Southern Europe are different from those of the other EU countries and, therefore, may respond to different motivations and local advantages. Moreover, it seems, at least at first sight, that SE regions are less competitive than other EU regions in the FDI attraction game, a result further confirmed by Fig. 6.1 which plots the relative attractiveness of each region with respect to the EU average on the vertical axis and to the corresponding national average on the horizontal axis.[6] By simultaneously considering each region's capacity to attract FDI relative to both the EU and the respective country average, four different groups of regions can be identified:

[6]SPIs shown in Fig. 6.1, have been computed using the number of foreign firms per million of inhabitants in order to capture the size effect. Then, they have been normalized by the EU average and the corresponding national averages in order to make it easier to compare across regions both within and across countries. This implies that the SPI varies between –1 and +1. It assumes the value of zero when a region hosts the same number of foreign firms per million of inhabitants as the EU or the corresponding national average.

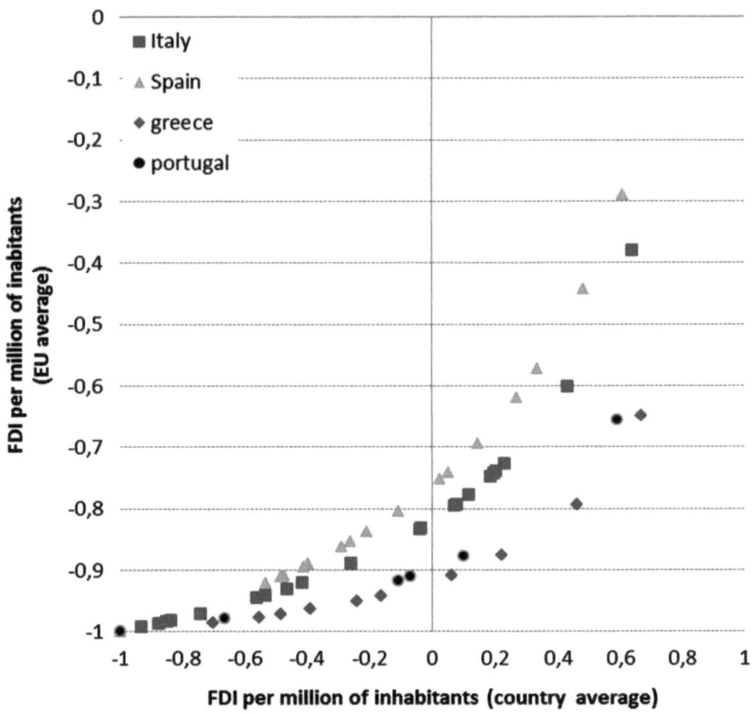

Fig. 6.1 The relative attractiveness of SE regions. Source: Own calculation from FDIRegio database

1. Regions performing better than the respective national mean and the EU mean. Southern European regions are not represented in this group.
2. Regions performing better than the respective national mean but that underperform compared with the EU mean. 22 out of 60 SE regions are included in this group.
3. Regions performing worse than the respective national mean but that perform better than the EU mean. This group does not encompass any SE regions.
4. Regions performing worse than the respective national mean and that underperform compared with the EU mean. 38 out of 60 SE regions are included in this group.

It is clear that all SE regions are less competitive than other EU regions, since none of them performs better than the EU average. Despite that, some regions have attracted a number of foreign firms per million of inhabitants above their respective national averages. These regions are those hosting the capital cities or the most important industrial centres in their own countries. Once again, a clear distinction emerges between Spain and Italy, which are closer to the EU average than Greece

Table 6.4 Drivers of FDI in the EU regions

Variables	Description	Source
Demand side variables		
GDP growth rate	% change in real regional value added (2002–2004)	Eurostat
Market accessibility	Weighted average of GDP of all European regions *j* other than *i*. The weights are the reciprocal of the bilateral distances between the respective capitals (2004)	Eurostat (GDP) DGRegio (bilateral distances)
Supply side variables		
Labour cost	Annual labour cost (average): salaries and wages (excluding apprentices and trainees) (2004)	Eurostat
Quality of governance	EU regional quality of governance index (2009). It ranges from zero (low quality) to 100 (high quality)	Charron et al. (2010)
Labour productivity	Value added per employee (2004)	Eurostat
Agglomeration variables		
Manufacturing size	Share of regional value added generated by manufacturing sectors	Eurostat
High skills	Corporate manager (ISCO-88/12) and professionals and scientists (ISCO-88/2) employment share on total regional employment (2004)	DGRegio
Agglomerated regions	Dummy variable, taking value of 1 for the agglomerated regions (city with >300,000 inhabitants and population density of about 150–300 inhabitant per km^2) and zero otherwise	Espon
Capital city	Dummy variable equals to one if the region includes the national capital and zero otherwise	

and Portugal. The next section is devoted to explain factors underlining these potential cross-geographical and cross-sectoral differences.

6.3 The Attractiveness of Regions: Methodology

Table 6.4 summarizes the main information about the explanatory variables considered in this study in order to analyse factors driving foreign firms' location choice. These variables may be classified into three broad categories: (1) demand side variables; (2) supply side variables; (3) agglomeration economies.

Demand Side Variables Studies focusing on the influence of demand side characteristics on foreign firms location choice stress the importance of market size and its accessibility and growth potential of host locations. The market size is usually proxied by GDP per capita (Coughlin and Segev 2000; Guimarães et al. 2000) in order to capture local purchasing power, or by a sum of distance-weighted GDPs of all locations different from the observed one in order to capture both market size and its accessibility (Head and Mayer 2004). Since it is likely that a foreign firm considers the size of the whole market and transport costs in order to decide where to set up a production plant in an integrated area like the EU (Barba Navaretti and Venables 2004), a measure of regional market accessibility seems more appropriate than a simple measure of local market size. Therefore, this contribution considers among the explanatory variables a market accessibility measure and the regional GDP growth rate. The idea is that foreign investors willing to exploit foreign markets prefer to locate in dynamic, large and well accessible regions (Neary 2002). Moreover, highly accessible markets are also preferred by firms engaging in vertical FDI, due to the large flows of trade in intermediate goods that characterize vertically fragmented FDI.

Supply Side Variables In their location decisions, firms are also motivated by labour market conditions, particularly, labour costs and the qualifications of the workforce. The labour cost, measured by the average wage rate, is included in several studies on FDI determinants, which usually find a negative relationship between FDI inflows and labour cost (Coughlin et al. 1991; Barbosa et al. 2004; Figueiredo et al. 2002; Holl 2004a, b; Woodward et al. 2006; Basile et al. 2009). Therefore, in this research, the proxy for labour costs is an average of annual labour cost in each EU region. The need for a workforce that is not only cheap but also skilled has also been discussed in several studies. Therefore, this research also includes labour productivity, measured by gross value added per employees, among the explanatory variables. FDI inflows are expected to be large in regions where labour costs are low and labour productivity is high. In addition to these traditional determinants for FDI flows, the influence of the business environment is usually considered. Therefore, an index of the quality of the local governance (Charron et al. 2010) has been introduced and a positive impact on regions' attractiveness is expected.

Agglomeration Economies The relevance of agglomeration economies as a driver for FDI inflows has been acknowledged by several studies (Basile et al. 2011; Devereux et al. 2007; Head et al. 1999). The literature usually distinguishes between urbanization economies and localized economies. While the former are external to firms and industries and relate to the positive effects of a diversified economic environment, the latter are external to firms but internal to industries and depend on the availability of a specialized labour market (Jacobs 1961, 1969), the proximity to suppliers and clients as well as the opportunity to reap technological externalities (Marshall 1890). Almost all empirical studies dealing with agglomeration economies conclude that foreign firms positively value a location that allows them to reap the benefits of agglomeration economies (Markusen and Venables 1999; Rodriguez-Clare 1996; Görg and Strobl 2001; Altomonte and Resmini 2002). However, when agglomeration reaches a critical value, congestion effects may arise thus reducing the attractiveness of a given location (Basile et al. 2011; Arauzo-Carod 2005; Viladecans-Marsal 2004). In this study, in order to capture the potential role of agglomeration forces in attracting FDI, two variables have been added: (i) the size of the manufacturing sector in total value added as a proxy for localization externalities; (ii) the share of corporate managers and professionals and scientists in total regional employment as a proxy for urbanization economies. Furthermore, two dummy variables have been included to control for urbanization. The first takes the value of 1 if the region hosts a city with more than 300,000 inhabitants and shows a population density of about 150–300 inhabitant per squared kilometre and zero otherwise. The second dummy, instead, takes the value of 1 only if the region hosts the national capital.

All these explanatory variables refer to 2004. This reflects, on the one hand, the fact that foreign firms need time to evaluate the characteristics of a location before making investments; on the other hand, this strategy helps in mitigating potential endogeneity problems. Table 6.8 in the Statistical Annex reports descriptive statistics of exogenous and endogenous variables for the whole sample and for SE regions.

Another important issue that should be accounted for in the analysis of FDI determinants is the existence of spatial effects, either in the form of spatial heterogeneity or spatial dependence. In order to control for possible spatial heterogeneity, the regression equation includes spatial fixed effects referring either to SE regions, or to single Southern European countries. The aim is to investigate not only whether and to what extent SE regions are, *ceteris paribus*, less attractive than other EU regions, but mainly whether this potential unattractiveness is due to characteristics common to the Southern European periphery or rather to country specific peculiarities. As for spatial dependence, the simplest ways to incorporate spatial dependence in a regression equation are the spatial lag model and the spatial error model (Anselin 1988).[7] According to the former, spatial effects occur through the dependent variable; i.e., foreign firms' location decisions are not independent and in choosing the location of a foreign production plant, a firm considers not only the characteristics of this location, but also where other foreign firms have been established. Furthermore, a change in any of the exogenous variables at any location will be transmitted to all other locations. This implies that changes in the location advantages in one region will affect FDI inflows not only in that location but also in neighbouring locations. The spatial error model, instead, accounts for the presence of spatially correlated omitted variables; that is, it tells us whether and to what extent a shock to FDI in a location spills over neighbouring locations.

Many factors can explain spatial dependence in FDI determinants. First of all, it may be the result of the activities of multinational firms, which may wish to serve multiple markets from a single location, as it is likely in integrated area such as the EU, or because they have fragmented the production process in several stages, each of which is carried out in a different location in order to exploit international input price differences (Baltagi et al. 2007; Blonigen et al. 2007). Moreover, spatial dependence may occur because foreign firms tend to cluster with other foreign firms producing at the same stage of the value chain or in different stages of it in

[7]Recently, more complex specifications have been developed in order to capture spatial patterns in data generating processes. Both the lag and the error models can be nested within one or more of these specifications. See Elhorst (2010) for a discussion on this.

order to exploit input-output linkages and technology spillovers or, more simply, because other foreign firms signal the presence of a business environment conducive for foreign investors (Pusterla and Resmini 2007; Basile et al. 2009; Braunerhjelm and Svensson 1996; Woodward 1992).

Although the theory supports a spatial lag specification, it is not possible to determine *a priori* whether spatially correlated omitted variables do exist. Therefore, a "specific-to-general approach" has been followed (Elhorst 2010; Florax et al. 2003). Hence, a non-spatial linear regression model has been estimated first by traditional OLS techniques, and then the potential spatial characteristics of the data have been incorporated.

A final remark concerns the spatial weight matrix used to accommodate spatial dependence. Given the objectives of this paper, the most appropriate structure for capturing the underlying spatial patterns of FDI inflows is a simple inverse distance matrix. Foreign investors entering Europe, in fact, are theoretically interested in the EU market as a whole rather than that of the host location or its neighbours, especially if it is a small territorial unit, such as a NUTS2 region. Moreover, the further the distance the more difficult it is to develop supplier and/or client linkages due a variety of reasons that can be broadly labelled as the costs of doing business at a distance. This implies that interactions may continue, depending on the degree of distance decay. Therefore, using a first order contiguity matrix or other more or less sophisticated forms of truncated spatial matrix would not be advisable from a theoretical point of view.

6.4 Results

6.4.1 Full Sample and European Vs. Non-European Sub-samples

In Table 6.5 we first assess the role of regional characteristics in attracting FDI in EU regions (column 1).[8] All coefficients have the expected sign, although they are not always statistically significant. In particular, the positive coefficients associated to market accessibility and growth prospect suggest that foreign firms concentrate where demand is high and dynamic, while the negative coefficient of the labour cost variable indicates that high wages discourage FDI. Costs advantages seem to be more important than productivity, which is not significant at the conventional levels. Agglomeration economies, instead, matter as indicated by the positive and significant coefficients of the manufacturing size and high skill variable, while urbanization is not among the drivers of FDI inflows. As expected, the quality of the local governance is also an important determinant of location.

[8]The dependent variable is the number of newly created foreign firms per million of inhabitants established in each EU26 NUTS2 region during the period from 2005 to 2007.

Table 6.5 Determinants of FDI in SE regions: basic model

	OLS									Spatial lag			Spatial error		
	(1)			(2)			(3)			(4)			(5)		
	Coeff.	Std. err.	Sig.	Coeff.	Std. err.	Sig.	Coeff.	Std. err.	Sig.	Coeff.	Std. err.	Sig.	Coeff.	Std. err.	Sig.
Market accessibility	0.27	0.071	***	0.25	0.070	***	0.25	0.069	***	0.17	0.065	***	0.22	0.072	***
GDP growth rate	0.13	0.020	***	0.13	0.019	***	0.13	0.017	***	0.09	0.018	***	0.11	0.019	***
Labour cost	−0.22	0.075	***	-0.18	0.071	*	−0.16	0.069	**	−0.18	0.061	***	−0.16	0.066	**
Labour productivity	0.15	0.169		0.38	0.174	**	0.38	0.190	**	0.39	0.173	**	0.38	0.188	**
Manufacturing size	9.95	2.727	***	9.95	2.600	***	9.44	2.594	***	8.81	2.522	***	8.93	2.496	***
High skills	11.88	1.727	***	9.95	1.556	***	9.79	1.489	***	7.29	1.362	***	9.43	1.505	***
Agglomerated regions	0.18	0.153		0.19	0.154		0.16	0.153		0.20	0.141		0.18	0.147	
Capital city	0.08	0.251		0.08	0.249		0.09	0.250		0.43	0.256	*	0.15	0.263	
Quality of governance	0.47	0.095	***	0.23	0.122	**	0.17	0.147		0.09	0.131		0.17	0.143	
SER	–	–		−0.68	0.213	***	–	–	–	–	–	–	–	–	
Italy	–	–		–	–		−0.72	0.343	**	−0.64	0.308	**	−0.78	0.343	**
Spain	–	–		–	–		−0.28	0.191		−0.17	0.186		−0.36	0.209	*
Greece	–	–		–	–		−0.94	0.442	**	−1.04	0.336	***	−1.30	0.398	***
Portugal	–	–		–	–		−1.36	0.359	***	−1.01	0.430	**	−1.12	0.472	**
Constant	0.44	1.401		−1.68	1.525		−1.84	1.719		−4.34	1.582	***	−1.76	1.693	
rho/lamba	–	–		–	–		–	–		0.82	0.142	***	0.87	0.122	***
R-squared/Variance ratio		0.66			0.68			0.69			0.71			0.65	
Log likelihood											−292.46			−295.53	
AIC test		–			–			–			616.92			623.05	
BIC		–			–			–			673.38			679.53	
n. of obs.		252			252			252			252			252	

***, **, * indicate significance at 1, 5 and 10%, respectively

After having defined the factors driving FDI inflows at the regional level, the capacity of SE regions to attract fewer or more foreign firms than other EU regions with similar observable characteristics has been investigated (column 2 of Table 6.5). In so doing, a dummy for SE regions has been included in the model; it indeed has a negative and significant coefficient, indicating that SE regions attract, *ceteris paribus*, fewer foreign firms than other EU regions with similar structural characteristics. It is interesting to note that, in this case, the coefficient of the labour productivity variable turns out to be significant. Alternatively, a dummy for each Southern European country has been considered (column 3). The findings indicate that only Spanish regions seem to be as attractive as other EU regions with similar characteristics, as indicated by the estimated coefficient, which is negative but not significant. Therefore, one can conclude that country specific effects affect the attractiveness of SE regions. It is worth noting that when country-specific fixed effects are included in the regression equation, the quality of governance becomes insignificant. This result depends on the fact that SE regions show the lowest quality of governance of the EU (see Table 6.8 in the Statistical Annex).

The results presented up to now may not be accurate because of the presence of spatial effects. Spatial diagnostics (see Table 6.9 in the Appendix) provide evidence on the existence of spatial dependence, although its nature cannot be precisely identified.[9] For that reason, both the spatial error and the spatial lag model have been estimated. Results are shown in columns (4) and (5) of Table 6.5, respectively. On the basis of the tests reported in the bottom of the table—i.e., the R^2, the log-likelihood and the AIC and BIC tests—spatial lag specification seems to be the most appropriate. As far as the standard FDI determinants are concerned, the results are robust to the inclusion of the spatial effects and are in line with the underlying theory. Moreover, the capital city dummy also displays some significance, indicating that regions hosting national capitals collect more foreign firms than other regions.

As a first attempt to see how the results for total inflows of FDI are robust to changes in FDI flows, the basic model has been re-estimated for two different sub-samples, i.e., FDI inflows from EU and non-EU countries. The reason to look at FDI originating from within or outside the EU is, on the one hand, to test for the relevance of the EU single market and, on the other hand, to investigate whether and to what extent FDI coming from different source countries share the same patterns. Table 6.6 shows the results of the spatial models only since these specifications are to be preferred over the OLS estimations (see spatial diagnostics in Table 6.9 in the Statistical Annex).

[9]As explained in the previous section, spatial patterns of FDI reflect the motivations at the base of the decision to undertake foreign investments. Researchers do not observe these motivations.

Table 6.6 Determinants of FDI in SE regions: intra-EU vs. Extra-EU FDI

	Intra-EU FDI						Extra-EU FDI					
	Spatial lag			Spatial error			Spatial lag			Spatial error		
	Coeff.	Std. Err.	Sig.	Coeff.	Std. Err.	Sig.	Coeff.	Std. Err.	Sig.	Coeff.	Std. Err.	Sig.
Market accessibility	0.16	0.065	**	0.21	0.071	***	0.18	0.072	**	0.25	0.082	***
GDP growth rate	0.08	0.018	***	0.09	0.20	***	0.09	0.019	***	0.11	0.021	***
Labour cost	−0.20	0.065	***	−0.18	0.069	**	−0.03	0.058		−0.004	0.057	
Labour productivity	0.46	0.176	***	0.44	0.189	**	0.08	0.178		0.07	0.195	
Manufacturing size	9.49	2.547	***	9.56	2.519	***	0.82	1.979		1.05	2.022	
High skills	6.57	1.409	***	8.59	1.538	***	8.75	1.312	***	10.20	1.535	***
Agglomerated regions	0.18	0.145		0.17	0.149		0.25	0.120	**	0.20	0.130	
Capital city	0.48	0.252	*	0.21	0.260		0.20	0.236		−0.08	0.250	
Quality of governance	0.05	0.096		0.12	0.144		0.15	0.118		0.23	0.130	*
Italy	−0.71	0.323	**	−0.85	0.357	*	−0.23	0.243		−0.39	0.281	
Spain	−0.15	0.189		−0.32	0.215		−0.27	0.189		−0.51	0.217	**
Greece	−0.97	0.329	***	−1.19	0.391	***	−0.67	0.259	**	−0.99	0.331	***
Portugal	−0.91	0.417	**	−1.01	0.458	**	−0.71	0.268	***	−0.81	0.321	**
Constant	−0.98	0.912		−2.21	1.718		−2.83	1.529	*	−1.52	0.769	**
rho/lambda	0.72	0.192	***	0.87	0.119	***	0.87	0.105	***	0.93	0.078	***
Variance ratio		0.66			0.60			0.78			0.64	
Log likelihood		−301.24			−303.59			−260.61			−268.37	
AIC test		634.47			639.19			553.22			568.73	
BIC test		639.19			695.67			568.73			625.20	
n. of obs.		252			252			252			252	

***, **, * indicate significance at 1, 5 and 10%, respectively

It turns out that our results are indeed sensitive to the sample selection. Main differences concerned patterns of extra-EU FDI, which seems to respond to a smaller set of location advantages, compared to intra-EU FDI. In particular, extra-EU FDI is sensitive to demand side variables, as well as to urbanization effects. Moreover, non-EU foreign investors perceive only Portuguese and Greek regions as less attractive than other EU regions, all other things being equal.

Overall the estimation results in Tables 6.5 and 6.6 allow us to conclude that:

- SE regions are, *ceteris paribus,* less attractive than other EU regions;
- SE regions' unattractiveness is mainly driven by Greek and Portuguese regions. Italian regions are perceived as less attractive than other EU regions only by intra-EU foreign investors;
- The bad quality of the institutions seems to be the most relevant factor at the base of the relative unattractiveness of SE regions.
- The standard determinants of FDI as well as the relative unattractiveness of SE regions are rather robust to the inclusion of spatial effects;
- Extra-EU foreign firms are attracted mainly by rich, accessible and dynamic markets, as well as by regions well-endowed with specific skills and an environment conducive for business;
- Intra-EU foreign firms follow a more complex pattern, being in search of a combination of relatively low production costs, good market access, and agglomeration economies.

6.4.2 Sectoral FDI

Previous results help in understanding which location advantages are able to drive the distribution of FDI across EU regions and, in particular, in SE regions. Since the magnitude of the effects these location advantages can exert on FDI flows may differ across sectors, it is useful to disaggregate FDI data. Therefore, the original sample has been split between the manufacturing and services sectors. Table 6.7 shows the results.

The findings confirm the existence of spatial patterns of FDI. In particular, the spatial lag specification seems appropriate to explain patterns of location of both manufacturing and services foreign firms (see Table 6.9 in the Statistical Annex), although for different reasons. Manufacturing firms are usually vertically integrated and significant flows of intermediates may occur among them. Location choices are not independent because of the need to minimize transportation costs. On the opposite side, the spatial distribution of foreign services suppliers is conditioned by proximity to clients given the non-tradability of several services. Therefore, they locate close to the richest markets, which, however, are spatially concentrated.

Table 6.7 Determinants of FDI in SE regions: Services vs. manufacturing FDI

	Services						Manufacturing		
	Spatial lag			Spatial error			Spatial lag		
	Coeff.	Std. Err.	Sig.	Coeff.	Std. err.	Sig.	Coeff.	Std. err.	Sig.
Market accessibility	0.22	0.068	***	0.27	0.074	***	0.07	0.057	
GDP growth rate	0.10	0.019	***	0.12	0.019	***	0.07	0.016	***
Labour cost	−0.14	0.062	**	−0.11	0.066	*	−0.20	0.062	***
Labour productivity	0.39	0.181	**	0.39	0.192	**	0.43	0.164	****
Manufacturing size	6.77	2.653	**	6.86	2.605	***	9.19	2.221	***
High skills	8.28	1.423	***	10.55	1.543	***	4.89	1.189	***
Agglomerated regions	0.25	0.143	*	0.22	0.147		0.13	0.131	
Capital city	0.58	0.281	**	0.29	0.280		−0.09	0.194	
Quality of governance	0.13	0.129		0.20	0.137		−0.19	0.126	
Italy	−0.86	0.322	***	−1.02	0.351	***	−0.47	0.285	
Spain	−0.181	0.215		−0.34	0.241		−0.29	0.180	*
Greece	−0.77	0.352	**	−0.99	0.415	**	−1.28	0.268	***
Portugal	−0.82	0.381	**	−0.87	0.418	**	−0.90	0.354	**
Constant	−0.26	0.743		−3.01	1.709	*	−6.24	2.301	***
rho/lamba	0.71	0.181	***	0.86	0.138	***	0.91	0.078	***
R-squared/Variance ratio		0.73			0.68			0.64	
Log likelihood		−307.93		−309.03			−254.74		
AIC test		647.86			650.06			541.47	
BIC		704.33			705.52			597.94	
n. of obs.		252			252			252	

***, **, * indicate significance at 1, 5 and 10%, respectively

More importantly, factors determining FDI in manufacturing and services are not the same, a result already highlighted by the literature (Casi and Resmini 2010). The main differences concern urbanization, which is, as expected, able to attract FDI in services but not in manufacturing. Moreover, manufacturing FDI responds more to supply side rather than to demand side location advantages, while the opposite occurs in the sub-sample of FDI in services.

The sectoral disaggregation confirms the relative unattractiveness of SE regions, with one not surprising exception. Italian regions are not less attractive than other EU regions in the sub-sample of manufacturing FDI. This result is consistent with the empirical evidence shown in Sect. 6.2.

6.5 Conclusions

This contribution investigated factors driving the distribution of FDI across EU regions and the relative (un)attractiveness of SE regions. In so doing, a distinction was made between intra- and extra-EU FDI, and manufacturing and services FDI in order to highlight firm and/or sectoral specificities in spatial patterns of FDI in the EU.

Without focusing on a single specification, a complex set of variables has been shown to determine FDI patterns in the EU. The results discussed above generally support the hypothesis that FDI has been driven by market considerations, even though the responsiveness of FDI to market variables differs between manufacturing and services foreign firms. Labour costs negatively affect FDI in all sectors, although they are not relevant for extra-EU foreign investors. The degree of urbanization exerts effects on inflows of FDI in the services sectors, while agglomeration economies are relevant for any kind of FDI.

Another interesting feature highlighted by the empirical analysis is the existence of spatial patterns in the distribution of FDI across EU regions, an issue not always considered in the analysis of the determinants of FDI. Spatial spillovers do exist and reflect the vertical organization characterising manufacturing production processes as well as the importance of agglomeration economies among foreign services providers, who consider the presence of other foreign suppliers in neighbouring regions as a signal of a business environment conducive for foreign investments. Moreover, it is important to bear in mind that spatial patterns of FDI in services are also affected by the intrinsic characteristics of services, which need the proximity between consumers and producers in order to be delivered. This implies that services providers follow the market rather than other potential local or foreign competitors; therefore, they cluster in core rather than peripheral regions.

The capacity of Southern European regions to attract FDI is, *ceteris paribus*, below the EU average. The least attractive regions are those belonging to Greece and Portugal, while Spanish regions are, generally speaking, perceived as attractive as other EU regions. As for Italian regions, their perceived unattractiveness seems to be limited to services FDI and intra-EU foreign investors.

This simple analysis suggests some preliminary conclusions about the causes of SE regions' FDI shortfall: the quality of local governance is not only very poor in these regions, but it seems also to reflect that of national institutions. This consideration is suggested by the behaviour of the quality of governance variable and country-specific dummies. The former, in fact, turns out to be insignificant when the latter are included in the regression equations.

Some policy implications can be drawn from these preliminary results, mainly for SE countries: in order to attract a high and sustainable level of FDI, the quality of local and national institutions should be reinforced and improved.

This basic empirical analysis leaves some questions open for further investigations. It particular, two policy issues are worth taking into consideration: the impact of the EU Cohesion policy and the effects of the Barcelona declaration and other neighbourhood policy instruments on regions' capacity to attract FDI.

Structural and Cohesion funds have been implemented to help laggard regions to transform and modernize in order to be able to compete within the EU Single Market. Therefore, regions receiving structural and cohesion funds should be, at least in principle, more attractive than other regions, provided that they have effectively used the EU funds. It has been demonstrated that structural funds have affected the location of industries in Europe (Midelfart-Knarvik and Overman 2002) while the impact on FDI inflows is still unclear (Basile et al. 2008; Breuss et al. 2010; Hubert and Pain 2002; Crozet et al. 2004), the main reason being the lack of detailed data either on the spatial distribution of FDI within Europe, or the amount of funds transferred to regions for different activities.

As for integration agreements, it is well known that preferential trade liberalization affects not only trade but FDI as well (Baltagi et al. 2008). One reason for the latter is the increasing importance of export platforms in multinational activity (Ekholm and Forslid 2001; Yeaple 2003). If tariffs are reduced or fully eliminated in a subset of economies, it becomes cheaper for multinationals to deliver goods to consumers inside the liberalizing area from export platforms within this area. Hence, we would expect the Barcelona declaration to make SE regions interesting locations for those multinationals, both European and non-European, willing to serve the Southern Mediterranean markets.

Further quantitative studies including these policy factors may provide essential clues for a better comprehension of the determinants of FDI in the southern peripheral European regions.

Statistical Annex

Table 6.8 Descriptive statistics

Variable	Obs.	Mean	Std. dev.	Min	Max
SE regions					
Market accessibility	57	2.7753	0.9670	1.2724	5.3234
GDP growth rate	57	2.0579	2.0092	−2.9000	8.1000
Labour cost	57	10.2549	0.2686	9.6289	10.6435
Labour productivity	57	10.4829	0.2977	9.7271	10.9821
Manufacturing size	57	0.0594	0.0302	0.0041	0.1386
High skills	57	0.1256	0.0311	0.0404	0.1999
Agglomerated regions	57	0.2807	0.4533	0.0000	1.0000
National capital	57	0.0702	0.2577	0.0000	1.0000
Quality of governance	57	−0.5554	0.7513	−2.5350	0.6346
All FDI	57	2.5022	1.2580	0.0000	4.8349
Extra-EU FDI	57	0.9565	0.9064	0.0000	3.3576
Intra-EU FDI	57	2.3887	1.2158	0.0000	4.5861
FDI in services sectors	57	1.9026	1.2548	0.0000	4.6564
FDI in manufacturing sectors	57	1.8315	1.0606	0.0000	3.8017
All sample					
Market accessibility	252	3.1049	1.3036	0.0000	8.4500
GDP growth rate	252	3.5607	2.8104	−2.9000	13.3186
Labour cost	252	10.1073	1.2003	5.5928	11.0751
Labour productivity	252	10.4661	0.6707	7.7962	11.8484
Manufacturing size	252	0.0599	0.0228	0.0041	0.1386
High skills	252	0.1676	0.0503	0.0404	0.3444
Agglomerated regions	252	0.2619	0.4405	0.0000	1.0000
National capital	252	0.0913	0.2886	0.0000	1.0000
Quality of governance	252	0.2893	0.9260	−2.5350	1.6949
All FDI	252	3.9475	1.4479	0.0000	8.5462
Extra-EU FDI	252	2.3460	1.4810	0.0000	7.9732
Intra-EU FDI	252	3.7240	1.3870	0.0000	7.7169
FDI in services sectors	252	3.4349	1.5790	0.0000	8.4618
FDI in manufacturing sectors	252	2.9810	1.1452	0.0000	6.0339

Table 6.9 Spatial diagnostics: all specifications

	Spatial error				Spatial lag			
	LM		Robust LM		LM		Robust LM	
	Coeff.	Sig.	Coeff.	Sig.	Coeff.	Sig.	Coeff.	Sig.
All FDI	14.16	***	3.17	*	18.75	***	7.76	***
Extra-EU FDI	22.22	***	5.01	**	40.64	***	23.43	***
Intra-EU FDI	15.87	***	3.63	*	18.03	***	5.79	**
FDI in Manufacturing industries	15.76	***	0.10		39.01	***	23.35	***
FDI in Services sectors	11.85	***	4.06	**	11.90	***	4.11	**

***, **, * indicate significance at 1, 5 and 10%, respectively

References

Altomonte C, Resmini L (2002) Multinational corporations as a catalyst for local industrial development. The case of Poland. Scienze Regionali (Italian J Reg Sci) 2002(2):29–57

Anselin L (1988) *Spatial econometrics: methods and models*. Springer

Arauzo-Carod J. (2005) Determinants of industrial location: an application for catalan municipalities. *Pap Reg Sci* 84(1): 105-120.

Baltagi B, Egger P, Pfaffermayr M (2008) Estimating regional trade agreement effects on FDI in an interdependent world. *J Econom* 145:194–208

Baltagi B, Egger P, Pfaffermayr M (2007) Estimating models of complex FDI: are there third-country effects? *J Econom* 140:260–281

Barba Navaretti G, Venables A (2004) *Multinational firms in the world economy*, Princeton University Press

Barbosa N, Guimarães P, Woodward D (2004) Foreign firm entry in an open economy: the case of Portugal. *Appl Econ* 36:465–472

Basile R., Benfratello L., D. Castellani (2011) Spatial clustering and nonlinearities in the location of multinational firms. Quaderno n 90, Quaderni del Dipartimento di Economia, Finanza e StatisticaUniversità di Perugia

Basile R, Benfratello L, Castellani D (2005) Attracting foreign investments in Europe—are Italian regions doomed? *Rivista di Politica Economica* 95(1):319–354

Basile R, Castellani D, Zanfei A (2009) National boundaries and the location of multinational firms in Europe. *Pap Reg Sci* 88(4):733–748

Basile R, Castellani D, Zanfei A (2008) Location choices of multinational firms in Europe: the role of national boundaries and EU policy. *J Int Econ* 74(2):328–340

Blonigen B, Davies R, Waddell G, Naughton H (2007) FDI in space: spatial autoregressive relationships in foreign direct investment. *Eur Econ Rev* 51:1303–1325

Braunerhjelm P, Svensson R (1996) Host country characteristics and agglomeration in foreign direct investment. *Appl Econ* 28:833–840

Breuss F, Egger P, Pfaffermayr M (2010) Structural funds, EU enlargement, and the redistribution of FDI in Europe. *Rev World Econ* 146(3):469–494

Bronzini R (2004) Foreign direct investment and agglomeration: evidence from Italy. Banca d'Italia Temi di discussione 526

Capello R, Fratesi U, Resmini L (2011) *Globalization and regional growth. Past trends and future scenarios*. Springer, Heidelberg

Casi L, Resmini L (2010) Evidence on the determinants of foreign direct investment: the case of EU regions. *Eastern J Eur Stud* 1:93–118

Charron N, Dijkstra L, Lapuente V (2010) Mapping quality of government in the European Union: a study of national and sub-national variation. QoG Working Paper Series 2010:22

Committeri M. (2004) Investire in Italia? Risultati di una recente indagine empirica", Banca d'Italia, Temi di discussione 491, Roma

Coughlin C, Segev E (2000) Foreign direct investment in China: a spatial econometric study. *World Econ* 23:1–23

Coughlin C, Terza J, Arrondee V (1991) State characteristics and the location of foreign direct investment within the United States. *Rev Econ Stat* 73:675–683

Crozet M, Mayer T, Mucchielli JL (2004) How do firms agglomerate? A study of FDI in France. *Reg Sci Urban Econ* 34(1):27–54

Devereux M, Griffith R, Simpson H (2007) Firm location decisions, regional grants and agglomeration externalities. *J Public Econ* 91(3–4):413–435

Egea MP, Lopez C (1991) Un estudio sobre la distribución geográfica de la inversión directa en España. *Información Comercial Española* 696(697):105–118

Ekholm K, Forslid R (2001) Trade and location with horizontal and vertical multi-region firms. *Scand J Econ* 103(1):101–118

Elhorst P (2010) Applied spatial econometrics: raising the bar. *Spat Econ Anal* 5(1):9–28

Eurostat (2013) International trade and foreign direct investment. Eurostat, European Commission
Figueiredo O, Guimarães P, Woodward D (2002) Home-field advantage: location decisions of Portuguese entrepreneurs. *J Urban Econ* 52:341–361
Florax R, Folmer H, Rey S (2003) Specification searches in spatial econometrics. The relevance of Hendry's methodology. *Reg Sci Urban Econ* 22:405–432
Golub S, Hajkova D, Mirza D, Nicoletti G, Yoo K-Y (2003) The influence of policies on trade and foreign direct investment. *OECD Econ Stud* 1:7–83
Görg H, Strobl E (2001) Multinational companies and productivity spillovers: a meta-analysis. *Econ J* 111(475):F723–F739
Guimarães P, Figueiredo O, Woodward D (2000) Agglomeration and the location of foreign direct investment in Portugal. *J Urban Econ* 47:115–135
Head K, Ries J, Swenson D (1999) Attracting foreign manufacturing: Investment promotion and agglomeration. *Reg Sci Urban Econ* 29(2):197–218
Head K, Mayer T (2004) Market potential and the location of Japanese investment in the European Union. *Rev Econ Stat* 86:959–972
Holl A (2004a) Start-ups and relocations: manufacturing plant location in Portugal. *Pap Reg Sci* 83:649–668
Holl A (2004b) Transport infrastructure, agglomeration economies, and firm birth: empirical evidence from Portugal. *J Reg Sci* 44:693–712
Hubert F, Pain N (2002) Fiscal incentives, European integration and the location of Foreign Direct Investment. *Manch Sch* 70(3):336–363
Iammarino S, McCann P (2013) *Multinationals and economic geography*. Edward Elgar, Cheltenham
Jacobs J (1961) *Death and life of great American cities*. Random House, New York
Jacobs J (1969) *The economy of cities*. Vintage, New York
Jordaan J. and V. Monastiriotis (2011), Regional distribution and spatial impact of FDI in Greece: evidence from firm-level data. GreeSE Paper No 44, Hellenic Observatory Papers on Greece and Southeast Europe
Markusen J, Venables A (1999) Foreign direct investment as a catalyst for industrial development. *Eur Econ Rev* 43(2):335–356
Mariotti S, Piscitello L (1995) Information costs and location of FDI within the host country: empirical evidence from Italy. *J Int Bus Stud* 26(4):815–841
Marshall A (1890) *Principles of economics*. Macmillan, London
Midelfart-Knarvik KH, Overman H (2002) Delocation and European integration. Is structural spending justified? *Econ Policy* 17:323–359
Mota I, Brandao A (2001) The determinants of location choice: single plants versus multi-plants. *Pap Reg Sci* 92(1):31–50
Neary P (2002) Foreign direct investment and the single market. *Manch Sch* 70(3):291–314
Petrakou M (2013) The determinants of foreign direct investment in the greek regions. *J Urban Reg Anal* 5(1):45–64
Pusterla F, Resmini L (2007) Where do foreign firms locate in transition countries? An empirical investigation. *Ann Reg Sci* 41(4):835–856
Rodrıguez X, Pallas J (2008) Determinants of foreign direct investment in Spain. *Appl Econ* 40:2443–2450
Rodriguez-Clare A (1996) Multinationals, linkages, and economic development. *Am Econ Rev* 86 (4):852–873
Viladecans-Marsal E (2004) Agglomeration economies and industrial location: city-level evidence. *J Econ Geogr* 4(5):565–582
Villaverde J, Maza A (2012) Foreign direct investment in Spain: regional distribution and determinants. *Int Bus Rev* 21(4):722–733
Woodward D, Figueiredo O, Guimarães P (2006) Beyond the Silicon Valley: University R&D and high-technology location. *J Urban Econ* 60:15–32

Woodward D (1992) Locational determinants of Japanese manufacturing start-ups in the United States. *South Econ J* 58:690–708
Yeaple SR (2003) The complex integration strategies of multinationals and cross-country dependencies in the structure of Foreign Direct Investment. *J Int Econ* 60(2):293–314

Laura Resmini is associate professor of Economic policy at the University of Milano-Bicocca and affiliated member of CERTeT, Center for Research on Regional Economics, Transport and Tourism at Bocconi University. She is the Treasurer of the European Regional Science Association (ERSA) and member of the Scientific Council of the Italian Section of the Regional Science Association International (AISRe). She is also co-editor of Scienze Regionali—Italian Journal of Regional Science and member of the Editorial Board of Papers in Regional Science. Throughout her professional life, she has been involved with various roles in several research projects, especially at European level. She is author of several papers published in refereed journals in the field of Foreign Direct Investment, Multinational corporations' location strategies and impact on local economic development.

Chapter 7
Regional Economic Development, Human Capital and Transport Infrastructure in Greece: The Role of Geography

Vassilis Tselios, Antonis Rovolis, and Yannis Psycharis

JEL Classification R11 • R40 • R58 • I25

7.1 Introduction

This chapter attempts to synthesise the various causal mechanisms which have been proposed in the literature to explain the relationship between regional development, human capital and transport investments in Greece, by increasing our understanding of the role that geography plays in the functioning and performance of regions. It will allow us to understand why economic activities tend to concentrate in specific Greek areas. The ultimate aim of the chapter is to draw some kind of potentially useful inference for regional policy makers whose primary concern is to guarantee both equity and efficiency.

Despite the abundance of theoretical and empirical literature dealing with the regional development, human capital and transport infrastructures nexus, we think that, specifically for the Greek economy, the reverse causality of this nexus has not been explored enough. Hence, this study not only sheds light on this relationship, but also contributes to the empirical analysis by providing descriptive analysis and mapping regarding the Greek case.

The remainder of the chapter is organised as follows. In Sect. 7.2, we debate regional economic development in Greece. In Sect. 7.3, we discuss the theoretical underpinnings of the human capital and economic development relationship and in Sect. 7.4 those of the transport investment and economic development relationship. In Sect. 7.5, we discuss whether we need additional drivers for the understanding of the association between regional development, human capital and transport

V. Tselios (✉)
University of Thessaly, Volos, Greece
e-mail: vtselios@prd.uth.gr

A. Rovolis • Y. Psycharis
Panteion University, Athens, Greece
e-mail: rovolis@panteion.gr; psycharis@panteion.gr

M. Fonseca, U. Fratesi (eds.), *Regional Upgrading in Southern Europe*, Advances in Spatial Science, DOI 10.1007/978-3-319-49818-8_7

infrastructure, examining the role of the first and second nature of geography. In Sect. 7.6, we draw out a number of policy implications with regard to the role of regional economic policy, and more specifically to the economic efficiency and equity issues. In Sect. 7.7, we conclude.

7.2 Regional Economic Development in Greece

Regional economic development is the application of economic processes and resources available to a region (Stimson et al. 2006). The term 'region' is a geographical sub-unit of the national economy and is used to refer to administrative areas and political jurisdictions (Armstrong and Taylor 2000). The standard measure of the performance of a regional economy is Gross Domestic Product (GDP) per capita, designed to measure the total output per capita in a particular region, including services (European Commission 1999). More specifically, GDP includes the total output of goods and services for final use produced by a regional economy, by both residents and non-residents, regardless of the allocation to domestic and foreign claims. GDP is a measure of aggregate income on a macro level, though it excludes transfers of income from individuals, companies and government in the form, for example, of social benefits (European Commission 1999). A region that has a low level of production might have a relatively high level of income due to large social security transfers, but it would still be a less favoured region (European Commission 2004: 25–26).

However, there are certain problems encountered in the use of GDP per capita as a measure of economic development, especially for city-regions. City-regions, such as the region of Attica, are underbounded regions, which are smaller than their Functional Urban Regions (FURs) (Cheshire and Hay 1988). The administrative definition of cities in Europe bears no constant relation to any functional definition (Cheshire and Hay 1988). The administrative definition of cities does not capture the economic sphere of influence of a city. Conversely, '*FURs are functional in that their boundaries are determined on the basis of economic relationships rather than history or political divisions*' (Cheshire and Hay 1988: 15). The bigger the city, the smaller the spatial units chosen, the greater the measurement bias is likely to be. For instance, the municipality of Athens is considerably smaller than the FUR of Athens. The fact that central cities are likely to provide public services that benefit populations living in the rest of the metropolitan area but working, studying or shopping in the central city (Greene et al. 1974) is not observable in large city-regions. The interdependencies between central cities and their suburbs are not captured. In city-regions, commuting by people who reside in other regions adds to the local workforce and GDP. The city-region's GDP per capita as a measure of income per capita is, therefore, overstated, while that of neighbouring regions is understated (European Commission 1999). Additional problems encountered in the use of GDP per capita as a measure of economic development within regions are: that GDP counts work that does not produce a net change or that results from repairing harm, such as a natural disaster (e.g., an earthquake); that cross-border trade within companies (e.g., to escape high taxation) distorts the GDP; and that if a region does not spend, but saves and invests in other regions, its GDP will decline in comparison to a region that spends borrowed money. Finally, GDP does not include deductions for depreciation of physical capital or depletion and degradation of natural resources. These features of GDP are very pronounced in the case of Athens, which extends its activities beyond its regional boundaries (Petrakos and Psycharis 2015a).

Figure 7.1 presents regional (i.e., prefectural NUTS III) GDP per capital in Greece for the year 2002. This figure shows that there are important asymmetries in the distribution of production and wealth across the Greek territory. Some of these observations stand out. First, the Greek economic space is dominated by the presence of the metropolitan area of Athens, which is included in the Attica Region,

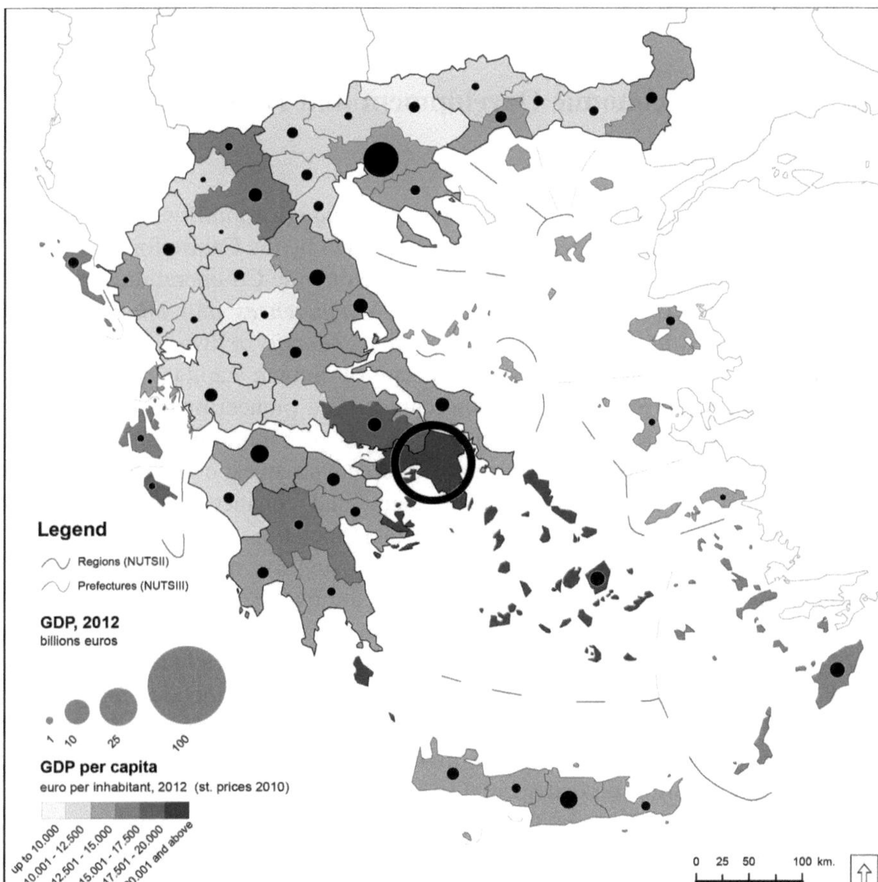

Fig. 7.1 Regional GDP per capita at NUTS III level in Greece (2012). Source: Eurostat, authors' elaboration

but functionally extends beyond that, embracing clusters of significant industrial activity located in a short distance beyond its borders in the neighbouring regions (Petrakos and Psycharis 2015b). Even without its 'satellites', the Attica region accounted for 36% of the national population and 50% of national GDP in 2012, maintaining a regional GDP per capita that is the highest in the country and 32% above the national average. Furthermore, Voiotia, adjacent to the Attica region, where it has been 'exposed to' a large part of the industrial activity of Attica, is the only continental region with GDP per capita above the country average (by 15%). Looking at the map of the country, the more relatively well-off areas are these on the 'S' axis, which starts from Thessaloniki, along the eastern coast of continental Greece until Athens and continues to the Northern cost of Peloponnese until Patras. Finally, it is evident that the majority of islands enjoy a higher GDP per capital relative to the country average with the Cyclades holding the second position in the ranking.

7.3 Regional Economic Development and Human Capital in Greece

A major force shaping economic development is *human capital*, which is considered a multidimensional concept. It has been defined by the Centre for Educational Research and Innovation and Organisation for Economic Co-operation and Development (1998: 9) as '*the knowledge, skills, competences and other attributes embodied in individuals that are relevant to economic activity*'. A number of economists have adopted the broad concept of human capital, including the work of Adam Smith in the eighteenth century. The pioneering work of Schultz (1961, 1962, 1963) views human beings as types of capital and investment. He treats human resources as a form of capital. People who invest in themselves extend the range of choice that is available to them, and enhance their welfare and, subsequently, the economic development of their society.

Schultz (1961) has classified human activities using five major dimensions. The *first* dimension is that of formally organised education at the elementary, secondary and tertiary levels. The cost of this type of human capital consists of the costs of the services of teachers, librarians and administrators. It also includes the costs of maintaining and operating the educational plant and the income foregone by students. The *second* dimension is the on-the-job training organised by firms. It differs from formal education in that investment is made within the workplace rather than in an institution that specialises in teaching (Becker 1962). The cost of this training is usually borne by employers and depends on the type of training and on the demand for different skills. The aim of such training programmes is to adjust the education of workers to the demand for new skills and abilities. Training is regarded as an important aspect of labour market flexibility. A lack of mobility, for instance, may inhibit the scope for firms to bring about changes in work practice and organisational structures (De Serres 2003; OECD 2003). The *third* dimension is the study programmes for adults that are not organised by firms, such as the extension programmes in agriculture that contribute to transmitting new knowledge and to developing skills among farmers. The *fourth* dimension is the migration of individuals and families to adjust to changing job opportunities. The movement of people from one sector to another changes their overall welfare. The *fifth* dimension of human capital is that of health facilities and services which includes all expenditures that affect life expectancy, strength and stamina, and the vitality of people, among others.

Economists, sociologists and geographers have extended the concept of human capital to many other areas. According to Becker (1962), an additional dimension of human capital concerns the acquisition of information about the economic system. Generally speaking, the economic system influences the efficiency, allocation and distribution of human resources. People can reduce the risk of their investment if they have a better knowledge of the market. Spence (1973) supports the notion that education may act as a ‘signal’ because of imperfect information which may generate temporary educational mismatch. For instance, the coexistence of a high incidence of overeducation among school-leavers and a lack of work experience reflects the educational mismatch (Hartog 2000). This type of mismatch conceptually differs from the skill mismatch that is the actual mismatch between acquired and required skills (Allen and van der Velden 2001). Hence, the acquisition of information about the economic system influences not only the distribution of human beings, but also the educational and skill mismatch. Benporath (1980) places emphasis on another dimension of human capital, the ‘personal’ or ‘specific’ human capital created by investments in reputation and personal relationships, which is known as the F-connection (i.e., families, friends and firms). Similarly, Becker (1962), Becker and Tomes (1986) and Becker and Barro (1988) have extended human capital to encompass marriage, fertility and family relations. Closely related to ‘specific’ human capital is the concept of social capital (Bourdieu 1993; Coleman 1988; Putnam 1993). However, social capital is generally understood to be a matter of relationships rather than the property of individuals (Schuller 2000). Thus, human capital focuses on the economic behaviour of individuals, while social capital on networks, norms and trust.

Educational attainment is the most used proxy for human capital as it can be defined in terms of various human attributes, such as the knowledge, skills and competences embodied in individuals that are relevant to economic activity. It is usually measured as the percentage of the population who have successfully completed various ‘levels’ of formal education. The term ‘level’ is defined in relation to the years of study and the age associated with an educational cycle. These indicators show how many people have completed each level of initial education. A related measure is the average number of years of schooling completed. It assumes that a year of education will add a constant quantity to the human capital stock, whether undertaken by a primary school child or a post-graduate student. However, these measurements do not take into account the quality of educational attainment. The ideal measures of human capital would be in terms of the output of education, but due to the difficulties of obtaining such measures, input measures tend to be used instead (Sianesi and Van Reenen 2003). Completion of educational levels is only broadly associated with certain forms of economically-relevant knowledge, skills and competence and does not look at the human capital stock attributed directly. Hence, such measures of regional differences in educational attainment cannot explain differences in adult literacy performance. In other words, they do not measure how much in practice such attributes are worth in economic terms. It should be noted here that neither proxy takes into account the fact that skills are lost through disuse. They ignore the depreciation of human capital which is often associated with unemployment and economic inactivity. A person's qualifications are kept for life, while the qualities required to gain them may depreciate over time (Centre for Educational Research and Innovation and Organisation for Economic Co-operation and Development 1998). To sum up, the proxies analysed are more measurements of the quantity and availability of a region's human resources (input measures), rather than measurements of the quality of human capital endowments (output measures). In measuring the quantity of education, one only gains a crude idea of skill differences (Hanushek and Kimko 2000).

Figure 7.2 shows the university graduates holding a postgraduate diploma in NUTS III regions in Greece and demonstrates that there are important differences in the level of education of people among regions. This figure shows that inequalities in concentration of the most educated human capital follow a similar pattern to the regional economic development and they are concentrated in the most urbanized areas of the country. In addition, these regions are the location of the largest universities and educational institutions in the country. Attica, which stands out as the most developed and the most urbanized area of the country, is the region with the highest percentage of graduates. Conversely, mountainous, remote and border regions which are lagging behind in terms of economic development also suffer from deprivation of educationally upgraded human capital. The correlation between economic wealth and educational level seem to be very high. This is further supported by all the educational indices. According to the Greek Population Censuses data, 49% of the population that has completed tertiary education and 64% of the population holding a post-graduate degree are concentrated in Athens Metropolitan Area (Petrakos and Psycharis 2015a). Thessaloniki, which is the second NUTS III region in this ranking, hosts 11% and 13% respectively. Together, these two regions host 60% of people holding a University degree and 77% of people holding a post-graduate degree (Petrakos and Psycharis 2015a).

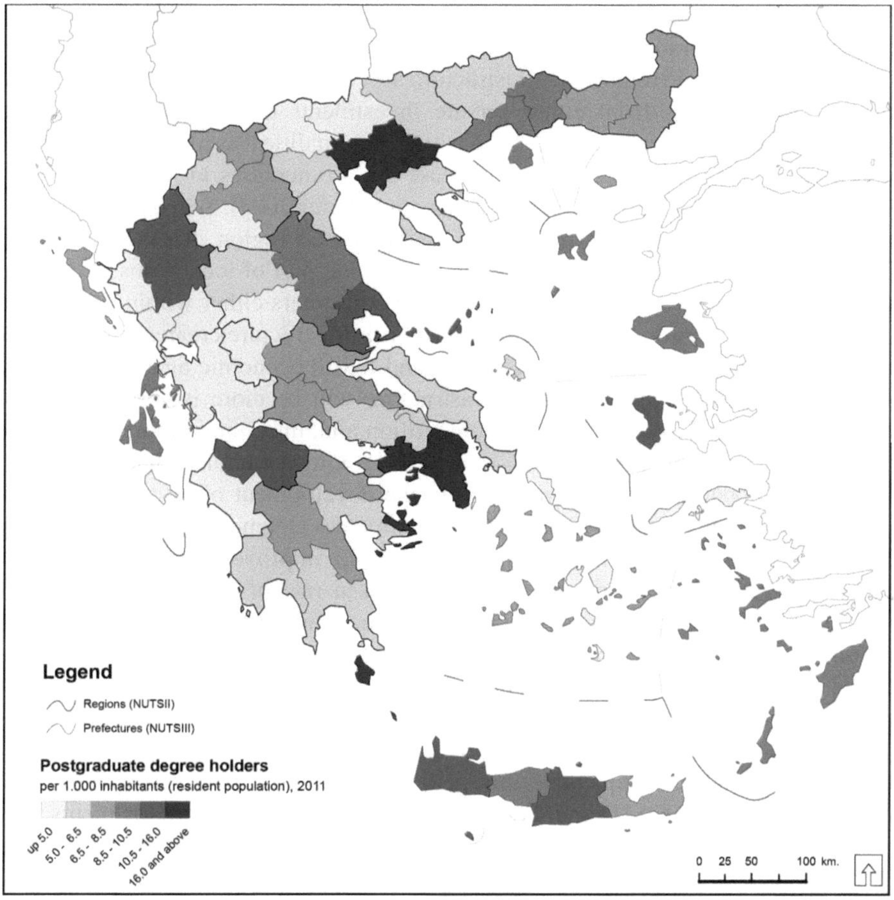

Fig. 7.2 University graduates in Greek prefectures (2011). Source: National Statistical Authority of Greece, Population Census 2011, authors' elaboration

7.4 Regional Economic Development and Transport Infrastructure in Greece

The relationship between regional economic development and transport infrastructure is a highly complex issue involving aspects of public-good provision, the generation of externalities and political decision-making (McCann and Shefer 2004). Most studies have accepted the position that transport infrastructures contribute positively to economic development. The pioneering studies of Aschauer (e.g., Aschauer 1989) concluded that public capital (including transport infrastructures) was a factor of enormous importance in explaining the evolution of economic performance in the United States. Later studies (e.g., Duffydeno and Eberts 1991) provided additional evidence for the results obtained by Aschauer.

The theoretical background on the positive relationship between transport infrastructures and economic development is multifarious. *First*, the net benefits associated with the public transport infrastructure are related to increases in the net local income, which stem from either private investments due to the reductions in transport costs and travel times or positive externalities as the income of the non-users of the infrastructure may increase due to increases in local demand on the part of the infrastructure users (McCann and Shefer 2004). *Second*, investments in transportation change the relative accessibility of a region. An increase in the level of connectivity implies a greater ability on the part of local firms to develop profitable market relationships with firms and consumers either within or between regions. In other words, a high quality transport infrastructure creates opportunities for interaction among firms and customers and for all economic agents. Firms that are located in areas with a better infrastructure will be more integrated into the market system and more exposed to competition and, thus, under more pressure to improve productivity (Deichmann et al. 2004). Greater choice, innovation and intellectual opportunities for agents imply the development of inter-regional and intra-regional linkages, and thus higher economic development (Vickerman 1991). When the road and rail infrastructure, for example, improves the relative accessibility of a region, it can provide for an increased rate of return on investments relative to other competing locations (McCann and Shefer 2004). Additional mobile resources (either capital or labour) from outside the region may be attracted to the area with the new infrastructure. This immigration of factors contributes to regional economic development. Based on this evidence, where transport infrastructure facilities are developed, it is easier for entrepreneurs to adopt new technologies and, consequently, this generates technical progress and regional economic development (Demurger 2001). *Third*, poor resource endowments may lead to limited access to educational and socioeconomic opportunities. Transport infrastructures offset some of the inherent disadvantages of lagging regions, because they connect remote regions to urban areas (Henderson et al. 2001). *Fourth*, transport infrastructures reinforce the cumulative causation process. Firms produce more efficiently and workers enjoy higher levels of welfare by being linked to large markets through a good transport infrastructure network. The large markets are, in turn, those where more firms and workers are located. *Fifth*, a good infrastructure network across regions might imply efficiency in the transportation of inputs (labour and capital) as well as potential increases in their price, and thus a higher growth rate. Transport facilities for both passengers and freight are usually critical to the competitiveness and prosperity of a region (European Commission 1999). Without a good infrastructure network, problems of both inefficiency and competitiveness may impede economic development (Demurger 2001). Therefore, infrastructure can contribute to economic development, either directly as a measurable final product, or indirectly as an intermediate input, because infrastructure enhances the productivity of all other inputs in producing output (Wang 2002) and it generates positive externalities. In other words, the first impact comes from the construction expenditure, while the second comes from the costs and revenues associated with its operation (Puga 2002).

However, some studies seem to contradict the widely accepted hypothesis that investment in the transport infrastructure always favours economic development and growth (Holtz-Eakin 1994; Holtz-Eakin and Lovely 1996). While a transport infrastructure may encourage development in under-developed regions, its construction alone will not be enough to bring about any desired economic changes (McCann and Shefer 2004). Other factors, such as the resource endowments of the region, the economic climate in the region, the prices of the input factors of production, government policies and underlying infrastructure tend to determine the economic viability of a region, far more than its transport infrastructures (McCann and Shefer 2004; Vickerman 1991). Complementary actions and policies need to be taken to ensure that lagging regions are in a position to profit from the opportunities created by improvements in road and rail transport (European Commission 1999). The benefits of a good transport infrastructure are not necessarily unlimited. If infrastructure investments increase the rate of growth, this does not imply that further investments will increase growth even more (Puga 2002). Some of the more central regions of the EU arguably face constraints on future economic development, despite high levels of transport infrastructure endowment, because of the inability of the structure in place to cope with further economic growth (European Commission 1999). The nature of road infrastructure tends to mean that there are capacity limits, beyond which negative externalities (e.g., congestion costs) start to dominate. Productivity will decline as congestion exceeds a certain threshold level (Glaeser and Kohlhase 2004). Hence, congestion on urban roads may have a negative impact on productivity and thus lead to a negative growth rate. The existing transport infrastructure may become obsolete because of high spatial movements of the population and business activity or a change in technology (McCann and Shefer 2004). According to Puga (2002: 396), a better connection between two regions with different economic development levels not only gives firms in a remote region better access to the inputs and markets of more developed regions, but also makes it easier for firms in richer regions to supply poorer regions at a distance, and can thus harm the industrialisation prospects of less developed areas. Finally, a network of transport infrastructures may indirectly influence regional economic development either positively or negatively, through other public infrastructures such as the public buildings for education and hospitals. It should also be noted that regional spillovers can exist insofar as the network can generate positive or negative external effects beyond the regions where infrastructures are located.

There are many characteristics that distinguish *road* from *rail* infrastructure. First of all, a motorway is a light transport infrastructure, while railway is a heavy one. According to Puga (2002), the road infrastructure is likely to have a more substantial effect on the spatial allocation of production, and hence on regional inequalities. Lynde and Richmond (1992) have argued that public capital can play an important complementary role in the productivity of the regional private sector. The complementary role of road infrastructures in productivity is more significant than the role of rail infrastructure, because the services of the former are mostly freely distributed to private producers. The sunk infrastructure cost of railways (especially high-speed rail) is higher than the cost of roads. The value of the transportation infrastructure can vary significantly, not only among different forms of transport, but also from sector to sector and firm to firm (McCann and Shefer 2004). For example, high-speed rail lines are generally not suitable for the transportation of goods, and are thus unlikely to have much effect on the location of industry (Puga 2002).

But, how can we *measure* transport infrastructures? According to the European Commission (1999), the simplest measure of infrastructure is the physical scale of provision in relation to the potential use. Physical measures of the existing transport stock are used, as in Biehl's (1986) analysis. Road stock is usually measured as the length of road-motorways per square kilometre, while rail capital is measured as the length of railways per square kilometre. Nevertheless, the physical scale measurement does not give a clear picture of infrastructure stock, because it is extremely difficult to approach an estimation of the qualitative characteristics of the infrastructure capacity (Rovolis and Spence 2002). Questions related to infrastructure measurements remain open to analysis in greater depth (European Commission 1999; Haughwout 1998, 2002).[1] Nevertheless, neither the indicators of scale nor of quality can convey how suitable the existing transport endowment in any region is to its regional development needs (European Commission 1999: 122).

The role of public transport infrastructure in regional development in Greece has not been systematically studied, however, there are several pieces of empirical research. The physical landscape of Greece, as argued later in this chapter, has some specific characteristics (mountainous areas, many islands, insularity, etc.) which have dictated the transportation networks in the country (Papadaskalopoulos and Christofakis 2008). Transport infrastructure in Greece has historically developed in several different phases. The most important period of public transport infrastructure construction was probably that of the Trikoupis administration (1882–1892), in which 2600 km of roads, 65 bridges, and most importantly the great bulk of railway network (still in use) were constructed; in 1893, the Corinth Canal was also completed (Christofakis 2007). The next important phase for investment in transport infrastructure was within the Venizelos administration during the first part of the twentieth century. Another phase in which important public works in transport were completed was during the fifties and sixties; actually, the main national highway that connects Athens and Thessaloniki, the backbone connecting Southern and Northern Greece, was constructed during this period.

The most recent developments in public transport infrastructure are interwoven into EU co-funded transportation projects. These projects were financed through the various European Community Support Frameworks, the Cohesion Fund, etc. Papadaskalopoulos and Christofakis (2008: 166) have argued that during this phase, and especially since the mid-nineties, Greek regional development strategy

[1]Indicators of quality are tricky to define. For the rail network, the extent of electrification and the number of separate tracks, which affect both the speed of the service and its carrying capacity, can be used to give a reasonable indication of quality (European Commission 1999: 122).

has shifted its focus from scale—projects to strategic infrastructure projects, many of which were transport infrastructure investment. For instance, during the 1994–1999 planning period the construction of major transport projects began, such as the motorway that connects Patra (in southwest Greece) to the Greek border with Turkey (northeast Greece) via Athens and Thessaloniki, the new Athens international airport 'Eleftherios Venizelos', the Rio-Antirio bridge (connecting Peloponnese to north western Greece), the Aktio-Preveza tunnel, and the significant urban transportation project of Athens Metro.

There are several studies analysing specific transportation projects in Greece, but there are rather few studies investigating the transportation infrastructure impact on Greek regional development. Rovolis and Spence (2002) have examined the effect of infrastructure investment on the productivity of the private sector (at the regional level); their overall finding is that public capital has a positive impact on regional private economy. Lambrinidis et al. (2005) examined the regional allocation of public infrastructure investment; their main findings is that the regional distribution of infrastructure investment was negatively associated with regional product per capita as well as with population size and population density, positively associated with the existing stock of infrastructure capital, and that infrastructure investment was linked to the political cycle (investment increased across prefectures in years preceding national elections). Rodríguez-Pose et al. (2012) show that public investment in infrastructure in general, and public investment in transport infrastructure in particular, had a significant impact on regional growth in Greece, highlighting the primary importance of the spillover effects. Moreover, recent evidence highlights that public infrastructure investment, and more particularly transportation infrastructure, does have an effect on regional specialization in Greece, even though it is not clear the direction that this effect works (Tsekeris and Vogiatzoglou 2013). On one hand, better transportation infrastructure entails improved market access, which in turn leads to a reduction of specialization of manufacturing; on the other hand, enhanced transport infrastructure facilitates higher specialization of manufacturing.

Figures 7.3 and 7.4 show the rail and road network in Greece. There are some important observations. First, the comparative assessment of these figures reveals the disproportional higher priority that has been given to development of the road network in Greece rather than the rail network. In addition the most advanced rail double tracked connection is that between Athens and Thessaloniki. Additionally, the road network is much thicker and covers the entire territory of the country. However, the main corridors of the country are those connecting the large urban centres which serve as the main nodes of economic activity in the country (Thessaloniki, Larissa, Athens, Patra). As a result the transport infrastructure seems to serve, but also to reinforce, the existing development axes and nodes in the country.

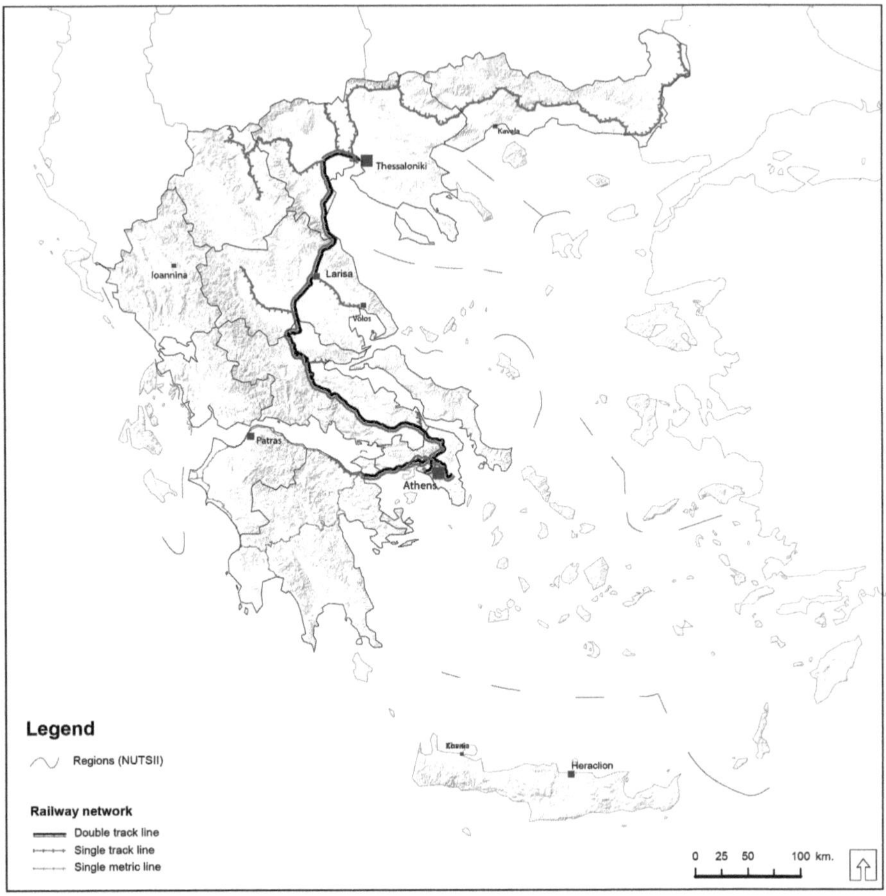

Fig. 7.3 Main rail lines network in Greece. Source: National Statistical Authority of Greece, authors' elaboration

7.5 Do We Need to Look for Additional Drivers?

The links between regional economic development, human capital and transport infrastructure are far less direct. This implies a need for the exploration of additional drivers. But, as there are a large number of drivers, we group them under two camps. The first camp places an emphasis on the physical geography of regions, known as the first nature of geography, while the second one stresses the geography of distance between economic agents, known as the second nature of geography. Using the first nature of geography framework, we will analyse the role of natural endowments, and using the second nature of geography framework, we will discuss the role of urbanisation. It is not the aim of this section to review this vast array of sources, but simply to focus on their impact on regional economic development.

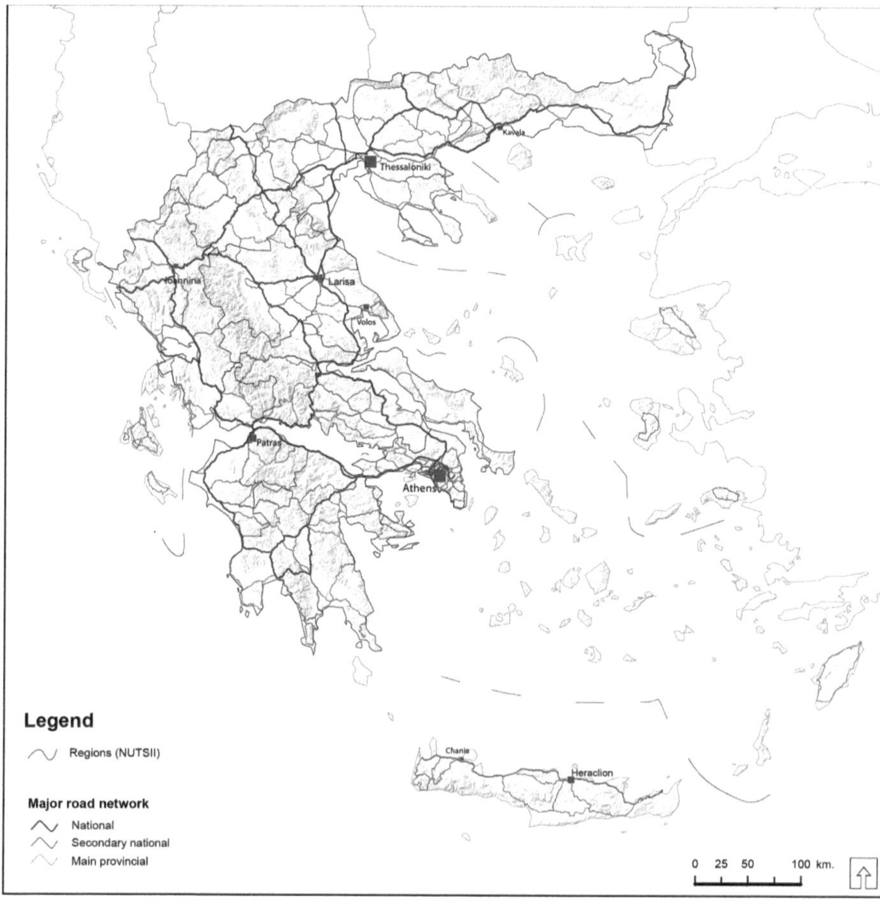

Fig. 7.4 Main road network in Greece. Source: National Statistical Authority of Greece, authors' elaboration

7.5.1 *First Nature of Geography Factors*

Adam Smith made a notable hypothesis that the physical geography of an area can influence its economic performance. Economic activity is geographically concentrated in particular areas with 'good' physical endowments, which induce factor inflows and thus increase income growth. The natural advantages of the regions are not uniformly distributed across all locations, causing regional disparities. Regions generally exploit their comparative advantage and the regional concentration of economic activities arises as regions produce and export products that are relatively intensive in the use of their abundant resource (Kim 1995). Hence, physical geography matters for the allocation of economic activities. Here, we will describe the role of climate, coastal proximity and the physical geography of coasts, and water and rivers.

A region's *climate* affects its economic development. First, disease ecology, agronomic processes and soil fertility can be influenced by climate and may, in turn, alter productivity (Mitchener and McLean 2003). For example, temperate climates favour productivity and economic development. Second, good weather is an amenity. For instance, cities with better weather than that of their countries in general have systematically higher rates of urban population growth (Cheshire and Magrini 2006). Third, changes in the occupational and wage structure are not independent of weather. For example, income inequality is higher in the Mediterranean countries which have many tourist resorts (e.g., the Greek islands) that offer part-time jobs, especially in the summer and for women and young people.

Coastal proximity and *the physical geography of coasts* crucially matter for economic development. Coastal regions enjoy a wider scope of the market than interior regions, which suffer from much higher transport costs. In China, for example, rapid growth and high efficiency take place in coastal cities, adding to the widening disparities of the interior. This shows that the socioeconomic benefits from city growth do not trickle down to rural areas (Naudé 2009). Another example is that landlocked African countries trade up to 92% less with one another than with coastal countries, as they need to cross numerous borders (Coulibaly and Fontagne 2006). The proximity gap of landlocked African countries is further increased by neighbouring countries that are economically performing poorly, often as a result of conflict (Collier 2006). Therefore "[L]andlocked countries may be particularly disadvantaged by their lack of access to the sea, even when they are no farther than the interior parts of coastal countries, because cross-border migration of labour is more difficult than internal migration, infrastructure development across borders is much harder to arrange than similar investments within a country, and coastal countries may have military or economic incentives to impose costs on landlocked countries" (Gallup et al. 1999: 184).

Water and *rivers* also matter for economic development. Access to navigable waterways directly affects productivity through transport costs, nutrition and population density. Africa has the lowest share of irrigated cropland in the developing world due to the relative scarcity of large rivers and alluvial plains (Sachs et al. 2004). Agriculture also depends more on access to fresh water than on access to the sea (Gallup et al. 1999).

In Greece the physical landscape, shown in Fig. 7.5, has, in one sense, dictated the spatial distribution of economic activity; this is apparent if Fig. 7.1 (prefectural GDP per capita) is examined in conjunction with Fig. 7.5, but also with Fig. 7.6 which presents population density in the Greek prefectures.

Figure 7.5 presents the altitude, along with road network and main urban centres across Greece. It is obvious that the physical landscape in very diverse with mountains, plains and islands. Two observations come out of this picture. First, the main urban centres of the mainland are at the coastal areas and located in the eastern part of the country. Comparing this figure with the previous Figs. 7.1, 7.2, 7.3 and 7.4 it is obvious that the there is a correlation between natural geography,

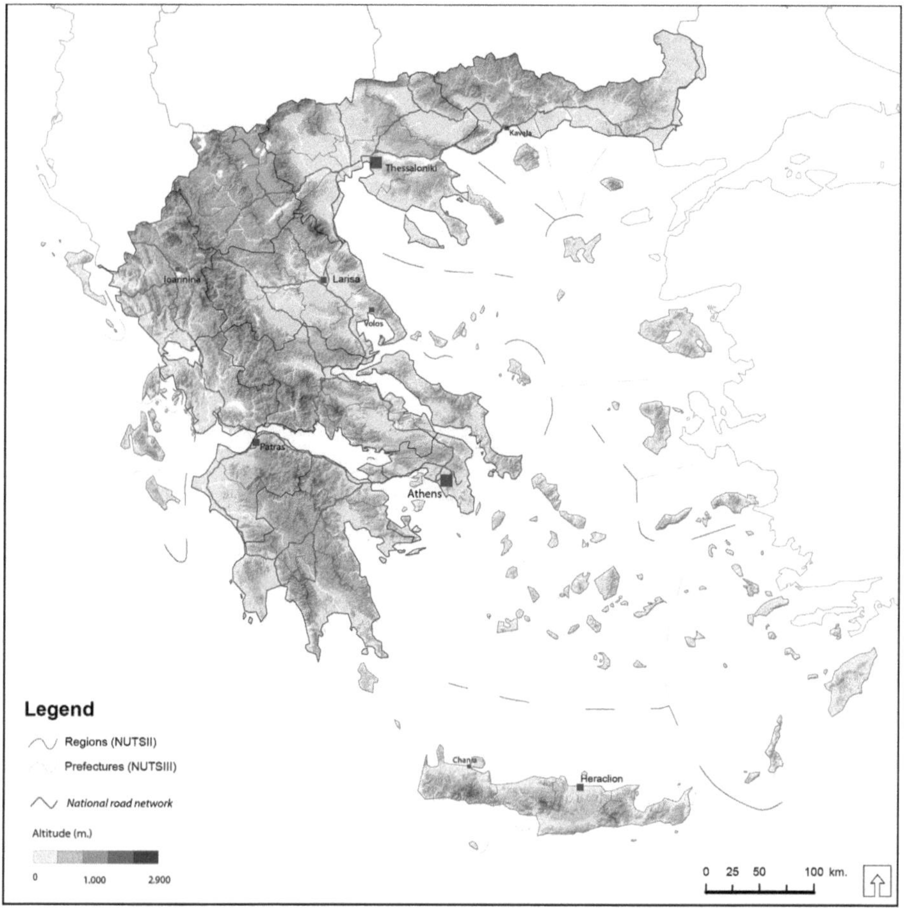

Fig. 7.5 Physical geography of Greece. Source: National Statistical Authority of Greece, authors' elaboration

concentration of people and production activity, transport infrastructures and level of economic development.

7.5.2 *Second Nature of Geography Factors*

Economic theory has ambiguous predictions about the likely effects of urbanisation through efficiency gains from low distance between economic agents. Here, urbanisation relates to features that depend on the spatial interaction between people and/or between firms in an area, but are not necessarily inherited (Naudé 2009). The role played by urbanisation in economic development and growth has been

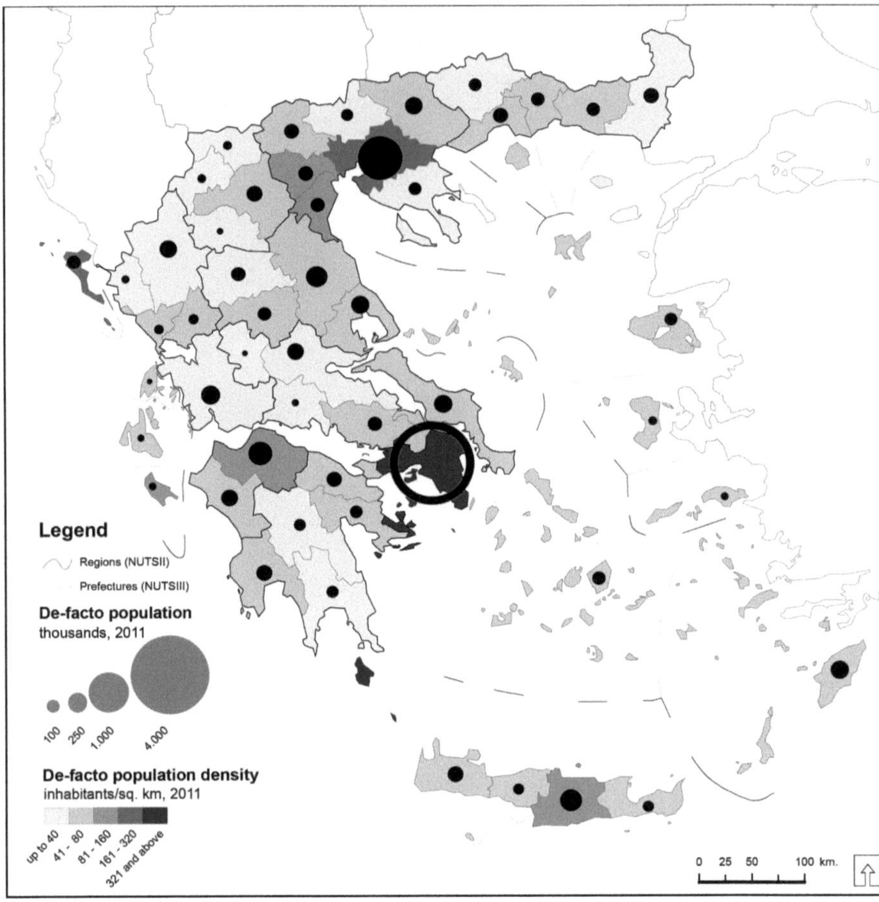

Fig. 7.6 Population density of Greek regions (2011). Source: National Statistical Authority of Greece, Population Census 2011, authors' elaboration

emphasised by urban economists, development economists, growth economists and economic historians, among others. The main conclusion is, without a doubt, that economic development and urbanisation are mutually self-reinforcing processes.

Urbanisation in one region is likely to spur economic development and growth because it reduces the costs of innovation, infrastructure, information and transactions in that region through technological and pecuniary externalities.[2] This trend is evinced most especially in the writings of the new growth and new economic geography theorists. Improvements in transport and communications processes tend to reinforce the clustering of economic activity by widening the market

[2]The former '*deal with the effects of nonmarket interactions that are realised through processes directly affecting the utility of an individual*', while the latter '*are by-products of market interactions*' and '*arise from imperfect competition*' (Fujita and Thisse 2002: 8).

range of any given centre and by helping to spark new rounds of specialisation in established urban areas (Scott and Storper 2003: 582). Cities allow goods, ideas and people to come together for the purposes of exchange and production (Polese 2005). This allows regions to reap the gains of trade and specialisation, increasing economic development and efficiency. Cities foster and facilitate flows of local knowledge, ideas and innovations, the creation of dense socioeconomic networks and the production of behavioural and cultural change. In cities, people have face-to-face contact, which is a fundamental prerequisite of tacit knowledge spillovers. Interaction between people promotes innovation, continually pushing up productivity, growth and efficiency (Jacobs 1970). Although the advent of new information and communication technologies has enormously increased the quantity, complexity and variety of the information and knowledge generated, face-to-face contact complements rather than substitutes for each other form of contact, such as an e-mail contact (McCann and Shefer 2005).

Urbanisation is likely to spur economic development and growth when its economic benefits outweigh its costs. On the one hand, the economic benefits of urbanisation arise due to the presence of knowledge spillovers among firms in an industry, a build-up of knowledge and ideas associated with historical diversity, the local competition of an industry, and the lower infrastructure, information, transaction, training and recruitment costs (Polese 2005). People may move to cities for reasons unrelated to their economic performance; for example, for the schools. On the other hand, the costs of urbanisation rise due to the commuting expenditures within cities, the substantial pollution and the pervasive traffic congestion (Bertinelli and Black 2004). The economic costs also rise from the pressure posed by geographic concentration on urban factor markets that bids up prices and from dispersed demand (Martin and Ottaviano 2001). Therefore, cities act as locations where technological, economic and social innovations are developed (Bräuninger and Niebuhr 2005), enhancing the economic chances and opportunities of working people.

Nevertheless, *reverse causation* in the positive development-urbanisation relationship is a subject of debate. Economic development is likely to foster agglomeration, because as the sector at the origin of innovation expands, new firms tend to locate close to that sector (Martin and Ottaviano 2001). The gains for a particular firm from being located in an urban area are scale economies due to greater market size, flexible and rapid input relationships and the presence of a large and diversified labour pool. The agglomeration of talented and educated individuals in specific areas encourages firms (e.g., research centres) to locate to those areas, and vice versa. According to the new economic geography context, the positive relationship indicates that the centripetal forces (knowledge spillovers and increasing returns to scale) are strong enough to offset the centrifugal forces (congestion and transportation costs).

The *city size* matters for the relationship between urbanisation and development. Large cities depend more on 'urbanisation' economies, while small cities depend more on 'localisation' economies (McCann and Shefer 2004). Large cities are locomotives of the national economies within which they are situated, in that they are the sites of dense masses of interrelated economic activities (Scott and Storper 2003). They also offer a wider selection and better quality of the producer services that are essential to technological innovation than the smaller cities. The level of urbanisation differs across space because only a few regions are able to attract investments in innovation and to acquire production capacity (Scott and Storper 2003). Uneven densities of agglomerations can influence the overall rates of regional economic development through locational interdependencies.

To sum up, conventional theories on the relationship between urbanisation and regional economic development and growth have favoured the view that a circular causation between growth and a concentration of economic activities sets in. However, the causal link between these two processes is not clear cut.

Figure 7.6 shows the NUTS III regions in Greece according to the population size. Regions of Attica (hosting the capital city of Athens) and Thessaloniki (hosting the city of Thessaloniki) which rank first and second in the population density are also regions with relatively higher levels of economic development. Furthermore, the most densely populated areas of the country are located across the eastern costal area of the country, as happens with the distribution of economic development. As a result, the map of population density resembles the development map of the country. Therefore, population density and level of economic development seems be correlated significantly across space. However, the direction of causality between density and development is far from conclusive. Finally, the Greek islands with lower population density show high levels of economic development. This is most probably due to the fact that in this case the first-nature geography impacts on the level of economic prosperity.

It should be mentioned here that the first and the second nature of geography can be complementary. First nature helps to explain initial differences in outcomes across regions, while second nature helps to account for ways in which those initial differences are magnified through positive and negative feedback (Puga 2002). A city might, for example, originally emerge because of cost advantages arising from differentiated geography, but then continue to thrive as a result of agglomeration economies even when the cost advantages have disappeared (Gallup et al. 1999: 184). In other words, first nature geography may give a region an initial advantage, which then becomes amplified by second nature agglomeration forces. Second nature of geography is important in explaining why areas with similar first nature of geography may end up at different levels of productivity and income (Naudé 2009).

7.6 Regional Economic Policy: Equity and Efficiency

The analysis of the relationship between regional economic development, human capital and transport infrastructures provides useful insights that may be vital in the planning of regional policy. Generally speaking, regional policy should seek a synergy in the achievement of both *efficiency* and *equity*. However, this may involve trade-offs in the extent to which the two goals can be attained. The pursuit of these goals is a matter of political choice (Wossmann and Schütz 2006).

The goals of European and Greek educational policy are twofold, encompassing both goals of efficient allocation and goals of equitable distribution. The goals of efficiency and equity are likely to be achieved at each level of formal education and are not trade-offs, since educational policies may advance both efficiency and equity in such a way that each complements the other. The concept of equity is more elusive because it has to do with scientific definitions of fairness and justice (Wossmann and Schütz 2006). Inequality in educational attainment should be tolerated only if it is due to differences in individual levels of effort (e.g., studying), but not if it is due to circumstances which are beyond a person's control (e.g., family background). Hence, a person's expected educational outcome should be a function only of his/her effort, but not of his/her circumstances (Wossmann and Schütz 2006). If this is the case, then individual abilities, along with certain specific traits and qualities, are likely to play the most prominent role in the income-education relationship. The existing studies (Rodríguez-Pose and Tselios 2009; Tselios 2008) highlight the fact that educational policies have an impact on welfare policies. The pursuit of the goal of equitable educational distribution is likely to decrease inequality in productivity and, thus, in income. Policy-makers can also address equity and/or efficiency through public investments. However, policy-makers should take into account the fact that externalities spill over the barriers of regional economies. Welfare and educational policies should account for the spillover effects with adjoining regions. Trade, migration, infrastructure and technological policies may also lead to geographically dependent regions. Factors such as labour force mobility, capital mobility, technology and transportation costs may be particularly important, because they directly affect regional interactions (Le Gallo et al. 2003). Income inequality can affect growth through investment in physical and human capital. Although some growth theories support the notion that more income inequality favours physical capital accumulation, because the rich agents have a higher marginal propensity to save compared to the poor suggests that the relationship between income inequality and growth depends on the stage of economic development (Galor 2000).

The relationship between income inequality within a nation and economic growth can also be investigated through political economy models (Perotti 1992). The basic argument for the negative effect of inequality on growth is that the higher the income inequality, the higher the rate of taxation, the lower the incentive to invest and the lower the growth rate (Bertola 1993). The argument in support of a positive effect, on the other hand, is that the higher the income inequality, the higher the rate of taxation, the larger the expenditure on public education programmes, and thus the higher the public investment in human capital and the higher the growth rate (Aghion and Bolton 1990). Hence, the trade-off between the incentive to invest (which is the fundamental mechanism of a *laissez-faire* economy) and the expenditure on public education programmes (which reflects a fundamental government policy of a command economy) determines the inequality-growth relationship. Finally, the effect of income inequality within a nation on economic growth also depends upon the effect of socio-political instability (Alesina and Perotti 1996). However, this channel plays a key role in the inequality-growth relationship of less-developed countries beset by political and social unrest or violence.

The empirical research that has been carried out on the effect of income inequality on economic growth is less unambiguous than the theory. Some studies find that inequality has a negative effect on growth (e.g., Barro 2000), while others find a positive effect (e.g., Forbes 2000). At a regional level, Rodríguez-Pose and Tselios (2010) have shown that the low interpersonal income and educational inequalities in Europe are likely to increase growth, but the size of their impact is small. European policy-makers, therefore, should take into account the fact that inequality is strongly related to growth, but the scale of the effect is relatively small, and thus the effectiveness of a regional policy to increase growth through inequalities is likely to be low. Educational inequality motivates and enables people to increase their investment in human capital in order to obtain higher educational qualifications, because they require qualifications that are not possessed by everyone so as to benefit from the higher returns on their skills. Income inequality enables people to acquire well-paid jobs, increasing competition in the labour market and, therefore, growth and efficiency. Public policies (e.g., tax policies) aimed at reducing income inequality may not be strong enough to produce negative incentives. The positive inequality-growth relationship highlights the fact that regional policies involve a trade-off, by either advancing growth efficiency to the detriment of educational and income equity or by advancing equity to the detriment of efficiency.

To sum up, the analysis shows the significance of a combined regional policy perspective that would address other policies such as labour market policies, educational policies, social policies, institutional policies and immigration policies. The combined policy should determine joined-up policy solutions, which encompass both the goal of economic efficiency and the goals of equitable income and educational distribution. The extent to which each of these goals should be pursued is a matter of political choice.

7.7 Some Concluding Remarks

The complex relationship between regional development, human capital and transport infrastructure has puzzled economists, economic geographers, and social scientists in general for a long time. The standard measure of regional economic development is GDP per capita. However, there are many conceptual problems with this. Even the definition of the spatial analysis unit, the region, is not always unproblematic; in the Greek context, for instance, the capital city, Athens, is much smaller than its Functional Urban Region.

Two of the major 'forces' that determine regional economic development are human capital (i.e., educational attainment) and transport infrastructure (i.e., road and rail infrastructure). There are however some other factors that shape and moderate regional economic development. As we have argued here, physical geography, a first nature geographical factor (in New Economic Geography parlance), and urbanization, a second nature geography factor, have influenced the economic development of Greek regions. The analysis of all these drivers of regional economic development should inform both national and European policies that affect directly, (for instance transport networks), or indirectly, (for instance, education policy), the fate of the regions.

Acknowledgements This chapter is based on research that has been co-financed by the European Union (European Social Fund) and Greek national funds through the Operational Program "Education and Lifelong Learning" of the National Strategic Reference Framework—Research Funding Program: THALES. Investing in knowledge society through the European Social Fund (grant number MIS 380421). We also thank Panagiotis Pantazis (MSc in Planning and Regional Development, PhD student) for the construction of the figures.

References

Aghion P, Bolton P (1990) Government domestic debt and the risk of default: a political economic model of the strategic role of debt. In: Dornbusch R, Draghi M (eds) Public debt management: theory and history. Cambridge University Press, Cambridge. Chapter 11

Alesina A, Perotti R (1996) Income distribution, political instability, and investment. Eur Econ Rev 40:1203–1228

Allen J, van der Velden R (2001) Educational mismatches versus skill mismatches: effects on wages, job satisfaction, and on-the-job search. Oxf Econ Pap New Ser 53:434–452

Armstrong HW, Taylor J (2000) Regional economics and policy. Blackwells, Oxford

Aschauer DA (1989) Is public expenditure productive. J Monet Econ 23:177–200

Barro RJ (2000) Inequality and growth in a panel of countries. J Econ Growth 5:5–32

Becker GS (1962) Investment in human capital – a theoretical analysis. J Polit Econ 70:9–49

Becker GS, Barro RJ (1988) A reformulation of the economic theory of fertility. Q J Econ 103:1–25

Becker GS, Tomes N (1986) Human capital and the rise and fall of families. J Labor Econ 4:S1–S39

Benporath Y (1980) The F-connection – families, friends, and firms and the organization of exchange. Popul Dev Rev 6:1–30

Bertinelli L, Black D (2004) Urbanization and growth. J Urban Econ 56:80–96

Bertola G (1993) Factor shares and savings in endogenous growth. Am Econ Rev 83:1184–1198

Biehl D (1986) The contribution of infrastructure to regional development. Final Report of the Infrastructure Studies Group to the Commission of the European Communities, Office for Official Publications of the European Communities, Luxembourg

Bourdieu P (1993) Sociology in question. Sage, London

Bräuninger M, Niebuhr A (2005) Convergence, spatial interaction and agglomeration effects in the EU: HWWA discussion paper 322, Hamburg Institute of International Economics

Centre for Educational Research and Innovation and Organisation for Economic Co-operation and Development (1998) Human capital investment: an international comparison. Organisation for Economic Co-operation and Development, Paris

Cheshire PC, Hay D (1988) Urban problems in western europe: an economic analysis. Unwin Hyman, London

Cheshire PC, Magrini S (2006) Population growth in european cities: weather matters – but only nationally. Reg Stud 40:23–37

Christofakis M (2007) Transports and regional development: the transport infrastructures policy (in Greek). Dionikos, Athens
Coleman JS (1988) Social capital in the creation of human capital. Am J Sociol 94:S95–S120
Collier P (2006) African growth: why a 'big push'? J Afr Econ 15:188–211
Coulibaly S, Fontagne L (2006) South-South trade: geography matters. J Afr Econ 15:313–341
De Serres A (2003) Structural policies and growth: a non-technical overview: OECD economics working paper no. 355. Organization for Economic Co-Operation and Development (OECD) – Economics Department (ECO)
Deichmann U, Fay M, Koo J, Lall SV (2004) Economic structure, productivity, and infrastructure quality in Southern Mexico. Ann Reg Sci 38:361–385
Demurger S (2001) Infrastructure development and economic growth: an explanation for regional disparities in China? J Comp Econ 29:95–117
Duffydeno KT, Eberts RW (1991) Public infrastructure and regional economic development – a simultaneous equations approach. J Urban Econ 30:329–343
European Commission (1999) The European regions: sixth periodic report on the socio-economic situation in the regions of the European Union. Official Publication Office, Luxembourg
European Commission (2004) A new partnership for cohesion: convergence, competitiveness, cooporation. Third report on economic and social cohesion. Office for Official Publications of the European Communities, Luxembourg
Forbes KJ (2000) A reassessment of the relationship between inequality and growth. Am Econ Rev 90:869–887
Fujita M, Thisse J-F (2002) Economics of agglomeration: cities, industrial location, and regional growth. Cambridge University Press, Cambridge
Gallup JL, Sachs JD, Mellinger AD (1999) Geography and economic development. Int Reg Sci Rev 22:179–232
Galor O (2000) Income distribution and the process of development. Eur Econ Rev 44:706–712
Glaeser EL, Kohlhase JE (2004) Cities, regions and the decline of transport costs. Pap Reg Sci 83:197–228
Greene KV, Neenan WB, Scott CD (1974) Fiscal interactions in a metropolitan area. D. C. Heath, Lexington, MA
Hanushek EA, Kimko DD (2000) Schooling, labor-force quality, and the growth of nations. Am Econ Rev 90:1184–1208
Hartog J (2000) Over-education and earnings: where are we, where should we go? Econ Educ Rev 19:131–147
Haughwout AF (1998) Aggregate production functions, interregional equilibrium, and the measurement of infrastructure productivity. J Urban Econ 44:216–227
Haughwout AF (2002) Public infrastructure investments, productivity and welfare in fixed geographic areas. J Public Econ 83:405–428
Henderson JV, Shalizi Z, Venables AJ (2001) Geography and development. J Econ Geogr 1:81–105
Holtz-Eakin D (1994) Public-sector capital and the productivity puzzle. Rev Econ Stat 76:12–21
Holtz-Eakin D, Lovely ME (1996) Scale economies, returns to variety, and the productivity of public infrastructure. Reg Sci Urban Econ 26:105–123
Jacobs J (1970) The economy of cities. Cape, London
Kim S (1995) Expansion of markets and the geographic distribution of economic activities – the trends in US regional manufacturing structure, 1860-1987. Q J Econ 110:881–908
Lambrinidis M, Psycharis Y, Rovolis A (2005) Regional allocation of public infrastructure investment: the case of Greece. Reg Stud 39:1231–1244
Le Gallo J, Ertur C, Baumont C (2003) A spatial econometric analysis of convergence across European regions, 1980-1995. In: Fingleton B (ed) European regional growth. Springer, Berlin
Lynde C, Richmond J (1992) The role of public capital in production. Rev Econ Stat 74:37–44
Martin P, Ottaviano GIP (2001) Growth and agglomeration. Int Econ Rev 42:947–968
McCann P, Shefer S (2004) Location, agglomeration and infrastructure. Pap Reg Sci 83:177–196

McCann P, Shefer S (2005) Agglomeration, economic geography and regional growth. Pap Reg Sci 84:301–309
Mitchener KJ, McLean IW (2003) The productivity of US states since 1880. J Econ Growth 8:73–114
Naudé W (2009) Geography, transport and Africa's proximity gap. J Transp Geogr 17:1–9
OECD (2003) Seizing the benefits from ICT in a digital economy. Meeting of the OECD Council at Ministerial Level, Paris, France
Papadaskalopoulos A, Christofakis M (2008) Transport and regional development: the pattern of spatial development in Greece due to the impact of the new transportation corridors. In: Coccossis H, Psycharis Y (eds) Regional analysis and policy: the Greek experience. Physica-Verlag, Heidelberg
Perotti R (1992) Income distribution, politics, and growth. Am Econ Rev 82:311–316
Petrakos G, Psycharis Y (2015a) Regional development in Greece (in Greek). Kritiki, Athens
Petrakos G, Psycharis Y (2015b) The spatial aspects of economic crisis in Greece. Camb J Reg Econ Soc 9:137–152
Polese M (2005) Cities and national economic growth: a reappraisal. Urban Stud 42:1429–1451
Puga D (2002) European regional policies in light of recent location theories. J Econ Geogr 2:373–406
Putnam RD (1993) The prosperous community: social capital and public life. Am Prospect 13:35–42
Rodríguez-Pose A, Tselios V (2009) Education and income inequality in the regions of the European Union. J Reg Sci 49:411–437
Rodríguez-Pose A, Tselios V (2010) Inequalities in income and education and regional economic growth in western Europe. Ann Reg Sci 44:349–375
Rodríguez-Pose A, Psycharis Y, Tselios V (2012) Public investment and regional growth and convergence: evidence from Greece. Pap Reg Sci 91:543–568
Rovolis A, Spence N (2002) Promoting regional economic growth in Greece by investing in public infrastructure. Environ Plann C Gov Policy 20:393–419
Sachs JD, McArthur JW, Schmidt-Traub G, Kruk M, Bahadur C, Faye M, McCord G (2004) Ending Africa.s poverty trap. Brook Pap Econ Act 1:117–240
Schuller T (2000) The complementary roles of human and social capital. In: International symposium on the contribution of human and social capital to sustained economic growth and well-being, Quebec City, Canada
Schultz TW (1961) Investment in human capital. Am Econ Rev 51:1–17
Schultz TW (1962) Reflections on investment in man. J Polit Econ 70:1–8
Schultz TW (1963) The economic value of education. Columbia University Press, New York
Scott AJ, Storper M (2003) regions, globalization, development. Reg Stud 37:579–593
Sianesi B, Van Reenen J (2003) The returns to education: macroeconomics. J Econ Surv 17:157–200
Spence AM (1973) Job market signaling. Q J Econ 87:355–374
Stimson RJ, Stough RR, Roberts BH (2006) Regional economic development: analysis and planning strategy. Springer, Berlin
Tsekeris T, Vogiatzoglou K (2013) Regional specialization and public infrastructure investments: empirical evidence from Greece. Centre of Planning and Economic Research, Discussion Papers, No. 130
Tselios V (2008) Income and educational inequalities in the regions of the European Union: geographical spillovers under welfare state restrictions. Pap Reg Sci 87:403–430
Vickerman RW (1991) Infrastructure and regional development. Pion, London
Wang EC (2002) Public infrastructure and economic growth: a new approach applied to East Asian economies. J Policy Model 24:411–435
Wossmann L, Schütz G (2006) Efficiency and equity in the European education and training systems: analytical report for the European commission, prepared by the European Expert Network on Economics of Education, Mimeo

Vassilis Tselios is an Assistant Professor of Regional Economics at the Department of Planning and Regional Development of the University of Thessaly. He is an economic geographer (PhD, London School of Economics) and his research centres around the spatial analysis of socioeconomic phenomena. He was a Lecturer in Economic Geography at the University of Southampton, a Research Associate at the Department of Economic Geography of the University of Groningen and at the Spatial Economics Research Centre of the London School of Economics and a Lecturer in Economic Geography at Newcastle University. Vassilis has also worked for the World Bank as Consultant for the International Trade Department.

Antonios Rovolis (economist, B.A. Athens, MA Sussex, PhD LSE) is associate professor of Spatial and Urban Economics at the Department of Economic and Regional Development, Panteion University of Athens. He has worked as a research fellow at the Queen Mary College, University of London, at the Institute of Regional Development and at the Institute of Urban Environment and Human Resources, Panteion University of Athens, and he has taught at Thessaly University and Harokopio University of Athens. He has been a visiting research fellow at Toronto University, McGill University, York University (Canada) and Concordia University.

Yannis Psycharis is a Professor of Regional Economic Analysis at the Department Economic and Regional Development, Panteion University of Social and Political Sciences, Athens, Greece. He has also taught at the Department of Planning and Regional Development of the University of Thessaly in Volos (2000–2009). He had been Senior Research Fellow at the LSE (2007–2008). He is the former Director of the Greek National School of Public Administration and Local Government (2010–2012) and is currently President of the Greek section of the European Regional Science Association. His research interests include regional economic analysis, regional policy, regional public finance and public administration.

Chapter 8
Globalisation, Delocalisation and Development: Conceptual Framework and Impacts on Southern European Countries

Athanasios Kalogeresis

JEL Classification F14 • F21 • F23

8.1 Delocalisation: Theoretical and Methodological Issues

8.1.1 General Framework and Tendencies

In the foreword to the 2013 edition of the European Competitiveness Report (European Commission 2013) the Director General of DG Enterprise and Industry, Daniel Calleja Crespo voiced a rather disturbing warning about the future of the European Economy: '*. . .(W)hat is new however is that in the last decade the shift away from manufacturing in Europe has accelerated, reaching a critical threshold below which the sustainability of the European economic and social model might be at risk.*'(European Commission 2013, p. 3)

The financial crisis and the growing relevance of Global Value Chains (GVC) for the sourcing of a growing share of tradable goods (or components of goods) seems to imply growing delocalisation pressures to countries and regions, particularly if the latter is viewed as a vehicle of deindustrialisation, adversely impacting exports of manufactures, which are considered central in the recovery of the EU economy (European Commission 2013).

The main aim of the chapter is the analysis of delocalisation in Southern Europe and its implications on the region's recovery and economic vitality. Apart from discussing the role of technology intensity and product quality/complexity, we aim to analyse the role of geography as a factor of resilience.

Methodologically, due to the complex nature of the concept of delocalisation, the article utilizes a wide array of secondary and some primary data. The former

A. Kalogeresis (✉)
School of Spatial Planning and Development, Faculty of Engineering, Aristotle University of Thessaloniki, Thessaloniki, Greece
e-mail: kaloger@plandevel.auth.gr

M. Fonseca, U. Fratesi (eds.), *Regional Upgrading in Southern Europe*, Advances in Spatial Science, DOI 10.1007/978-3-319-49818-8_8

aims to analyse various facets of delocalisation, such as international trade, FDI, outsourcing and trade in value added. The main sources of the secondary data used are UNCTAD for FDI and trade related data, EUROSTAT for outsourcing data and OECD for trade in value added data. In addition to secondary macro data, the article attempts to analyse locational responses to the crisis pressures of a small sample of Greek firms.

The last few decades have been a period of significant redrawing of the global economic landscape; for instance, the share of the global total Gross Value Added (GVA) of developing economies increased from 21% in 2003 to 35% in 2011 (UNCTADStat). However, in many ways this is a landscape often reminiscent of the old international divisions of labour, since there are considerable parts of the word where growth appears stagnant. The Gross Value Added (GVA) of the developing countries of Africa, America and Oceania remained fairly steady throughout the period, as opposed to the Asian developing countries, which currently account for 70% of the developing countries total, up from 51% in 1970 (UNCTADStat, own calculations).

This change is nowhere more evident than in the analysis of the trends of industry, which is in the forefront of developing countries catch-up efforts, and the strides made by specific countries. By 2011 46% of the global industry GVA was accounted for by developing countries (up from 15% in 1970), while a single developing country (China) accounted for 17% of global industry GVA, having doubled its share in less than a decade (the respective share in 2001 was 7%, (UNCTADStat, own calculation).

This huge shift is, to a very large extent, due to a changing pattern of global trade, where trade in final products is gradually becoming less significant, while trade in intermediate products, parts and more recently, tasks (Grossman and Rossi-Hansberg 2008) is fast becoming the main component of global trade flows. During the last decades trade in intermediate goods and services has fluctuated between 50% and 75%, accounting for the largest part of total trade (Sturgeon and Memedovic 2011; WTO 2013, p. 183).

An interesting point is made by Zhu and Pickles (2014) in that the development of GVCs and global production networks (GPNs) (both of which are inextricably tied to delocalisation) in developing countries is widely considered to have benefited (or taken advantage of) the governance capacity deficits of these countries, as globalisation *'destabilized the governance of nation state and local institutions through its footloose sourcing practices'* (Zhu and Pickles 2014, p. 44). In many ways the same can be considered to be true also for developed countries, as the types of activities relocated have apparently changed during the last decade from predominantly labour intensive, low cost activities to a more varied mix encompassing all business activities, even those that were traditionally considered to be the basis of developed counties' competitive advantage, such as R&D and headquarters (Contractor et al. 2010; Manning et al. 2008). The increasingly footloose character of such activities causes increasing concerns in developed countries, putting intermediate regimes such as those of Southern European countries under pressure (Kalogeresis and Labrianidis 2010).

8.1.2 What Is Delocalisation?

Delocalisation is a term that has come to mean quite a few, often rather different, things. Delocalisation can correspond to the sum of FDI and international subcontracting (Amighini and Rabellotti 2006; Labrianidis and Kalantaridis 2004); it can also be identified with the diffusion of an industry or activity to a 'less developed place', implying that this place lies outside the country of origin, although not always necessarily so (Storper 2009). To Pickles and Smith (2011, p. 171) the term refers to something involving '*...the fragmentation of tasks and the division of labour across geographical space, often with the relocation of labour-intensive elements of the production process to lower-cost locations, while core competencies (product design, network coordination, brand ownership, fabric research and development, and so on) are assumed to be more spatially inflexible, tied as they are to human capital resources and knowledge networks*'. Zhu and Pickles (2014, p. 45) identify delocalisation with outsourcing, or the 'Go out' policy of Chinese manufacturing towards the vast Chinese hinterland.

Why, then, didn't all of these authors use the relatively clearer and more straightforward term 'relocation' (OECD 2007)? We believe there are two main reasons. The first is that relocation is a term that focuses on the individual firm. The second is that the role of geography as a crucial determinant of the location of industry is implicit and often explicit in the use of the term delocalisation. Here geography extends far beyond the natural or even human resources of a specific territory to the social or political trajectories shaping the decisions of firms. As such, firms are the building blocks of local or trans-local production systems and delocalisation can be seen as the movement of '*...production activities away from the local and/or national system*' (Mazzanti et al. 2011, p. 421).

We understand *delocalisation as the spatial restructuring of industry on an international scale*. However, as we analyse further down, the establishment of some type of foreign activity is neither a necessary nor a sufficient condition for the existence of delocalisation.

As the term suggests, delocalisation must be understood in relation to localisation. In economics or geographical economics literature, localisation usually refers to 'spatial co-localisation' (Antonietti et al. 2013; Holmes 1999), therefore making empirical verification rather easy. In Economic Geography the term refers to specific type of economies (localisation economies), shaping industrial agglomeration or spatial clustering (Amin and Thrift 1992; Boschma and Lambooy 1999; Malmberg and Maskell 2002), two terms whose interpretations remain quite 'fuzzy' (Malmberg and Maskell 2002; Markusen 1999). Hence, localisation refers to the existence of networks of relations that bind or embed firms to wider institutional assemblages or regions.

Although delocalisation is shaped by the relocation decisions of individual firms, very often environmental (territorial) or sectoral factors are considered to be equally, if not more important than the individual decision making firm. Hence, in some of the literature on delocalisation (Bellandi and Caloffi 2008; Biggiero

2006; Sammarra and Belussi 2006) it is the territorial system that constitutes the main object of enquiry. Although territorial systems may be the most appropriate level of analysis to identify the impacts of delocalisation, they are extremely difficult to study using secondary data. It is firms as actors with '...*a tangible and important stake in the business environments where they are located in ways that go far beyond taxes, electricity costs, and wage rates*' (Porter 2000, p. 16), which constitute the main building blocks of local economies. Issues such as firm embededdness, local forward and backward linkages, and knowledge creation, circulation and sharing highlight the significance of the firm to local productive systems and hence to regions. Through this viewpoint, a firm delocalizes when it eliminates local linkages, or becomes less embedded.

8.1.3 How (and Why) Do Firms Delocalize?

Firms delocalize to take advantage of more favourable cost structures in other areas or countries. Technological innovations and lower trade costs allow production to be fragmented and components to be produced in geographically distant areas, creating new opportunities for international specialisation by tapping into appropriate institutional settings or resource endowments. The welfare gains come from the more efficient utilisation of resources brought about by component specialisation (Arndt 1999). More recent work (Grossman and Rossi-Hansberg 2008) has highlighted the possibility of even finer divisions of labour into 'tasks' and the welfare implications of such extreme fragmentation.

Conceptually, the decision to delocalize can be explained either through the viewpoint of the transaction cost theory, or the resource approach, or the interplay of the two.

Each firm is a bundle of resources, which constitute the building block of the many variants of Penrose's (1959) resource–based theory aiming to analyse firm growth. For Penrose, productive resources, and especially the services they offer are not general and unspecified categories accessible to all firms. Hence, they are particularly important, since they constitute the base of firm differentiation. While resources may be similar, the way firms combine their services can hardly be identical, explaining the existence of different products.

The unique combinations of firms' resources, accumulated experience, entrepreneurship and unused productive services can explain the direction of expansion at home or abroad (Kay 2000). In this case the critical decision about whether to make or buy largely depends on whether the firm's capabilities are superior to those of potential suppliers.

The alternative explanation can be traced to the work of Coase (1937) on the boundaries of the firm: outside the firm, it is price movements that direct production, which is coordinated through a series of exchange transactions in the market; within a firm, these market transactions are eliminated and it is the entrepreneur–coordinator who directs production.

On the basis of the works of Williamson (1975, 1985), for whom transaction costs, asset specificity and incomplete contracts play a central role, Grossman and Helpman (2002) argue that the decision about whether to make or buy is a trade–off between the cost of running a large and less specialized organisation and the costs involved in finding partners and incomplete contracting, which, in turn depends on asset specificity.

A constant reconfiguration of the boundaries of the firm through external (Cowling and Sugden 1987; Dicken and Thrift 1992) or internal (O'Neill and Gibson-Graham 1999) pressures makes the choice of mode of delocalisation less relevant. We do not consider FDI and outsourcing to be equipollent, primarily since the resources required for each of these can differ quite substantially. However, there are various mechanisms at work that are constantly altering this imparity, such as the feverish competition between countries and regions in attracting FDI and the constant efforts to create more liberal and hospitable international FDI regimes. Therefore, rather than studying FDI or outsourcing, and while we consider the choice of mode as important, we are interested in explaining the decision of firms to move part of their activities abroad and we are searching for underlying mechanisms and implications that are common in the two modes.

Of particular interest are efforts to combine the two seemingly opposing views (the resource-based and the transaction costs) of the firm (Argyres 1996; Broedner et al. 2009; Jacobides and Winter 2005) aiming to cover a wider array of firms, sectors and environments.

Further insight into why production systems delocalize can be gained from understanding the factors leading to localisation.

Firms' decisions about where to locate depend on the ways technology and knowledge spread in the global economy and innovation is created. The main sources of localisation are Marshall's (1920) local externalities based on horizontal and vertical specialisation and Arrow's (1962) learning by doing, highlighting the role of being at, or near where 'things happen'. The role of knowledge is clearly central in understanding these processes, and despite a long history of efforts to explain the growth inducing character of technology and knowledge (Arrow 1962; Young 1928) it was Romer (1986) and the endogenous growth model that established increasing returns as the principal source of long-run economic growth under resource constraints. The increasing returns of knowledge depend on its character as a non-rival and partially excludable good, both of which imply that it can be reused without loss and flow everywhere.

Although these three types of externalities are usually treated as one single force behind agglomeration and growth, collectively called 'Marshall–Arrow–Romer' (MAR) externalities, operating through knowledge spillovers in an industry (Glaeser et al. 1992; Henderson 1997), Storper (2009) argued that Romer (R) externalities should be treated separately from the Marshall–Arrow (MA) component. Specifically, he claimed that the MA externalities account for the creation of innovation through knowledge spillovers and exchange at 'definite territorial scales'. Then, the Romer model explains how the initial local monopoly rents are bid away by competition at the economy wide level.

Therefore, innovation tends to be created in specific locations as a result of MA externalities. The localized character of such innovation will tend to give rise to cumulative processes of innovation and growth, as the regions that initially create such monopoly rents will most likely be better positioned for the next wave of innovations. However, at the same time R externalities will tend to spread at economy-wide or even international levels, leading to an upward growth spiral of innovation creation (by leading regions) and catch up (by lagging regions). Convergence in such a system is not guaranteed, although there may be occasional episodes of convergence, or even a—not smooth—sequence of convergence as countries make the transition from a low level of development to a rich country group (Puga and Venables 1999).

8.1.4 Causes of Delocalisation

Delocalisation usually involves some kind of physical relocation of some of the firm's activities, but not always; i.e., firms switching from manufacturing to trade or other service activities usually become detached from the local production system. Conversely, the relocation of an activity does not by definition constitute delocalisation. Consider for example a firm deciding to relocate a labour intensive activity to a lower labour cost country. The impact of such a movement is by no means straightforward. At the level of the firm itself, the movement may result in the freeing of scarce or underutilized resources; at the level of the cluster (and consequently, the locality), internationalisation may lead to either delocalisation or relocalisation, as a result of the complex interactions between local and global systems (Amin and Thrift 1992). According to Bellandi and Caloffi (2008) the outcome is a result of two types of variables. The first is the time horizon of the movement (i.e., short-term market strategies as opposed to long-term industrial and trade strategies), while the second is the industrial configuration, referring to the extent of 'co-ordination' of local and foreign firms and clusters: the more concerted the move, the more likely both localities and clusters will benefit, leading to delocalisation.

This implies that there may well be instances of unexpected outcomes, e.g., when some type of movement leads to relocalisation instead of delocalisation; in other words, to the strengthening of a local productive system instead of its weakening. Naturally, such phenomena largely depend on the wider systemic changes, such as the largely ongoing international financial crisis.

The viewpoint and timeframe determine the perceived impacts of delocalisation. One possible scenario is described by Storper (2009), contesting the dominant idea in local and regional studies that "... *the more a supply chain is localized, the more developmental benefits for a locality can be captured over time through expansion of the activity*". Apart from the ample evidence against the validity of such a thought (Arndt 1999; Puga and Venables 1999) in a long term perspective, a policy aimed at localizing value chains would block the mechanism of comparative advantage, severely limiting welfare for all countries involved. This idea expresses a fundamental bias against long-distance linkages and commodity chains that are highly fragmented over different territorial jurisdictions. In simple accounting terms, it has some short-term empirical validity, in that the more localized the value chain, the more of it will be captured locally for a given increment of increase in output of the activity in question.

Going from the development perspective to the other end of the spectrum, i.e., the firm, allows for a more complete understanding of the impacts of delocalisation. Studying the firm allows for an appreciation of how outsourcing, delocalisation or relocalisation, viewed as determinants of reconfiguration of local productive systems, which usually (but not always) take the form of '*sectoral and activity "succession" and intrasectoral innovation, improvements in quality, and vertical differentiation*' (Storper 2009, p. 3) affect local productivity levels, which is what eventually matters towards local or regional development.

Empirically, the relationship between outsourcing and productivity seems to point to an overall positive relationship. Most of the studies find a strong association between firm productivity and the decision to get involved with foreign sourcing (Fariñas and Martín-Marcos 2010; Tomiura 2007), and a positive impact of outsourcing on labour and total factor productivity (Amiti and Wei 2005; Girma and Görg 2004; Görg et al. 2008; Görg and Hanley 2003; Jabbour 2010).

Most of this, generally optimistic, literature ignores issues of welfare distribution and justice. Hence, labour productivity gains usually come from high skilled labour, while labour demand is considerably reduced due to offshore outsourcing of materials (Görg and Hanley 2005). In addition, Houseman (2007) voices her concern about problems in the measurement of productivity, as well as the relatively more serious inconsistency between the surges of productivity in the American economy during the last decades and the level of wages in the economy.

On the other hand, a pure transaction costs view, according to which cost reductions through value chain disintegration and relocation will lead to overall firm productivity increases, and, in the long run, create a regional advantage, may be considerably limiting, given the extensive nature of market imperfections and failure. Along these lines Broedner et al. (2009) argue that '*the reduction of the vertical range of manufacturing ... has a strong negative impact on a firm's labour productivity*'. Apparently, there are some limits beyond which further disintegration will affect a firm's competences.

It is more or less clear that directly measuring delocalisation is a daunting task. Numerous international organisations (Eurostat 2015, OECD, UNECE, and WTO) are directing their efforts towards various aspects of GVCs in order to overcome this problem (Sturgeon 2013).

8.2 Delocalisation in Southern Europe: A Macro Approach

The picture for Southern Europe is a highly fragmented one, since there is very little relevant data that covers all four countries (Portugal, Spain, Italy and Greece). Using several data sources on FDI, trade (particularly changes in trade specialisation), Trade in Value Added, European Outsourcing and data from a survey studying the delocalisation of Greek firms, we will try to assess the level and impacts of delocalisation.

8.2.1 Foreign Direct Investment (FDI)

The first metric used is FDI. Outward and inward FDI depend on rather different factors. Inward FDI depends on the wider global trends and is highly conditioned by the receiving country attractiveness, which, in turn, depends on a vast array of factors (Dunning 1998, 1993; Dunning and Lundan 2008). Incumbent FDI may be driven out of the economy especially if it is of the market-seeking type, given a shrinking domestic demand. On the other hand, resource seeking FDI may benefit if the cost of the resource(s) that initially attracted them to the country declines. In the case of firms in search of host countries, crises often create significant opportunities in the form of fire-sale FDI as has been the case with the Asian crisis, and Mexico before that (Krugman 2000).

The impact of a crisis on outward FDI will tend to depend on: the type of FDI (horizontal—vertical), with the former operating as a shock absorber, particularly if the host country is not affected by the crisis, while the latter can be expected to be more severely affected, as low domestic demand may lead to lower demand for the intermediate product supplied by the affiliate. The more tied the affiliate is to the requirements of the parent the greater the pressure caused by the crisis will be. Another significant factor is the embededdness of the firm in its home economy. Highly internationalized MNEs will tend to scan the domestic and foreign environments for opportunities and threats. Having long absorbed any 'foreignness' disadvantages, such firms may more easily decide to move core (in terms of value creation and appropriation) parts abroad.

The Hellenic Bottling Company (Ball and Stamouli 2012) and FAGE (Ball and Stamouli 2012; GreekReporter.com 2012), Greece's largest bottling and dairy companies respectively, relocated their headquarters in 2012 to Switzerland and Luxembourg, while the Italian company FIAT (now FIAT-Chrysler), one of the largest car manufacturers globally, recently moved its headquarters to the Netherlands and its tax domicile to Britain (Flak 2014). In all cases the firms claimed that production and employment in the former home countries would not be affected, however the overall impacts of such moves are always hard to assess, not least because that usually evades the crucial 'what if' question, i.e., what would happen had the relocations not taken place.

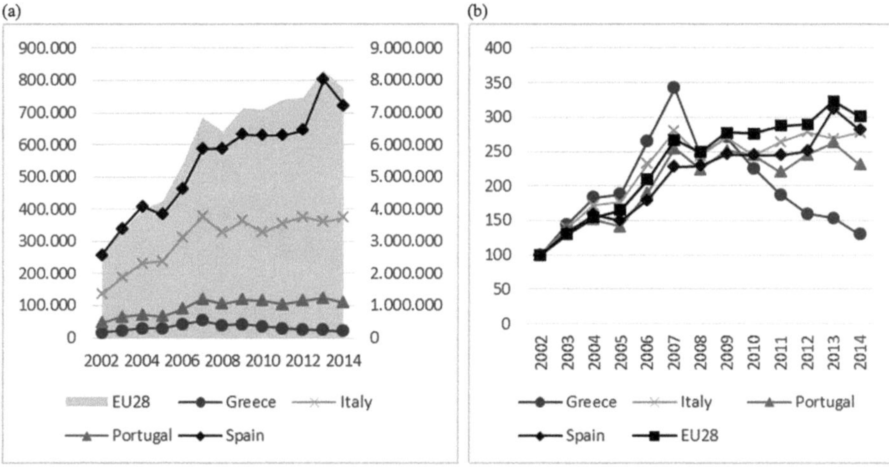

Fig. 8.1 FDI inward stocks (**a**) and their evolution (**b**) (2002 = 100). Source: UNCTAD (2015a)

Inward FDI (in terms of stocks) seems to have followed a pattern resembling that of "Developed Europe" as a whole, although the wider Southern European region seems to recover more slowly than Europe (Fig. 8.1). Greece is the country which fluctuates the most, displaying a sharp pre-crisis increase, followed by a prolonged decline post-crisis. The reluctance of foreign direct investors to invest in Greece can be an indication of the fact that the continuing debt crisis is mostly a trust crisis. In terms of the regulatory framework Greece, Portugal, Italy and Spain (in that order) are systematically the worst performing European countries in terms of quality and efficiency of their regulatory system[1]

The quality of the regulatory system is reflected in the perceived international competitiveness of the countries. According to the World Economic Forum's rankings, the four Southern European countries highlight the disparities in competitiveness in Europe as a whole (Schwab 2013, p. 27).

On the contrary, outward FDI seems to have risen in the area more quickly than in "Developed Europe" (Fig. 8.2), and, with the exception of Spain, it seems to have been less affected by the crisis. This should not be unexpected since widespread austerity has led to a 'massive negative demand shock' (Kitson et al. 2011, p. 299) leading firms to search for foreign markets.

[1]According the World Bank's 'Doing Business' 2013 rankings (http://www.doingbusiness.org/rankings), among 31 OCED countries, Greece, Italy, Span and Portugal were ranked at 30, 29, 27 and 19 respectively.

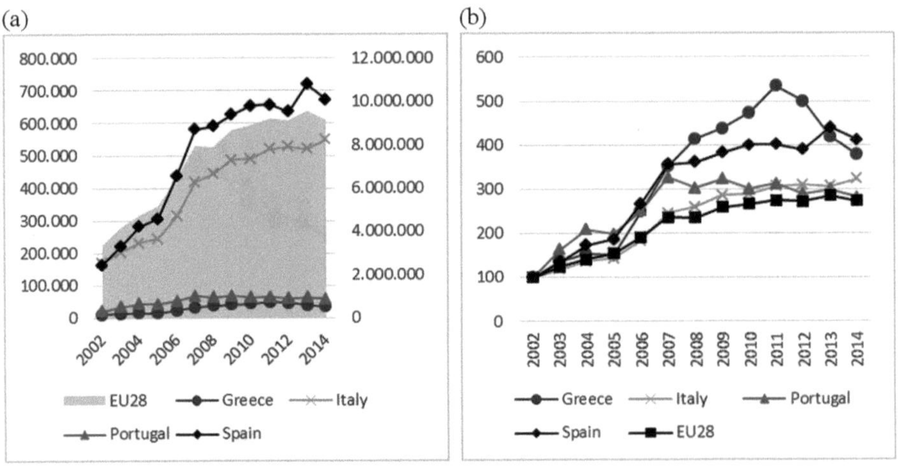

Fig. 8.2 FDI outward stocks (**a**) and their evolution (**b**) (2002 = 100). Source: UNCTAD (2015a)

8.2.2 *International Trade*

Moving on to data on international trade, Southern European countries are consistently less open than the average European country. In fact, in terms of the ratio of total trade as a share of GDP, Greece and Italy were the least open European countries, while Spain and Portugal were also near the bottom of the European ranking (Fig. 8.3). Naturally, the implications of this measure are very different between large and small countries. Hence, the low figures of Italy and Spain can be—at least partly—attributed to their sizeable internal markets and the consequent scale economies, which allows for greater diversity in both final and intermediate products. The pattern of limited openness is, nevertheless, still visible, since, along with France, the two Southern European 'large' countries are systematically the least open larger European countries.

The impact of the crisis appears to be very similar in all countries, with Greece displaying the slowest recovery.

The merchandise trade specialisation index compares the net flow of goods (exports minus imports) to the total flow of goods (exports plus imports), and is also known as 'normalized trade balance by product'. The range of values is between -1 and 1; positive values indicate that an economy has net exports (hence it specializes in the production of that specific product) and negative values means that an economy imports more than it exports (net consumption). This index removes bias of high export values due to significant re-exports activities, thus it is more suitable to identify real producers rather than traders. The normalized trade

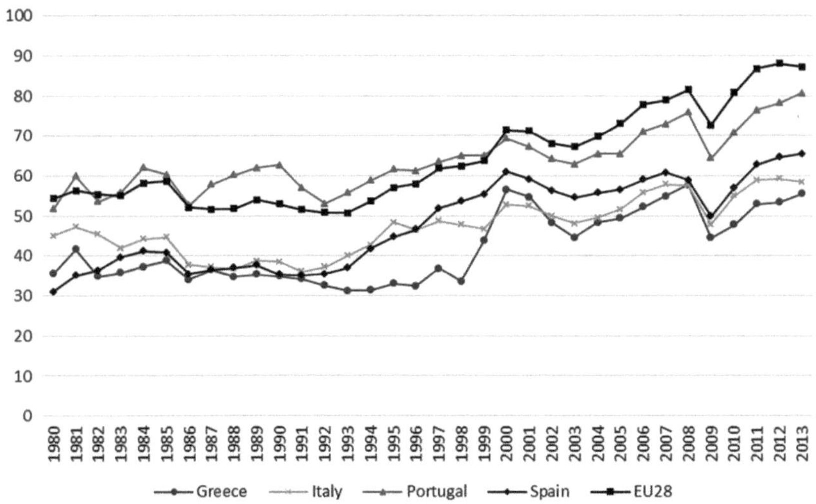

Fig. 8.3 Trade openness of Southern European countries. Note: Trade openness: sum of exports and imports as percentage of nominal gross domestic product (GDP). The indicators are calculated for total trade in goods and services. Source: UNCTAD (2015b)

balance is suitable to make comparisons across countries and product groups by removing the bias due to the size of an economy.[2]

By focusing on four main groups of products (grouped by skill/technology content) the trade specialisation index allows for a dual comparison. On the one hand we can see the medium-term evolution of the economies' structure, while assessing the relative competitiveness of the countries.

There is a rather clear divide between the four countries, with Greece and Portugal performing considerably worse than Italy and Spain (Fig. 8.4). Moreover,

---

[2]Formula of trade specialization index: $TSI_{ji} = \frac{X_j^i - M_j^i}{X_j^i + M_j^i}$

TSI_{ji} = the index of trade specialization of economy j for goods i in a specific period
i = product or product groups
j = economy (country or country group)
X_j^i = economy's j exports of goods i
M_j^i= economy's j imports of goods i

As the index shows the normalized trade balance at the product level and does not take into account the size of the trade, then products having low trade values may have high index numbers. This may lead to incorrect conclusions of specialization in trade. However, as those low trade values are considered important information to have, instead of removing those values they are kept but thoroughly footnoted. They are defined by having values less than a defined threshold. In order to set the threshold, first the significant products are specified (the ones that make up the cumulative market share up to 95% of total exports and imports). The lowest value of those significant products is considered as a threshold.

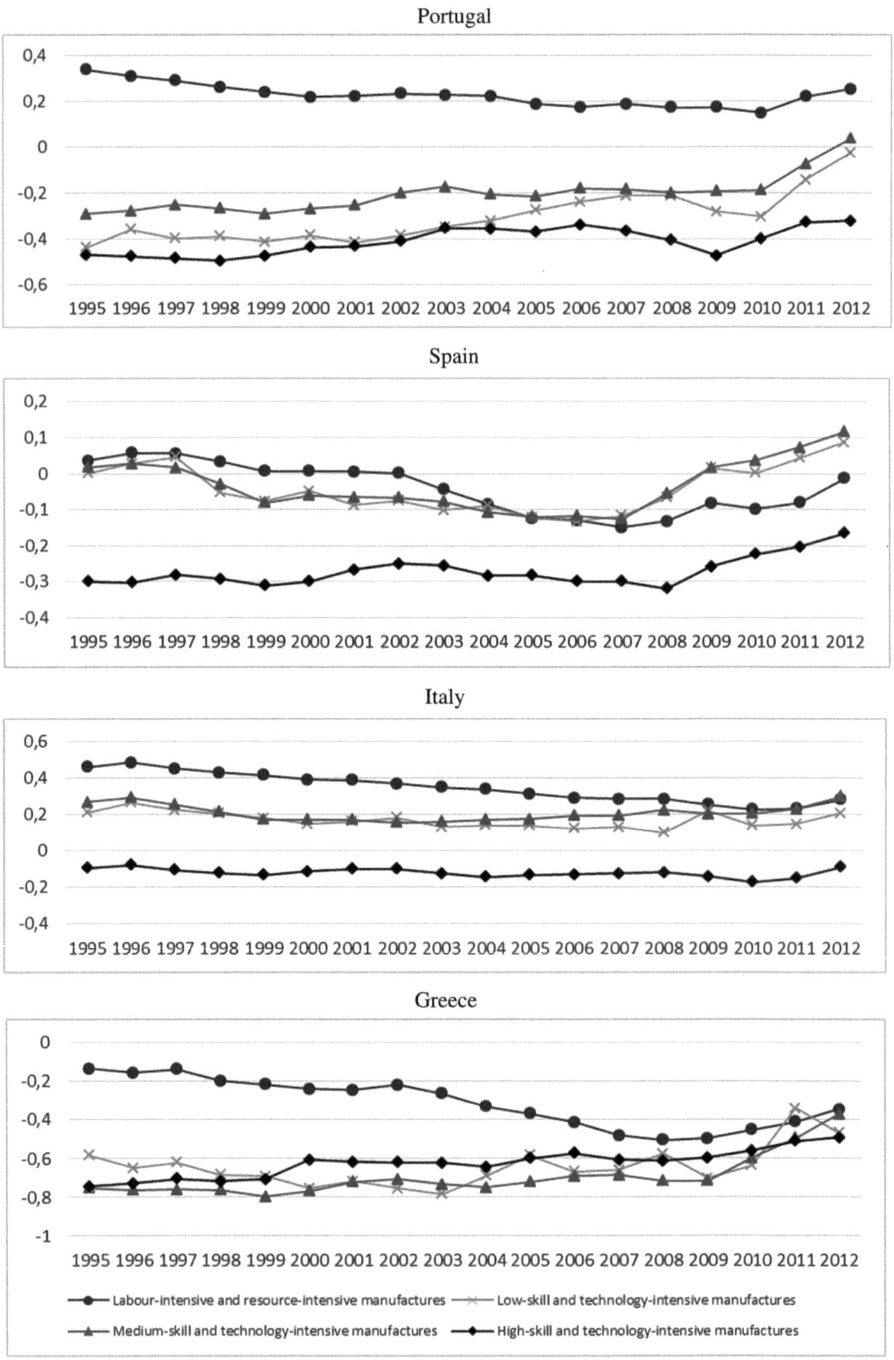

Fig. 8.4 Merchandise trade specialisation index. Source: UNCTAD (2015c)

Greece and Portugal are the two countries displaying a clear specialisation in labour intensive and resource intensive manufactures until the early 2000s. However, the magnitudes were completely different, since in the case of Portugal the index for the specific sector was positive throughout the period, while it was negative for Greece.

Portugal is the country that has changed the least, while Greece is the extreme opposite; although still not specialized in any particular sector, the country seems to be moving forward towards a more balanced industrial mix. In other words, Greece is a weak performer throughout. However, the relatively higher technology sectors are gradually gaining in importance.

Overall Italy appears to be the best performer followed by Spain. Both countries share a specialisation (much more systematic and persistent in the case of Italy) in all industry groups except high tech manufactures.

In terms of a sectoral outlook in a sector whose performance is very likely related to delocalisation, in 1995 Greece had a specialisation in five out of seven subsectors of the clothing sector (Fig. 8.5). By 2005 the specialisation was maintained in two subsectors, only one of which involved textile clothing, while currently, the country specializes in only one subsector.

Trade in Value Added (TiVA) reflects a number of aspects of the increasing interconnectedness of national economies and the blurring of the once clearer domestic character of products. The data currently available is provided by a joint OECD-WTO initiative based on national Input-Output (I-O) tables in conjunction with international trade data. Although still in many ways a work in progress, the

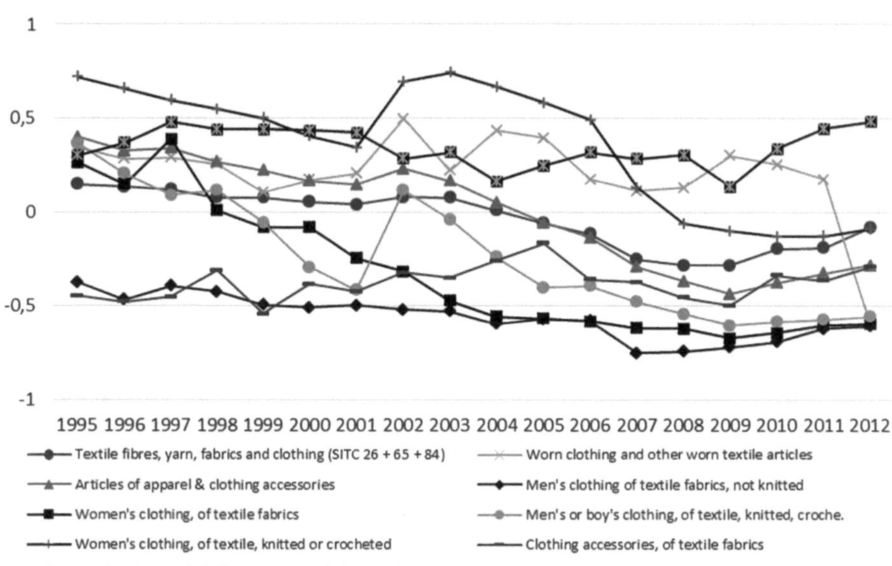

Fig. 8.5 Clothing sectors in Greece: Merchandise trade specialisation index. Source: UNCTAD (2015c)

data may inform us about the value added content of a Euro of imports or exports by value adding industry and country. Although TiVA is but one input in the effort to understand phenomena such as outsourcing, GVCs and delocalisation, it can prove to be a rather valuable input, as it may very well alter our view on the trade balance positions of countries, as well as the relative "goods" and "bads" of foreign content.

Foreign Value-Added embodied in Final Domestic Demand shows for a final good or service (purchased by households, government, non-profit institutions serving households, or as investment) how much value added is foreign and where it originates. It shows how industries abroad (upstream in a value-chain) are connected to consumers at home, even where no direct trade relationship exists. It can most readily be interpreted as 'imports of value-added'. Considering the four Southern Europe countries and two other countries from the North of Europe—Finland and Poland—the share of GDP declined between 2008 and 2009, reflecting the overall contraction in international trade (Fig. 8.6). Due to the market size effect and the greater variety of domestic sources of intermediates in larger countries, size appears to be a considerable determinant with smaller countries displaying higher shares (Greece and Portugal vis-à-vis Italy and Spain). However, its impact is moderated by other factors such as the relative openness of economies (Poland's share nearly doubled within the last 15 years—a period during which the Polish economy was opening up).

Is a high share of foreign VA in domestic final demand a negative sign? Although a definitive answer is difficult to come by, it could depend on the combined effects of two factors, namely the sector breakdown and the balance between foreign value added in domestic final demand and domestic value added embodied in foreign final demand. Hence, both Finland and Poland are considerably more 'open', while at the same time display a surplus (more domestic VA

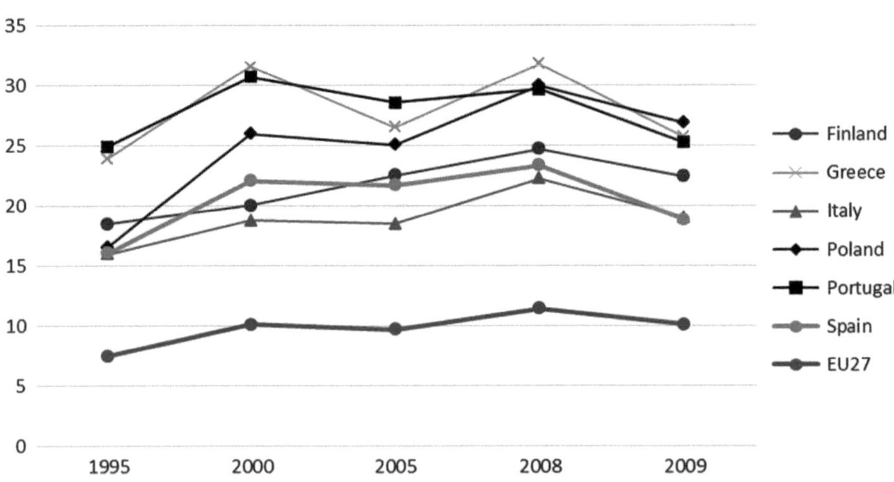

Fig. 8.6 Foreign value added embodied in domestic final demand as a % of GDP (total value added). Source: OECD (2015)

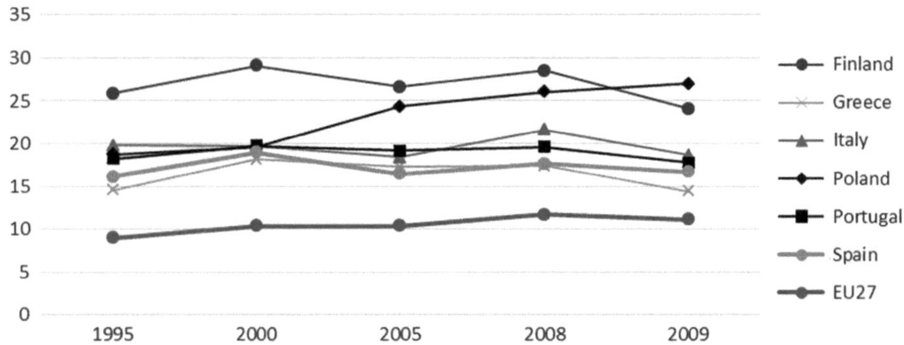

Fig. 8.7 Domestic value added embodied in foreign final demand as a % of GDP (total value added). Source: OECD (2015)

embodied in foreign final demand than foreign VA in domestic final demand) (Fig. 8.7).

8.3 An Assessment of the Impact of the Crisis on Greek Firms

In order to assess the impacts of the crisis on the delocalisation of Greek firms we performed a number of interviews with a panel of representatives from Greek firms Based on an older (Labrianidis 2008; Kalogeresis and Labrianidis 2008) survey conducted in 2006 which aimed to understand delocalisation and uncover its impacts on the firm, industry and spatial level, the current survey, conducted in 2012, enabled us to gain a good understanding of the impact of the crisis on firms that were already, one way or the other, delocalised (Table 8.1).

Our original sample consisted of firms involved in a wide array of modes of production—and/or employment—transferred abroad.[3] Such a conceptualisation focuses on the sourcing decisions of the firm, largely ignoring the possibility of *delocalisation* (understood as the various impacts on local productive systems) that can be caused by such movements.

In turn, the current wave focuses on the impact of the crisis on both the performance as well as the sourcing strategies of firms that were already involved in delocalisation. The survey is based on a rather compact semi-structured telephone questionnaire addressed to a subsample of the Greek firms that were contacted in 2006 as part of the original survey.

[3]Foreign Direct Investment (FDI); outsourcing; subcontracting; firms that traditionally bought the intermediate product (that is, never produced it in-house and therefore never stopped producing it) and are now outsourcing it; and horizontal FDI, which is very often not considered a component of delocalisation, since it involves the movement of production abroad.

Table 8.1 Responses to the telephone survey

Sector	Responses	% of original sample
Software	12	60
Electronics	11	52
Clothing	11	35
Footwear	4	50
Total	38	48

Table 8.2 Employment change among respondents

		Employment change 2008–2012 (employees)	
		Average	Total
Sector	Clothing	−20.29	−142.00
	Electronics	−4.45	−49.00
	Footwear	−12.75	−51.00
	Software	−3.00	−27.00
Respondent is affiliate	No	−9.72	−282.00
	Yes	6.50	13.00
Respondent is parent	No	−8.48	−178.00
	Yes	−9.10	−91.00
Respondent undertakes subcontracting	No	−8.00	−96.00
	Yes	−9.11	−173.00
Respondent assignes subcontracting	No	−4.11	−74.00
	Yes	−15.00	−195.00

Overall, 48% of the original sample responded to the new questionnaire. The highest non-response rates were recorded in the clothing sector. Those that did not respond can be divided into two main groups. The first group includes firms whose existence we failed to verify (18.75% of the firms), while the second includes firms that are in operation but declined to respond. The clothing sector clearly stands out as the worst represented one.

In terms of employment change during the crisis, it seems that the vast majority of firms reduced employment, although it is clear that the employment losses were more severe in the 'low tech' sectors (clothing and footwear). The average clothing firm lost 20.29 employees during the period, a figure which sharply contrasts with the software sector, where the respective figure was 3 (Table 8.2).

It appears that being an affiliate of a foreign firm is a significant source of strength, since the group of foreign affiliates is the only one where employment was increased.

In terms of the types of changes in production since 2008 (an approximation for the beginning of the crisis) there seem to be a number of distinct strategies

Table 8.3 Production change since 2008 by firm size and sector

		Has production changed since 2008?			
		No		Yes	
		Count	%	Count	%
Sector	Clothing	4	50.0	4	50.0
	Electronics	5	45.5	6	54.5
	Footwear	1	25.0	3	75.0
	Software	3	33.3	6	66.7
	Total	13	40.6	19	59.4
Employment size	1–9	1	25.0	3	75.0
	10–19	3	60.0	2	40.0
	20–49	9	52.9	8	47.1
	50–99	0	0.0	4	100.0
	100–249	0	0.0	2	100.0
	250–499	0	0.0	0	0.0
	Total	13	40.6	19	59.4
Region	Attiki	9	40.9	13	59.1
	Thessaloniki	4	40.0	6	60.0

(Table 8.3). The most prevalent one is specialisation, while considerably fewer firms are opting for diversification and development of new products and activities.

In terms of the role of the crisis in the changes in production, only two of the 16 firms whose production was altered claimed that the crisis was irrelevant. The remaining 14 firms identified a small number of aspects of the crisis that led to the change in production. The most prevalent ones were dwindling domestic demand, lack of liquidity and the effects of the decline of other sectors of the domestic economy (mainly construction).

In only one firm that responded to the specific question was the foreign participation eliminated during the last 5 years. Specifically, a small software firm located in Attica, which during this period completely diversified into a commercial firm.

Not surprisingly, very few firms managed to increase their turnover (20% of the sample—Table 8.4). With the exception of footwear firms, which are clearly under considerable pressure, there is no clear picture of any trends identifying any kind of resilience.

Table 8.4 Change in turnover since 2009

		Considerably lower		Lower		Same		Higher		Considerably higher	
		Count	Row N%	Count	Row N%	Count	Row N%	Count	Row N%	Count	Row N%
Sector	Clothing	2	25.0	2	25.0	1	12.5	2	25.0	1	12.5
	Electronics	1	9.1	5	45.5	3	27.3	0	0.0	2	18.2
	Footwear	3	100.0	0	0.0	0	0.0	0	0.0	0	0.0
	Software	1	12.5	6	75.0	0	0.0	0	0.0	1	12.5
	Total	7	23.3	13	43.3	4	13.3	2	6.7	4	13.3
size	1–9	2	66.7	0	0.0	0	0.0	0	0.0	1	33.3
	10–19	1	20.0	3	60.0	0	0.0	0	0.0	1	20.0
	20–49	3	17.6	9	52.9	4	23.5	0	0.0	1	5.9
	50–99	0	0.0	1	33.3	0	0.0	1	33.3	1	33.3
	100–249	1	50.0	0	0.0	0	0.0	1	50.0	0	0.0
	250–499	0	0.0	0	0.0	0	0.0	0	0.0	0	0.0
	Total	7	23.3	13	43.3	4	13.3	2	6.7	4	13.3
Region	Attiki	6	28.6	11	52.4	1	4.8	1	4.8	2	9.5
	Thessaloniki	1	11.1	2	22.2	3	33.3	1	11.1	2	22.2

8.4 Conclusions: Discussion

In one of the most classic books on Southern Europe of the early 1980s Alain Lipietz (1987), while describing the common elements of the 'European periphery', identified the rather clear differences of three of the countries: *'One immediately assumes that (in relative terms), Greece is closest to the 'old international division of labour' (producing and exporting primary commodities), that Portugal is characterized by a form of 'primitive Taylorization' (exporting cheap industrial goods, and with a weak home market) and that only Spain represents a fully developed form of 'peripheral Fordism'.*(Lipietz 1987, p. 123)

Nearly 30 years later could one, equally succinctly, describe the region's elements of 'unity' and 'diversity'? Apparently, 30 years of participation in the core European institutions have done a lot to change the economies of the countries of the region; however, the issue of convergence with the European 'core' is still debatable.

So, where do we stand on the issue of delocalisation? Both the theory and the evidence appear rather fuzzy. According to international trade theory, it seems that more fragmentation may induce growth; however the role of market size impacts, timing of entry, infant industry arguments, as well as path dependences tend to blur the regularities of trade economics. If issues such as learning capacities, local innovations systems, entrepreneurial densities, oligopolistic conditions or more generally, the temporal, spatial, social and organisational particularities were unimportant then, participation in Global Value Chains would, more or less automatically, put firms and regions on upgrade paths. In reality, though, upgrade is not at all automatic and depends on very idiosyncratic factors (Hardy et al. 2011; Starosta 2010; Tokatli 2012).

Southern Europe is still an introverted part of the Union, whose countries are still focused on producing medium to low tech products and constitute an area of low competitiveness. In addition to these endogenous characteristics, there appear to be exceptionally strong centripetal locational forces at work in Europe, a process that seems to have accelerated since the crisis.

Nonetheless, it would be naïve to consider the region homogenous, as there are considerable factors of diversity at work, size being the most obvious one. Greece is currently faced with a crisis that is considerably more internal that external, and is in much greater need for a new development model, which will be more or less inevitable after the current destruction.

References

Amighini A, Rabellotti R (2006) How do Italian footwear industrial districts face globalization? Eur Plan Stud 14:485–502. doi:10.1080/09654310500421105

Amin A, Thrift N (1992) Neo-marshallian nodes in global networks. Int J Urban Reg Res 16:571–587. doi:10.1111/j.1468-2427.1992.tb00197.x

Amiti M, Wei S-J (2005) Service offshoring, productivity, and employment: evidence from the United States (Working Paper No. WP/05/238), IMF Working Papers

Antonietti R, Cainelli G, Lupi C (2013) Vertical disintegration and spatial co-localization: the case of Kibs in the metropolitan region of Milan. Econ Lett 118:360–363. doi:10.1016/j.econlet.2012.11.031

Argyres N (1996) Evidence on the role of firm capabilities in vertical integration decisions. Strateg Manag J 17:129–150. doi:10.1002/(SICI)1097-0266(199602)17:2<129::AID-SMJ798>3.0.CO;2-H

Arndt SW (1999) Globalization and economic development. J Int Trade Econ Dev 8:309–318. doi:10.1080/09638199900000018

Arrow K (1962) The economic implications of learning by doing. Rev Econ Stud 29:155–176

Ball D, Stamouli N (2012) Bottler spills out of Athens. Wall Street J. http://www.wsj.com/articles/SB10000872396390444657804578050713958952022. Accessed 29 Dec 2015

Bellandi M, Caloffi A (2008) District internationalisation and trans-local development. Entrep Reg Dev 20:517–532. doi:10.1080/08985620802462108

Biggiero L (2006) Industrial and knowledge relocation strategies under the challenges of globalization and digitalization: the move of small and medium enterprises among territorial systems. Entrep Reg Dev 18:443–471. doi:10.1080/08985620600884701

Boschma RA, Lambooy JG (1999) Evolutionary economics and economic geography. J Evol Econ 9:411–429. doi:10.1007/s001910050089

Broedner P, Kinkel S, Lay G (2009) Productivity effects of outsourcing: new evidence on the strategic importance of vertical integration decisions. Int J Oper Prod Manag 29:127–150. doi:10.1108/01443570910932020

Coase RH (1937) The nature of the firm. Economica 4(16):386–405

Contractor FJ, Kumar V, Kundu SK, Pedersen T (2010) Reconceptualizing the firm in a world of outsourcing and offshoring: the organizational and geographical relocation of high-value company functions: relocation of high-value functions. J Manag Stud 47:1417–1433. doi:10.1111/j.1467-6486.2010.00945.x

Cowling K, Sugden R (1987) Market exchange and the concept of a transnational corporation: analysing the nature of the firm. Br Rev Econ Issues 9:57–68

Dicken P, Thrift N (1992) The organization of production and the production of organization: why business enterprises matter in the study of geographical industrialization. Trans Ins Brit Geogr 17:279–291

Dunning JH (ed) (1993) The theory of transnational corporations, United Nations library on transnational corporations. International business and the world economy; set A, vol 1. Routledge, London

Dunning JH (1998) Location and the multinational enterprise: a neglected factor. J Int Bus Stud 29:45–66

Dunning JH, Lundan SM (2008) Multinational enterprises and the global economy, 2nd edn. Edward Elgar Publishing, Cheltenham

European Commission (2013) European competitiveness report 2013: towards knowledge driven reindustrialisation. Publications Office of the European Union, Luxembourg

Eurostat (2015) International sourcing statistics—all activities (iss)

Fariñas JC, Martín-Marcos A (2010) Foreign sourcing and productivity: evidence at the firm level. World Econ 33:482–506. doi:10.1111/j.1467-9701.2010.01264.x

Flak A (2014) Fiat Chrysler headquarters will be in London, CEO confirms. Reuters, London

Girma S, Görg H (2004) Outsourcing, foreign ownership, and productivity: evidence from UK establishment-level data. Rev Int Econ 12:817–832. doi:10.1111/j.1467-9396.2004.00483.x

Glaeser EL, Kallal HD, Scheinkman JA, Shleifer A (1992) Growth in cities. J Polit Econ 100:1126–1152

Görg H, Hanley A (2003) International outsourcing and productivity: evidence from plant level data. The University of Nottingham research paper series: Globalisation, Productivity and Technology Research Paper 2003/20

Görg H, Hanley A (2005) Labour demand effects of international outsourcing: evidence from plant-level data. Int Rev Econ Financ 14:365–376
Görg H, Hanley A, Strobl E (2008) Productivity effects of international outsourcing: evidence from plant-level data. Can J Econ/Revue canadienne d'économique 41:670–688. doi:10.1111/j.1540-5982.2008.00481.x
GreekReporter.com (2012) FAGE moves its headquarters from Greece to Luxemburg
Grossman GM, Helpman E (2002) Integration versus outsourcing in industry equilibrium. Q J Econ 117(1):85–120
Grossman GM, Rossi-Hansberg E (2008) Trading tasks: a simple theory of offshoring. Am Econ Rev 98:1978–1997. doi:10.1257/aer.98.5.1978
Hardy J, Micek G, Capik P (2011) Upgrading local economies in Central and Eastern Europe? The role of business service foreign direct investment in the knowledge economy. Eur Plan Stud 19:1581–1591. doi:10.1080/09654313.2011.586180
Henderson V (1997) Externalities and industrial development. J Urban Econ 42:449–470. doi:10.1006/juec.1997.2036
Holmes TJ (1999) Localization of industry and vertical disintegration. Rev Econ Stat 81:314–325. doi:10.1162/003465399558102
Houseman S (2007) Outsourcing, offshoring and productivity measurement in United States manufacturing. Int Labour Rev 146:61–80. doi:10.1111/j.1564-913X.2007.00005.x
Jabbour L (2010) Offshoring and firm performance: evidence from French manufacturing industry. World Econ 33:507–524. doi:10.1111/j.1467-9701.2010.01265.x
Jacobides MG, Winter SG (2005) The co-evolution of capabilities and transaction costs: explaining the institutional structure of production. Strateg Manag J 26:395–413. doi:10.1002/smj.460
Kalogeresis A, Labrianidis L (2008) Delocalisation and development in Europe: conceptual issues and empirical findings. In: Labrianidis L (ed) The moving frontier: the changing geography of production in labour-intensive industries. Ashgate, Aldershot, pp 23–58
Kalogeresis A, Labrianidis L (2010) Delocalisation and development: empirical findings from selected European countries. Compet Chang 14:100–123
Kay N (2000) The resource-based approach to multinational enterprise. In: Pitelis CN, Sugden R (eds) The nature of the transnational firm. Routledge, London, pp 140–161
Kitson M, Martin R, Tyler P (2011) The geographies of austerity. Camb J Reg Econ Soc 4:289–302. doi:10.1093/cjres/rsr030
Krugman P (2000) Fire-sale FDI. University of Chicago Press, Chicago
Labrianidis L (ed) (2008) The moving frontier: the changing geography of production in labour-intensive industries, Ashgate economic geography series. Ashgate, Aldershot
Labrianidis L, Kalantaridis C (2004) The delocalisation of production in labour intensive industries: instances of triangular manufacturing between Germany, Greece and FYROM. Eur Plan Stud 12:1157–1173
Lipietz A (1987) Mirages and miracles: the crisis in global Fordism. Verso, London
Malmberg A, Maskell P (2002) The elusive concept of localization economies: towards a knowledge-based theory of spatial clustering. Environ Plan A 34:429–449. doi:10.1068/a3457
Manning S, Massini S, Lewin AY (2008) A dynamic perspective on next-generation offshoring: the global sourcing of science and engineering talent. Acad Manag Perspect 22:35–54
Markusen A (1999) Fuzzy concepts, scanty evidence, policy distance: the case for rigour and policy relevance in critical regional studies. Reg Stud 33:869–884. doi:10.1080/00343409950075506
Marshall A (1920) Principles of economics, 8th edn. Macmillan, London
Mazzanti M, Montresor S, Pini P (2011) Outsourcing, delocalisation and firm organization: transaction costs versus industrial relations in a local production system of Emilia Romagna. Entrep Reg Dev 23:419–447. doi:10.1080/08985620903233986
O'Neill P, Gibson-Graham JK (1999) Enterprise discourse and executive talk: stories that destabilize the company. Trans Inst Br Geogr 24:11–22
OECD (2007) Offshoring and employment: trends and impacts. OECD, Paris
OECD (2015) OECD-WTO Trade in Value Added (TiVA)—May 2013

Penrose ET (1959) The theory of the growth of the firm. Basil Blackwell, Oxford
Pickles J, Smith A (2011) Delocalisation and persistence in the European clothing industry: the reconfiguration of trade and production networks. Reg Stud 45:167–185. doi:10.1080/00343401003601933
Porter ME (2000) Location, competition, and economic development: local clusters in a global economy. Econ Dev Q 14:15–34. doi:10.1177/089124240001400105
Puga D, Venables AJ (1999) Agglomeration and economic development: import substitution vs. trade liberalisation. Econ J 109:292–311. doi:10.1111/1468-0297.00433
Romer PM (1986) Increasing returns and long-run growth. J Polit Econ:1002–1037
Sammarra A, Belussi F (2006) Evolution and relocation in fashion-led Italian districts: evidence from two case-studies. Entrep Reg Dev 18:543–562. doi:10.1080/08985620600884685
Schwab K (2013) The Global Competitiveness Report 2013–2014. World Economic Forum
Starosta G (2010) Global commodity chains and the Marxian law of value. Antipode 42:433–465. doi:10.1111/j.1467-8330.2009.00753.x
Storper M (2009) Roepke lecture in economic geography—regional context and global trade. Econ Geogr 85:1–21. doi:10.1111/j.1944-8287.2008.01001.x
Sturgeon T (2013) Global value chains and economic globalization: towards a new measurement framework
Sturgeon T, Memedovic O (2011) Mapping global value chains: intermediate goods trade and structural change in the world economy (Working Paper No. 05/2010). UNIDO, Vienna
Tokatli N (2012) Old firms, new tricks and the quest for profits: Burberry's journey from success to failure and back to success again. J Econ Geogr 12:55–77. doi:10.1093/jeg/lbq046
Tomiura E (2007) Foreign outsourcing, exporting, and FDI: a productivity comparison at the firm level. J Int Econ 72:113–127. doi:10.1016/j.jinteco.2006.11.003
UNCTAD (2015a) Foreign direct investment: inward and outward flows and stock, annual, 1980–2014
UNCTAD (2015b) Goods and services trade openness indicators, annual, 1980–2013
UNCTAD (2015c) Merchandise trade specialization index, annual, 1995–2012.
Williamson OE (1975) Markets and hierarchies: analysis and antitrust implications: a study in the economics of internal organization. Free Press, New York
Williamson OE (1985) The economic institutions of capitalism: firms, markets, relational contracting. Free Press, New York
WTO (2013) International trade statistics 2013. WTO, Geneva
Young AA (1928) Increasing returns and economic progress. Econ J 38:527–542. doi:10.2307/2224097
Zhu S, Pickles J (2014) Bring in, go up, go west, go out: upgrading, regionalisation and delocalisation in China's apparel production networks. J Contemp Asia 44:36–63. doi:10.1080/00472336.2013.801166

Athanasios Kalogeresis is Assistant Professor at the School of Spatial Planning and Development, Faculty of Engineering, Aristotle University of Thessaloniki, where he teaches economic geography, urban and regional planning and globalization. His research interests and recent work evolve around two main themes, namely, local and regional development and various aspects of the organization of production (spatial, social, institutional and cultural). Within these broad themes, he has worked and published in a number of specific areas, such as the creative economy; the analysis of new forms of (multinational) organization of economic activities; the role of multinational production and trade in knowledge spillovers; relations between international and local productive systems, the sources of regional disparities and the role of human capital and human capabilities.

Chapter 9
The Impact of Regional and National Policies in the Development of the Italian Mezzogiorno

Guido Pellegrini

JEL Classification R11 • R12 • R58

9.1 Introduction

After the Second World War, the Southern regions of Italy (the Mezzogiorno) underwent a period of exceptional growth. However, this period ended after the oil crisis and now the Mezzogiorno is the largest backward region within the EU-15. A huge amount of literature is devoted to finding the main reasons why the Mezzogiorno did not evolve like the rest of the country (see Iuzzolino et al. 2011 and the literature cited therein). In this paper I propose that the implemented policies were essential or critical in influencing the rise and then the decline of the southern economy. The analysis is based on the strict association between the implementation of certain policies and the results in terms of output and employment growth. The link is not estimated by an econometric model, but I connect the dynamics of economic and social indicators to the policy's changes. I examine the impact of Italian regional and national policies on social and economic development of the Mezzogiorno. The study has an historical dimension, analysing the relationship between economic policies and growth in the South of Italy from the fifties to the nineties, and it is focused on the recent "new regional policies", and the effect of the national programmes on the regional divide.

The literature on Italian economic disparities, or on the "Southern question", and the role of the policy actions is immense, and cannot be synthesised in few words. Several references can be found in Eckaus (1961), Saraceno (1974), Gerschenkron (1965), Castronovo (1975), Toniolo (1988), Romeo (1988), Zamagni (1993), Cafiero (1996), Cohen and Federico (2001), Fenoaltea (2006), Ciocca (2007), Vecchi (2011). Recent references to the impact of public policies on regional divide

G. Pellegrini (✉)
Department of Social Sciences and Economics, Sapienza University of Rome, P.le Aldo Moro, 5, Rome 00185, Italy
e-mail: guido.pellegrini@uniroma1.it

M. Fonseca, U. Fratesi (eds.), *Regional Upgrading in Southern Europe*, Advances in Spatial Science, DOI 10.1007/978-3-319-49818-8_9

are in Trigilia (1992), Rossi (1998), Del Monte and Giannola (1997), Barca and Ciampi (1998), Felice (2007a), Viesti (2009), Mauro and Pigliaru (2011), Cannari et al. (2010), Barucci et al. (2011), Iuzzolino et al. (2011, 2013). In recent years the availability of more and better quantitative data than in the past allows for comparing regional development and policy outcomes: time series on regional GDP, sectoral productivity, industrial value added (with detailed sectoral and territorial disaggregations), the local components of public spending, the geographical distribution of educational levels, health, and poverty have been collected and published, especially in the works of Daniele and Malanima (2007), Felice (2007b), Federico (2007), Vecchi (2011), and in the Bank of Italy's project on the reconstruction of the Italian National Account. These new resources are used in this paper to focus on the decisive periods in Italian regional and economic history, linking the development with the effective policies in the period.

The results of the analysis show that the policies are essential in explaining the economic development of the southern regions in Italy, and the dynamic of the convergence process. However, the effect has been both positive, such as when the welfare actions were extended to the whole country, or negative, as in the case of policies against immigration, or oriented to the support of war industries in the North, or the abolition of the "wage cages". In the focus on the "new regional policy" the paper suggests that the larger effects are imputed to the lower quality of public expenditure in the South and the decline of the intensity and quality of public services in this area (see also Iuzzolino et al. 2011). The significant disparity in the supply of many public services affects competitiveness and growth differentials. The institutional framework defining the role of the regions, especially those in the South, and of the Central Governments can explain part of the weakness of the public action. The recent institutional innovations have determined a sort of imbalance between the role of the regions, especially those in the South, and Central Governments. This led to a fragmentation of effort and excessive consensus at the local rather than the national level. Moreover, there was a deficiency of political impulse, with the reduction and the procrastination of several policies for the development of the Mezzogiorno. The most obvious symptom was the continued reduction of financial resources dedicated to the South, which reduced the achievement of objectives.

The paper is structured in the following way. The first two sections places the Italian regional divide in context, giving a brief overview of its social and economic origins from the country's unification in the second half of the nineteenth century, and exploring the causes underlining the "golden age of convergence" of the South in the fifties and sixties. The third section analyses the role of public policies in the halting of the convergence process in the seventies and eighties, opening the path to a protracted period in which regional income and output gaps have remained more or less constant. The fourth section describes the crisis of regional policy at the beginning of the nineties, the characteristics of the following new regional policy, and its effects on regional differences. The fifth section explores the role of national policies and the differences in the supply of public services on the growth of the southern region. Some comments on the relationship between national and regional policies, and how they affect the development of the whole country, conclude the paper.

9.2 The Origin of the Regional Divide

Italy has been characterized in its economic development by marked geographical disparities. This has been a distinct feature of several countries, in Europe as outside Europe, but in Italy we have registered a persistent backwardness of the regions making up the South. However, the economic divide is a feature of roughly the last century. Actually, Italian macro-areas and regions at unification (1861) and for the first two decades thereafter, were uniformly poorer, all basically still agricultural economies, even if we could have observed different degrees of backwardness in terms of the size of industry, infrastructure, living conditions, and human capital. In the estimates by Daniele and Malanima (2007), the per capita product in the Mezzogiorno was equal to the level of the Centre and North in 1861, dropping to 88% in 1900 (Fig. 9.1).

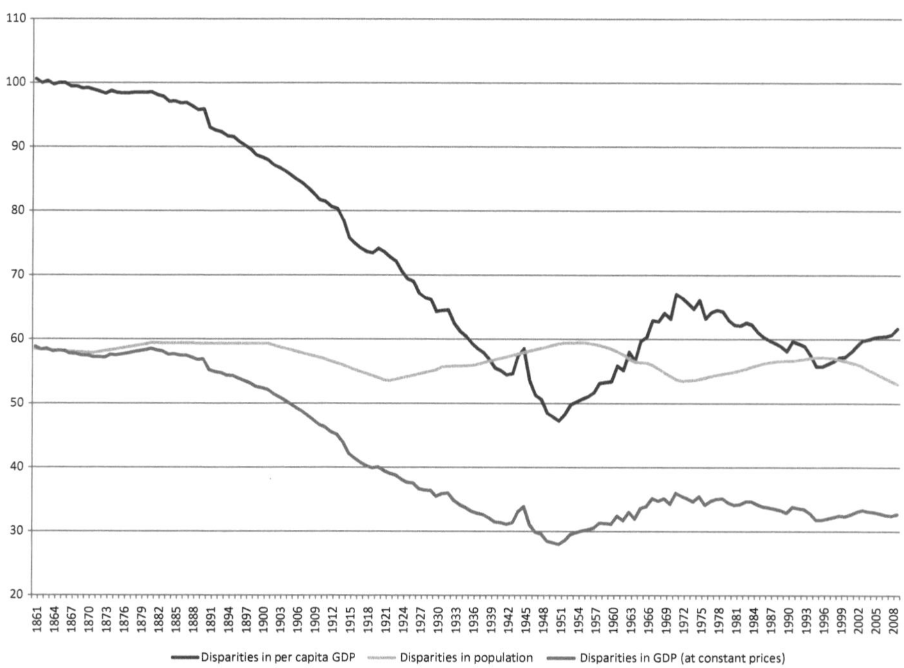

Fig. 9.1 Disparities in population, GDP (at 1911 constant prices), and GDP per capita between Mezzogiorno and Center-North (Mezzogiorno as percentage of Center-North). Source: Iuzzolino et al. (2011)

As noted by Iuzzolino et al. (2011), the relative uniformity of per capita income did not mean, however, that the living conditions of the national population were similar across regions. The diffusion of "well-being" was lower in the southern regions than in the country as a whole: Amendola et al. (2011) point out that the share of the population classified as poor at the unification was equal to 52% in the South and 37% in the Centre and North.

The differences in the preconditions for industrial development were also large. The advantages were mostly polarized in some cities and areas in the North-West, favoured by particularly promising environmental, economic and social conditions for industrialization. The widening of the development gap started in the decades around the turn of the century, when industrialization was concentrated in the "industrial triangle" of Milan, Turin and Genoa and bordering zones. The rapid development of the textile industry was also followed by the rise of more modern industries, like light manufacturing but also steel and chemicals.

Even if the awareness of the existence of a "southern question" came very early on, the government policies were not oriented to the reduction of the differences but, in some sense, contributed to the enlargement of the gap. On one side, the financial investments associated with public policy were low compared to European standards: up to the First World War, overall spending by the central government and local administrations rarely exceeded one fifth of GDP. Moreover, central government spending consisted very largely of interest on the public debt and armaments. Attention to defence entailed not only heavy current spending (naturally greater in the North, along the country's borders) but also major support for Italian industry. Furthermore, the most important public programme, the building of an extensive rail network, does not appear to have had any significant impact on the more distant (southern) regions' access to interregional markets. Finally, the effects both of fiscal unification and taxation and spending across regions also fostered rather than fought the emergence of these disparities.

On the other side, as pointed out by Iuzzolino et al. (2011), social and education spending was minimal. Social solidarity and health care were in the hands of private bodies or mutual societies, which for historical reasons were more common in the North. Education was charged to municipal budgets, and its expansion was affected by differences in fiscal capacity. This is one of the main reasons why the regional literacy gap did not narrow, but widened.

Nevertheless, up until the First World War the country's surprising development was not only limited to the North-West, but involved the entire territory, albeit with varying intensity. For instance, life expectancy at birth increased by more than 16 years on average and by 6 years even in the region with the worst performance. The growth of industry, though concentrated in the North-West, had effect on all parts of the country. Therefore, as late as the mid-1920s, the scale of regional development disparities was not particularly unusual by European standards, and in the meantime the awareness of the question of southern industrialization increased.

The disparities strongly increased in the period that followed. In the estimates by Daniele and Malanima (2007), the gap grew from 25% at the beginning of the twenties to 45% in 1940 and 50% in 1948. In the years between the two World Wars, dominated by the Fascist government in Italy, policy actions not only blocked the beginnings of convergence, but also transformed the North-South disparity into a long-lasting critical gap. Actually, the per capita output difference between the South and the rest of the country widened more rapidly during the Fascist years than during the initial era of Italian industrialization. The economic policy choices that negatively affected the regional convergence were basically two: on one side, emigration abroad was blocked, and Fascist policies first discouraged and then banned any form of internal migration, which could have accompanied the differences in income and economic structure between regions. On the other side, available capital was concentrated in the industries already established in the North-West: first with the abnormal growth of the war industry; then with the repeated rescue operations in the 1920s. Finally, the birth of the Institute for Industrial Reconstruction (IRI) in 1933 transferred to the State a major part of the Italian banking sector and manufacturing. As Iuzzolino et al. (2011) noted, the Second World War and post-war reconstruction in the late 1940s continued to act in the same direction. During the war the modest industrial apparatus of the South was hit much harder than that of the North. At the end of the war the gap of the South was the widest in its history (53% in 1951).

9.3 The Golden Age of Convergence

In 1951, the southern economy was in disastrous condition. Iuzzolino et al. (2011) point out that southern industry's share of value added amounted to just over 11% of the national total, well under half of its share in 1911; for every thousand inhabitants the South had just 43 full-time equivalent workers, compared to 77 for the North-East and 171 for the North-West; and labour productivity at current prices was almost 40 points lower than the Italian average, and 54 points lower than in the North-West.

However, beginning in 1951 the South underwent a period of exceptional growth, the highest in its history. From 1951 to 1971 per capita GDP in the South rose at an average annual rate of 5.8%. The South was outperformed significantly only by Japan, and slightly by Greece and Spain. Even if the whole country grew quickly, the output gap between South and North was reduced significantly. All the southern regions took part, if to differing extents.

What are the reasons for this exceptional development? An important cause was the removal of the policies responsible for the artificial containment of migration and of the sectoral distribution of the public spending. The combined effect of those dynamics and of the new economic policy approaches would produce the first considerable convergence between North and South, stimulated by the extraordinary increase in productivity. The modernization process was intense in both agriculture and industry, the latter following with a lag of some years. The share of per capita income of the South increased from 47% in 1952 to 67% in 1971, more than 24 points in two decades, more than a point each year.

The role of national and regional policies was essential in the development. It was not only the removing of the barrier to the free trade and movement of factors with the creation of a truly integrated national market, the result of a radical decrease in transport and transaction costs, but the strong impact was also due to the active policies oriented to the reduction of the regional divide. There were specific southern development programmes, where the key player was the Southern Italy Development Fund, which for the first decade focused on the infrastructure endowment for agriculture, water supply and government services and from the 1960s on extended its action to direct industrial promotion. The overall intervention of the Fund was valued at 6.6 trillion lire in 1970, to which one must add the funds appropriated by the regions of Sicily and Sardinia to additional projects. As noted in Iuzzolino et al. (2011), the impact of the Fund was of fundamental importance to the economy: in 1971 the investment rate in the South was 37%, nearly twice as high as the 21% rate of the Centre and North. Therefore, investment in the South was 58% of the amount invested in the rest of Italy, although regional GDP was only 36%.

The national programmes, oriented to increase the welfare in the entire country, also had a role: the welfare, health and education systems were strengthened. These policies were not expressly targeted at the weakest regions, but spending on them was proportionate to population, not output, so while their per capita effect was similar in North and South, their impact in relation to aggregate economic activity was greater in the South. The result of the increase in per capita public spending was an implicit transfer of substantial resources to the population of the South.

The result was a strong increase in productivity, especially in the manufacturing sector, from 76% to 99% of that of the Centre-North. Productivity grew both within sectors and in the economy as a whole, as a result of the changing sectoral composition of economic activities. An important part in the productivity catching up was played by the many new large plants, driven by public subsidies or the impetus imparted by public industry. Bodo and Sestito (1991) signal that direct employment in state-owned corporations in the South rose from 40,000 in 1960 to 150,000 in 1975.

The positive assessment of the Fund's activity and of regional development policy should not hide the feebleness of the stimulus that it provided for self-sustained growth. The expansion of the capacity to supply goods basically served the industrial sector, and consumer demand occurred in other parts of the country. No internal southern market had ever existed, and certainly none did in the 1950s and 1960s. The geography of the South and the lack of good transport networks, with the consequent absence of a tradition of interregional trade within the South, meant that for small southern manufacturers the "internal market" was strictly local. Therefore, the expansion of the southern industrial base proved insufficient in number of enterprises and in maintaining equilibrium in the labour market. The differential in unemployment rates, which had been practically eliminated by the mid-1960s, widened again to nearly 3 percentage points in 1971.

On the other side, the southern market became highly important to northern Italian industry. Iuzzolino et al. (2011) point out that access to a growing domestic market enabled northern firms to achieve economies of scale that proved to be a major factor for success on the international market, while southern firms were often reduced to a local dimension: in 1959 the South took 70% of the Centre and

North's net exports; net imports from the rest of Italy and the rest of the world came to 24% of southern GDP at current prices in 1951 and 38% in 1963, reducing to 30% in 1970.

9.4 The Limit of the Regional Policies in Seventies and Eighties

The South's convergence process came to a sudden halt around 1970: in the decades that followed, regional income and output gaps remained more or less constant. The question is why the convergence stops and if there was a role of regional policies in the slowing down.

During this period, the Italian economy was affected by three important shocks: a rise in the cost of energy, a rise in labour costs, and depreciation of the currency. Industry in the South, given its size and sectoral and technological characteristics, was more exposed to adverse economic developments and less able to follow the new paths that Italian industry would take following the oil shock.

The reaction to rising labour costs was an accentuated decentralization of production. At the end, significant competitiveness gains occurred in smaller firms, especially in industrial districts. However, the manufacturing in the South was only marginally affected by these developments. As described in Iuzzolino et al. (2011), the decentralization of production followed economic criteria of geographical contiguity and swept through the Centre and North-East, but the South participated in it to a far lesser extent. Convergence between the North-East and North-West was completed, and the Centre also made up ground. The gap between the South and the rest of the country increased.

Even if these dynamics were caused mainly by external events, national and regional policies were at work, but unfortunately often in the wrong directions.

First of all, the competitiveness of southern industry was negatively affected by the abolition in 1968 of "wage cages", which differentiated wages geographically. Employers were compensated by having a portion of their social security contributions bill charged to the state budget, a scheme that would absorb growing portions of the public resources earmarked and that was eliminated from 1995 onwards. Labour costs in the South moved into line with the national average, but in a context of significantly lower levels of productivity.

The negative effect was also due to the decline of the intensity and quality of public policy programmes. Southern development action, though formally extended, became less incisive, less concentrated, technically poorer and more subject to political influence, increasingly focused on ordinary investment that definitively eradicated its quality of additionality. The extraordinary public expenditure for the South came to 0.7% of GDP in the 1950s and 1960s and 0.9% in the 1970s. It was reduced to 0.65% in 1981-86, rose to 0.75% through 1993 and then to 0.8% thereafter. Thus, in the end the reduction in public intervention may have played a role in convergence. But the question is broader, going to the nature of development policy in a backward region of a developed country as compared with the situation in an underdeveloped country proper. There are fewer instruments available, and reconciling the industrial development of the rich and poor areas is complicated.

This problem influenced the changes in political priorities. The huge exodus from agriculture and the development, even if incomplete, of a modern industrial apparatus was followed, at the same time, by a remarkable increase in per capita income. The "Southern question" converted from a fight against poverty to a remedy for a lack of jobs: regional income differentials were (and are) dominated by huge differences in employment rates, and not primarily by the productivity gap. Especially up to 1992, many current public programmes sought to compensate for the lack of work and mitigate situations of social hardship. Iuzzolino et al. (2011) note that they proved ineffective, however, both because they were often designed for a particular exchange between politicians and final beneficiaries, and owing to the simultaneous lack of structural measures to reduce the imbalance between labour demand and supply.

Finally, another negative factor that is broadly linked to the policy choices was the creation of the regions. Until the 1980s regional governments had no significant role in the implementation of local development policy, save for the five special-statute regions. Starting in the mid-1970s a number of functions were devolved to the regions and a good number of officers seconded from the central government, resulting in increasing decentralization of territorial policies and programmes. Mauro and Pigliaru (2011) find that the process had a significantly negative differential effect for the South. The reason is that the decentralization of programmes makes them more vulnerable to local pressures and interest groups and, in a broader sense, more sensitive to the level and quality of social capital, lower in the Southern regions.

These aspects contributed to the halt the convergence process. This does not mean that the industrial apparatus of the South became insignificant, but it was unable to accelerate growth with respect to the rest of the country, and suffered from the acute problems of internal and external competitiveness. The effects of the reduction in quantity and quality of the regional policies reinforced these developments.

9.5 The Crisis in 1992 and the New Regional Policy

1992 was a crucial year from a social and political point of view: a dramatic crisis of the public finances was coupled with the crisis of the political system in general. The Italian economic system faced a strong devaluation until Italy qualified for the European single currency, whereas strong competition came from the new emerging countries.

In the presence of a strong fiscal effort, the credibility of southern development policy sank: the amount of money and the low quality of public policy programmes devoted to the South, increasingly subject to political influence, was strongly questioned. In 1992, in order to prevent a negative vote in a national referendum, the Southern Italy Development Fund and its activities were definitively liquidated and its technical personnel, many of them highly skilled, were dispersed in a range of general government bodies. The ending of special investment for the South came after a long period of stagnation, which coincided with the fiscal adjustment effort of the mid-1990s that hit the South hard. The reduction, or elimination, of investment policy was an important factor in the halt in convergence (Barucci et al. 2011). Investment played an important part in the South's post-war catch-up, and its disappearance had a negative effect in the subsequent period.

The paralysis of the Italian regional policy lasted through 1995, when Law 488/1992 for the funding of selected investment projects went operational. The charging of southern employers' social contributions to the central government budget was phased out under a 1994 agreement with the European Commission, and no offsetting policy measure was taken. The impact of restrictive fiscal policy was especially heavy for the economy of the South, which was more dependent on public resources.

During these same years the European Union's economic and social cohesion policy took shape with the Community Support Frameworks. In 1995 the first structural funds planning cycle began. The discretionary powers of the member states were considerably reduced; the criteria, calendar and procedure for the assignment of funds were established; progressively, power was shifted to the Regions, which since the 1970s had been exercising some powers formerly assigned to the Southern Italy Development Fund.

However, in the second half of the 1990s, following the closure of "old" regional policy represented mainly by the Cassa del Mezzogiorno, a new development aid policy ("New Regional Policy", NRP) was put in place, based on mobilizing local actors around local development projects (Barca and Ciampi 1998). The sources of changes were mainly two: the coherence with EU's regional policy, required by the EU Commission and a greater appreciation of the importance of local systems of small businesses in the Mezzogiorno, which, in the presence of the vacuum of the regional policy, unveiled some form of auto-sustaining growth.

The NRP was a clear example of place-based action to promote regional growth. The aim was to encourage above all the development of "social capital" by stimulating efficient forms of cooperation between local public and private actors. It gave special attention to the involvement of local communities in the policy design, exploiting local knowledge. For that, it made a great effort to develop an extensive information system on local economies, which has be used to measure regional policy performance.[1]

[1]The database "Indicatori di contesto chiave e variabili di rottura" was a joint effort of Istat and the Ministry of the Economic Development to serve as a quantitative support for the Objective 1 2000–2006 programming period. It has become an important tool for the analysis of regional imbalances.

An important characteristic of NRP was that some statistical indicators were used in an outcome-based financing scheme. The "conditionality" approach, strongly appreciated by the EU Commission, conditioned the amount of money distributed to the region by the results of the policy with respect to the targets, named "obiettivi di servizio". In the implementation of the "conditionality" approach, public funds were disbursed on the basis of the results obtained by local governments in four areas: education, child- and elderly-care, waste disposal, and water provision. The incentive scheme was based on 11 quantitative indicators. The ex-post assessment of the policy indicated some positive results (e.g., improving the quality of administrative procedures) but also some critical aspects emerged. On one side, the achievement of the target was also influenced by external factors that were out of the control of local governments, affecting the credibility of the all scheme. On the other side, very specific objectives encouraged opportunistic behaviour, when local government concentrated its efforts on reaching the objectives subject to conditionality, disregarding other important services.

While this NRP generated much hope, energies and expectations after the negative experiences of the Cassa del Mezzogiorno, in the end the results were also disappointing (Cannari et al. 2010). Clear shortcomings came from the setting of too many and confused priorities, that resulted in overlapping responsibilities. On the other side, not enough attention was paid to the effects of ordinary policies in the South. However, the quality of public services was generally worse than in the Centre North, and regional policies alone cannot offset these effects: additional capital expenditure in the South was about ½ of total capital expenditure in the area, but only about 5% of total public spending in the South (Cannari et al. 2010).

Another problem was related to the ineffectiveness of incentive schemes. Trigilia (2012) points out that, despite NRP's apparent focus on public goods, the majority of the aid ended up destined toward incentives for single firms (which averaged 7 billion Euros per year in the period 1996–2009). In the period 2000–2006 the total aid destined for the Mezzogiorno from the EU's structural funds (including national co-financing) amounted to 45 billion Euros, the vast majority of the aid.

Empirical work on the utility of providing direct incentives to business points to modest effects and highly critical performances. The Bank of Italy's 2008 survey of 4000 companies indicates that additional investment amounted to no more than 30% of subsidies, but only 6% excluding changes in timing of projects (De Blasio and Lotti 2008). The results of "Patti territoriali", a typical new local program of NRP, showed that dynamics of employment and plants in municipalities within the Pacts did not differ from those of similar municipalities outside the Pacts. The ineffectiveness could reflect some shortcomings due to the mismanagement of the program: lengthy procedures, uncertainty about funding and policies, and few financial resources. Recent research on other policy instruments devoted to increasing new private capital at the local level, like Law 488/92, indicates better performances (Bernini and Pellegrini 2011; Cerqua and Pellegrini 2014).

In the end, the data available underscore that the NRP was also unable to overcome the South's difficulty in keeping up with even the slow growth of the rest of the country. Per capita output, equal to 59.6% of that in the Centre and North in 1991, increased to 61.6% in 2007, gaining only a percentage point per decade. And even this minimal gain was due entirely to demographics: in terms of output alone the gap widened, as southern GDP slipped from 33.8% to 32.7%.

9.6 National Policies, the Provision of Public Services and Growth

The previous analysis shows that public policies were central, for better or worse, in determining the scope and the dimension of the economic and social gap between the South and the rest of the country. But the regional policies (the "place-based" policies), explicitly oriented to the economic and social development of the backward areas, cannot be blamed for all the differences. During this period, powerful territorial effects from general, national policies (i.e., central government programmes for the entire country but whose effects differ from region to region) were at work.

On one side, the nationwide extension of several policy interventions on some economic factors for the country's growth and on social aspects of welfare, such as schooling, health programmes including compulsory vaccination, and the building of infrastructure, enabled the South to share in national development. This development was in part inclusive: a number of public programmes ensured that income differences were no longer accompanied by unsustainable social disparities (Cannari et al. 2010). Thus the fact that since the 1970s the income and output gap has remained virtually unchanged does not mean the South has not made progress. Actually, the southern Italian regions have managed to keep pace with one of the most advanced areas of Europe. The totally obvious conclusion is that living conditions in the South today are better than 30 years ago. There is still a difference in the quality of these public services, such as education or health, but now the "Southern question" is no longer associated with huge poverty, illiteracy or early death. This is a great success story of social development, and it depends in part on the existence of national public services, whose upkeep implies redistributive transfers between territories. However, some differences in "well-being" remain if they are measured by the more sophisticated indicators. If we look more closely at the present, observing students' educational attainment rather than just the illiteracy rate, or at life expectancy without disability rather than infant mortality, or at felonies that indicate organized crime rather than total crimes, alarming dimensions of the disparity emerge (Iuzzolino et al. 2011).

On the other side, the significant disparity between the South and the rest of the country in the provision of many public services has affected (and is affecting today) competitiveness and growth differentials. Recent studies by the Bank of Italy (Cannari and Franco 2011) show that, while the intensity of public action has become relatively similar from region to region (excluding the major outlays on pensions, a good deal higher in the Centre and North), the quality of public services is significantly lower in the South.

Several examples and case-studies are reported in Cannari et al. (2010). For instance, the gap in transport and communication is wide: the proportion of non-electrified railways with only one platform in the South is approximately double that of the North, whilst only 18% of Italy's high speed network is found in the South; in terms of the road network, there are only 17 km of motorway per 1000 km^2 in the South (and only 13 on the islands), compared with 32 in the North-West of Italy and 23 in the North-East.

The quality of local public services is much lower in the southern regions: the water supply is interrupted three times as frequently in the South than it is in the North; electricity, twice as frequently.

Strong differences are also found in nation-wide public services: in education, where in the Mezzogiorno 23% of students do not finish high school (compared with 16% in the North); in the justice system, where the time to resolve cases is longer by 40% in the Mezzogiorno in comparison with the rest of the country; in the provision of health systems, where in the Mezzogiorno hospitals and clinics are in shorter supply, and those there offer significantly worse care, meaning that many patients travel northwards when they are in need of medical attention. An important problem is also the poorer state of public safety and legality in the southern regions. In some parts of the South these phenomena were already present at the time of national unification, in others they have spread in recent decades, in others still they are practically absent.

The importance of national compared to regional policy is given by their relative financial size. Cannari et al. (2010) show that regional policies have a very low weight with respect to national ones. Total general government per capita primary expenditure in the period from 2004 through 2006 averaged 9800 € in the South, 10,800 € in the rest of the country. The difference depends mainly on current spending, in particular pension transfers. Capital expenditure, which is explicitly targeted to sustain long-term growth, counts for only a tenth of total spending. On a per capita basis, average capital spending in the South was about 10% higher than in the rest of Italy. But if we also count investment by state-owned corporations, such as the State Railways, the difference vanishes (Viesti 2009).

There are lights and shadows on the role of the public sector in the South, especially in the last 30 years. Many observers underscore the distortions of public action, especially of regional policies, and hold it responsible for throttling growth. However, several studies and undeniable facts show that, while the intensity of public action has become relatively similar from region to region, the quality of public services is significantly lower in the South, negatively affecting economic and social development.

The institutional framework defining the role of the regions, especially those in the South, and of the central governments is at the base of the distribution of policy responsibilities and the level of decentralization in Italian administrations; it can explain part of the weakness of the public action. From this point of view, the recent institutional innovations have determined a sort of imbalance between the role of the regions, especially those in the South and the central governments. The principle of subsidiarity, the change of Title V of the Constitution, the direct dialogue with the Commission, but also the advent of a new regional management comparable in quality to the national one has encouraged the regions to plan entire projects only within their administrative boundaries. The central administration, on the other hand, showed several difficulties in combining national and regional policies, often failing to impose principles of national interest. This led to a fragmentation of effort and excessive consensus at the local level rather than at the national level. Moreover, vertical institutional cooperation between regional and local governments has remained complex, because the administrative decentralization was only partially carried out, and because forms of centralization of decision-making that characterized, and sometimes still characterize, administrative centres, were reproduced at the regional level.

However, the complex relationship between central governments and local governments should not make us forget that the reduction of interventions in the South is mostly due to the central government. The previous analysis showed that it is precisely the central government's lack of spending which explains at least part of the non-realization of major projects in the South. The possibility of an adequate policy intervention requires additional expenditure to avoid substitutions between ordinary and new policy intervention, beyond the formal adjustments. This was only partially true in Italy.

Last but not least there was a deficiency of political impulse, with the reduction and the procrastination of several policies for the development of the Mezzogiorno dropped from the key priorities of the various governments. The most obvious symptom was the continued reduction of financial resources dedicated to the South, which has helped to influence, as already mentioned, the achievement of objectives. After an initial phase, to be situated in 1998–1999, of a strong consensus on the new regional policy, there has been a continuous lack of actions to be taken in the protagonists of the political scene, except for a few individual figures of the national leadership, such as Carlo Azeglio Ciampi.

9.7 Conclusions

In the last 60 years, there were two major types of public spending which were directed towards the Mezzogiorno: funds specifically dedicated to economic development, and funds which form a more general part of spending on public policy programs (especially welfare provisions). According to many analysts, the regional policies (and in recent years, the New Regional Policy launched at the end of the nineties) should be blamed as the main cause of the unsatisfactory performance of the economy in the Mezzogiorno. This paper has a different position: even if regional policies are important, the fundamental effect is, in our opinion, rather attributable to general policies, particularly those with significant regional effects.

Moreover, the national dimension of the problem has also affected the effectiveness of regional policy. It is the paradigmatic case of organized crime: in the South it alters the conditions of competition, increasing the cost to the community, promoting the spread of a culture of illegality, and hindering the formation of social capital and trust between citizens and between citizens and institutions.

Therefore, despite the introduction of forms of "conditioning" related to the achievement of targets in the quality and offer of public services, there exists a problem of enforcement of rules that can only be assured by a good government. In the South, it is still not there. Moreover, just to increase the share of resources devoted to public investment, reducing the share of inefficient financial incentives is not in itself a sufficient condition to usefully support regional growth, if you do not remove the malfunctioning of the market. There are cases, among those just mentioned, which depend much more strongly on general policy than on regional policy.

In our opinion, the failure to narrow the gap between North and South in the last 20 years is attributable to areas that primarily ask the responsibility of national policies and where the backwardness of the South is pronounced, like justice, education and human capital, and crime. These areas are largely outside the control of territorial policies. In the presence of unequal conditions in the North and in the South, the same economic policy measure has different effects in the two areas. For instance, if government is inefficient in the South, the same rule will produce different results with respect to the rest of the country. Similarly, if the social and economic contest is different (and worse in the South), even efficient administrations generally will get different results: if young people come from uneducated families and live in areas where crime is widespread, it is more difficult for them to obtain the same results in the PISA test achieved by the young people who come from wealthy and highly acculturated families, even if the quality of teachers and school infrastructures were exactly the same.

The whole history of Italy's regional differences shows that the essential role of national policy in development should be reconsidered. The reduction of the gap requires that some essential services, like education, justice, security and health care, should have the same quality throughout the country. In many cases, the quality of public services is worse in the South. Sometimes, but not always, even spending per capita is lower than in the rest of the country. So there are situations where it may be necessary to increase spending in the South, and others where it is instead necessary to gain efficiency. Cannari et al. (2010) give some examples: it may be necessary to use more resources in the South for the fight against organized crime to ensure the same conditions of security throughout the country or to spend more money to reward teachers who work successfully in areas where students demonstrate high levels of early school leaving and social conditions less favourable to learning. In health care, there is clearly a problem of inefficiency if per capita expenditures higher than in the North lead to often poorer services. In this case the problem is not the amount of resources but the quality of the results.

To ensure the same quality of essential services in all areas of the country it is necessary that the South goes back to being a national issue. The good regional policies are not enough: it is crucial to place the South at the centre of national economic policy, and then also to allocate the resources of regional and national policies with the aim of reducing regional disparities.

Acknowledgement Many of the observations and analysis presented in this paper draws from discussions with my co-authors and from the work done with them together. I am highly indebted especially to Luigi Cannari, Giovanni Iuzzolino, Marco Magnani, Delio Miotti and Gianfranco Viesti for this and thank them for many insights and suggestions they offered in their collaboration.

References

Amendola N, Brandolini A, Vecchi G (2011) Disuguaglianza. In: Vecchi G (ed) In ricchezza e in povertà. Il benessere degli italiani dall'Unità ad oggi. Bologna, Il Mulino

Barca F, Ciampi CA (1998) La Nuova Programmazione e il Mezzogiorno. Donzelli, Roma

Barucci P, Miotti D, Pellegrini G (2011) I divari territoriali in una prospettiva storica: dall'unità d'Italia ad oggi. In: Pescosolido G (ed) Cento anni di attività dell'Associazione Nazionale per gli Interessi del Mezzogiorno d'Italia e la questione meridionale oggi. Rubettino editore, pp 123–153

Bernini C, Pellegrini G (2011) How are growth and productivity in private firms affected by public subsidy? Evidence from a regional policy. Reg Sci Urban Econ 41:253–261

Bodo G, Sestito P (1991) Le vie dello sviluppo. Il Mulino, Bologna

Cafiero S (1996) Questione meridionale e unità nazionale (1861-1995). La Nuova Italia Scientifica, Roma

Cannari L, Franco D (2011) Il Mezzogiorno: ritardi, qualità dei servizi pubblici, politiche. Stato e Mercato (1): 3–40

Cannari L, Magnani M, Pellegrini G (2010) Critica della ragione meridionale. Il Sud e le politiche pubbliche. Roma-Bari, Laterza

Castronovo V (1975) La storia economica. In Storia d'Italia. Dall'unità ad oggi. Da contadini ad operai. Einaudi, Torino

Cerqua A, Pellegrini G (2014) Do subsidies to private capital boost firms' growth? A multiple regression discontinuity design approach. J Public Econ 109(C):114–126

Ciocca P (2007) Ricchi per sempre? Una storia economica d'Italia (1796-2005). Torino, Bollati Boringhieri

Daniele V, Malanima P (2007) Il prodotto delle regioni e il divario Nord-Sud in Italia (1861-2004). Rivista di politica economica marzo-aprile 2007, pp 267–315

Cohen e Federico (2001) Lo sviluppo economico italiano: 1820-1960. Il Mulino, Bologna

De Blasio G, Lotti F (eds) (2008) La valutazione degli aiuti alle imprese. Il Mulino, Bologna

Del Monte A, Giannola A (1997) Istituzioni economiche e Mezzogiorno nell'economia italiana. La Nuova Italia Scientifica, Roma

Eckaus RS (1961) The North-South differential in Italian economic development. J Econ Hist, XXI(3):285–317

Federico G (2007) Ma l'agricoltura meridionale era davvero arretrata? Rivista di politica economica marzo-aprile 2007, pp 317–340

Felice E (2007a) Divari regionali e intervento pubblico. Il Mulino, Bologna

Felice E (2007b) I divari regionali in Italia sulla base degli indicatori sociali. Rivista di politica economica marzo-aprile 2007, pp 359–405

Fenoaltea S (2006) L'economia italiana dall'Unità alla Grande Guerra. Laterza, Rome Bari

Gerschenkron A (1965) Il problema storico dell'arretratezza economica. Einaudi, Torino

Iuzzolino G, Pellegrini G, Viesti G (2011) Convergence among Italian Regions, 1861-2011, Quaderni di Storia Economica, n. 22, 2011, Banca d'Italia, Roma

Iuzzolino G, Pellegrini G, Viesti G (2013) Regional convergence. In: Toniolo G (ed) The Oxford handbook of the Italian economy since unification, Jan 2013
Mauro L, Pigliaru F (2011) Social capital, institutions and growth: further lessons from the Italian regional divide, CRENOS, working paper, no. 3
Romeo R (1988) Breve storia della grande industria in Italia 1861-1961. Il Saggiatore, Milano
Rossi S (1998) La politica economica italiana. Laterza, Roma-Bari
Saraceno P (1974) Il meridionalismo dopo la ricostruzione (1948-1957), Monografie Svimez. Giuffrè, Roma
Toniolo G (1988) Storia economica dell'Italia liberale 1850-1918. Il Mulino, Bologna
Trigilia C (1992) Sviluppo senza autonomia. Effetti perversi delle politiche nel Mezzogiorno. Bologna, Il Mulino
Trigilia C (2012) Why the Italian Mezzogiorno did not Achieve a Sustainable Growth, Cambio, Anno II, N. 4/Dicember 2012, pp 137–148
Vecchi G (2011) In ricchezza e in povertà. Il benessere degli italiani dall'Unità ad oggi. Il Mulino, Bologna
Viesti G (2009) Mezzogiorno a tradimento. Il Nord, il Sud e la politica che non c'è. Laterza, Roma-Bari
Zamagni V (1993) Dalla periferia al centro. La seconda rinascita economica dell'Italia 1861-1990. Il Mulino, Bologna

Guido Pellegrini is Full Professor in Statistical Methods for Regional Policies and Statistics at the Department of Social Sciences and Economics, Sapienza, University of Rome (Italy). Previously, he was Economist at the Research Department of Bank of Italy, where he managed the Regional Analysis Unit. He participated in several projects and committees on European and national policy evaluation, in Italy and abroad. He was the Scientific Director of the evaluation of several national and regional programmes and policies. Recently, he collaborated in the definition of national and regional strategies for smart specialisation in Italy. He has published numerous papers in international journals and books on policy evaluation, industrial and regional policies, economic growth and convergence among regions, local development and economic statistics.

Part III
Regional Upgrading II: Human Capital, Education, Labour Market and Migration

Chapter 10
The Role of Education in Regional Labour Markets: Evidence from Two Fragile Economies

Enrique López-Bazo, Vassilis Monastiriotis, and Elisabet Motellón

JEL Classification I26 • J64 • R12

10.1 Introduction

Disparities across economies are sizeable and persistent within the European Union. This is so, regardless of the measure that is used to proxy for the level of social and economic development (e.g., EC 2010). In the case of the labour market, it is well known that the incidence of unemployment varies enormously between member states as a result of differences in the functioning of that market but also in the fundamentals of the economy in each country. Less flexible institutions and higher regulation have been claimed to produce more unemployment in the southern EU countries, particularly during downturns (OECD 2012). In this context, Greece and Spain are two paradigmatic cases in the EU with regard to their high levels of unemployment. In 2012, one out of four individuals in the labour force were unemployed in these two countries. This is in sharp contrast with figures on unemployment in countries such as Austria, the Netherlands and Germany (around 5%). Actually, the Greek and Spanish unemployment rates are far above those in other southern economies such as Italy and Portugal, and in Ireland, which was also strongly affected by the economic crisis.

If differences across economies in labour market institutions and regulation were the sole reason behind the disparities in the incidence of unemployment, we should

E. López-Bazo (✉)
AQR, University of Barcelona, Avda. Diagonal 690, 08034 Barcelona, Spain
e-mail: elopez@ub.edu

V. Monastiriotis
European Institute and Hellenic Observatory, LSE, Cowdray House, Houghton Street, WC2A 2AE, London, UK
e-mail: v.monastiriotis@lse.ac.uk

E. Motellón
Open University of Catalonia, Avda. Tibidabo 39-43, 08035 Barcelona, Spain
e-mail: emotellon@uoc.edu

M. Fonseca, U. Fratesi (eds.), *Regional Upgrading in Southern Europe*, Advances in Spatial Science, DOI 10.1007/978-3-319-49818-8_10

not observe significant differences within countries; that is to say between regions in a country with similar institutional frameworks. However, this is not the case. As is shown in this chapter, the order of magnitude of regional disparities in unemployment rates in Greece and Spain is similar, or even larger, than the one between EU countries. As an example, in the spring of 2012 unemployment in Dytiki Makedonia was 30%, twice the figure of 14.7% in the Greek region with the lowest unemployment rate, Ionia Nisia. Similar regional differences exist in Spain, with the unemployment rate in Andalusia (34.6%) being more than double that of the Basque Country (14.9%).

Alongside the differences in unemployment, economies in the EU also differ in terms of the level of wages earned by workers. Wages in some countries are higher to compensate for differences in the cost of living, but also because of differences in the level of firms' productivity, and in institutions of the labour market, e.g., the system of collective bargaining (Peeters and den Reijer 2011). Whatever the case, the average hourly earnings in Greece and Spain are below the EU27 and the Euro area—both in nominal and in real terms. Actually, leaving aside the central and eastern member states, these two countries, jointly with Portugal, are at the bottom of the list of EU member states with regard to the wage level. Of course, significant regional disparities in wages exist also within countries in the EU (Duranton and Monastiriotis 2002; García and Molina 2002; Pereira and Galego 2011). As we show later in this chapter, in Greece and Spain such disparities are also very sizeable and, importantly, they have been quite persistent during the crisis, despite the overall trend of declining average wages following the crisis in the two countries.

Developments in unemployment and wages are important both at the aggregate and at the individual level—reflecting conditions of labour market dynamism and labour market success, respectively. The link between wages and unemployment (especially in relation to the interplay between the individual and aggregate levels) has been widely discussed in the literature, often with conflicting predictions about the nature as well as the direction of the relationship (e.g., from the theory of compensating differentials proposing that high wages are induced by *high* unemployment as a compensation for it; to the theoretical explanations of the wage curve, which suggest that high wages are induced by *low* unemployment, either via efficiency wage considerations or via union bargaining power) (Nijkamp and Poot 2005). Our interest in this chapter, as we explain below, is not directly in the relationship between these two variables, but rather in how these two variables respond, both at the aggregate and the individual level, to the human capital endowments of regions and individuals and especially how this response varies across space (for different regions) in any particular point in time and over the business cycle. By looking at both wages and unemployment we can obtain a more spherical picture about the role of education for the regional labour markets on the aggregate and for allocating individual workers into jobs: both in the sense of affecting one's chances of getting a job (unemployment) and in the sense of affecting the quality of the job obtained (as proxied by the wage). Our focus is on the cases of Greece and Spain, two countries with known problems of regional disparity and a substantially accentuated impact from the recent crisis.

In this context, the first objective of this chapter is to describe regional disparities in the labour market performance of the two countries during the period covering the economic boom from the early years of the last decade to the great recession that was sparked by the Eurozone crisis at the start of this decade. This is of interest since it is well known that the crisis hit these two economies with particular virulence due to their macroeconomic imbalances and the weaknesses of their economic structures. This resulted in adjustments in employment and wages in industries, and in connection with this also in regions, that were among the most dynamic during the booming period.

Arguably, an important factor in processes of adjustment, and in the determination of equilibrium outcomes with regard to wages and unemployment more generally, has to do with the human capital endowment available to each (regional or national) economy and thus with the level of education of individuals residing in each economy. Thus, as a second objective, in this chapter we provide evidence of the effect of the individuals' level of education on unemployment and wages in each region. Under the assumption that the higher the level of educational attainment of an individual, the lower her chances are to be unemployed and the higher the wage she earns, our hypothesis is that, ceteris paribus, regions with high endowments of education had less unemployment and a higher wage level—and increasingly so, in relative terms, during the crisis. This implies that the regional distribution of individuals' education would be a key driver of disparities in labour market outcomes and in regional responses to the crisis.

That said, the contribution of education to favourable economic outcomes, both at the individual and at the aggregate/regional level, should not be taken as fixed across space. In contrast, it is reasonable to expect that this contribution will vary—sometimes widely—across labour markets of different fundamentals, different structural characteristics and different capacities. Following this line of thought, our contribution in this chapter aims, in addition to the above, to provide evidence on the variability of the impact that education has on unemployment and wages, depending on the region. Our hypothesis is that education acts as a mechanism for sorting individuals participating in the labour market into employment or unemployment, and that for the salaried workers it positively affects wages through improvements in worker's productivity. In other words, education plays a role for allocating workers to jobs—both in a dichotomous sense (employment vs. unemployment) and in terms of job quality (as proxied by the level of wages). However, the strength of these two effects is shaped by region-level characteristics, causing the sorting mechanism and the wage return to be more intense in some regions than in others. Although we do not investigate empirically which region-level characteristics may be responsible for the variations that we document across regions, it is intuitive to expect that these will relate to both geographical and labour market parameters—for example, accessibility and inter-regional labour mobility, or—and perhaps most notably—sectoral structure/specialisations and labour market thickness/density.

The empirical evidence on regional unemployment rates and wage levels in Greece and Spain, from 2002 to 2012, is based on micro-level data from the Labour Force Survey and the Structure of Earnings Survey. These data also allow us to compute a measure of educational attainment for individuals in each region, which is used to estimate the corresponding effect of education on the probability of being unemployed and on the wage return to schooling. These estimates are then used to assess regional disparities, not simply in the levels of education but also in the *effect* of education with respect to both unemployment and wages.

Our analysis reveals some common and interesting patterns in the two countries. In both countries, sizeable disparities exist not only in wages and unemployment but also in average human capital endowments (years of schooling). But while average years of schooling, both for the employed and for the labour force as a whole, increased notably during the crisis—consistent with expectations about intensified sorting and bumping-down when demand collapses—regional disparities in these remained rather stable, showing persistence across the business cycle. In turn, unemployment differentials seem to have followed a pro-cyclical trend in both countries, rising in the pre-crisis period but declining during the crisis. Pro-cyclicality also characterizes the evolution of regional wage disparities in Spain—but not in Greece. The role of education as a sorting mechanism during the crisis is further manifested by our analysis of the impact of education on the probability of unemployment and on individuals' wages. We find that the marginal effect of education on an individual's probability of being employed has increased dramatically during the crisis—albeit with significant differences across regions. In contrast, returns to education (and thus the contribution of education to obtaining a better job) have increased much more modestly and—importantly—for a large number of Greek regions, especially in the northern parts of the country, they have actually declined with the crisis. The rest of the chapter is organized as follows. The source of the datasets and the details on the selected samples and the periods under analysis are provided in the next section. Section 6.3 describes the distribution of wages and unemployment rates in the two countries under analysis and examines the extent of regional disparities in these aggregates. It also pays attention to the evolution over the period under analysis. A similar description regarding the individuals' endowment of education is provided in Sect. 6.4. Sections 6.5 and 6.6 look in turn into the effect that education has on unemployment rates and wages (respectively), based on estimates from an econometric analysis of unemployment probabilities and returns to schooling. In these two sections we first introduce the empirical model used to obtain the estimate of the effect of education and then summarize the main results, stressing both the regional variability and the changes over the time period. Finally, the discussion and interpretation of the results and some concluding comments are provided in Sect. 6.7.

10.2 Datasets

Micro-level data is required to study the effect of individuals' education on their labour market performance (with regard to the likelihood of being employed or unemployed, and with respect to their wage level). Since we are interested in the effect of education in each of the Greek and Spanish regions, the source of the micro-data must ensure representativeness at the territorial level; that is to say, the sample for each region needs to represent the corresponding population. In the case of the effect of educational attainment on the probability of being unemployed, such information is available from the Labour Force Survey (LFS). The LFS also includes information on wage earnings in the Greek sample, while in the case of Spain such information is obtained from the Structure of Earnings Survey (SES), as the Spanish LFS does not contain information on individuals' wages. The Greek LFS is conducted under the auspices of the Hellenic Statistical Authority (ELSTAT) on a quarterly basis. The Spanish LFS is produced by the Spanish National Institute for Statistics (INE) also on a quarterly basis, while the SES is conducted every 4 years and, for the analysis conducted here, covers the years 2002, 2006 and 2010.[1] To maximize the comparability of the effects of education on unemployment and wages in Spain, we selected the same years for the LFS data. Thus, our analysis of unemployment is based on LFS data for 2002, 2006, 2010 and 2012 in both countries; our analysis of wages for Greece is based on the same data-source and for the same years; while our analysis of wages for Spain is based on the SES data and covers only the years 2002, 2006 and 2010. Concerning the LFS data, as in similar studies in the literature, we selected the information corresponding to the second quarter of each year (March–May). We assume that the second quarter is the least affected by seasonal fluctuations, that particularly affects regions specialized in tourism and related services and in activities of the primary sector. In any case, it should be noted that the evidence reported in the following sections on the effect of education on unemployment is robust to the selection of any of the other quarters.

The LFS provides information on the working status of individuals participating in the labour market, i.e., whether they are employed or unemployed. It also contains information regarding the highest educational level attained by the individual, the age at which the individual completed their continuous full-time education, and other personal and household characteristics that are considered to exert an effect on working status (e.g., gender, nationality, age, and number of household members). The spring quarter of the Greek LFS surveys includes around 31,000 households (approximately 76,000 individuals). After restricting our sample to individuals aged between 16 and 65, and some further data cleaning, we are left

[1]SES data are also available for Greece although access to this data is restricted and at the time of writing this chapter such data were not available to us. In any case, as we show later, the impact of the crisis in Greece, in contrast to what happened in Spain, unfolded largely after 2010 and thus the use of LFS data, which covers the years up to 2012 is imperative.

with around 50,000 individuals for each of our study years, of which around 18,000 are salaried employees (wage earners).[2] In Spain, the LFS sample includes approximately 60,000 households, equivalent to around 180,000 people interviewed in each quarter. In our analysis, the selected sample includes individuals aged between 16 and 65 that after some data cleaning, results in a sample of around 110,000 individuals in each of the study years. As indicated above, the design of the LFS ensures that the samples are representative of the national as well as the regional populations for each of the 13 Greek and 17 Spanish NUTS2 regions, allowing us to obtain reliable estimates of the effect of education on the probability of being unemployed at the regional level in the two countries.

In turn, the SES is also produced by the INE according to the standards defined by EUROSTAT in a statistical operation that covers the entire European Union. This survey provides information on wages and the effective working time for all individuals in the sample. It also includes information about an extensive set of worker characteristics (including the highest educational level attained) and of firm characteristics. We purged the original sample provided by the INE to remove outliers and to ensure comparability of the information in the three periods analysed. In that regard, it should be noted that the sample for 2002 did not include workers in firms with less than 10 employees, so in this study we decided to standardize the information regarding the 3 years analysed, removing observations for workers in establishments with less than 10 employees in the samples for 2006 and 2010. Something similar was done with respect to sectors of activity covered by the SES in each of the 3 years. Employees of the public sector were not included in the analysis, since this sector was incorporated in the survey for 2010.[3] From the sample provided by the INE for each of the 3 years, we selected the observations for the full-time employees aged 65 years or less, from all Spanish regions with the exception of Ceuta and Melilla, which are two small Spanish cities in the North of Africa and thus with peculiar characteristics. The final sample used in our analysis of the effect of education on wages for the Spanish regions is of 120,593 individuals in 2002, 155,754 in 2006 and 127,202 in 2010. As indicated above for the case of the LFS, the design of the SES also ensures the representativeness of the sample for each of the Spanish NUTS2 regions, allowing us to obtain a reliable estimate of the returns to education in each region.

Using the information in the SES for each individual, we calculated the gross hourly wage as the gross wage (before taxes and including the worker's

[2]Our working-age sample is 50,529, 48,605, 49,076 and 38,151 for the years 2002, 2006, 2010 and 2012 respectively. Wage-earners for the same years are 17,188, 17,978, 17,861 and 11,363. Note that in 2012 total sample size drops to 25,000 households (61,000 individuals).

[3]For Greece, the LFS data cover all employees in all sectors. This adds crucial detail in the information processed in this chapter, as small-firm employment in Greece accounts for a large part of total salaried employment. To keep consistency with the wage data for Spain, we exclude public-sector workers from the Greek sample. The implication, however, is that the wage data for Greece are not directly comparable with those of Spain. We account for this in our subsequent discussion of the two country cases in Sects. 6.3 and 6.6.

contribution to the social insurance system) paid by the firm in the month of October of the corresponding year divided by the number of hours actually worked by the employee during that month (the result of multiplying the weekly hours provided in the survey by the average number of weeks in a month, 4.429). The wage includes the base salary and extra payments related to the job and the workplace conditions, such as bonuses for seniority, knowledge, specific training, work during the night and holidays, dangerous tasks, toxicity, and productivity. However, it does not include payments for overtime work, since the SES does not provide all the information required for its proper inclusion in the calculation of the payment per hour actually worked. A similar approach has been taken for the calculation of hourly gross wages in Greece. In the Greek LFS wage data refer to weekly gross earnings (including bonuses but excluding overtime pay) and are reported in bands of 250 €. We divided the mean value of the wage income bands per observation by the reported usual weekly hours to create a pseudo-continuous wage variable.[4] This is an approach typically used in the case of wage data from the Greek LFS and, as has been shown elsewhere (Christopoulou and Monastiriotis 2014, 2016), it provides consistent results in a wage-equations context. As mentioned already, given these differences in the measurement and coverage of the wage data in the two datasets, the average regional wage levels that we derive are not directly comparable between the two countries (the use of small firms in the Greek data will tend to produce lower average wages than in Spain) and the same can be argued for the estimated returns to schooling in the two countries, to the extent that the latter vary by firm size. This, however, does not affect the main aim of our analysis, that is, assessing the extent of regional disparities, and their evolution over time, *within* each country with regard to average wages and the returns to schooling.

10.3 Wage and Unemployment Regional Disparities

As a first step in our analysis, this section examines the wage level and the unemployment rate in each region of the two countries for the years under analysis. Beyond the particular figure for each region and year, the main aim is to provide evidence on the magnitude of the regional labour market disparities in Greece and Spain, and how they evolved during the recent expansive and recessive periods. Table 10.1 summarizes the information for the Greek regions; that information for Spain is in Table 10.2.

Figures for Greece in Table 10.1 indicate that the average nominal wage of private sector workers in the entire country rose during the expansion and the early

[4]For the top, open-ended band, we set the upper limit to 2.250 € (calculated as the lower limit of the open interval plus two times the width of the closed intervals). We also experimented with other 'mean' values for this band, but this did not influence the substance of the results we obtain.

Table 10.1 Wage per hour (€) and unemployment rate (%) in the Greek regions

	2002		2006		2010		2012	
	Wage	Urate	Wage	Urate	Wage	Urate	Wage	Urate
Anatoliki Mak.	3.73	10.89	4.71	12.21	5.20	14.77	4.79	24.76
Kentriki Mak.	3.87	11.50	4.86	10.01	5.44	13.16	5.11	25.67
Dytiki Mak.	4.15	15.11	4.79	15.46	5.55	15.18	5.26	30.76
Ipeiros	3.66	12.58	4.67	9.57	5.48	12.84	4.82	22.97
Thessalia	3.67	11.77	4.64	8.67	5.37	11.88	5.04	22.86
Ionia Nisia	3.42	7.49	4.77	14.29	5.11	12.87	5.03	14.92
Dytiki Ellada	3.92	11.60	4.91	9.70	5.29	11.52	4.91	24.83
Sterea Ellada	4.15	10.56	5.00	9.32	5.74	12.04	5.19	28.76
Attiki	4.28	9.80	5.18	8.32	6.03	11.86	5.83	24.38
Peloponnisos	3.95	9.35	4.64	8.56	5.38	10.57	4.71	20.48
Voreio Aigaio	4.11	10.36	4.70	10.01	5.23	8.58	4.83	22.45
Notio Aigaio	3.63	16.34	5.02	8.20	5.80	12.75	4.45	17.32
Kriti	3.74	7.53	4.69	6.48	5.58	11.35	5.04	23.56
Greece	4.05	10.64	4.98	9.24	5.72	12.23	5.40	24.20

Table 10.2 Wage per hour (€) and unemployment rate (%) in the Spanish regions

	2002		2006		2010		2012
	Wage	Urates	Wage	Urates	Wage	Urates	Urates
Andalusia	7.50	18.93	8.10	12.73	11.06	27.93	34.00
Aragon	7.99	5.87	9.21	5.78	11.30	14.29	18.78
Asturias	7.34	10.39	8.40	8.12	10.93	16.44	21.14
Balearic Isl.	6.50	6.92	8.31	6.69	10.80	19.98	21.29
Canary Isl.	6.14	11.28	7.05	11.49	9.45	29.70	33.42
Cantabria	6.49	9.80	8.04	6.74	10.84	13.93	17.56
Castile Leon	6.43	10.75	8.46	8.41	10.61	16.43	19.89
Castile La Mancha	7.02	9.38	7.87	8.99	10.42	21.48	28.82
Catalonia	8.56	9.60	10.11	6.51	11.95	17.85	22.12
Valencia	6.68	11.16	8.23	7.86	10.65	23.89	27.24
Extremadura	6.49	18.72	6.63	13.74	9.44	22.52	33.45
Galicia	6.42	12.09	7.80	8.68	9.72	15.71	21.22
Madrid	8.96	6.96	10.53	7.03	11.89	16.53	19.04
Murcia	6.45	11.32	7.65	7.94	10.74	21.35	26.26
Navarre	8.78	5.14	10.25	5.60	11.64	10.99	16.60
Basque C.	9.61	9.39	11.09	7.15	13.61	10.47	14.65
La Rioja	6.75	7.60	8.01	6.14	9.28	12.28	22.80
Spain	7.90	11.25	9.25	8.58	11.32	20.21	24.78

Note: The data on wages for the Spanish regions are not available for 2012.

stages of the crisis, from 2002 to 2010. In turn, the impact of the crisis in the Greek economy caused a decrease in the average wage in 2012. A similar pattern in the evolution of the wage level is observed in all the Greek regions. It is interesting to note that despite the dramatic effects of the crisis, the wage at the end of the period under analysis was above the level in 2006 in the country as a whole and in most of its regions. The exceptions include Notio Aigaio where the wage in 2012 was 11% lower than the level in 2006, and Dytiki Ellada with the same level in both years.

In fact, regional disparities in wages were clearly affected by the situation of the Greek economy over the period under analysis. For instance, the average wage in Attiki in 2002 was 25% higher than that in Ionia Nisia, which was at the bottom in the regional ranking of that year. Attiki ranked first in the other 3 years under analysis. However, neither the gap nor the region with the lowest wage level remained stable. The wage gaps between Attiki and Thessalia in 2006, and Attiki and Ionia Nisia in 2010, were 12 and 18%, respectively. In contrast, the wage in Attiki was as much as 31% higher than the level in Notio Aigaio in 2012. Figures on wages in Table 10.1 also reveal that the period of expansion and the impact of the great depression modified the relative situation of a large number of regions. The most striking evidence of churning in the regional distribution is that of Notio Aigaio, a region which relies greatly on tourism and which is thus highly dependent on fluctuations in the economic cycle. This region was the second at the bottom of the list in 2002, with a wage level that was 18% lower than the one in Attiki. During the boom, it experienced a notable improvement in the wage level that led it to be ranked second in 2006 and 2010, with wage levels only 3 and 4% lower than in Attiki. However, the crisis had a stronger impact on Notio Aigaio, causing a sharp decrease in its wages which led the region to the lowest position in the ranking, and a gap with respect to Attiki that was as wide as the above-mentioned, 31%.

The coefficient of variation, as a simple but useful measure of regional dispersion in wage levels, decreased quite substantially from 6.6% in 2002 to 3.6% in 2006, and increased from that year on, to 4.8% in 2010 and 6.6% in 2012. So, it seems that a certain process of convergence in regional wages came to an end as a result of the crisis.

The information in Table 10.1 also provides evidence on unemployment rates. In the country as a whole they were around 10% in the expansive period, rising to a bit more than 12% in 2010. But it was in 2012 when the destruction of jobs caused by the crisis led the Greek unemployment rate to as much as 24%. With almost no exceptions, the same pattern in the evolution of unemployment is observed in the Greek regions, though the changes were more dramatic in some regions that, as will be discussed later, caused variations over time in the amount of regional disparities. In the first part of the period (2002–2006), unemployment rates declined in most regions, although by no means in all—thus resulting in an overall widening of the regional distribution of unemployment, as the most dynamic regions appear to have benefited more from the expansion of the economy nationally. The increase in unemployment in 2010 and, particularly, in 2012 did not prevent the persistence of a substantial gap between regions with the highest and lowest rates (15.2% in Dytiki Makedonia vis-à-vis 8.6% in Voreio Aigaio in 2010, and 30.8% in the former region versus 17.3% in Notio Aigaio in 2012). Nevertheless, with a few exceptions (mainly, Notio Aigaio and Peloponnisos, the largest increases in unemployment between 2006 and 2012 occurred in the regions that had originally below-national unemployment rates (Kriti, Sterea Ellada, Attiki, Thessalia). As a result, the increase in the country-average unemployment rate was combined with a decrease also in disparities, as measured by the coefficient of variation, during the years of the crisis. The coefficient of variation went down from 0.24 and 0.27 in 2002 and 2006, to 0.14 and 0.17 in 2010 and 2012.

The average wage and the unemployment rates in Spain and in each of its regions are shown in Table 10.2. Figures for the country as a whole reveal that the average nominal wage increased over the period for which data for Spain is available. Interestingly, the average nominal hourly wage in 2010, when the crisis already had exerted its initial effects in the Spanish economy, was 22% higher than the level in 2006, far above the 8% inflation rate in that period.

On the other hand, Table 10.2 provides clear evidence on the extent of regional wage disparities in Spain. At the beginning of the last decade, the average wage levels in Catalonia, Madrid, Navarre and the Basque Country were about 50% higher than that observed for regions with the lowest levels, the Canary Islands, Castile Leon, Extremadura, Galicia and Murcia. With few exceptions, the ranking of regions was maintained throughout the decade, although the dispersion decreased over the period, particularly since the beginning of the crisis. In 2002, the coefficient of variation provides a value of 0.14, only slightly above the one in 2006 which amounts to 0.13. This is in contrast with the value for 2010, which decreases to 0.10. In line with this, the wage gap between regions with extreme levels exceeded 60% in 2006, falling to just under 50% in 2010. The figures for the last year suggest that the reason behind the decline in the degree of regional inequality is on the moderate increase in the regions that have traditionally presented higher average wages. Thus, the deviation from the Spanish average in Catalonia, Madrid and Navarre was less in 2010 than in previous periods. The exception is the Basque Country, which was able to maintain the distance with respect to the wage level in the rest of the country.

With regard to the figures for the unemployment rate in Spain, Table 10.2 shows a marked cyclical evolution, with continuous decrease over the expansion and rapid rebound following the recession at the end of the decade. As a result, one out of four individuals participating in the labour market were unemployed in the spring of 2012. When compared with the unemployment figures in Greece, it is evident that the crisis hit Spain much earlier than Greece (with unemployment rising to 12.2% in Greece versus 20.2% in Spain in 2010), although both countries converged to similar unemployment rates by 2012.

As in previous decades, Andalusia and Extremadura were the Spanish regions showing the highest unemployment rates in 2002, with a value slightly below 20%, substantially higher than in the country as a whole (11.2%). This is in sharp contrast with rates between 5% and 7% observed in Aragon, Balearic Islands, Madrid and Navarre. Unemployment went down in the whole of Spain in 2006, largely as a result of the decrease in regions with persistently high rates. In fact, the decline in regions that had lower rates in 2002 is negligible, suggesting the existence of a natural rate of unemployment in these regions, of around 6%. As a result, regional differences in unemployment rates decreased in 2006 compared to those observed in 2002 (the coefficient of variation went down from 0.34 to 0.28), although there were no significant changes in the ranking (Andalusia, Extremadura and the Canary Islands stayed among the regions with higher rates, whereas Aragon, Balearic Islands and Navarre are among those showing lower rates). As mentioned above, the unemployment rate in the country as a whole rose almost 12 points to over 20% in 2010. Regions with historically high rates, such as Andalusia, Extremadura and the Canary Islands contributed significantly to that increase, with unemployment rates doubling (and in some cases almost tripling) compared to their 2006 values. Other regions, whose labour market benefited largely from the expansive period, also made a significant contribution. For instance, unemployment rates in the Balearic Islands, Castile La Mancha, Valencia and Murcia rose from about 8% to 20% or more. By contrast, the unemployment rate in other regions stood at values clearly below average, with Navarre and the Basque Country having rates slightly above 10%, almost half the national average. In any case, and despite regional asymmetries in the response to the crisis, the overall extent of disparities remained similar in 2010 to that observed in 2006 (the coefficient of variation remained at 28% in 2010). The deepening of the recession in 2012 caused further increases in the unemployment rate in all regions that, ultimately, provoked a reduction in the coefficient of variation, to a value of 0.25.

All in all, the simple descriptive analysis confirms the evidence reported in studies for previous periods on the existence of outstanding regional disparities in wages and unemployment rates in Greece and Spain. With the crisis, regional disparities in both unemployment and wages seem to have declined mildly in Spain; but in Greece disparities appear to have followed an upward trend as the crisis intensified (in 2012). In the next section we look at whether a similar picture, with regard to regional disparities and their evolution over time, characterizes the distribution of education endowments in the two countries.

10.4 Regional Endowments of Education

To measure the regional levels in the endowment of education, and the extent of cross-regional disparities in it, we have relied as before on the micro-data derived from the LFS and SES databases. For all regions in the two countries we have computed the average years of schooling (a well-known synthetic measure of educational attainment), for the 4 years under analysis. Results for the active population and for the wage earners are summarized in Tables 10.3 and 10.4 for, respectively, Greece and Spain.

The level of educational attainment increased over the period under analysis in the two countries, both for the active population and the wage earners. Years of schooling of the active Greek population increased by 1.2 years between 2002 and 2012, which corresponds to an increase of more than 10% in a decade. A similar improvement in the endowment of education in this country is observed for the group of wage earners. The rise in the measure of education was somewhat lower in

Table 10.3 Average years of schooling of active, and wage earners populations in the Greek regions

	Actives				Wage earners			
	2002	2006	2010	2012	2002	2006	2010	2012
Anatoliki Mak.	10.22	11.10	11.47	11.51	10.36	11.01	11.68	12.26
Kentriki Mak.	11.94	12.42	12.78	13.04	12.05	12.41	12.65	13.15
Dytiki Mak.	11.16	11.81	11.97	12.39	11.23	11.52	12.07	12.61
Ipeiros	11.23	11.72	11.92	12.20	11.36	11.29	11.77	11.62
Thessalia	11.10	11.89	12.33	12.55	11.34	11.61	12.30	12.42
Ionia Nisia	10.67	11.09	11.53	11.68	10.63	11.38	11.40	11.70
Dytiki Ellada	10.68	11.62	11.91	12.12	10.82	11.51	11.90	12.20
Sterea Ellada	10.61	11.53	11.73	12.20	10.56	11.29	11.29	11.98
Attiki	12.93	13.49	13.75	14.09	12.61	13.06	13.30	13.87
Peloponnisos	10.98	11.44	11.75	12.07	11.57	11.67	11.84	12.01
Voreio Aigaio	11.26	12.11	12.35	12.33	11.46	11.80	12.12	11.76
Notio Aigaio	10.90	11.72	11.53	12.31	10.57	11.40	11.38	12.68
Kriti	11.14	11.92	11.83	12.16	11.43	11.90	11.59	12.36
Greece	11.80	12.45	12.72	13.03	11.95	12.37	12.63	13.16

Table 10.4 Average years of schooling of active, and wage earners populations in the Spanish regions

	Actives				Wage earners		
	2002	2006	2010	2012	2002	2006	2010
Andalusia	10.13	10.82	10.92	11.00	10.43	10.20	11.35
Aragon	11.07	11.72	11.70	11.75	10.46	10.65	11.40
Asturias	11.09	11.57	11.99	12.15	10.46	10.87	11.34
Balearic Isl.	10.50	10.95	11.05	11.29	9.39	9.34	10.45
Canary Isl.	10.40	10.83	10.77	10.93	9.65	9.28	10.70
Cantabria	10.96	11.72	12.09	12.15	9.88	10.41	11.24
Castile Leon	10.80	11.32	11.62	11.78	9.85	10.56	11.01
Castile La Mancha	10.16	10.61	10.88	11.03	10.19	10.05	10.52
Catalonia	11.17	11.52	11.43	11.69	10.69	11.17	11.58
Valencia	10.69	11.30	11.29	11.47	10.00	10.15	11.03
Extremadura	10.14	10.83	11.01	10.97	10.36	9.81	11.10
Galicia	10.43	11.38	11.65	11.67	10.15	10.24	11.09
Madrid	11.92	12.10	12.26	12.36	11.68	11.58	12.09
Murcia	10.60	10.75	10.65	10.88	10.23	9.95	10.95
Navarre	11.45	12.01	12.34	12.03	10.95	10.78	11.29
Basque C.	11.72	12.50	12.73	12.76	11.46	11.69	11.99
La Rioja	10.80	11.40	11.86	11.95	9.35	9.09	9.92
Spain	10.88	11.39	11.47	11.60	10.67	10.77	11.46

Spain for the actives—about 0.7 years over the entire period—and similar for wage earners—a rise of 0.8 years between 2002 and 2010. The comparison of the figures for the active population in the two countries also reveals a higher endowment of education in the Greek economy. At the beginning of the analysed period, there was a gap favourable to Greece of about 1 year (11.8 vis-à-vis 10.9) that increased over the time period to 1.4 years in 2012. The gap for wage-earners was even wider, particularly during the expansion (a maximum of 1.6 years in 2006).[5]

As for the regional differences in the individuals' endowment of education, Table 10.3 shows that average years of schooling in densely populated Greek regions, such as Attiki and Kentriki Makedonia, tend to be well above the levels in the less developed areas. Actually, the gap between these regions and Anatoliki Makedonia Ionia Nisia, or Sterea Ellada (as wide as about 2.5 years in some cases) confirms the existence of far from negligible differences across regions in the level of educational attainment. On the other hand, the evolution of the coefficient of variation for the regional endowments of education suggests that disparities remained stable over the period under analysis. In the case of the active population the coefficient takes a value of 0.06 in 2002 and 0.05 in the other 3 years, whereas for wage earners it amounts to 0.05 in 2002 and 0.04 in the other years. That is to say, there seems not to be a change in the degree of regional disparities in the level of educational attainment in Greece induced by the great recession.

A similar conclusion on regional disparities is derived from the information in Table 10.4 for Spain. Traditionally rich regions such as Madrid, the Basque Country, and Navarre are better endowed than the less developed areas in the southern part of the country (Andalusia, the Canary Islands, Extremadura, and Murcia). The gap between the regions with extreme values is between 1.5 and 2 years, depending on the period and the group of individuals, while the ranking is rather stable over the period under analysis. With respect to the evolution of the global level of disparities, the coefficient of variation for the years of schooling in the Spanish regions remains stable at 0.05 over the entire period for the active population, whereas it just shows minor changes for wage earners (0.06, 0.07, and 0.05 respectively for 2002, 2006, and 2010).

Summing up, the simple descriptive evidence in this section confirms that Greek and Spanish regions also differ in terms of the average endowment of education; but this time it appears that regional disparities in education endowments have remained stable during the expansive period and were not particularly affected by the crisis. In contrast, as should be expected, in both countries the educational endowment for wage earners went up with the crisis, reflecting the fact that employment opportunities (for salaried employment) increased for the more educated (relative to the rest) in both countries during the crisis—a result reflecting

[5]However, it should be kept in mind that the source of the Spanish data on actives is different to the one of wage earners. Despite using a similar methodology to compute the years of schooling in both cases, comparability cannot be guaranteed as the sample of wage earners does not include workers in firms with less than 10 employees in Spain. Therefore, the comparison should be made with caution.

some degree of sorting on the basis of education. This is something that we examine formally in the next section.

In particular, in the remainder of this chapter we move on to examine at the individual level the effect that education exerts on an individual's probability of unemployment and on her wage level across the different regions of Greece and Spain—thus departing from most of the previous literature, which has analysed this question using aggregate regional magnitudes. To do so, we revert to an econometric analysis using a human-capital approach involving the estimation of (a) probit regressions on the probability of unemployment and (b) a set of Mincerian wage regressions on individual wages. The next two sections present our estimation method and empirical results from these two sets of analysis.

10.5 The Regional Effect of Education on Unemployment

10.5.1 Empirical Model

The empirical specification is based on the idea that an individual i in region r is unemployed when her propensity of being in such labour status (U_{ir}^*) is above a threshold, that for simplicity it is set at 0:

$$\begin{aligned} U_{ir} &= 1 \text{ if } U_{ir}^* = \beta^r Educ_{ir} + X_{ir}\delta^r + \mu_{ir} > 0 \\ U_{ir} &= 0 \text{ otherwise} \end{aligned}$$

The propensity of unemployment is a latent variable and, thus, unobservable. Instead, we observed if the individual i in region r is unemployed ($U_{ir} = 1$) or not ($U_{ir} = 0$), depending on her propensity of being above or below the threshold. We assume that the propensity of unemployment for each individual in each region depends on a set of personal and household observable characteristics, grouped in X_{ir}, and on the level of individual's educational attainment, $Educ_{ir}$. Instead of imposing a uniform regional effect of education and the other observable characteristics on the propensity of unemployment, the empirical model includes specific coefficients for each region, β^r and δ^r. That is to say, the change in U^* caused by a 1-year increase in education is allowed to differ across regions.

The propensity of unemployment for individual i in region r also depends on unobservable characteristics that are captured by the random component μ_{ir}. Under the assumption of normality of this error term, the estimation of the effect of education on the probability of unemployment can be obtained by a probit model such as:

$$prob(U_{ir} = 1) = \Phi(\beta^r Educ_{ir} + X_{ir}\delta^r)$$

The estimates of the coefficients β^r and δ^r are used to compute the marginal effect of education for individuals in region r, defined as the change in the probability of unemployment that results from increasing the level of education by a year for these individuals while keeping all other individual characteristics at sample mean values.

The control variables included in X in the probit specification for the probability of unemployment are dummy variables for the gender, the nationality (native- versus foreign-born), the marital status (married versus other situations), being head of household, and having children under 9 years old. We also included as continuous variables the number of children (under 16 years old) in the household, the number of household members, and the number of members of the household that were employed other than the surveyed individual. The specifications used to obtain the estimates for the whole of Greece and Spain also included regional dummies.

10.5.2 Results

Our analysis produces a large number of results, which are difficult to report due to space reasons. Given our interest in the role of education, here we only report the marginal effects corresponding to the years of schooling, although the entire set of effects is available from the authors upon request. The results contain two main features: first, the contribution of education to lowering individuals' chances of unemployment appear to rise with the overall level of unemployment (especially over time) and is stronger in Spain than in Greece—suggesting an important role for labour market structure in the relationship between education and unemployment; second, regional differences in this contribution are quite large in both countries and both in periods of expansion and contraction—suggesting in turn an important role for the production structure and regional characteristics also outside the labour market.

The results of the estimate of the marginal effects of education in Greece and each of its regions are summarized in Table 10.5. For the country as a whole, an additional year of schooling contributed significantly to decrease the likelihood of unemployment in the 4 years under analysis. However, the magnitude of the effect evolved over time. It increased from −0.19 percentage points in 2002 to −0.22 points in 2006, and to −0.45 points in 2010. The reduction in the probability of unemployment reached a maximum of 1.1 percentage points in 2012, when the unemployment rate in Greece increased dramatically (see Table 10.1).

However, the significant total effect in the Greek economy hides outstanding regional variation in the impact of education on unemployment. This is clear from

Table 10.5 Marginal effect of schooling on the probability of unemployment in the Greek regions

	2002	2006	2010	2012
Anatoliki Mak.	0.0030**	0.0014	−0.0031	−0.0075***
KentrikiMak.	−0.0007	−0.0047***	−0.0052***	−0.0092***
Dytiki Mak.	−0.0039	−0.0134***	−0.0109***	−0.0189***
Ipeiros	−0.0005	−0.0022	−0.0033*	−0.0118***
Thessalia	0.0023	−0.0025	−0.0023	−0.0104***
Ionia Nisia	−0.0015	−0.0114***	0.0021	−0.0043
Dytiki Ellada	0.0001	0.0007	−0.0008	−0.0045
Sterea Ellada	0.0001	−0.0039**	−0.0027	−0.0072**
Attiki	−0.0017	−0.0050***	−0.0075***	−0.0105***
Peloponnisos	−0.0008	−0.0013	−0.0017	−0.0035
Voreio Aigaio	0.0004	0.0042	−0.0054*	−0.0100*
Notio Aigaio	−0.0042	−0.0021	−0.0052	−0.0032
Kriti	0.0022*	0.0017	0.0005	−0.0072***
Greece	−0.0019***	−0.0022***	−0.0045***	−0.0107***

Note: ***$p<0.01$, **$p<0.05$, *$p<0.1$

the maps in Fig. 10.1, where the size of the circles represents the magnitude of the marginal effect of education on unemployment, for those regions where it is statistically significant. Leaving aside results for 2002, in which the estimated effect is very small in all regions, and is even significantly positive in Anatoliki Makedonia and Kriti, we observe that the number of regions where education has a statistically significant effect on unemployment—which is thus also stronger than that estimated for the country as a whole—is rather limited. For instance, in 2006 the marginal effect was −1.34 percentage points in Dytiki Makedonia and −1.14 points in Ionia Nisia, but in 8 out of the 13 Greek NUTS2 regions, there were no differences in the propensity of unemployment between individuals with different levels of education, once controlling for other characteristics. A similar picture is derived from the estimates for 2010, though there are a few changes in the regions with a significant effect (Dytiki Makedonia, Kentriki Makedonia and Attiki are now the regions with the strongest coefficients). More interesting are the results for the last year under analysis, since the size of the reduction in the chances of being unemployed associated to the level of education increased substantially in all but one region (Notio Aigaio). Actually, in all but four regions the marginal effect is statistically significant for 2012, in contrast with what is observed for the previous years. Still, the generalized increase in the size of the effect did not prevent differences across regions in the impact of education in the last year under analysis. The estimated marginal effect equals −1.89 percentage points in Dytiki Makedonia and −1.18 in Ipeiros, whereas it is not significantly different from zero in Ionia Nisia, Dytiki Ellada, Peloponnisos, and Notio Aigaio.

To properly assess the extent of these disparities, it is useful to calculate the difference in the probability of unemployment for similar individuals who differ only in their level of education in various regions. In the case of Dytiki Makedonia

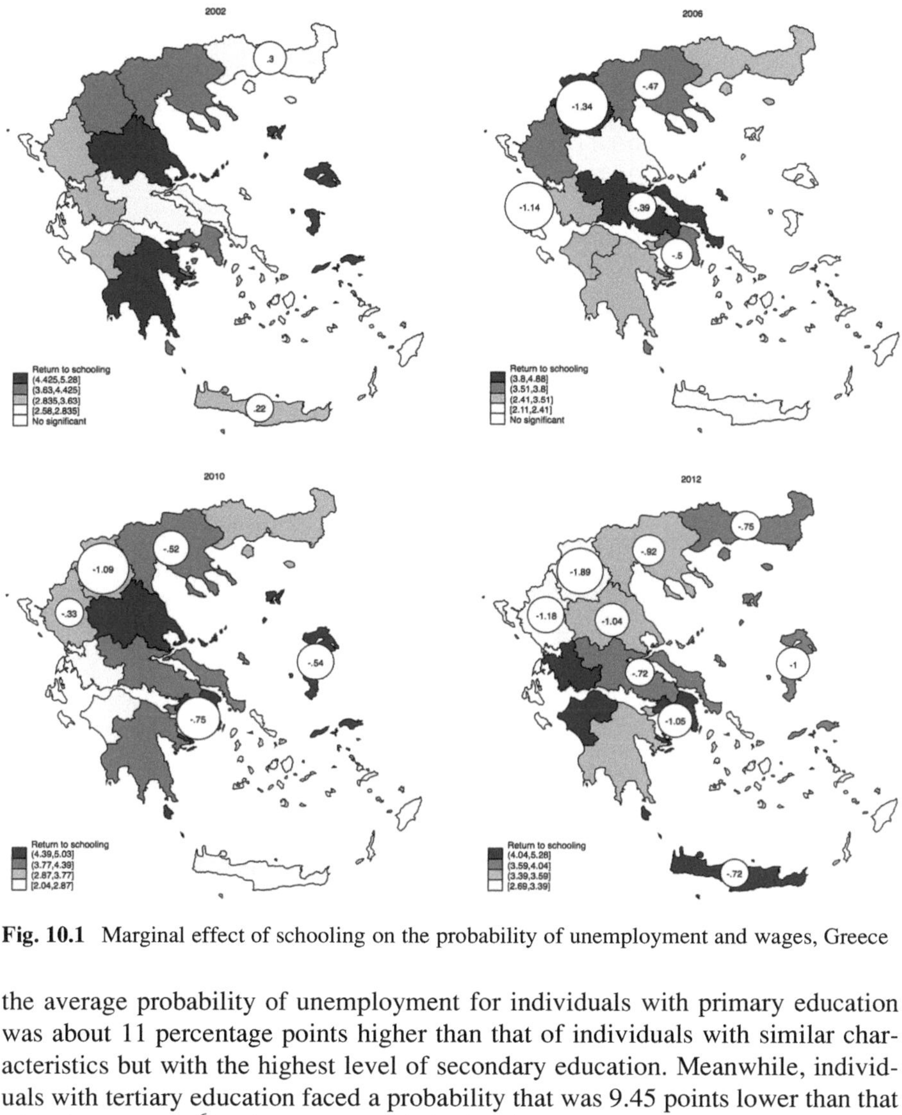

Fig. 10.1 Marginal effect of schooling on the probability of unemployment and wages, Greece

the average probability of unemployment for individuals with primary education was about 11 percentage points higher than that of individuals with similar characteristics but with the highest level of secondary education. Meanwhile, individuals with tertiary education faced a probability that was 9.45 points lower than that of the latter group.[6] In sharp contrast, in Ionia Nisia and the other regions mentioned above there was no difference in the probability of unemployment between similar individuals with primary, high secondary, and tertiary education, since the marginal effect of schooling is not statistically different from zero for these regions. This shows a peculiar dysfunction in those labour markets, as even with a substantial rise

[6]In computing the difference in the probability of unemployment between levels of education, we have used 6 years between primary and the high level of secondary schooling, and 5 years between the latter level and tertiary education. The figures in the text result from multiplying these amounts by the corresponding estimate of the marginal effect.

Table 10.6 Marginal effect of schooling on the probability of unemployment in the Spanish regions

	2002	2006	2010	2012
Andalusia	−0.0143***	−0.0110***	−0.0276***	−0.0286***
Aragon	−0.0014	−0.0024**	−0.0113***	−0.0147***
Asturias	−0.0028	−0.0022	−0.0105***	−0.0207***
Balearic Isl.	−0.0068***	−0.0042***	−0.0160***	−0.0213***
Canary Isl.	−0.0074***	−0.0072***	−0.0269***	−0.0197***
Cantabria	−0.0000	−0.0000	−0.0127***	−0.0172***
Castile Leon	−0.0041***	−0.0036***	−0.0154***	−0.0164***
Castile La Mancha	−0.0063***	−0.0063***	−0.0215***	−0.0261***
Catalonia	−0.0057***	−0.0040***	−0.0169***	−0.0184***
Valencia	−0.0050***	−0.0062***	−0.0219***	−0.0214***
Extremadura	−0.0177***	−0.0137***	−0.0226***	−0.0293***
Galicia	−0.0034**	−0.0024*	−0.0122***	−0.0149***
Madrid	−0.0026**	−0.0046***	−0.0133***	−0.0129***
Murcia	−0.0046**	−0.0063***	−0.0168***	−0.0176***
Navarre	−0.0002	−0.0049***	−0.0098***	−0.0107***
Basque C.	−0.0050***	−0.0043***	−0.0111***	−0.0109***
La Rioja	−0.0054**	−0.0041**	−0.0126***	−0.0130***
Spain	−0.0066***	−0.0058***	−0.0181***	−0.0196***

Note: ***p<0.01, **p<0.05, *p<0.1

in unemployment, as shown earlier, education continues to be non-influential in sorting individuals between employment and unemployment.

Regarding the results of the effect of education on unemployment in Spain and its regions, these are summarized in Table 10.6. The estimated effects confirm a negative relationship between the two magnitudes, which seems to be stronger in 2010, when unemployment rates were much higher than in previous years. An additional year of education decreased the likelihood of unemployment in Spain as a whole by 0.66 and 0.58 percentage points in 2002 and 2006 respectively. The effect rose to 1.81 percentage points in 2010 and to 1.96 points in 2012. Compared with the effect of education in Greece, the magnitude of the reduction in the probability of unemployment associated to an additional year of schooling in Spain appears much higher both during the expansive period and once the crisis started hitting the two countries. As a matter of example, the contribution of an additional year of education in reducing the probability of being unemployed was almost twice in Spain than in the Greek economy at the end of the period under analysis—suggesting that education functions as a signal and/or a sorting mechanism, much more effectively in Spain than in Greece.

In any case, estimates of the marginal effect for the Spanish regions, depicted in the maps in Fig. 10.2, reveal that the impact of education on the propensity of unemployment was far from regionally uniform. In 2002, the effect in Andalusia and Extremadura stood at −1.43 and −1.77 percentage points, whereas no

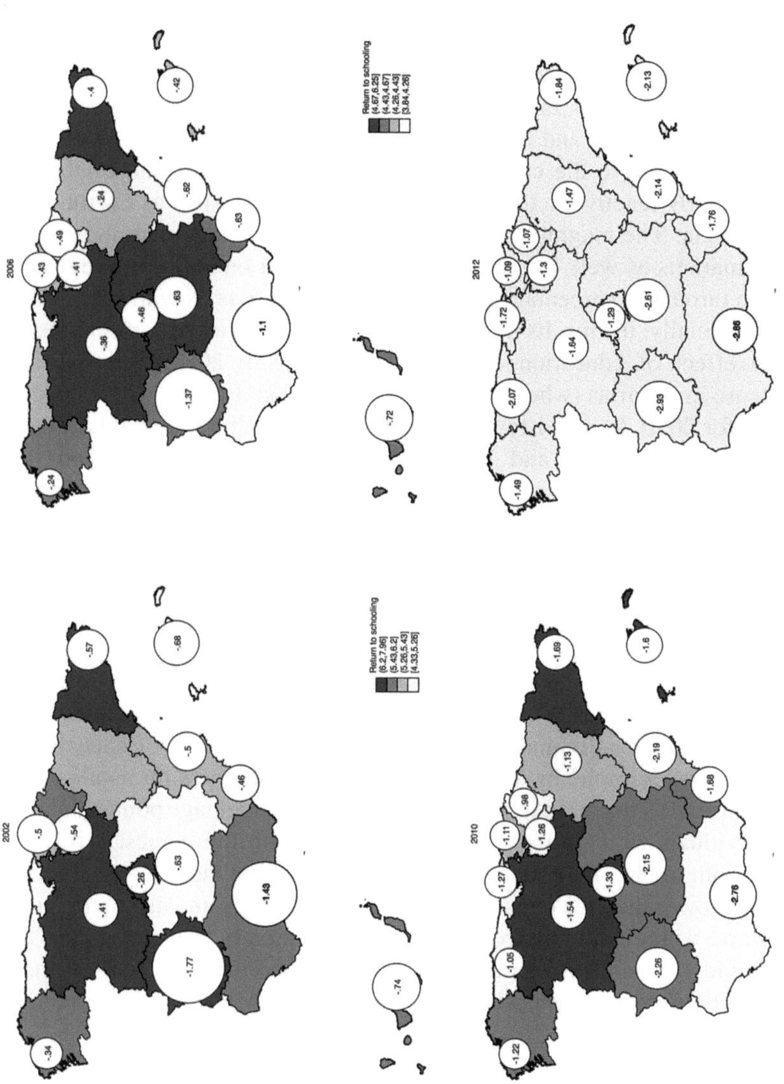

Fig. 10.2 Marginal effect of schooling on the probability of unemployment and wages, Spain

significant impact of education was observed in regions such as Aragon, Asturias, Cantabria and Navarre. A similar pattern in the regional distribution of the effects is observed for 2006, although again there are some changes in the group of regions with no significant effects.

In turn, the sizeable increase in the effect of education on the likelihood of unemployment is observed for all regions in 2010. But, once again, the regions with the highest rates of unemployment are those with the largest magnitude for the marginal effect of education. An additional year of education is associated with a reduction in the probability of unemployment close to 3 percentage points in Andalusia, the Canary Islands, and Extremadura. In addition, the size of the effect in 2010 is also clearly above the country-average in other regions whose labour market was particularly reactive to the early stages of the crisis, such as Castile La Mancha and Valencia. The magnitude of the effect rose in regions with the most dynamic labour markets as well, but to values that are about one third of the ones mentioned above (around 1 percentage point in Aragon, Asturias, Navarre, and the Basque Country). Finally, the results in Table 10.6 reveal that, with few exceptions, the size of the effect of education continued increasing in 2012. The rise is particularly intense in Asturias (where the effect of education doubled with respect to that estimated for 2010, from -1 to -2 percentage points), the Balearic Islands, Cantabria, Castile La Mancha, and Extremadura. In contrast, a reduction is observed for the Canary Islands, whereas values in the other regions have remained rather similar for the last 2 years under analysis.

All in all, the evidence from the estimates of the marginal effect of education on the likelihood of unemployment in the Spanish regions indicates that the magnitude of the effect evolved with the business cycle and with the rate of unemployment. It also confirms that the effect on the likelihood of unemployment of the individuals' endowment of education varies greatly across regions. As in the analysis of the results for Greece, it is useful to calculate the difference in the probability of unemployment for similar individuals who differ only in their level of education in various regions. For example, in 2012 the average unemployment probability of individuals with primary education in Extremadura was 17 percentage points higher than that of individuals with similar characteristics but with the highest level of secondary education. In turn, individuals with tertiary education faced a probability that was 14 points lower than the one of the latter group. These same differences in the case of Navarre were 6 and 5 percentage points respectively. This represents a far from negligible regional difference in the effect that education has on the likelihood of unemployment, even when compared to the actual unemployment rates observed in each region.

Summing up, the results for Greece and Spain point to a large regional heterogeneity in the effect that education has on individuals' propensity to be unemployed. Although intuitively one would expect that first- and second-nature geography factors may be responsible for this heterogeneity (e.g., location/accessibility and specialisations/production structure, respectively), it is particularly interesting to note that the magnitude of the effect is greatest in those regions (and years) where unemployment rates are higher. This is consistent with the view that education acts as a sort of insurance against unemployment, or a sorting device when the economy is far from its full-employment equilibrium, the effect being stronger in regions that suffer most from imbalances in the labour market. In those cases, the possession of education favours individuals with a high endowment of education, presumably both because they are more productive and because they are more likely to be employed in occupations and sectors less affected by job losses.

Nevertheless, the comparison of results for Greece and Spain, particularly in 2012 when the unemployment rates were similar in the two countries, indicates that the benefits associated with higher education are larger in the Spanish labour market. Differences in the transmission mechanisms of the crisis in the two countries may at least partly account for this differential between Greece and Spain. In Greece, the crisis originated from, and affected more, the public sector, where levels of education are typically higher—thus releasing a relatively highly-educated workforce which was unable to find alternative employment in conditions of austerity and economic depression. In Spain, the crisis emerged predominantly in the construction sector, thus affecting predominantly—at least in the first instance—the less educated segment of the workforce. At least to some extent, however, the difference ought to be due also to more substantive differences in the functioning of the labour markets of the two countries—especially as the differential appears in our data well before the eruption of the crisis. In this line of explanation, it would appear that the demand for educated labour in Spain, relative to the supply of educated workers, is stronger than in Greece. Whether this represents evidence of a healthier skilled-job creation in Spain, or of over-education in Greece, is something that we cannot examine with the available data—although both explanations seem plausible. In this vein, it is also important to note that the regional differences in the derived conditional probabilities are much larger than the observed regional differences in levels of education. This suggests that, as far as education is concerned, unemployment differentials across regions have more to do with the ability of the regional labour markets to utilize the available labour force skills (as proxied by years of schooling) than to attract and retain such skills. In other words, regional differences in the education endowment are a less prevalent explanation of regional unemployment differentials compared to regional differences in the effective use of the educational stock endowed to each region.

10.6 The Regional Effect of Education on Wages

10.6.1 Empirical Model

As noted earlier, the estimate of the effect of schooling on wages in each of the regions is obtained by means of a Mincerian wage equation in which the (log) wage of individual i in region r, w_{ir}, depends on the years of schooling, $Educ_{ir}$, and a set of other observed characteristics, grouped in Y_{ir}, that in one way or another affect productivity:

$$\ln(w_{ir}) = a^r + \tau^r Educ_{ir} + Y_{ir}\varphi^r + \varepsilon_{ir}$$

where a^r is a region-specific intercept and ε_{ir} is the error term that accounts for the effect of unobservable factors affecting the wage of worker i in region r. The return to a year of education in a region r is given by the τ^r coefficient, which is estimated from the equation above using the sample of private-sector wage earners in region r, for each of the years analysed (i.e., excluding public-sector employees).

Following common practice, our vector of observable characteristics Y_{ir} includes variables that are typically hypothesized to affect productivity or to capture the accumulation of productivity gains during one's work-history. This includes variables measuring labour market experience and job-tenure (years since leaving continuous full-time education and years since started on the present job, respectively)—both included in both linear and quadratic form to capture the diminishing character of this accumulation process. It also includes a dichotomous male/female variable, to account for the known differences in wages between genders, that is to say the lower wages earned by women in comparison with their male counterparts.

Despite the availability of information on other characteristics, such as occupation, firm size and industry, in the SES and the LFS datasets, our choice has been to use this parsimonious specification presented above and not to include in our analysis these additional variables. This is because, as also indicated in some previous literature (e.g., Pereira and Martins 2004), such variables typically included in what is often referred to as 'extended Mincerian wage equations' are in fact *the channels* through which workers with more education obtain the return to their educational investment. In this sense, including them in our regressions would tend to 'over-explain' the observed wages and thus to under-estimate the full returns to education which is the object of our analysis. By using the parsimonious Mincerian specification, we are able to measure regional differences in the returns to education that are due to all possible factors, including factors such as differences in occupational and sectoral structures, in firm sizes, and so forth. It should be noted, however, that in any case, the findings that we obtain with our parsimonious specification are qualitatively very similar to the ones we obtain when we extend our model to include controls for more characteristics: generally, as should be expected, the estimation of wage equations incorporating these other characteristics results in lower estimates of the return to education; however, this effect is quite horizontal across regions and thus the conclusions drawn about regional differences are not altered. We turn to the discussion of our findings next.

10.6.2 Results

Similar to what was found for the case of unemployment, our results for the case of the wage returns to education suggest a relative decline in booming years and intensification during the crisis. This is consistent with the view of education operating as a sorting mechanism, which is less intensive when the economy is closer to full employment but becomes stronger in times of slack. Additionally, however, and again as was the case before, returns (and thus the sorting mechanism associated with education) appear to be stronger in Spain than in Greece, across the business cycle; while regional disparities in these returns also appear to be larger in the case of Spain than in Greece.

We present the summary results for our estimated returns to education, for each region and year analysed, in Table 10.7 for Greece and Table 10.8 for Spain. For the Greek economy as a whole, the estimated return to education declined marginally from 2002 to 2006 (3.8% and 3.5% respectively), rose quite fast in 2010, to slightly above 4%, and continued to rise, albeit moderately, in 2012 to 4.3%. Therefore, the return to schooling in the private sector of the Greek economy decreased during the economic boom and rose during the recession. However, as is clear from the maps in Fig. 10.1, which are based on the information from Table 10.7, this estimate for the entire country hides interesting regional variations, in connection with both the magnitude of the return and its evolution over the period. It is observed that, in 2002, the return to schooling in Thessalia and Voreio Aigaio was above 5%, far beyond the return in Anatoliki Makedonia (2.6%) and Ionia Nisia (1.7%, non-statistically significant). A gap of a similar magnitude is also observed between the regions with the highest and lowest returns in the other 3 years under analysis, despite the particular evolution of the return in each region. As a matter of example, the return in Sterea Ellada shows a dramatic increase in 2006, up to 4.9% from 2.7% in 2002, whereas the percentage in Voreio Aigaio decreased from 5.2% to 1.1% (a value that it is not statistically different from zero). Sizeable changes are observed also for 2010, whereas the figures for 2012 suggest that the intensification

Table 10.7 Return to schooling in the Greek regions

	2002	2006	2010	2012
Anatoliki Mak.	0.0258***	0.0325***	0.0377***	0.0367***
Kentriki Mak.	0.0366***	0.0365***	0.0405***	0.0359***
Dytiki Mak.	0.0368***	0.0477***	0.0309***	0.0339**
Ipeiros	0.0358***	0.0361***	0.0296***	0.0274***
Thessalia	0.0528***	0.0238***	0.0455***	0.0358***
Ionia Nisia	0.0170	0.00435	0.0287***	0.0285**
Dytiki Ellada	0.0360***	0.0351***	0.0204***	0.0458***
Sterea Ellada	0.0274***	0.0488***	0.0439***	0.0404***
Attiki	0.0416***	0.0380***	0.0503***	0.0528***
Peloponnisos	0.0469***	0.0337***	0.0425***	0.0344***
Voreio Aigaio	0.0521***	0.0108	0.0445***	0.0364**
Notio Aigaio	0.0266***	0.0211***	0.0247***	0.0269**
Kriti	0.0293***	0.0241***	0.0286***	0.0421***
Greece	0.0382***	0.0347***	0.0417***	0.0427***

Note: ***$p<0.01$, **$p<0.05$

Table 10.8 Return to schooling in the Spanish regions

	2002	2006	2010
Andalusia	0.0573***	0.0422***	0.0514***
Aragon	0.0543***	0.0430***	0.0522***
Asturias	0.0480***	0.0438***	0.0506***
Balearic Isl.	0.0496***	0.0443***	0.0686***
Canary Isl.	0.0582***	0.0451***	0.0616***
Cantabria	0.0433***	0.0418***	0.0498***
Castile Leon	0.0622***	0.0492***	0.0648***
Castile La Mancha	0.0526***	0.0508***	0.0629***
Catalonia	0.0644***	0.0539***	0.0662***
Valencia	0.0532***	0.0426***	0.0582***
Extremadura	0.0776***	0.0464***	0.0621***
Galicia	0.0620***	0.0467***	0.0639***
Madrid	0.0796***	0.0625***	0.0789***
Murcia	0.0533***	0.0450***	0.0627***
Navarre	0.0594***	0.0401***	0.0433***
Basque C.	0.0535***	0.0427***	0.0552***
La Rioja	0.0448***	0.0384***	0.0401***
Spain	0.0608***	0.0485***	0.0635***

Note: ***$p<0.01$

of the crisis in 2011/12 did not cause an increase in the return to education in the majority of Greek regions. On the contrary, for almost all regions, the estimated return in 2012 is similar and in some cases even lower than the one obtained for 2010. Actually, results show that the moderate increase in the return to education nationally during this period was driven by the rise in the return of just a couple of regions, Dytiki Ellada and Kriti. In any case, as already mentioned above, the crisis does not seem to have affected the amount of regional disparities in the wage return to schooling in Greece.

As in the case of the results regarding regional disparities in the impact of education on unemployment, it is useful to compare the change in the wage level, in different regions, of similar workers that just differ in the level of educational attainment. As in that case, we have computed the wage gap between workers with primary, high secondary and tertiary education (which corresponds to differences of 6 and 5 years of schooling, respectively). The results for 2012 reveal that in Attiki the wage earned by a worker with high secondary education was 32% higher than that earned by a similar worker with primary education. In turn, in 2012 a worker with tertiary education in that region earned a wage that was 26% higher than the similar worker with high secondary schooling. These differences are far more pronounced than those in the Greek region with the lowest return to schooling. In Notio Aigaio, the wage of the representative worker with tertiary education was 13% higher than that with high secondary, whereas the latter earned 16% more than the representative worker with only primary education.

The estimates of the return to schooling in Spain and its regions are in Table 10.8. For the whole of Spain, the return is estimated at 6.1% in 2002, falling to 4.6% in 2006. This drop of around a third in the wage increase associated with an additional year of education, in the short period of 4 years, probably has its origin in the peculiar circumstances of the labour market in Spain in this period, particularly in sectors such as construction, and in the high level of over-qualification of the workforce. However, the impact of the economic crisis seems to have changed that trend, since the estimate of the return for 2010 grew to 6.4%, which is a level above the one observed in 2002. Therefore, the evolution of the return to schooling in Spain was similar to that in Greece, although the magnitude of the changes observed within the period under analysis are larger in Spain than in Greece. The effect of education on wages seems to be also much higher in Spain, particularly in 2002 and in 2010 (50–60% higher). It will be interesting to compare the returns for 2012 when the Spanish data become available. If there was a further increase in the return in Spain in 2012 as a result of the deepening of the recession, it could be the case that the gap in the return would have widened even further. Interestingly, the distance between the two countries in the estimated returns is lower at the peak of the boom period.

The same trend over the decade is observed for each of the Spanish regions, although there are some differences in the intensity of the drop in the first part of the period and of the increase after the impact of the crisis. For example, the estimated value for 2010 in the Balearic Islands lies well above that obtained in 2002, while in Extremadura the increase between 2006 and 2010 was not large enough to counterbalance fully the decrease in the first part of the last decade, leading to a value for the return in 2010 that is clearly below that in 2002. In any case, the results in Table 10.8 and the corresponding maps in Fig. 10.2 confirm that the regional heterogeneity in the return to education in Spain is far from negligible, being observed both in periods of growth and recession. In 2002, the return was close to 8% in regions as different among them as Madrid and Extremadura. In contrast it was just between 4% and 5% in the Balearic Islands, Cantabria and La Rioja. The gap lessened slightly in 2006, with Madrid and Catalonia showing the highest return (6.3% and 5.4%, respectively), and Navarre and La Rioja the lowest (around 4%). The latter two regions were also at the bottom of the list in 2010, partly as a result of the limited increase in the return since 2006. At the top, Madrid still leads the ranking in the last year analysed, with a return of about 8% (similar to the one at the beginning of the decade).

To end with the discussion on the results regarding the regional estimates of the return to schooling in the Spanish regions, it is worth mentioning that the wage gap between workers with primary and high secondary education in Madrid in 2012 was close to 50%, whereas that for workers with tertiary and high secondary education was 40%. The corresponding gaps were much narrower in La Rioja, of 24% and 20% respectively. Therefore, these figures confirm that, as in the case of Greece, there are considerable disparities between Spanish regions in the effect of the individual's endowment of education on the wage she earns. Again, however, these differences appear much higher in Spain than in Greece.

Beyond the regions that lead or close the list of the returns to schooling in the two countries, our aim with the figures in Tables 10.7 and 10.8 has been to show the different impact that education has on the wage earned depending on the region in which the individual works. Overall, the evidence from the two countries confirms that there are notable disparities in the return to education made by individuals earning a wage in each of these regions, which add to the disparities discussed in the previous section in reference to the effect of education on the propensity to be employed or unemployed. Moreover, the high regional heterogeneity in the return to education suggests that regional differences in wage levels in the two countries are not explained solely by differences between regions in the endowment of education, but also by differences between regions in the wage rewards associated to any given level of education.

10.7 Concluding Comments

There are two main issues that our analysis in this chapter sought to examine. On the one hand, the labour market responses to the boom-and-bust cycle of the last decade and the particular role played in this by education. On the other hand, the regional differentiation in labour market outcomes (wages, unemployment) and fundamentals (education endowment), including the role that education plays in intermediating these outcomes at the regional and national level (marginal effect on the probability of unemployment and wage returns to education). Further, by examining these issues jointly for two southern European countries that have been severely affected by the crisis, we were able to gain insights about the relative importance of these factors in a comparative fashion.

The starting point of our analysis was the examination of the regional dispersion and temporal evolution of unemployment rates and average private-sector wages in our two study-countries. In line with what is known from previous studies (Petrakos and Psycharis 2004; Monastiriotis 2011, 2014; López-Bazo and Motellón 2012, 2013), labour market outcomes have been found to vary markedly across regions in both Greece and Spain. Although the crisis seems to have instigated a process of convergence (albeit marginally so), disparities have been sizeable throughout the 2000s and remain so today. This suggests quite clearly a disequilibrium condition in both countries, with employment opportunities and salaried incomes being persistently unequal across space—which in turn is bound to reflect problems in the functioning of equilibrium mechanisms, such as migration, cross-regional capital flows, and the cross-regional transmission of price signals.

Levels of education have also been found to be quite diverse across space in both countries, although here the differences are not so pronounced as in the case of wages and unemployment. In a way, this finding acted as a direct motivation for our subsequent analysis, which focused on the role, not of individual characteristics, but of the returns to these characteristics—in the form of contributions both to the incidence of (un)employment and to an individual's wage compensation. These two variables (wages and unemployment) are obviously related both at the individual and the aggregate level; but for our analysis here they represent essentially two aspects of labour market success, one relating to the quality of a job (wages) and the other to the probability of securing a job in the first place (unemployment). Our analysis has clearly demonstrated that the contribution of education to these measures of labour market 'success' varies widely across regions in both countries.

Interestingly, however, there are some notable differences between the two countries in the role (and perhaps also in the extent) of education in the labour market. Greece appears to have slightly higher averages in terms of years of schooling, both in general (active population) and in its private-sector salaried employees. At the same time, however, education in Greece appears to have a much more muted role in sorting people between employment and unemployment and in determining the level of wages received by each wage-earner. Indeed, even at the height of the crisis (in 2012), where one would expect labour market sorting to be at its strongest, in five out of the 13 Greek NUTS2 regions education appears to play no statistically significant role in directing people into employment—while nationally it only makes a marginal contribution to an individual's employment chances. This contrasts starkly with the case of Spain, where an additional year of education appears to lower the unemployment probability of an individual by 2 percentage points—or by between 1.0% and 2.8%, depending on the region where the individual is located.[7]

As noted earlier, these differences may be attributable to two sets of factors. On the one hand, the particular transmission mechanisms of the crisis in the two countries: in Spain, the crisis came predominantly through the low-skill sector (mainly construction), thus disproportionately hurting the lower-educated, who experienced faster rises in unemployment and larger reductions in their wages; in contrast, in Greece the recession came through the austerity measures implemented by the government, which were more horizontal, or even progressive, in nature, thus affecting in the first instance the more educated by far. On the other hand, and especially under the light of the observation that country differences in the wage-returns and unemployment-penalties of education existed also well before the crisis, a more plausible explanation for these differences seems to be one concerning the vibrancy of labour demand and of skilled-job creation in particular. In this line of thought, the relatively weaker role of education in the Greek labour market may be taken to signal an over-representation of low-quality/low-education jobs in the economy, at least relative to the level of educational qualifications available in the workforce. This interpretation is also supported by the cross-regional evidence, in both countries, where we find that the returns to education (in terms of both wages and employment probabilities) are typically higher in regions of more vibrant labour demand and a higher technological content in their production mix (e.g., industrial

[7]Similar differences are found for the case of the wage-returns to education, although, as noted earlier, in this case our results are not directly comparable due to differences in the composition of the relevant samples and the measurement of the wage variable.

and metropolitan regions). This seems to indicate directly that structural (e.g., sectoral specialisations) and functional characteristics of the regions play an important role in the contribution of education in determining labour market 'success', either directly or through their effect on the functioning of the regional labour markets and of the vibrancy of labour demand there. The importance of this is amplified when considering the fact that actual differences in levels of education, both between countries and across regions, are generally rather marginal.

In closing, a comment is due on the role of education in the adjustment process in the regional economies of the two countries studied here. As has also been shown elsewhere, in both countries unemployment rates have increased substantially with the crisis, somewhat faster in Spain and slightly later in Greece, but in both cases reaching rates nearing or surpassing a quarter of the active population. In contrast, the adjustment of wages has been much slower and smaller, with wages in Greece declining somewhat compared to 2010 but generally remaining well above their pre-crisis levels (e.g., compared to 2006) and wages in Spain being still higher in 2010 (the last year for which we have relevant data) compared to 2006 (even in real terms). This, despite significant wage cuts regulated in the Greek economy and the natural downward pressure on wages that one would expect to take place given the vast rise of unemployment in both countries. Quite evidently, this may be taken as a signal of poor functioning of essential labour market adjustment mechanisms in the two countries, and in particular of wage adjustability (flexibility) both across space and over time—although it is also partly accounted for by compositional changes in salaried employment (e.g., a sharper decrease in the number of salaried workers at the bottom of the wage distribution during the crisis).

Combined with the previous conclusion about the nature of labour demand, it appears to us that our analysis, although descriptive in nature, has allowed us to reveal some key labour market issues and weaknesses, particularly in Greece but also in Spain. In both countries, labour market adjustment in response to the crisis has taken place significantly more on the quantity side (unemployment) rather than through prices (wages). In both countries, education has played a role in mediating the impact of the crisis (i.e., helping, in relative terms, individuals with more years of schooling), but this role has not been even across space and has generally functioned better in regions which already possessed some advantages in terms of production structure and levels of development. And in both countries, the high incidence of unemployment does not appear to be so much related to regional handicaps in terms of actual educational endowments as it is related to an apparent inability, in most Greek regions and in a large number of Spanish regions, to sufficiently utilize the educational endowment available to each region. In this sense, and as a general conclusion emanating from our analysis in this chapter, it seems that addressing the problems of unemployment (nationally) and regional disparities (in labour market performance more generally) in our two study-countries (and perhaps more broadly, in the European South) would more likely require policies targeting the *functioning* of the labour market rather than ones focusing on the human capital *endowments* of these countries and their regions. In essence, given the spatially disparate and generally low (especially in Greece) effect that education has been found to have on labour market outcomes across our two samples, it appears that an educational endowment deficit (at least in terms of quantity) is not amongst the main weaknesses of the labour markets studied here—and that, thus, efforts aimed at addressing the pressing issues of unemployment and declining wages ought to be directed more towards appropriate labour market and industrial policy interventions, i.e., policies concerning labour mobility, the regional transmission of price signals, and the qualitative upgrading (in terms of both resilience/diversification and skill-content/knowledge-intensity) of existing production structures.

Acknowledgments The authors wish to acknowledge financial support from the European Community's Seventh Framework Programme (FP7-SSH-2010-2.2-1) under grant agreement n° 266834, SEARCH Project. EL-B and EM wish also to thank the support of the Spanish Ministry of Economics and Competitiveness, National Program of R&D, under the project ECO2014-59493-R.

References

Christopoulou R, Monastiriotis V (2014) The Greek public sector wage premium before the crisis: size, selection and relative valuation of characteristics. Br J Ind Relat 52(3):579–602

Christopoulou R, Monastiriotis V (2016) Public-private wage duality during the Greek crisis. Oxf Econ Pap 68(1):174–196

Duranton G, Monastiriotis V (2002) Mind the gaps: the evolution of regional inequalities in the UK, 1982-1997. J Reg Sci 42(2):219–256

European Commission (2010) Investing in Europe's future. Fifth report on economic, social and territorial cohesion, Luxembourg

García I, Molina J (2002) Inter-regional wage differentials in Spain. Appl Econ Lett 9:209–215

López-Bazo E, Motellón E (2012) Human capital and regional wage gaps. Reg Stud 46 (10):1347–1365

Lopez-Bazo E, Motellón E (2013) The regional distribution of unemployment. What do micro-data tell us? Pap Reg Sci 92(2):383–405

Monastiriotis V (2011) Making geographical sense of the Greek austerity measures: compositional effects and long-run implications. Camb J Soc Econ Reg 4(3):323–337

Monastiriotis V (2014) Convergence through crisis? The impact of the crisis on wage returns across the Greek regions, Region et Developpement, No 39, pp 35–66

Nijkamp P, Poot J (2005) The last word of the wage curve? J Econ Surv 19(3):421–450

OECD (2012) Employment outlook 2012. Paris

Peeters M, den Reijer A (2011) On wage productivity, wage flexibility and wage co-ordination – a focus on the wage impact of productivity in Germany, Greece, Ireland, Portugal, Spain and the United States, MPRA Paper No. 31102

Pereira J, Galego A (2011) Regional wage differentials in Portugal: static and dynamic approaches. Pap Reg Sci 90(3):529–548

Pereira PT, Martins PS (2004) Returns to education and wage equations. Appl Econ 36 (6):525–531

Petrakos G, Psycharis Y (2004) Regional development in greece. Kritiki, Athens. [in Greek]

Enrique López-Bazo is full professor of applied economics at the University of Barcelona and member of the Regional Quantitative Analysis Research Institute (AQR). For more than 25 years, his research has been mainly in the area of regional and urban economics, having spawned numerous papers published in recognised journals and edited volumes. He serves on the editorial board of different international journals in the field of applied economics and spatial economics. He was a visiting research at the London School of Economics, the Free University of Amsterdam and the European Commission.

Vassilis Monastiriotis is Associate Professor of Political Economy at the European Institute, London School of Economics (UK). He is Director of the LSE Research Unit on Southeast Europe and holds affiliations with LSE's Department of Geography and Environment, the Hellenic Observatory and the ESRC Spatial Economics Research Centre. His main research interests are on regional and national labour markets, regional and local socioeconomic disparities, economic growth and macroeconomic policy, economic integration and the political economy of reforms. He has published numerous articles in economics and regional science journals and received various distinctions including the Moss Madden Medal in Regional Science (2008). He has a PhD in Economic Geography (LSE), an MSc in Economics (University of Macedonia) and a BSc in Economics (Aristotle University of Thessaloniki). He is Co-editor of Spatial Economic Analysis (Taylor & Francis) and Committee Member of the British and Irish Section of the Regional Science Association International.

Elisabet Motellón is reader of economics at the Open University of Catalunya and member of the Regional Quantitative Analysis Research Institute (AQR) at the University of Barcelona. Her research focuses on the empirical analysis of labor economics combined with elements of spatial economics. She has published her work in this field in recognised journals.

Chapter 11
Human Capital Formation and the Missing Regional Upgrading in the EU Periphery: The Role of Migration and Education-Job Mismatch

Nicola D. Coniglio and Francesco Prota

JEL Classification J24 • J61 • O15 • O18 • R58

11.1 Introduction

Why does the supply of human capital (in peripheral regions) not create its own demand? This question is the cornerstone of the present chapter. The starting point of our contribution is the observation that although several decades of national and EU-level investments in human capital formation have considerably increased the supply of highly skilled and educated individuals in peripheral regions, in almost all these regions the availability of a relatively cheap and well-educated labour force has not triggered a significant productive upgrading. On the contrary, rather than stimulating the demand of human capital in the periphery, generally the excess supply of highly skilled individuals has been 'absorbed' through internal or international outmigration or has generated what seems to be a colossal 'brain waste' with widespread over-education and job mismatch.

The aim of this chapter is to shed light on the complex channels which link human capital investments, spatial mobility and regional upgrading in peripheral regions. For this purpose we analyse—using original datasets collected by the authors—two different locally funded human capital investment policies implemented by two neighbouring Italian Mezzogiorno regions, Basilicata and

N.D. Coniglio (✉)
Dipartimento di Scienze Economiche e Metodi Matematici, Università degli Studi di Bari "Aldo Moro", Bari, Italy

NHH Norwegian School of Economics, Bergen, Norway
e-mail: nicoladaniele.coniglio@uniba.it

F. Prota (✉)
Dipartimento di Scienze Economiche e Metodi Matematici, Università degli Studi di Bari "Aldo Moro", Bari, Italy
e-mail: francesco.prota@uniba.it

M. Fonseca, U. Fratesi (eds.), *Regional Upgrading in Southern Europe*, Advances in Spatial Science, DOI 10.1007/978-3-319-49818-8_11

Apulia. Both policy measures draw resources from the European Social Fund and from the regional fiscal budget.

The first policy is aimed at fostering human capital accumulation in Basilicata, a small region in the South of Italy. The policymakers of Regione Basilicata started to support human capital formation at the beginning of the 1990s, providing generous subsidies to young highly qualified graduates who intended to invest in specialised training and educational activities by attending post-graduate courses inside or outside the region. We analyse, following an early contribution of Coniglio and Prota (2008), the 'leakage' of human capital associated with this regional policy through out-migration. This first 'story' allows us to underline the high risks of failure of policies which push a single 'side' of the human capital market, i.e., its supply, without considering measures that at the same time stimulate its demand. Promoting linkages between the beneficiaries of the regional support and local productive entities—for instance by means of internships—significantly reduces the probability of outmigration.

The second 'story' is drawn from another human capital investment policy implemented by a larger and more industrialized neighbouring region, Apulia (Borse di ricerca). In this case there is an explicit attempt by the regional policymakers to act on both the supply and the demand of qualified workers by linking young beneficiaries with higher education and research institutions, and with (local) firms.[1] An ex post evaluation of this policy shows that only 10% of the individual beneficiaries are working outside the region. In this case human capital leakage through migration is limited, but our empirical analysis shows that there is a rather severe education-job mismatch in terms of both people being engaged in precarious employment forms (flexible or part-time) and a (low) level of competences required in their actual occupation. Somewhat paradoxically, we find that the higher the individual competences (measured by the holding of a PhD degree), the higher the likelihood of not using these skills in the current job or to be unemployed or employed in highly precarious occupations.

These two policy cases indicate, in our opinion, that severe market failures characterize the 'absorption' of human capital in the local economy rather than its formation.

The rest of the chapter is organized as follows: In Sect. 11.2 we discuss the absence of a clear correlation between the economic performance of regions and their human capital endowment. Section 11.3 reports the econometric analysis based on the policy measures aimed at boosting human capital formation in the two Mezzogiorno regions. In the final part of the chapter we discuss the factors which limit the role of human capital in peripheral economies and draw some policy implications.

---

[1]A requisite for the grant of the financial support, labelled Borse di Ricerca, was the setting up of a triangular partnership between a 'researcher' (the final beneficiary of the policy), a University department or a research institute (scientific partner) and a productive unit (generally an innovative firm). The aim of the policymaker was to enhance the accumulation of competences 'suitable' for direct productive use in the local economy and boost the likelihood that the human capital formed was absorbed by the local economy.

11.2 Human Capital Endowment in the EU Periphery

The evolution of regional income disparities within Europe has received considerable attention both from an academic and a policy point of view. The panorama over the last decade and a half has been one of national convergence and regional stability or even divergence in income levels.[2] Achieving economic and social cohesion by reducing disparities between regions is one of the fundamental objectives laid out in the European Union Treaty. Given the wide scholarly agreement on the fact that human capital is one of the key factors behind economic growth and that, therefore, disparities in human capital endowment across regions can reduce the potential for convergence of the European Union peripheral regions, one of the main fields of investment across all cohesion policy programmes has been human resources (education, training, employment and social inclusion schemes financed by the ESF).

The educational stock, even as result of the policies aimed at fostering human capital accumulation at a regional level, has increased across the European peripheral regions in the last decades. Figure 11.1 shows the growth between 2000 and 2010 of the number of persons aged 25–64 and 20–24 with upper secondary or tertiary education attainment and the growth of the GDP per capita.[3] Interestingly, there does not seem to exist a clear correlation between the economic performance of regions and their human capital endowment.

An adequate educational stock is a necessary but not sufficient condition to foster economic convergence. Adopting a long term perspective, Felice (2012) shows the high degree of regional convergence in human capital across Italian regions and the ups and downs in the process of regional convergence in income levels.[4] Notwithstanding the significant closure of the North-South gap in terms of educational levels, spatial disparities in economic development remain the main open problem in the national history of Italy (Iuzzolino et al. 2011).

Indeed, if human resources in less developed regions are left inactive or not used to the best of their capacity in the workplace (skill mismatch) or 'lost' as a result of migration towards more developed regions, the passage from human capital endowment to economic growth is not achieved.

[2]Several authors have pointed towards a growing evidence of the emergence of convergence clubs, resulting in increasing polarization and lower economic cohesion across Europe (López-Bazo et al. 1999).

[3]In order to minimize problems of spatial autocorrelation, all data is standardized nationally (Armstrong 1995; Rodríguez-Pose 1999; Magrini 1999). Thus, the variables indicate how well a region is doing relative to the national average.

[4]The author shows that the association between regional convergence in human capital and income has been discontinuous pointing to the fact that the road moving from the former to the latter is, at best, 'bumpy'.

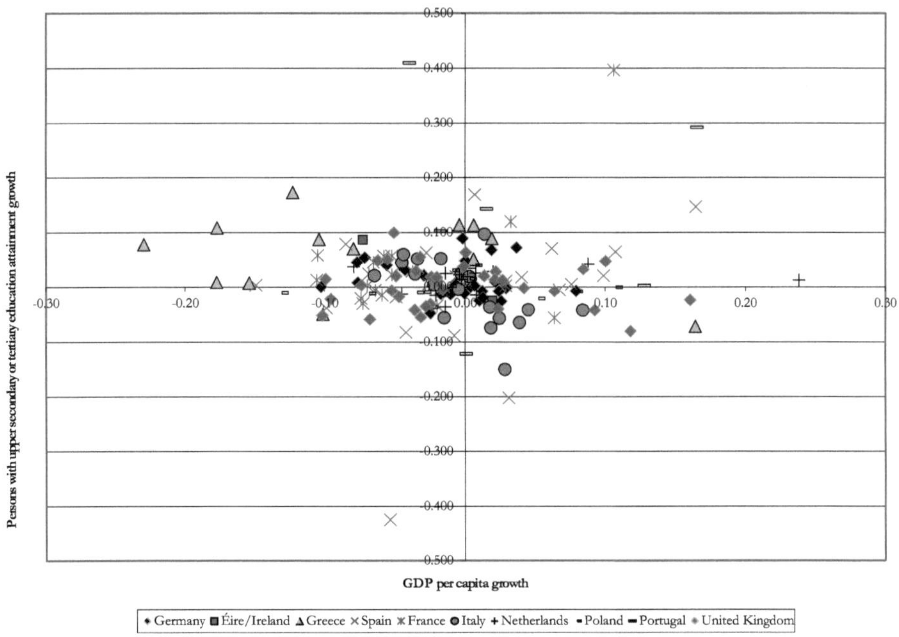

Fig. 11.1 Education attainment and economic performance of European regions, 2000–2010. Source: Authors' elaborations on Eurostat data

Skill mismatch is one of the main challenges faced by modern economies. Empirical evidence suggests that skill underutilization is a widespread phenomenon which has several negative implications: it may lead to skills loss and a waste of the resources that were used to acquire these skills; in addition, over-skilled workers earn less than workers who are well-matched to their jobs and tend to be less satisfied at work. At the same time, workers with low levels of skills are found to be employed in jobs which appear to have relatively high skills demands. Under-skilling is likely to affect productivity and slow the rate at which more efficient technologies and approaches to work can be adopted.

As shown in Table 11.1, job mismatch—defined as employment in a job requiring qualifications and competences below those possessed by the workers—is severe both in Southern and Northern European countries. Overall, job mismatch characterizes 29% of the workforce in the Netherlands—the best performing labour market among the countries included in the table—and a peak of 47% in Italy. With some notable exceptions—Belgium, the Netherlands and, marginally, Spain and France—female workers are generally more likely to be mismatched compared to male workers.

Table 11.1 Job mismatches in Europe—2000

	Incidence of job mismatches by country (%)	Incidence of job mismatches for females (%)	Incidence of job mismatches for males (%)	Incidence of job mismatches by level of education ISCED 3–4 (%)	Incidence of job mismatches by level of education ISCED 5–6 (%)
Belgium	32	28	36	43	26
Denmark	38	41	34	44	30
Greece	40	40	39	47	35
Spain	34	33	34	46	31
France	35	34	35	40	29
Italy	47	48	46	50	36
Hungary	35	39	32	36	33
Netherlands	29	25	33	29	29
Austria	32	34	29	32	31
Slovenia	31	33	29	33	26
Finland	31	32	29	32	29
Sweden	37	38	36	44	27

Source: Authors' elaborations on Eurostat data
Note: ISCED 3–4: Upper secondary education and Post-secondary non-tertiary education; ISED 5–6: Tertiary education (first stage) and Tertiary education (second stage)

The occurrence of mismatch is likely to be more severe in peripheral regions where labour market failures are more severe and hence the allocation of workers in such areas is less efficient compared to core regions. This is particularly true for highly skilled and educated individuals residing in less-developed regions since (given the reduced number of job opportunities) they might be more inclined to accept 'mismatched' jobs in order to avoid the costs of spatial mobility (Hensen et al. 2009).

Another challenge for the accumulation of human capital in peripheral regions is the high net out-mobility of the highly educated individuals. As is well documented in economic literature, highly skilled and educated workers represent a very mobile population group: more talented and skilled individuals have a higher propensity to migrate than the rest of the population (Coniglio and Prota 2008). Regional integration of labour markets may increase workers' incentive to spatially relocate, in particular from peripheral to central regions. Haapanen and Tervo (2012), examining the inter-regional migration of university graduates in Finland, show that out-migration is much higher among graduates in the more peripheral universities than in the metropolitan centres. Flows of graduates towards the economic centre of the country are found in Germany and the Netherlands, too (Busch and Weigert 2010; Venhorst et al. 2011).

In what follows we explore in more detail some 'challenges' for the implementation of human capital accumulation policies in peripheral regions by means of two 'policy cases' drawn from the Italian Mezzogiorno.

11.3 On the Effectiveness of Public Investments in Human Capital in the EU Periphery: A Tale from Two Italian Regions[5]

In what follows we discuss how the spatial mobility of human capital and its sub-optimal employment might reduce the role played by publicly-financed measures aimed at boosting regional competitiveness by generating and maintaining human capital. We use individual-level information from two policy experiences implemented in two distinct southern Italian regions, Basilicata and Puglia. Our aim is not that of evaluating the impact of the two policy measures,[6] but to shed light on the factors which lead to the sub-optimal results.

11.3.1 Policy Case 1: On the Out-Migration of Human Capital from Peripheral Regions

Public investments in human capital—whether or not locally financed—are motivated by a clear expected 'trajectory': increase human capital accumulation by augmenting the base of highly qualified individuals and, in turn, promote the upgrading of the regional economic systems. The case for public intervention is justified by the existence of collective (often localized) returns from human capital which go beyond private ones. How effective are these policies in peripheral areas? The 'policy case' analysed here is focused on a first element which might 'derail' the policy from its expected trajectory: out-migration from peripheral regions.

---

[5]The data used for the empirical analysis contained in this section are derived from two surveys designed and conducted by the authors. The questionnaires were sent to all the individuals who benefited from the two regional policy measures. In the case of the policy measure '*Borse di formazione*' (Region Basilicata) the survey was conducted between 2007 and 2008, while in the case '*Borse di ricerca*' (Region Puglia) it was conducted in 2012. The response rates were, respectively, 40% and 60%. An accurate analysis of the non-responses was conducted in order to investigate the degree of representativeness of the sampled individuals. The non-responding individuals were found to be not significantly different on most of the relevant characteristics—demographics, migration patterns, skills, gender, employment rate etc.—vis à vis the responding ones. Note also that in the case of the '*Borse di formazione*' (Region Basilicata), given the almost automatic access to the funding once the candidate had the formal requirements requested, it is highly plausible that the sample is representative of the entire population of highly educated individuals residing in this Mezzogiorno region.

The survey questionnaires and a detailed description of the survey methodology adopted are available upon request from the authors.

[6]We acknowledge that our analysis cannot shed light on the causal effects of the two policy measures and hence their relative degree of effectiveness. In fact, we lack information about those individuals that could have applied to the measures but did not. Nevertheless, we argue that it is important to investigate the channels through which the (potential) human capital created is depleted: spatial mobility and education-job mismatches of the beneficiaries.

The regional policymaker in Basilicata pursued a policy aimed at fostering human capital in this relatively small Mezzogiorno region starting from the beginning of the 1990s. Since then, several thousand young graduates, in a region of around 600,000 inhabitants, have benefitted from the locally-funded policy and pursued post-graduate studies in all disciplines in Italian and foreign higher education institutions. The financial effort has been substantial: considering only the period 2000–2005, the cost of the policy measure was 26.6 million € for approximately 2.5 thousand beneficiaries. A survey was conducted between 2007 and 2008 in order to gather a rich set of information on the post-policy performances of the beneficiaries.

In what follows we use information on 839 beneficiaries in order to investigate the characteristics of those beneficiaries who left the region (out-migrants). In fact, 45.6% of the beneficiaries of the regional policy resided and worked outside Basilicata at the time of the survey; the number of migrants is lower than that found in our previous study on the policy beneficiaries between 1991 and 2001 (58%; see Coniglio and Prota 2008).

Summary statistics of the variables employed in the analysis are reported in Table 11.2. Table 11.3 shows probit estimates on the probability of residing in the home region (Basilicata). We find that males are more likely to stay in the home region; a finding that confirms a higher likelihood of migration for female highly educated individuals.[7] Evaluated at the baseline group, the likelihood of staying is 9.5% higher for males compared to females. Note that, in line with our findings, an alarmingly low participation rate and a very high unemployment rate is observed across all Mezzogiorno regions for the female component of the workforce. As noted in Faggian et al. (2007), female workers might be more inclined to migrate in order to avoid the consequences of a gender gap in employment opportunities. We do not find significantly different effects of age and of the marks obtained during bachelor studies on the probability of staying in the home region when we consider the whole sample (which includes employed and unemployed individuals). Note that Models 1 and 2 include a dummy variable equal to 1 when the individual beneficiaries are unemployed. The positive and highly significant coefficient of this variable suggests that the unemployed are more likely to stay in the home region. The latter result is in line with the 'contracted' migration hypothesis which suggests that individuals typically move after having already assured a job offer and only seldom migrate to search for job opportunities in other destinations. When only employed individuals are considered (Model 3) we find that a higher age—measured at the time of the postgraduate course financed by the regional authority—is associated with a lower probability of residing in the home region. The effect is non-linear as shown by the positive and significant effect of age square. The results are weaker in Model 4 where the sample excludes a small sub-sample of individuals with a high-school diploma (this type of beneficiary is younger on average).

[7]Similar results were found by Faggian et al. (2007) in their analysis on the spatial mobility of UK graduates.

Table 11.2 Policy case 1. Human capital investment policy of Regione Basilicata (Italy). Summary statistics of variables employed in the probit analysis

Variable	Description	Mean	Std. dev.
Home region (dependent variable)	Individual residence/work in the home region	0.456	0.498
Male	Male	0.435	0.496
Age	Age at the time of attending the postgraduate course	28.2	3.7
Age squared	Squared value of age	808.3	230.6
Marks	Final mark of the bachelor degree (between 66 and 110)	101.4	10.5
Business studies	Degree in economics or business studies	0.245	0.431
Law studies	Degree in law or political sciences	0.176	0.381
Engineering studies	Degree in engineering or architecture	0.145	0.352
Humanities studies	Degree in humanities	0.244	0.43
Other studies	Degree in other subjects	0.09	0.285
High school diploma	Individual's highest degree at the moment of the scholarship was a high school diploma	0.086	0.28
University away	Undergraduate studies attended outside the home region[a]	0.45	0.5
Master away	Postgraduate studies attended outside the home region[a]	0.63	0.48
University and Master away	Both undergraduate and postgraduate studies outside the home region[a]	0.37	0.48
University home/ Master away	Postgraduate studies only attended outside the home region[a]	0.26	0.44
University away/ Master home	Undergraduate studies only attended outside the home region[a]	0.08	0.27
Internship home	Internship of the financed postgraduate programme was done in the home region	0.24	0.43
Preference home	Basilicata was the preferred location of residence	0.44	0.49
Year of the master programme	The year when the master programme has been attended	5.29	1.9
Unemployed	Unemployed at the time of the survey	0.289	0.453

[a]Home region includes Basilicata and two neighbouring regions (Puglia and Campania)

Those beneficiaries with an educational background in business/economic studies are less likely to reside in the home region; this result confirms the finding of our previous study (Coniglio and Prota 2008) and is related to the lack of employment opportunities for graduates in those disciplines within the region.

The positive and significant coefficient on the high-school diploma dummy suggests that individuals with less education are, ceteris paribus, more likely to stay home: evidence of positive self-selection of out-migration flows often observed in empirical studies on internal migration.

Possibly, the most relevant determinants of the probability of residing in the home region are related to the location where the human capital investment

Table 11.3 Promoting and maintaining human capital: a probit analysis on the probability of staying in the home region of the regional policy beneficiaries

	Mod. 1	Marginal effects	Mod. 2	Marginal effects	Mod. 3—employed	Mod. 4—no diploma
Male	0.382*** (0.127)	0.095*** (0.031)	0.383*** (0.127)	0.096*** (0.031)	0.459*** (0.15)	0.406*** (0.132)
Age	−0.261 (0.179)	−0.065 (0.045)	−0.253 (0.180)	−0.063 (0.045)	−0.617** (0.302)	−0.357* (0.210)
Age squared	0.004 (0.003)	0.001 (0.0007)	0.004 (0.003)	0.001 (0.0007)	0.010** (0.005)	0.005 (0.003)
Marks	0.0097 (0.009)	0.002 (0.002)	0.010 (0.009)	0.0026 (0.0023)	0.011 (0.0106)	0.007 (0.010)
Business studies	−0.296* (0.170)	−0.074* (0.042)	−0.29* (0.17)	−0.073* (0.042)	−0.460** (0.197)	−0.321* (0.172)
Law studies	0.082 (0.180)	0.021 (0.045)	0.086 (0.180)	0.021 (0.045)	−0.052 (0.207)	0.071 (0.182)
Engineering studies	−0.185 (0.191)	−0.046 (0.048)	−0.187 (0.191)	−0.047 (0.047)	−0.214 (0.213)	−0.176 (0.192)
High school diploma	0.718* (0.425)	0.179* (0.105)	0.719* (0.426)	0.180* (0.106)	0.508 (0.508)	
University away	−0.219* (0.130)	−0.055* (0.032)				
Master away	−0.248* (0.145)	−0.062* (0.036)				
University and Master away			−0.49*** (0.176)	−0.12*** (0.043)	−0.561*** (0.20)	−0.489*** (0.18)
University home/Master away			−0.335* (0.176)	−0.084* (0.044)	−0.535*** (0.20)	−0.324* (0.183)
University away/Master home			−0.399* (0.242)	−0.100* (0.060)	−0.218 (0.296)	−0.398 (0.244)
Internship home	1.144*** (0.181)	0.286*** (0.0414)	1.134*** (0.181)	0.283*** (0.041)	1.248*** (0.21)	1.170*** (0.19)
Preference home	0.413*** (0.126)	0.103*** (0.031)	0.414*** (0.126)	0.104*** (0.031)	0.366** (0.145)	0.420*** (0.129)
Year of the master programme	−0.0532 (0.033)	−0.0133 (0.008)	−0.053 (0.033)	−0.013 (0.008)	−0.054 (0.036)	−0.060* (0.03)
Unemployed	1.284*** (0.151)	0.321*** (0.032)	1.287*** (0.152)	0.322*** (0.032)		1.315*** (0.16)
Constant	2.549 (2.976)		2.410 (2.981)		7.826* (4.679)	4.535 (3.509)
Observations	663		663		470	600
LL	−293.4		−293.05		−217.83	−278.55
Pseudo R2	0.358		0.359		0.241	0.314

Note: Standard errors in parenthesis. Significant at: *10%; **5%; ***1%. Marginal effects for dichotomous variables are computed as discrete change from 0 to 1 activities took place. In Model 1 we consider whether individuals' bachelor and post-graduate locations were undertaken outside the region. In addition, we consider the location of the internship period at the end of the postgraduate programme financed by the regional authority. Individuals with a university degree obtained outside the home region are 5.5% less likely to remain home; the effect of pursuing postgraduate courses outside the region is slightly higher (6.2%).[8] It is interesting to note the very strong association between an internship period in the home region and the likelihood to remain (+28.6%). In fact, one possible way to interpret the reduced overall out-mobility found in this study compared to our previous analysis (Coniglio and Prota 2008) is the stronger emphasis given by the region to the facilitation of internships in Basilicata.[9]

Note also that in order to capture individuals' preferences toward the home location, we include in the analysis a dummy variable, 'Preference home', which is equal to 1 when Basilicata was their preferred option during the job market search after the completion of the postgraduate course. These revealed preferences toward the home location are—not surprisingly—positively related with the probability of residing in the home region.

In Model 2, we assess the combined effects of location choices during the graduate and post-graduate studies. When both university and master studies are carried out outside the region, the beneficiaries are, ceteris paribus, 12.2% more likely to migrate compared to an individual who has completed both courses in the region. Mobility only for the financed postgraduate course translates into an 8.4% higher probability of residing outside the region while mobility for the attainment of the bachelor degree is only associated with a 10% higher likelihood of migration. Obviously one should be careful in interpreting these as causal effects given the fact that past mobility choices might reveal a higher attitude/preference for geographical mobility.

The analysis provides a general message that promoting more (high quality) local opportunities for human capital accumulation and boosting ties with local potential employment (for example, through internship programmes) might translate into a reduced skilled out-migration from peripheral areas.

Although from an individual point of view out-migration is generally highly desirable—in fact those who migrate in our sample are significantly more likely to be employed and get higher wages—often mobility is a constrained choice which entails individual costs. Such costs are generally neglected in the existing literature. In our sample 88.2% of the policy beneficiaries who reside outside the region would be willing to return to the home region if a similar job position was available. How valuable is this 'home attachment'? We asked these beneficiaries to attach a monetary value to the option to relocate in the home region (with similar job

[8]The definition of the home region in this case includes the two neighbouring regions Puglia and Campania as a location for graduate and postgraduate studies. In fact, the institution of a local University in Basilicata is rather recent and not all subjects are covered by this relatively small university.

[9]Only 15% of the beneficiaries in the early phase of the policy attended an internship period in the home region compared with 24% of the beneficiaries between 2000 and 2005.

conditions except the salary). Interestingly, 41% of the migrants would trade a reduction in monthly salary, which is on average equal to 17.1%, with the possibility to return to Basilicata. At sample mean this is equivalent to an annual reduction of approximately 4,000 €. Clearly this 'monthly cut' includes perceived differences not only in amenities but also in real wages between the current residences and the home location; still we believe that this is important information about the possible welfare gains of 'moving jobs' to the periphery.[10] In fact when the (efficiency) cost of moving jobs to the periphery is not substantial and the local supply of qualified individuals is large enough there might be Pareto improvements to be reaped. These Pareto improvements are likely to be (partly or completely) blocked by large coordination costs which prevent private agents (in particular, firms) to 'move' jobs to the periphery; one corollary of this consideration is the need to reinforce human capital accumulation policies with investment attraction policies which leverage the local supply of skilled and qualified individuals.

11.3.2 Policy Case 2: On the Education-Job Mismatch in Peripheral Regions

The second 'policy case' we analyse is about the second element which might 'derail' human capital accumulation policies from their expected trajectory: education-job mismatch.

In this analysis, we examine the factors correlated with mismatch in the case of a sample of highly skilled individuals who received financial support from the Apulian regional government to realize an applied research project in cooperation with a firm and a research centre within the region. A survey of the beneficiaries of this policy measure was conducted by the authors during 2012 in order to evaluate the performances of the beneficiaries.[11]

In order to measure the match between education level and current job we focus on two specific aspects of the education-job mismatch: (i) flexible or part-time job versus permanent and full-time job (an aspect less studied in the literature); (ii) the usefulness of acquired competences in the current occupation.

Summary statistics of the variables employed in both the analyses are reported in Table 11.4. For the first exercise, our dependent variable is, therefore, a mismatch indicator we order from completely/severely mismatched (unemployed/in training) to matched (permanent and full-time job). The rationale is the consideration that

[10]Admittedly moving some type of jobs to the periphery might entail significant efficiency costs when agglomeration effects are at work. Nevertheless, it must be recognized that improvements in transportation and communication infrastructures and technologies have changed the geography of production in many sectors and have reduced the costs of relocating some jobs/tasks out of core regions.

[11]See footnote 5.

Table 11.4 Policy case 2. Human capital investment policy of Regione Puglia (Italy). Summary statistics of variables employed in the ordered probit analysis

Variable	Description	Mean	Std. dev.
Mismatch_indicator_1 *(dependent variable in Table 10.5)*	1 = unemployed (completely mismatched); 2 = in training (severely mismatched); 3 = flexible or part-time job (moderately mismatched); 4 = permanent and full-time job (matched)	2.427	1.043
Mismatch_indicator_2 *(dependent variable in Table 10.6)*	The usefulness of acquired competences in the current occupation (1= useless; 2 = less useful; 3 = useful; 4 = very useful)	2.299	1.335
age_ln	Age at the time of the research project (log)	3.530	0.156
sex	Male = 1; female = 0	0.433	0.496
marks	Final mark of the bachelor degree	106.175	5.396
Engineering_d	Degree in engineering or architecture	0.352	0.478
agriculture_d	Degree in agricultural sciences	0.157	0.364
biology_d	Degree in biology	0.229	0.421
chemistry_d	Degree in chemistry	0.027	0.163
law_d	Degree in law or political sciences	0.048	0.214
business_d	Degree in economics or business studies	0.044	0.206
other_d	Degree in other subjects	0.140	0.348
phd	Individual holding a PhD	0.369	0.483
migrant	Individual not resident in Apulia	0.027	0.163
borsa_year	The year when the research project was realized (2006 = 1; 2009 = 0)	0.553	0.498
Pub_StrongRole	Interaction effect between a measure of the quality of the research project (publication) and a measure of the involvement of the two partners in the project	0.061	0.241
emp_partner_company	The employer is the firm partner of the project	0.141	0.349
emp_partner_research_center	The employer is the research centre partner of the project	0.215	0.412
public_sector	The employer is in the public sector	0.514	0.502
research_network	The research centre played a leading role in creating the network	0.863	0.344
skills_evaluation	Beneficiaries evaluation of the research project in terms of accumulation of competence	4.242	0.798

returns on human capital investments are maximized in permanent and full-time jobs, while precarious work is associated with less security, career prospects and lower salaries [see Hensen et al. (2009) for a similar analysis on Dutch graduates].

An ordered probit model is used to estimate the determinants of the mismatch. The marginal effects of the estimates on the probability of being in the matched category are summarized in Table 11.5.

Table 11.5 Education-job mismatch: flexible or part-time job versus permanent and full-time job (ordered probit regression)

	Completely mismatched	Severely mismatched			Moderately mismatched			Matched		
	Mod. 1—mfx	Mod. 1—mfx	Mod. 2—mfx	Mod. 3—mfx	Mod. 1—mfx	Mod. 2—mfx	Mod. 3—mfx	Mod. 1—mfx	Mod. 2—mfx	Mod. 3—mfx
age_ln	0.085 (0.161)	0.013 (0.024)	0.029 (0.037)	−0.003 (0.013)	−0.055 (0.104)	0.134 (0.162)	−0.054 (0.258)	−0.043 (0.081)	−0.163 (0.195)	0.056 (0.271)
sex	−0.018 (0.047)	−0.003 (0.007)	0.000 (0.010)	0.000 (0.003)	0.012 (0.030)	0.001 (0.045)	0.002 (0.065)	0.009 (0.024)	−0.001 (0.055)	−0.002 (0.068)
marks	−0.008* (0.005)	−0.001 (0.001)	−0.001 (0.001)	−0.001 (0.001)	0.005* (0.003)	−0.005 (0.004)	−0.014** (0.007)	0.004* (0.002)	0.006 (0.005)	0.015** (0.007)
engineering_d	−0.235*** (0.063)	−0.043*** (0.016)	−0.016 (0.016)	−0.007 (0.008)	0.126*** (0.033)	−0.083 (0.086)	−0.162 (0.129)	0.151*** (0.053)	0.099 (0.100)	0.169 (0.134)
chemistry_d	−0.264*** (0.038)	−0.091*** (0.027)	−0.003 (0.023)	0.000 (0.009)	−0.068 (0.128)	−0.014 (0.130)	0.005 (0.158)	0.423** (0.177)	0.017 (0.153)	−0.005 (0.166)
biology_d	−0.081 (0.072)	−0.014 (0.015)	0.012 (0.024)	0.006 (0.011)	0.049 (0.040)	0.041 (0.064)	0.076 (0.091)	0.047 (0.048)	−0.053 (0.087)	−0.082 (0.101)
agriculture_d	−0.123* (0.070)	−0.024 (0.018)	−0.011 (0.013)	−0.003 (0.005)	0.067** (0.031)	−0.070 (0.116)	−0.093 (0.159)	0.081 (0.060)	0.080 (0.129)	0.096 (0.163)
law_d	−0.127 (0.089)	−0.028 (0.027)	−0.006 (0.018)	−0.002 (0.005)	0.061** (0.025)	−0.037 (0.137)	−0.076 (0.216)	0.093 (0.095)	0.043 (0.154)	0.079 (0.220)
business_d	−0.068 (0.111)	−0.012 (0.025)	−0.016 (0.010)	−0.004 (0.004)	0.039 (0.055)	−0.194 (0.240)	−0.193 (0.253)	0.041 (0.081)	0.209 (0.246)	0.196 (0.254)
phd	0.109** (0.053)	0.014** (0.007)	0.006 (0.012)	0.003 (0.005)	−0.072** (0.037)	0.027 (0.046)	0.058 (0.066)	−0.051** (0.024)	−0.033 (0.058)	−0.061 (0.070)
migrant	−0.228*** (0.056)	−0.070** (0.032)	−0.012 (0.011)	−0.004 (0.004)	0.021 (0.082)	−0.102 (0.155)	−0.194 (0.214)	0.276* (0.160)	0.114 (0.165)	0.198 (0.216)
borsa_year	−0.257*** (0.050)	−0.032*** (0.010)	−0.016 (0.015)	−0.004 (0.006)	0.166*** (0.038)	−0.057 (0.042)	−0.061 (0.064)	0.124*** (0.027)	0.072 (0.055)	0.065 (0.069)
Pub_StrongRole			−0.020** (0.010)	−0.005 (0.005)		−0.324** (0.154)	−0.379* (0.221)		0.344** (0.156)	0.384* (0.222)
emp_partner_company			−0.021** (0.011)	−0.003 (0.004)		−0.240** (0.112)	−0.067 (0.103)		0.261** (0.115)	0.070 (0.106)

(continued)

Table 11.5 (continued)

	Completely mismatched	Severely mismatched			Moderately mismatched			Matched		
	Mod. 1—mfx	Mod. 1—mfx	Mod. 2—mfx	Mod. 3—mfx	Mod. 1—mfx	Mod. 2—mfx	Mod. 3—mfx	Mod. 1—mfx	Mod. 2—mfx	Mod. 3—mfx
emp_partner_research_center			0.047 (0.031)	0.023 (0.020)		0.086*** (0.031)	0.158*** (0.052)		−0.133*** (0.047)	−0.181*** (0.061)
public_sector				0.010 (0.010)			0.183** (0.080)			−0.194** (0.084)
Observations	284	284	175	138	284	175	138	284	175	138
Pseudo R-squared	0.084	0.084	0.154	0.254	0.084	0.154	0.254	0.084	0.154	0.254

Standard errors in parentheses
*** $p<0.01$, ** $p<0.05$, * $p<0.1$

The set of control variables include: (i) individual characteristics such as age, sex and migrant status, (ii) detailed information on educational background (marks obtained, subject of study, education level, location of studies), (iii) information on the research project (degree of involvement of the two partners, nature of the network, beneficiaries' evaluation of the project, results produced by the project), (iv) (if employed) job characteristics (sector and employer).

The percentage of people with a permanent and full-time job is slightly more than 12%, while around 60% of the respondent are engaged in a flexible or part-time job (another 30% is unemployed or in training).

According to our estimates, gender and age of beneficiaries are not significantly correlated with mismatch. Marks obtained during bachelor studies have a (weak) positive effect on the likelihood of being in the matched category. The individuals with an educational background in engineering or chemistry are more likely to be engaged in a permanent and full-time job[12]. This result confirms the heterogeneity of mismatch by subject of degree. One possibility for skill mismatching is that individuals are not studying the 'right' type of graduate studies. In other words, the choice of higher education made by individuals does not correspond to the needs of the labour market in terms of field of study.

Somewhat surprisingly, we find that the higher the individual competences (measured by holding a PhD degree), the higher the likelihood of being unemployed or employed in highly precarious occupations. As documented in other studies (Hensen et al. 2009), geographic mobility seems to reduce education-job mismatches, even if it is important to underline that in our sample the percentage of people working outside the region is small.

Interestingly, if the beneficiary works at the firm which was the partner of the research project (emp_partner_company), her probability of being in the matched category increases by 26%, while on the contrary this probability decreases by 13% if her employer is the research centre partner of the project (emp_partner_research_center). This negative effect is stronger (-18%) when controlling for the possibility that the employer is in the public sector (public_sector).

Another way to look at the determinants of mismatch is to examine the answer to the question "in your current job, how useful are the skills acquired during the financed research project?". The dependent variable is ordered in increasing usefulness of the skills acquired (from 1, useless, to 4, very useful). An ordered probit model is used to estimate the determinants of mismatch. The marginal effects are reported in Table 11.6.

As for the previous analysis, gender and age of beneficiaries are not significantly correlated with mismatch, while marks obtained during bachelor studies have a (weak) positive effect on the likelihood of declaring that the skills have been very useful. The individuals with an educational background in engineering are more

[12]Note that this finding might be related to a higher propensity in this sector to use full-time contracts. We acknowledge an anonymous referee for suggesting this interpretation.

Table 11.6 Education-job mismatch: the usefulness of the skills acquired (ordered probit regression)

	Useless		Less useful		Useful		Very useful	
	Mod. 1—mfx	Mod. 2—mfx	Mod. 1—mfx	Mod. 2—mfx	Mod. 1—mfx	Mod. 2—mfx	Mod. 1—mfx	Mod. 2—mfx
age_ln	−0.069 (0.199)	−0.011 (0.199)	0.000 (0.002)	0.000 (0.001)	0.008 (0.023)	0.001 (0.023)	0.061 (0.175)	0.010 (0.175)
sex	−0.058 (0.058)	−0.058 (0.058)	0.000 (0.001)	0.000 (0.001)	0.006 (0.006)	0.007 (0.007)	0.052 (0.052)	0.051 (0.052)
marks	−0.008 (0.006)	−0.010* (0.006)	0.000 (0.000)	0.000 (0.000)	0.001 (0.001)	0.001 (0.001)	0.007 (0.005)	0.009* (0.005)
Engineering_d	−0.259*** (0.086)	−0.268*** (0.086)	−0.003 (0.005)	−0.004 (0.005)	0.020** (0.008)	0.021** (0.008)	0.242*** (0.086)	0.251*** (0.086)
chemistiy_d	−0.214 (0.164)	−0.245 (0.154)	−0.010 (0.018)	−0.014 (0.021)	0.004 (0.017)	0.000 (0.024)	0.219 (0.197)	0.259 (0.197)
biology_d	−0.083 (0.096)	−0.108 (0.096)	−0.000 (0.002)	−0.001 (0.003)	0.008 (0.008)	0.010 (0.007)	0.076 (0.090)	0.099 (0.092)
agricultuie_d	−0.172* (0.098)	−0.168* (0.098)	−0.004 (0.006)	−0.004 (0.006)	0.011** (0.005)	0.011** (0.005)	0.165 (0.102)	0.160 (0.103)
law_d	−0.091 (0.149)	−0.053 (0.154)	−0.001 (0.005)	−0.000 (0.003)	0.007 (0.007)	0.005 (0.012)	0.085 (0.148)	0.048 (0.145)
business_d	0.048 (0.164)	0.033 (0.165)	−0.001 (0.005)	−0.000 (0.003)	−0.006 (0.024)	−0.004 (0.023)	−0.041 (0.136)	−0.029 (0.138)
phd	0.067 (0.063)	0.045 (0.064)	−0.001 (0.001)	−0.000 (0.001)	−0.008 (0.008)	−0.006 (0.008)	−0.058 (0.054)	−0.039 (0.055)
migrant	−0.300** (0.119)	−0.306*** (0.117)	−0.021 (0.020)	−0.023 (0.021)	−0.009 (0.029)	−0.012 (0.031)	0.330** (0.166)	0.341** (0.167)
borsa_yeai	−0.120** (0.060)	−0.116* (0.060)	0.001 (0.002)	0.001 (0.002)	0.014* (0.008)	0.014* (0.008)	0.105** (0.052)	0.101* (0.052)
skills_evaluation		−0.074** (0.037)		0.000 (0.001)		0.009* (0.005)		0.065** (0.033)

research_network		0.159** (0.079)		0.004 (0.005)		−0.010** (0.005)		−0.153* (0.083)
Observations	282	282	282	282	282	282	282	282
Pseudo R-squared	0.038	0.049	0.038	0.049	0.038	0.049	0.038	0.049

Standard errors in parentheses
*** $p<0.01$, ** $p<0.05$, * $p<0.1$

likely to be associated with a positive evaluation of the skills acquired as well as people who migrated (with respect to this variable, the previous caveat still holds).

The scientific side of the triangular partnership seems to be the weak one; in fact, when the leading role in creating the network has been played by the research centre (research_network), the evaluation of the usefulness of the skills is more likely to be negative. One possible explanation of this finding can be found in the recent difficulties of the Italian public research system (mainly the Universities) to absorb the young highly educated and skilled people. The increasing supply of labour at the post-graduate level does not meet the low demand of labour in research departments as a consequence of low investments in research. A complementary explanation might be related to the tendency of research institutions to prioritize abstract and theoretical knowledge over more applied knowledge and hence reduce, at least in the short term, the direct employability of the newly-acquired human capital.

Finally, we find a positive correlation with the 'quality' of the research project as perceived by the beneficiaries in terms of accumulation of competences (skill_evaluation).

The analysis of this second case provides further support, in terms of policy implications, to the previous consideration that it is necessary to reinforce human capital accumulation policies with investment attraction and startup promotion policies which leverage the local supply of skilled and qualified individuals.

11.4 The Missing Regional Upgrading and the Low Absorptive Capacity of the Peripheral Regions: Concluding Remarks

Human capital is a fundamental ingredient for the upgrading of the regional production structure and, in turn, for the competitiveness of peripheral regions. Policies at regional, national and EU levels have devoted substantial efforts to boost the 'stock' of this necessary but, unfortunately, not sufficient ingredient. The tale of the two stories presented in this work points to the need to work jointly on both sides of the human capital market: promote the demand of human capital at least as much as its supply. The emphasis on the demand side—and its coordination with supply side interventions—has been, in our opinion, weak and in many cases lacking so far in the policy arena. Without linking the two sides there is a very high risk of 'human capital leakages' through out-migration of highly skilled and qualified individuals from the peripheries. In addition, the policy implemented by Apulia Region—where an explicit attempt to involve the 'demand side' (firms and research institutions) was made—highlights how relevant another risk of failure is: that of generating a 'human capital waste' due to a mismatch between the competences acquired and those required by the local economy.

Boosting the demand for highly qualified workers of firms in the economic periphery is possible but it is likely to be, like all processes which involve a 'cultural' change, a rather slow process. Firms are highly heterogeneous in their response to these 'policy stimuli' and hence the policy design should be made in a way to target the more 'receptive firms' rather than being too broad. In fact, the case study on Apulia shows that when a firm was strongly involved in the definition of the research project financed by the policymaker, the likelihood of a mismatch was substantially reduced. Participation of firms at 'zero costs' (and effort) in the partnership with an individual beneficiary was not a key to success.

Are human capital promotion policies in the EU periphery predestined to be ineffective in terms of upgrading the productive system? In our opinion, in order to boost the effectiveness of these measures, policymakers should start to leverage the availability of abundant (and even relatively cheap) qualified workforce for 'moving' qualified job opportunities in the periphery. In several cases inducing behavioural changes in local firms which have a structural low demand of qualified workers might be more difficult than attracting new players and/or boosting the creation of new innovative firms. Investing millions of Euros in educating new scientists and engineers and not using the results of this policy measure as a tool for attracting firms that make use of this scarce factor of production is a common policy failure.[13] Many potential investors would value much more this kind of location incentive rather than the transitory financial support that is the cornerstone of investment attraction policies in the EU periphery.

Several observers claim that migration out of the periphery toward core regions is 'efficient' both at macro and at individual levels. At the macro level, while this is true for jobs/tasks characterized by increasing returns to scale in production and positive agglomeration externalities, not all 'qualified jobs' are characterized by these features. Individual migrants do benefit from migration but geographical relocation towards a core region is not a 'cause' for an improved job market outcome but a 'venue' that leads to it. One element which is often under-evaluated in the existing literature is the individual cost of out-migration. In fact, for many individuals, migration is not a choice but a necessity. In our study on Basilicata, 88.2% of those actually residing outside the region would be willing to return to the home region if a similar job position was available. Interestingly, among them 46.7% would even accept a lower salary in the home region. Moving some of these jobs back to the periphery—those for which a peripheral location will not imply severe reduction in production efficiency—might lead to a conspicuous Pareto improvement for firms, workers and local communities.

[13]In both policy cases analysed in this study, the contribution of the regional authorities has helped human capital formation of several thousands of brilliant young graduates; many of them have completed their studies in the best higher education and research institutes around the globe.

References

Armstrong HW (1995) An appraisal of the evidence from cross-sectional analysis of the regional growth process within the European Union. In: Vickerman RW, Armstrong HW (eds) Convergence and divergence among European regions. Pion Limited, London, pp 40–65

Busch O, Weigert B (2010) Where have all the graduates gone? Internal cross-state migration of graduates in Germany 1984–2004. Ann Reg Sci 44:559–572

Coniglio N, Prota F (2008) Human capital accumulation and migration in a peripheral EU region: the case of Basilicata. Pap Reg Sci 87(1):77–95

Faggian A, McCann P, Sheppard S (2007) Some evidence that women are more mobile than men: gender differences in the U.K. graduate migration behavior. J Reg Sci 47(3):517–539

Felice E (2012) Regional convergence in Italy, 1891-2001: testing human and social capital. Cliometrica 6:267–306

Haapanen M, Tervo H (2012) Migration of the highly educated: evidence from residence spells of university graduates. J Reg Sci 52(4):587–605

Hensen MM, de Vries MR, Cörvers F (2009) The role of geographical mobility in reducing education-job mismatches in the Netherlands. Pap Reg Sci 88(3):667–682

Iuzzolino G., Pellegrini G., Viesti G. (2011) Convergence among Italian Regions, 1861-2011. Banca d'Italia, Quaderni di Storia Economica, 22

López-Bazo E, Vayá E, Mora AJ, Suriñach J (1999) Regional economic dynamics and convergence in the European Union. Ann Reg Sci 33:343–370

Magrini S (1999) The evolution of income disparities among the regions of the European Union. Reg Sci Urban Econ 29:257–281

Rodríguez-Pose A (1999) Convergence or divergence? Types of regional responses to socioeconomic change. Tijdschrift voor Economische en Sociale Geografie 90:363–378

Venhorst V, Van Dijk J, Van Wissen L (2011) An analysis of trends in spatial mobility of Dutch graduates. Spat Econ Anal 6(1):57–82

Nicola D. Coniglio obtained a PhD in Economics from the University of Glasgow (UK) and a doctorate at the University of Milan—Bicocca. Nicola is currently associate professor in Economics at the University of Bari (Italy). He is the Italian director of the Erasmus Mundus—Master in Economics of Globalisation and European Integration. His research interests include urban and regional economics, industrial policy, economics of migration, international trade and factor mobility and the economic consequences of climatic changes. He was awarded with the EPAINOS prize for the best research work presented by a young scholar at the European Regional Science Association meetings in 2003 and 2004.

Francesco Prota (PhD in Agricultural and Environmental Economics) is Lecturer in Economics at the University of Bari "Aldo Moro". His research interests include regional economics and international economic integration, development economics, public policy evaluation and innovation economics. Francesco is the author of several articles in economics journals. He has also written two books: *Senza cassa. Le politiche di sviluppo del Mezzogiorno dopo l'Intervento straordinario* (Il Mulino, 2012; coauthor G. Viesti) and *Le nuove politiche regionali dell'Unione Europea* (Il Mulino, 2008; coauthor G. Viesti). Besides serving as referee for international journals, he is Associate Editor for *Regional Studies, Regional Science.* Since 2011, Francesco has been acting as consultant to UNIDO (United Nations Industrial Development Organization) on cluster development and FDI in Africa. He has also a long track record of collaboration with different Italian government departments and agencies.

Chapter 12
Ageing and Migration: Some Reflexions on the Effects of the Economic and Financial Crisis on Demographic Trends in Portuguese Regions

Maria Lucinda Fonseca, Diogo de Abreu, and Alina Esteves

JEL Classification J11

12.1 Introduction

The ageing of the Portuguese population is a long-term trend that began years ago but has become more evident and worrying in the present decade.

The role of international migration in demographic issues has gained significant ground in migration policy debates since the mid-2000s. A growing number of studies about the future of the European population emphasize the role of immigration in the European demographic dynamics (EC 2006, 2009; Lanzieri 2011; Giannakouris 2010; Lutz and Scherbov s/d; Bijak et al. 2013).

In 2006, the EU Commission committed itself that every 2 years a European Forum on Demography would be held with the purpose of analysing the demographic trends and reviewing the position of the EU and its member states in responding to demographic change.

Portugal is keeping up with this trend and recent studies on population change, fertility and migration have examined the increasing importance of international migration in population change (Valente Rosa et al. 2004; Magalhães and Peixoto 2008; Abreu and Peixoto 2009; Abreu 2012; Muysken 2008). Growing concerns with the sustainability of the social security system led the Portuguese government to commission research on the evolution of the birth rate and possible measures to

M.L. Fonseca (✉) • D. de Abreu • A. Esteves
Centro de Estudos Geográficos, Instituto de Geografia e Ordenamento do Território, Universidade de Lisboa, Edifício IGOT – Rua Branca Edmée Marques, 1600-276 Lisbon, Portugal
e-mail: fonseca-maria@igot.ulisboa.pt

M. Fonseca, U. Fratesi (eds.), *Regional Upgrading in Southern Europe*, Advances in Spatial Science, DOI 10.1007/978-3-319-49818-8_12

remove the obstacles to the wanted fertility, in which the role of migration comes into play (Azevedo 2014).[1]

According to Statistics Portugal and the 2011 Census (INE 2012), 82.4% of the foreign citizens living in Portugal are aged between 15 and 64 and only 5% are 65 or older, whereas for the nationals those proportions are respectively 65.5% and 19.6%. According to the demographic statistics, in 2012, 12.1% of all births in the country were from foreign mother, father or both, and this proportion grew steadily throughout the last decade (8.5% in 2002).

Considering the relative youth of the migrant population, the higher birth rates of some communities and the regional disparities in its settlement patterns, the presence of foreign groups may attenuate the population loss and ageing in some regions of Portugal, giving a valuable contribution to regional development by feeding the economic activity with working-age population.

However, the economic and financial crisis the country is going through has had a deep effect on the recent evolution of migration flows to and from Portugal. The rising unemployment led to a reduction of labour inflows, expansion of return flows to the origin countries and even re-emigration to other countries, perceived as offering better opportunities. Moreover, on the outflows side, there has been a growing emigration of Portuguese workers that is reaching similar levels to those observed in the 1960s (Fonseca and McGarrigle 2014; Malheiros 2011; Peixoto 2012; Marques 2009; Pires et al. 2010; Santos 2013).

The goal of this chapter is to explore these processes, illustrating the link between economic growth, international migration flows and demographic change in Portugal in the last decades, giving particular attention to the most recent dynamics, mainly after the emergence of the economic and financial crisis in 2008. In order to anticipate the demographic trends at the regional level, forecasting models were developed, taking into account different scenarios of natural population change, economic growth and migration flows. The paper is composed of four main parts and starts by giving a general picture of the main demographic trends in Portugal, focusing on the relevance of migration for demographic change. In the second part, the role of international migration for the growth of the Portuguese economy is analysed, whereas in the third section the population projections according to different scenarios up to 2050 are presented. The fourth part includes a regionalization of the previously mentioned demographic scenarios at the NUTS 3 level. The chapter ends with some concluding remarks.

[1]Due to continuous population decline, demographic issues have indeed reached a moment's high in Portugal. Statistics Portugal and the Foundation Francisco Manuel dos Santos conducted a nation-wide survey to fertility in order to understand the values, attitudes and socioeconomic factors underpinning the decision of procreation (INE/FFMS 2014).

12.2 Main Demographic Trends in Portugal: The Increasing Importance of Migration in Demographic Change

Throughout the last 40 years the Portuguese demographic evolution shows a convergence with the EU's average. The total fertility rate (TFR) had a sharp decline, from 3.01 in 1970 (well above the replacement level) to 2.25 in 1980 and 1.56 in 1990. This declining trend has continued and in 2013 it was only 1.21. This is the lowest figure ever in Portugal and the lowest among the EU member states.

Improvements in living standards as well as universal access to the National Health Service have also led to a continuous increase in life expectancy at birth. Indeed, the life expectancy at birth in Portugal has increased during the period 1970–2013 by 12.87 years, reaching an average of 80.00 years for the total population, 76.91 years for men and 82.79 years for women.

The continuous decline of the birth rate and the increase of life expectancy at birth are visible in the population ageing. The recently released results for 2013 show a country with an old age dependency ratio[2] of 30.3, well above the EU28 average (27.5), an index of renewal of the active population[3] of 86.2 much lower than the figure for 2001 (142.4) and a declining proportion of young people (only 14.6% are aged 14 or less against 16.2% in 2001). The 2% population growth between the 2001 and 2011 censuses was possible due to the remarkable increase of foreign citizens in Portugal (rate of change of 70% between the two censuses[4]) who smoothed not only the population decline and ageing, but also the decreasing birth rate. If it was not for the presence of an average of 400,000 non-nationals between 2002 and 2012, representing approximately 4.0% of the total resident population, Portugal would be an even older country.

Indeed, in the last half a century, migration has been a very important component of the population change with a simultaneous decrease of the role of natural growth. This component was particularly important in the 1960s and 1970s (rate of natural increase of 122.2‰ and 85.9‰, respectively) but its relevance dwindled in the following decades with a positive net migration (rate of net migration 1991–2001: 40‰; 2001–2011: 18‰) that clearly overcame the natural component (Table 12.1).

Considering the last 10 years, the way migration flows influenced the evolution of the population in Portugal was quite different throughout the decade and worth

---

[2]The old age dependency ratio is the ratio between the total number of elderly persons of an age when they are generally economically inactive (aged 65 and older) and the number of persons of working age (from 15 to 64).

[3]Relation between the population who is potentially entering the labour market and the population that is leaving it. In potential terms, in 2011, for each 100 people leaving the labour market, only 94 joined in.

[4]The figures from the 2001 and 2011 censuses conducted by Statistics Portugal differ from those disseminated by the Immigration and Borders Service for the same years, being the main reason for the disparities the criteria used to collect the data.

Table 12.1 Components of population change in inter-census periods, 1960–2011

Rates per 1000 people			
Decades	Population change	Natural increase	Net migration
1960–1970	−25.8	122.2	−148.0
1970–1981	126.5	85.9	40.6
1981–1991	3.5	35.5	−32.0
1991–2001	48.4	8.3	40.0
2001–2011	19.7	1.7	18.0

Source: 1960, 1970, 1981, 1991, 2001 and 2011 INE census data; INE Statistical Yearbooks (several years)

analysing in more detail. Considering the most recent decade, the population variation between 2001 and 2009 (from 10,394,669 to 10,573,479, i.e., 1.72%) was essentially due to the positive net migration that compensated the very low natural growth rate which has been increasingly negative since 2007 (from −0.01% in 2007 to −0.23% in 2013). That is, for most of the period, the inflows exceeded the outflows and even compensated for the negative natural change until 2009, allowing Portugal to have a small population growth. However, the onset of the economic crisis of 2008 has had a direct impact on the migration flows to and from Portugal with less people choosing it as a country of residence and more people leaving for other destinations seen as more attractive, both in Europe and on other continents. Since 2010 emigration has been higher than immigration and thus, the migratory flows are reinforcing the already negative natural population loss.

Emigration has been a structural feature of the Portuguese society, and despite the fluctuations observed in the 1990s, especially in the temporary outflows, the figures were rather low in this decade and in the early 2000s, probably due to the good economic performance of the nation's economy[5] (Peixoto 1993; Arroteia 2011). Despite the breaks in the statistical series that render a longitudinal comparison more difficult, temporary and permanent emigration have been growing steadily since 2011 with the temporary outflows higher than the permanent ones (Fig. 12.1).

In Fig. 12.1, it can also be observed that since 1993, the temporary emigration has been always higher than the permanent kind. According to Peixoto (2004), the real identity of the temporary emigrants may have changed across time. They often used the temporary migrant status because it was the only legal way to have access to the labour market in the hosting countries. After returning to Portugal, they would leave several times until they obtained a permanent status. More recently, researchers admit that a significant proportion of these individuals are indeed

[5]Between 1991 and 2007, the GDP's real growth rate was always positive (except in 1993 and 2003) and often above the EU average in the early 1990s. Moreover, in the same period, the unemployment rate was kept below the two-digit figure, reaching a maximum of 8.0% in 2007 and was frequently below the EU average (Source: Fonseca and Malheiros 2003; Fonseca and McGarrigle 2014).

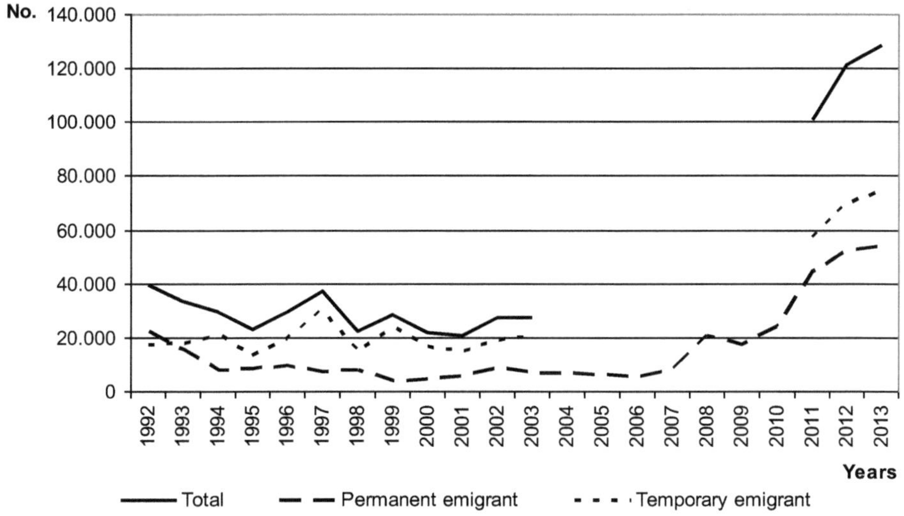

Fig. 12.1 Emigration from Portugal: total, temporary and permanent, 1992–2013. Source: Statistics Portugal and PORDATA. Note: The data between 1992 and 2007 were collected in the survey of the outflows and from 2008 onwards in the Annual Estimations of Emigration. Both sources are from Statistics Portugal

temporary workers who emigrate for restricted periods in order to maximize their income abroad.

Regarding immigration, the effects of the economic and financial crisis are reflected in the decrease of the inflows to Portugal, as well as in return flows to sending countries or re-emigration to other destinations of a growing number of foreigners (Fonseca and McGarrigle 2014; Pires et al. 2010).

12.2.1 Regional Disparities

The population loss and ageing is not evenly distributed across Portugal and noteworthy regional disparities can be found. The migratory gains of the first half of the 2001–2011 period were not equally distributed throughout the country, with foreign citizens opting for the areas with higher economic dynamics to settle down (Fonseca et al. 2013; Malheiros and Esteves 2013; Reis et al. 2010). Regions like the metropolitan areas of Lisbon and Porto and the Algarve were more often chosen by immigrants, who not only increased the resident population but also smoothed the population ageing through their younger age structure and higher birth rates. According to the 2011 census, 82% of the foreign citizens living in Portugal were aged between 15 and 64 years and those aged 65 or older only accounted for 5%. For the total resident population, the correspondent values were 59% and 20%, respectively (INE 2012). Considering the birth rates, again the foreign population overcomes the figures for the Portuguese nationals: in 2001, the feminine birth rate (number of live births per 1000 women) for Portuguese women was 20.4‰ whereas for women with a foreign citizenship it reached 55.8‰ (Valente Rosa et al. 2004). For 2011 the difference between the two groups persists but with lower rates as a result of population ageing (16.5‰ and 51.0‰ respectively).

Considering the location quotients[6] of foreign residents, they are more notably over-represented in the NUTS 3 of Grande Lisboa and Algarve, but also in Península de Setúbal, Oeste and Alentejo Litoral (Fig. 12.2).

Despite this spatial concentration in the three mentioned regions, it should also be noted that the migrants who arrived in the more recent migratory flows of the 2000s (Brazilians, Ukrainians and nationals from other Eastern European countries and from the former USSR) are slightly more dispersed throughout the territory compared to the citizens coming from the Portuguese-Speaking African Countries (PALOPs) and from the Asian continent. Although in small figures, the presence of Brazilians, Romanians, Ukrainians and Moldovans in the interior parts of Portugal contributed to the slowdown of population loss and ageing. However, vast areas of Portugal, namely the interior north and centre, the Alentejo region, the mountain areas of the Algarve, and some municipalities of the Autonomic Regions of the Azores and Madeira lost population and increased their demographic ageing index. The regions with a more severe negative population change were the NUTS 3 of Beira Interior Norte, Serra da Estrela and Pinhal Interior Sul (between −8% and −12%) which largely coincide with the geographical units with higher proportion of people aged 65 or older, but Alto Trás os Montes and Beira Interior Sul also have to be added (proportions between 27.9% and 33.6%)—Figs. 12.3 and 12.4. The NUTS 3 in the littoral, presenting more economic dynamics and labour market opportunities had population gains: up to 5% in the case of NUTS 3 of Grande Porto, Cávado, Ave and Tâmega and between 5% and 14% for Grande Lisboa, Península de Setúbal, Oeste, Algarve and the archipelago of Madeira. Some of these regions also have small proportions of ageing people (the archipelago of Madeira, for example) but in others, like the Oeste, 20% of the residents are aged 65 and older[7] (Fig. 12.4).

[6]According to Statistics Portugal, the location quotient is calculated as follows: $LQ = (X_{rj}/X_r)/(X_{pj}/X_p)$, being X_{rj} the population of the group j in the territorial unit r; X_r the total population of the territorial unit, X_{pj} the population of the group j in the territorial unit p; X_p the total population of the unit p.

[7]According to Statistics Portugal, the ageing population is the population aged 65 or older.

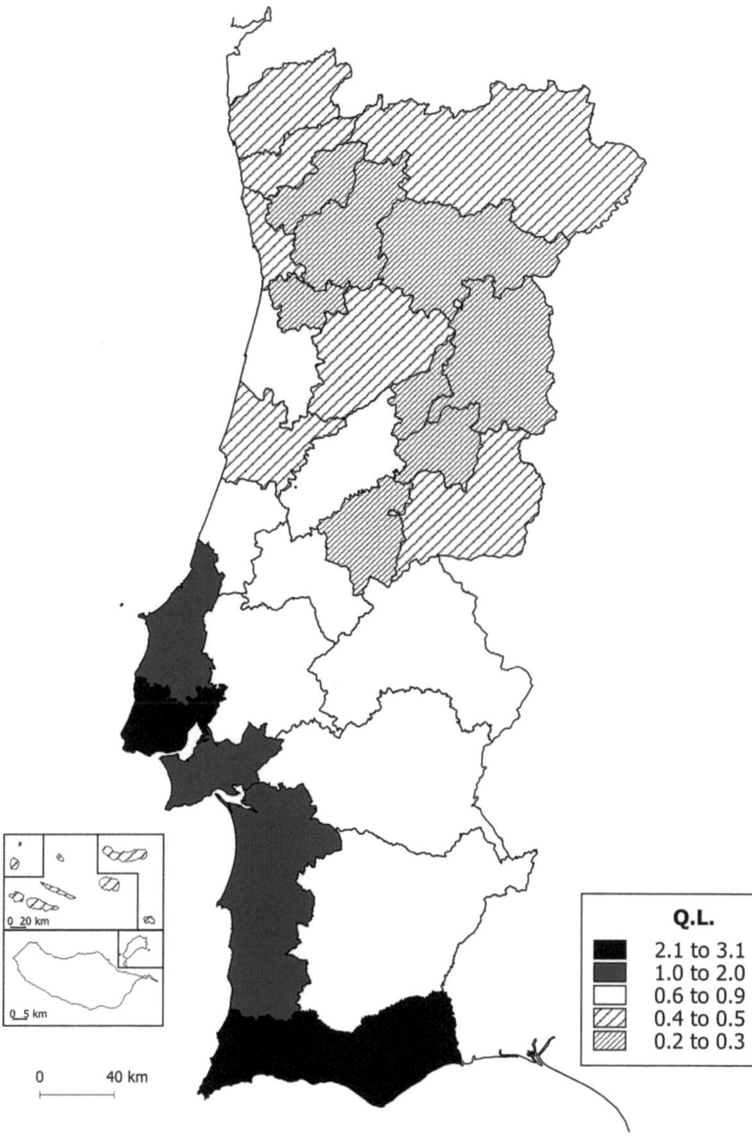

Fig. 12.2 Location quotients of foreign residents, 2011, NUTS 3. Source: INE 2012, with the authors' elaboration

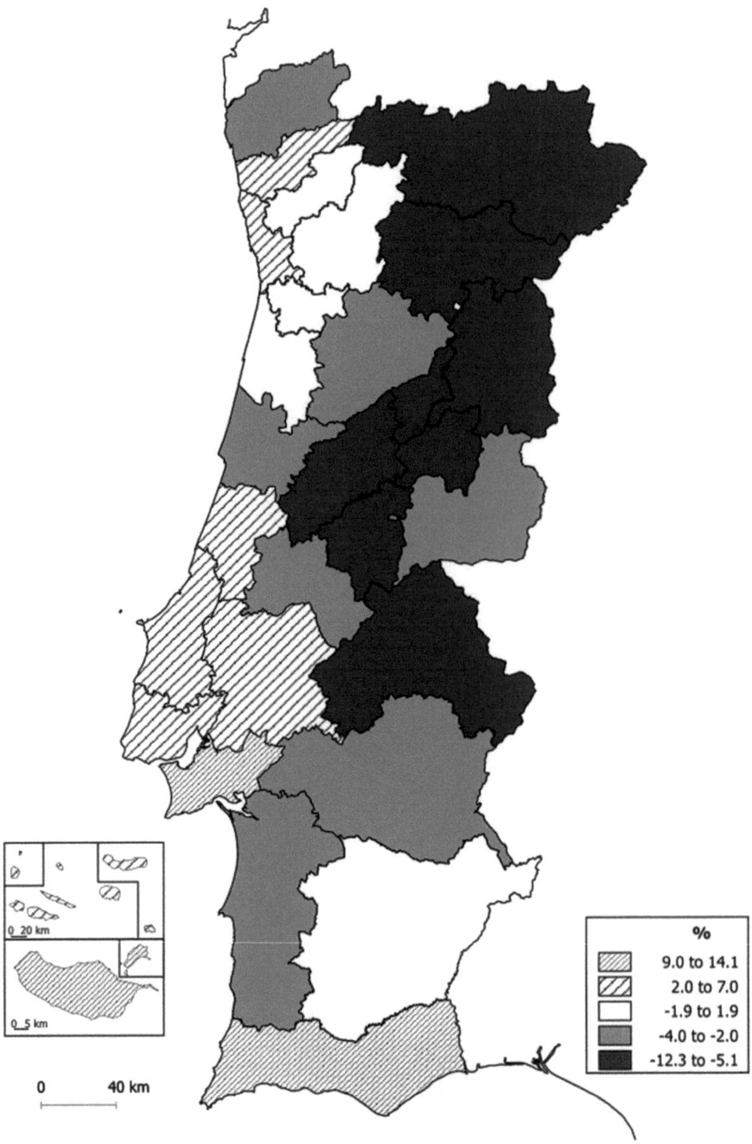

Fig. 12.3 Population change 2001–2011 (%), (NUTS 3). Source: INE 2012, with the authors' elaboration

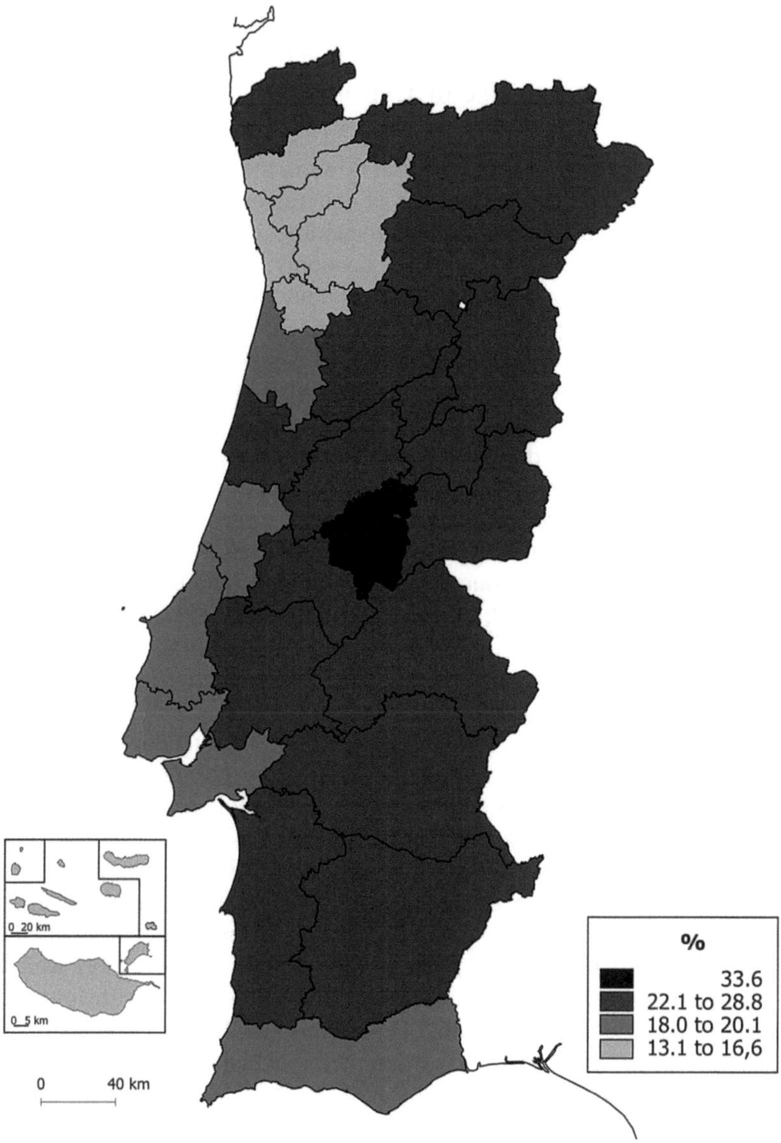

Fig. 12.4 Ageing population on the total population, 2011 (%), (NUTS 3). Source: INE 2012, with the authors' elaboration

12.3 International Migration and Growth of the Portuguese Economy: A Model Based on the Extensive Use of Labour

Considering the relevance of the migration flows in the evolution of the population living in Portugal, it is worth looking at the factors that have constrained or influenced their evolution. From a long-standing emigrant nation, due to the structural features of the Portuguese economy, regional asymmetries and geo-economic unbalances between Portugal and the destination countries, the country evolved to being a host of foreign citizens from the second half of the 1970s onwards (Baganha 1994; Arroteia 2011; Fonseca 2005; Fonseca et al. 2003; Pires et al. 2010). The decolonization process in Africa in 1974–76 led to a boom of arrivals of Africans from the former colonies until the early eighties. The rate of increase was fairly good during the 1980s and there was a diversification of geographical origins (Asians from Pakistan, India and China, and South Americans, mostly Brazilians) pointing to a more important role of the Portuguese labour market in the recruitment of foreign workers and closely associated with the good economic performance of the country, especially after joining the EU in 1986, and until 1991 (Baganha et al. 1999; Fonseca and Malheiros 2003).

Indeed, the European funds of the Community Support Frameworks allowed for major public works in Portugal in the fields of transportation, construction, communication and energy, just to name a few (Fonseca et al. 2002; Góis and Marques 2007; Malheiros and Esteves 2013). There was a simultaneous increase in the foreign direct investment and a modernization of the Portuguese economy, with the tertiary sector assuming a predominant role in the country's creation of wealth.

However, a service-oriented economy may not be associated with high productivity and skills. As stated by experts from several fields "the Portuguese economy of the new millennium is an intensive user of labour force, more so than other productive factors. Therefore, its model of growth is conventionally called extensive." (Reis et al. 2010, p. 23). Mota et al. (2004) add that the sectors which grew more significantly created huge amounts of low-skilled jobs, with low levels of productivity and productivity growth.[8] This means that there was abundant offer on the side of the labour market which was satisfied by a higher participation of women and import of foreign workers (Baganha et al. 1999; Reis et al. 2010). As noted by other authors, informality, heavy segmentation and seasonality of some sectors are important features of the Portuguese labour market (Carvalho 2007; Peixoto 2008; Fonseca and McGarrigle 2014) and immigrants, due to their flexibility and ability to adapt to new and more precarious situations, were essential to feed the intermittent cycles of economic growth of the nineties and 2000s. Reis et al. (2010) explain that

[8]Besides its extensive character, the model was also dual in the sense that a small and geographically concentred nucleus of activities of the industrial and tertiary sectors and also of the knowledge branch, with higher productivity and highly-skilled jobs, was consolidated (Mota et al. 2004).

for the Portuguese economy, immigration changed the ratios measuring the availability of active labour force *vis-a-vis* the resident population because immigration is associated with employment search and therefore, to mobility of active-age people between countries.

Considering that labour is a variable of adjustment in face of the economic cycle,[9] in contexts of economic crisis like the one Portugal is experiencing, when confronted with lack of jobs, national and foreign workers leave and look for better opportunities in other places. Moreover, potential migrants in the home country receive negative feedback from relatives and friends living in Portugal who advise them to opt for a more prosperous country (Fonseca et al. 2014). Therefore, not only have the outflows increased but there has also been a simultaneous reduction of the inflows.

Despite the challenges in measuring emigration, Malheiros (2011) points to a figure close to 70,000 exits per year in the second half of the 2000–10 decade whereas a recent report from the Observatory of Emigration (Pires et al. 2014) mentions 95,000 Portuguese emigrants between 2010 and 2012, a remarkable increase closely linked to the worsening of the situation in Portugal due to the growing sovereign debt.[10] Compared to previous periods of emigration, three features are quite new: (a) the framework of mobility has changed and a significant proportion of emigration occurs in the free-circulation area of the EU; (b) a substantial part of this emigration is done on a temporary basis, meaning it is not permanent; (c) the relative weight of skilled or highly educated emigrants in the total outflows is higher (Malheiros 2011; Pires et al. 2014).

Concerning the inflows, since 2008 there has been a continuous decrease in the first residence permits issued to foreign citizens. From the peak of close to 73,000 in 2008, the Immigration and Borders Service states in the annual report slightly more than 33,000 permits issued in 2013 (SEF 2009, 2014). The stock is also dwindling since 2009 when slightly more than 454,000 documented foreigners, representing 4.3% of the resident population, were registered by the same office (SEF 2014).[11] In 2013, the 401,320 documented foreign citizens accounted for 3.8% of the residents in the country. The evolution of the first permits issued and also of the stock shows a diminishing attractiveness of Portugal as a hosting nation, which in demographic terms means descending inflows of childbearing-aged people. This, combined with

---

[9]Reis et al. (2010) clarify that the Portuguese economy is highly dependent on huge volumes of labour due to the lack of positive articulation of labour with other strategic dimensions of production like improvement of skills and higher investment in R&D.

[10]Between 2010 and 2014, the Portuguese economy was bailed-out with the intervention of a troika, an entity composed by experts from the European Commission, the European Central Bank and the International Monetary Fund.

[11]The growing number of requests of for Portuguese citizenship since the publication of the Organic Law no. 2/2006 (17th April), also known as the Nationality Law, may partly justify the shrinking stock of foreigners in the country. In 2006, 4447 grants of Portuguese citizenship were given whereas in 2012 the figure totalled 21,819 (Eurostat).

a soaring number of outflows, mostly in the similar age-bracket, will aggravate the country's population ageing and loss.

Considering the relevance of international migration in the country's demographic dynamics and also in the Portuguese regions, observed in the most recent decades as well as the strong association between the evolution of economic growth and migratory flows from and to Portugal, we will try to anticipate the regional evolution trends (at the NUTS 3 level) of the population and demographic ageing in the next section. The calculations will present results until the mid-twenty-first century for mainland Portugal based on different scenarios of economic evolution and migratory flows.

12.4 Population Projections to 2050

Despite the limitations, and ultimately, the uncertainty inherent to forecasting, population projections using different scenarios of natural demographic change, economic growth and migration flows can show diverse pictures of the expected evolution of a country's population. No matter how enticing it is, seeing into the future is not really possible, however, "... the momentum of demographic processes links the future with the past in clear and measurable ways" (Smith et al. 2001, p. 2), and computing one's knowledge of the past and expectations for the future in terms of births, deaths, inflows and outflows into a mathematical model, can give us reasonably accurate predictions.

Using a model specifically built for this paper (MIGLF), the evolution of the population residing in mainland Portugal was forecasted using a cohort-component model with restrictions on some of the demographic and economic features that enabled us to assess the impact of the change of some variables on all the others. The model considers 16 age groups in 5-year brackets (from [0–4] ... [70–74] and >= 75) divided by gender, totalling 32 demographic cohorts. The population projections are calculated and presented for the NUTS 1 level (1 territorial unit), NUTS 2 level (5 territorial units), and NUTS 3 level for continental Portugal (28 territorial units),[12] and for the 2011–2051 period with 5-year intervals. Inputting different rates at the demographic and economic levels, it was possible to produce a set of four scenarios. They all run with the fertility and mortality rates specific to each age group for the 2001–2011 decade, which allows us to calculate the effects of the changes in the other variables.

[12]Besides the mainland, Portugal comprises two archipelagos enjoying the status of Autonomic Regions—Madeira (261,313 inhabitants in 2013) and Azores (247,440 inhabitants in 2013).

12.4.1 Scenarios of Population Projection

Scenario A considers the average fertility and mortality rates specific to each age group of the 2001–2011 decade and does not take into account any migration flows. These fertility and mortality rates correspond to crude rates that are lower than the observed ones due to the decrease of the relative weight of the more fertile age cohorts. This scenario will be used as a baseline for the possibilities of demographic evolution of the other scenarios.

Scenario B combines the same fertility and mortality rates of scenario A with the average migration rates observed in the 2001–2011 period. The assumption is that this scenario represents the evolution trend of migration.

Scenario F corresponds to the evolution trend of the active population. It brings together scenario A (baseline) with the variation of the working-age people that was observed between 2001 and 2011. It represents a scenario in which the economic growth, although moderate, would be expected if the figures for the 2001–2011 would have been kept in the future.

Scenario G combines the specific fertility and mortality rates of the 2001–2011 period with the change in the proportion of the working-age population induced by the "economic crisis", in a differentiated way: (i) for the 2011–2021 time span, the model considers the proportion of the working-age population of the 2006–2011 period, when the financial and economic crisis began and was acutely felt in Portugal; (ii) after 2021, a moderate recovery is admitted, considering similarly as in scenario F, the variation of the working-age people that was observed between 2001 and 2011.

12.5 Results

The results show that according to three out of the four scenarios described above (A—without migration; B—with the migration levels of the 2001–2011 period and G—which takes into account the effects of the crisis) there will be a strong trend of reduction of the resident population in mainland Portugal (Fig. 12.5). The situation is more acute for scenarios A and G with the population decreasing from 10 million people in 2011 to a figure close to 7.8 million people in 2051. The difference rests in the speed of this reduction, which is higher in scenario G, especially at the beginning of the period being studied.

More precisely, it is possible to observe that according to scenario A, the Portuguese population has a 21.8% decrease in the 40-year time span between 2011 and 2051. According to scenario B, a loss of population is also expected, but smaller than in the previous one: the population will dwindle from 10.05 million in 2011 to 8.64 million in 2051 (Fig. 12.5).

Scenario F is the only one forecasting a demographic growth until 2046 followed by a decrease in the decade 2040–51. When compared with scenario B, the results

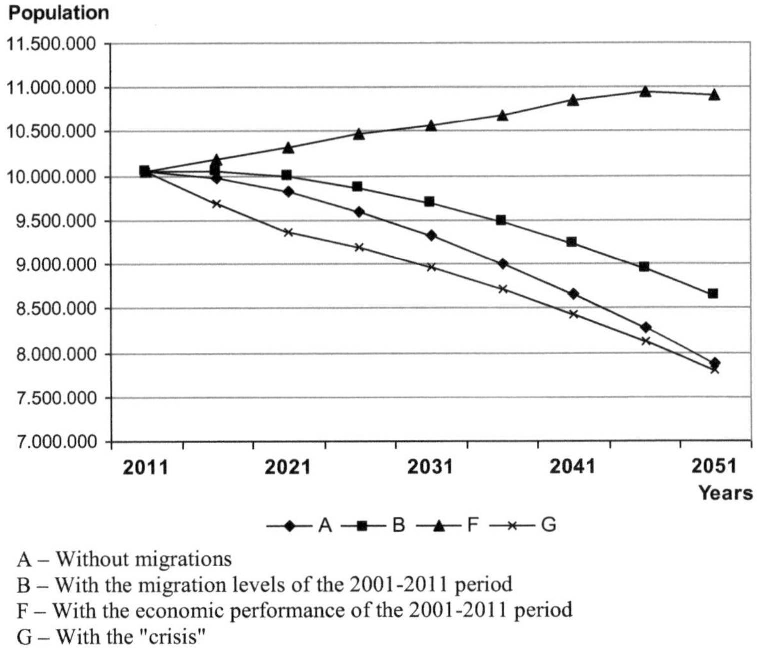

Fig. 12.5 Evolution of the total population in mainland Portugal according to the four scenarios of the MIGLF model, 2011–2051. A—Without migrations; B—With the migration levels of the 2001–2011 period; F—With the economic performance of the 2001–2011 period; G—With the "crisis"

of this scenario indicate the number of migrant workers that Portugal would need to keep a production system close to stagnation (considering that it admits a working-age population growth similar to the one observed between 2001 e 2011).

In scenario G, the effects of the present "crisis" in the evolution of the Portuguese population were identified. The results of this scenario show a strong trend for the reduction of the working age population and the increase in the percentage of people aged 65 or older (Fig. 12.5). Comparing this scenario with scenario F it is possible to have an idea of the demographic impacts of the crisis, namely on international migration flows (immigration and emigration).

As one can see in Fig. 12.6, all scenarios put into evidence the strong ageing trends of the Portuguese population and, consequently, the difficult conditions of sustainability of the national social security system.

Although these results are not comparable with the population projections for the 2012–2060 period published by Statistics Portugal (INE 2014), because they are based on slightly different assumptions, it is worth mentioning that Statistics Portugal's projections also indicate a trend towards the reduction of the resident population. In addition, like the MIGLF projection models, they equally show the expected changes in the population's age structure pointing to a continuous and strong demographic ageing in Portugal (INE 2014).

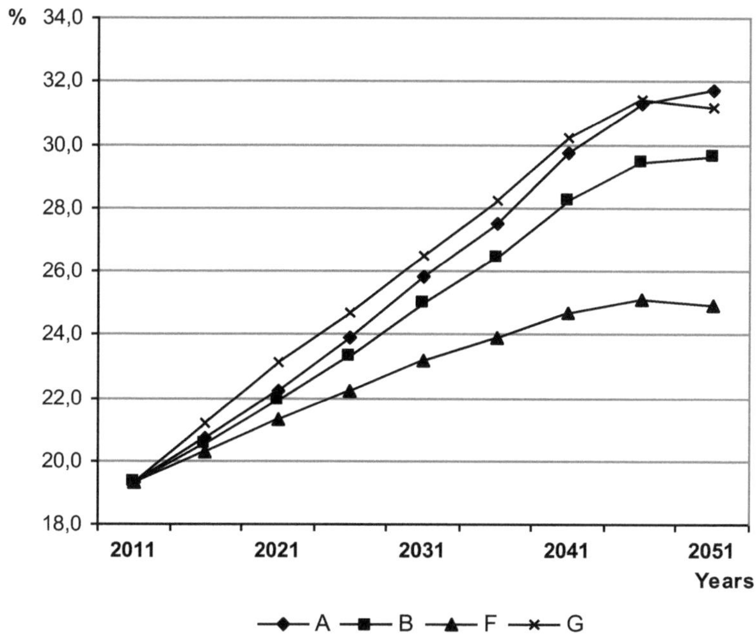

Fig. 12.6 Evolution of the proportion of ageing people (>=65 years) according to the four scenarios of the MIGLF model, 2011–2051. A—Without migrations; B—With the migration levels of the 2001–2011 period; F—With the economic performance of the 2001–2011 period; G—With the "crisis"

With 19.3% ageing population in 2011, and in case there are no migrations (scenario A), the proportion of ageing people (aged 65 or older) in 2051 will reach 31.7%. Even considering the migration levels of the 2001–2011 decade (scenario B), the proportion of ageing residents will be quite high (29.6%). Moreover, the effect of the crisis on the economy (scenario G) will produce very similar effects in the levels of ageing population comparatively to the scenario without migrations (31.2% of the population will be aged 65 or older). The "crisis", causing a significant reduction in immigration and a resuming of emigration will represent, in 2051, a 6.3% difference in the proportion of ageing people, relative to scenario F.

The challenges associated with a growing proportion of ageing people in European societies, namely the sustainability of the social security system, can also be seen in the population support ratio (PSR), that is, the ratio of working-age (15–64 years) to retirement-age persons (65 or older)—Fig. 12.7. In 2001, the PSR was 4.10 and it had already dropped to 3.42 ten years later. In 2051, even considering the most favourable scenario (scenario F), which is very unlikely to

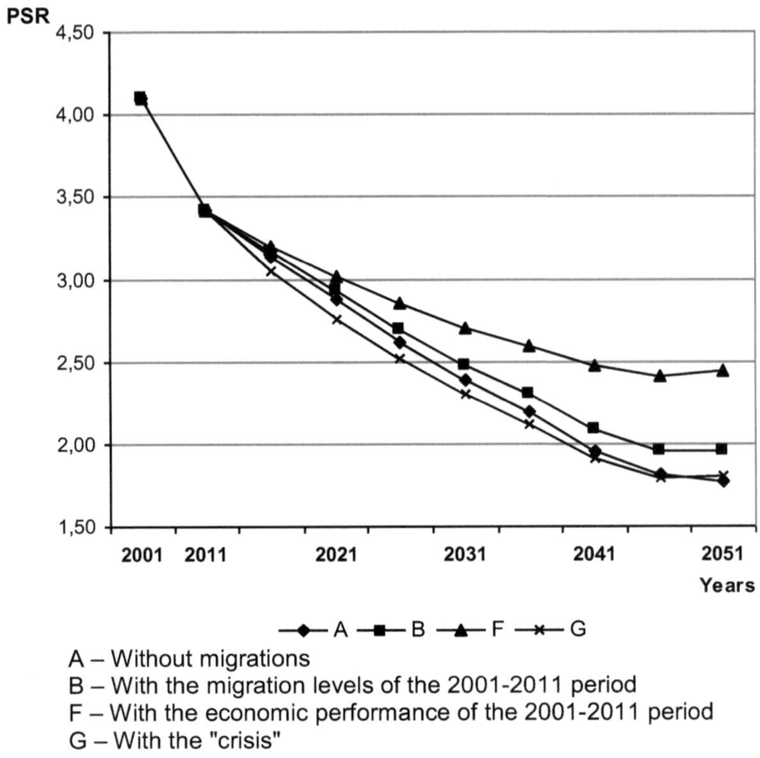

Fig. 12.7 Evolution of the PSR according to the four scenarios of the MIGLF model, 2011–2051. A—Without migrations; B—With the migration levels of the 2001–2011 period; F—With the economic performance of the 2001–2011 period; G—With the "crisis"

occur; there will be 2.44 working-age individuals for each retirement-age person. According to scenario G, the most likely to take place, the PSR will be only 1.8.

Across the scenarios, the least critical period in terms of the rate of change of the PSR is 2041–2051, during the course of which the decrease slows down a bit.

It is also important to have a look at the proportion of young people forecasted in the four scenarios of the MIGLF model because they are a remarkably relevant part of the population issue and influence the ageing process at the base of the age pyramid (Fig. 12.8).

The number of youth (population aged <=14) will decrease considerably, especially in scenarios A, B and G but the concomitant variation of the share of the total population makes this loss relatively less important. A trend towards stagnation at the end of the studied period of time is observable, mostly from 2030 onwards. In scenarios F and G, a certain trend of growth in the proportion of young people in the total resident population is expected (Fig. 12.9).

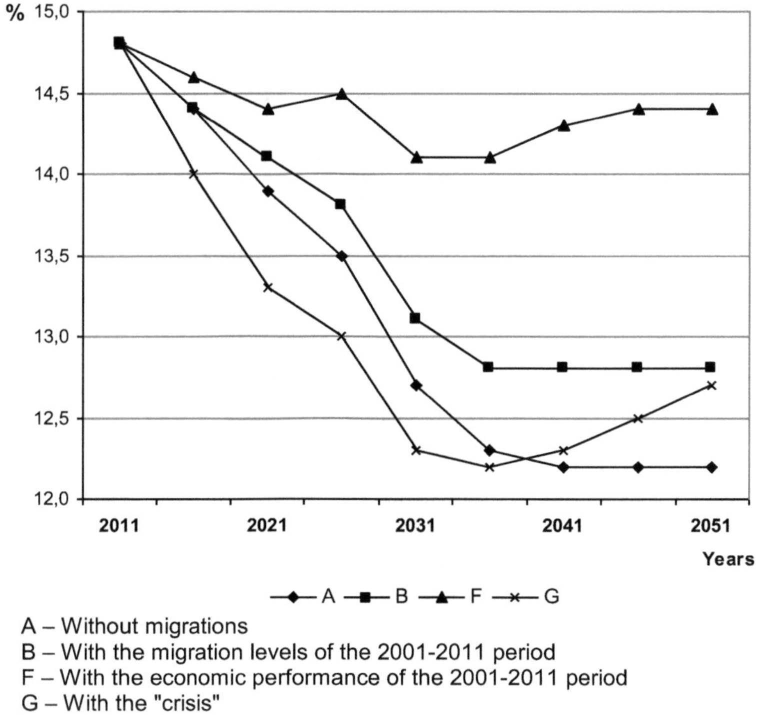

Fig. 12.8 Evolution of the proportion of young people (aged <=14 years) according to the four scenarios of the MIGLF model, 2011–2051. A—Without migrations; B—With the migration levels of the 2001–2011 period; F—With the economic performance of the 2001–2011 period; G—With the "crisis"

12.6 Regionalization of the Scenarios at the NUTS 3 Level

Figures for the country level often hide interesting regional disparities due to distinct local and regional structures of the population, often associated with different levels of fertility, mortality and migrations. In scenario A (without migrations) the rate of change of the total population for mainland Portugal is −21.7% but there is a profound regional differentiation at the NUTS 3 level ranging from Tâmega with −12.6% to Pinhal Interior Sul with −45.1% (Fig. 12.9). All the territorial units located in the interior present higher negative variations compared with those located along the coast, which show a huge population loss if dependent exclusively on the natural balance.

Presuming that the migratory volume of the 2001–2011 decade will be maintained during the 2011–2051 period, the results of scenario B show a negative population change, although quite smaller (−14.0%) than in scenario A. The regional contrasts are much more acute, ranging from a remarkable growth in the

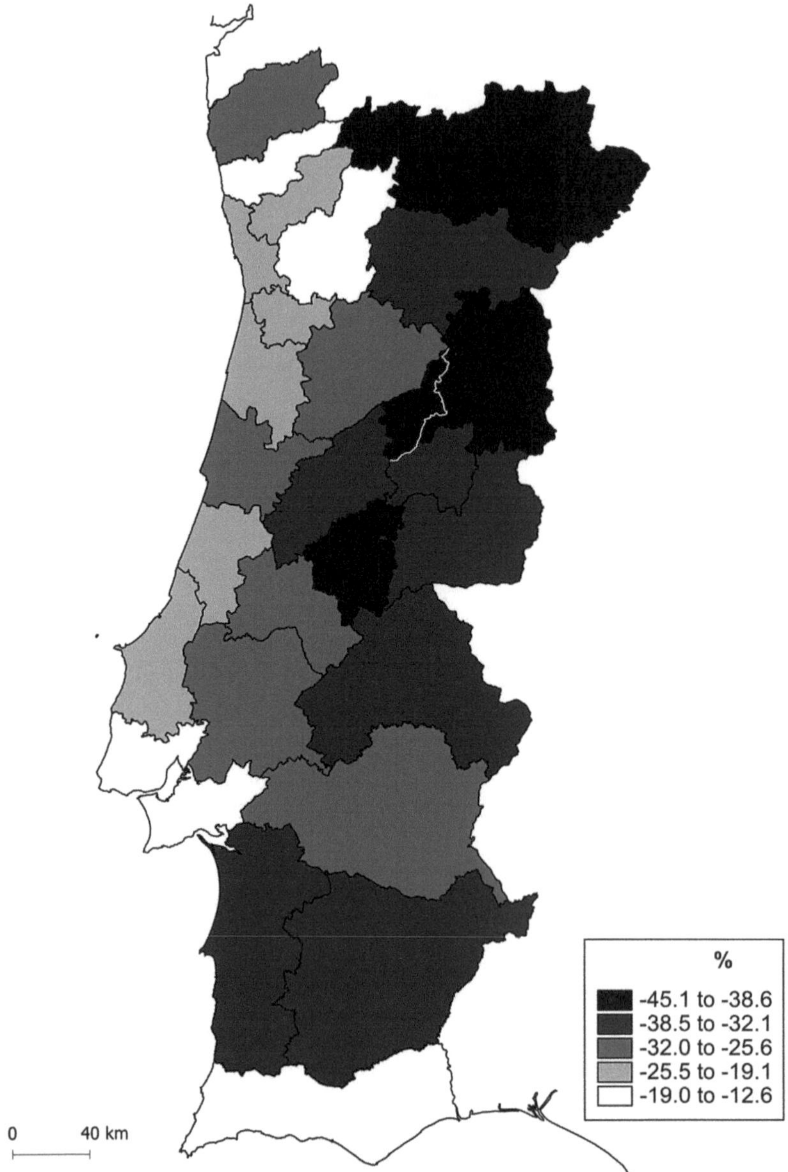

Fig. 12.9 Regional variation of the population, 2011–2051 (%): scenario A

Algarve (57.8%) to a severe decline in Serra da Estrela (−57.5%). Thus, migrations have an impact on the increase of regional contrasts (Fig. 12.10).

In scenario F (with the economic performance of the 2001–2011 period), Portugal will see its population increasing 8.6% and the variations of the population

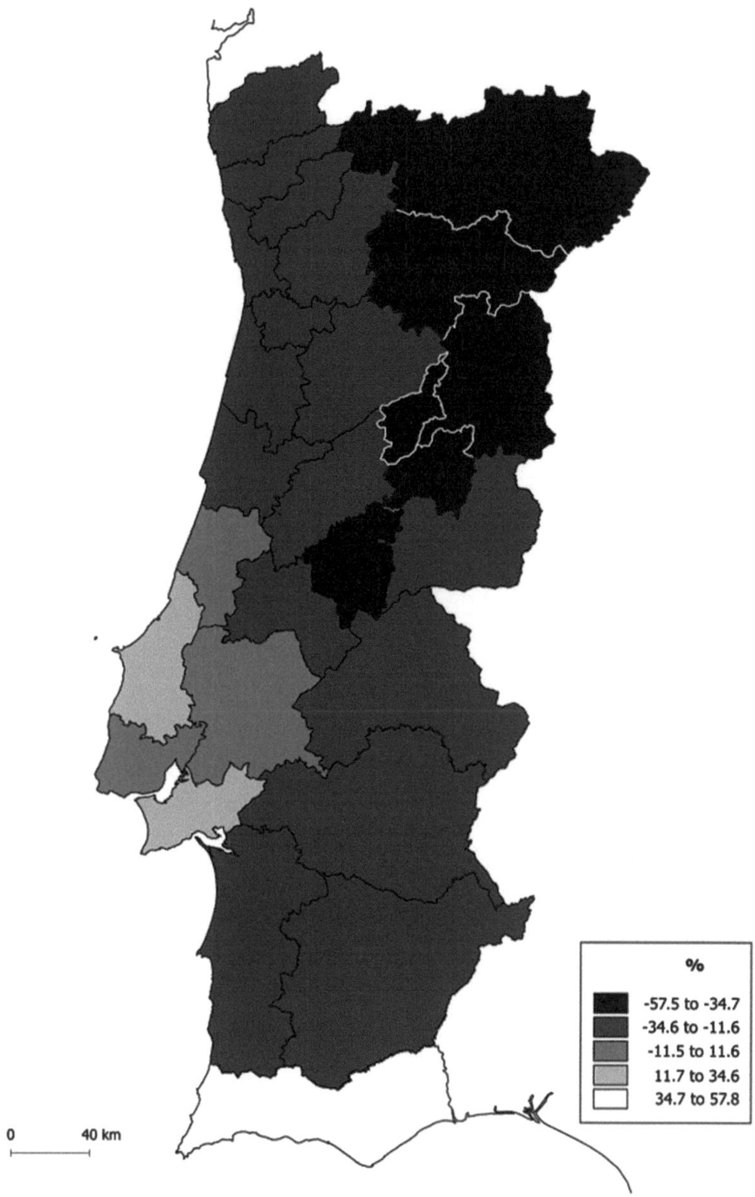

Fig. 12.10 Regional variation of the population, 2011–2051 (%): scenario B

between 2011 and 2051 show a smaller amplitude comparatively to the previous two scenarios (Fig. 12.11). The main losses are still in the interior regions of the country. The Metropolitan Area of Lisbon, the Algarve and the NW region (Porto,

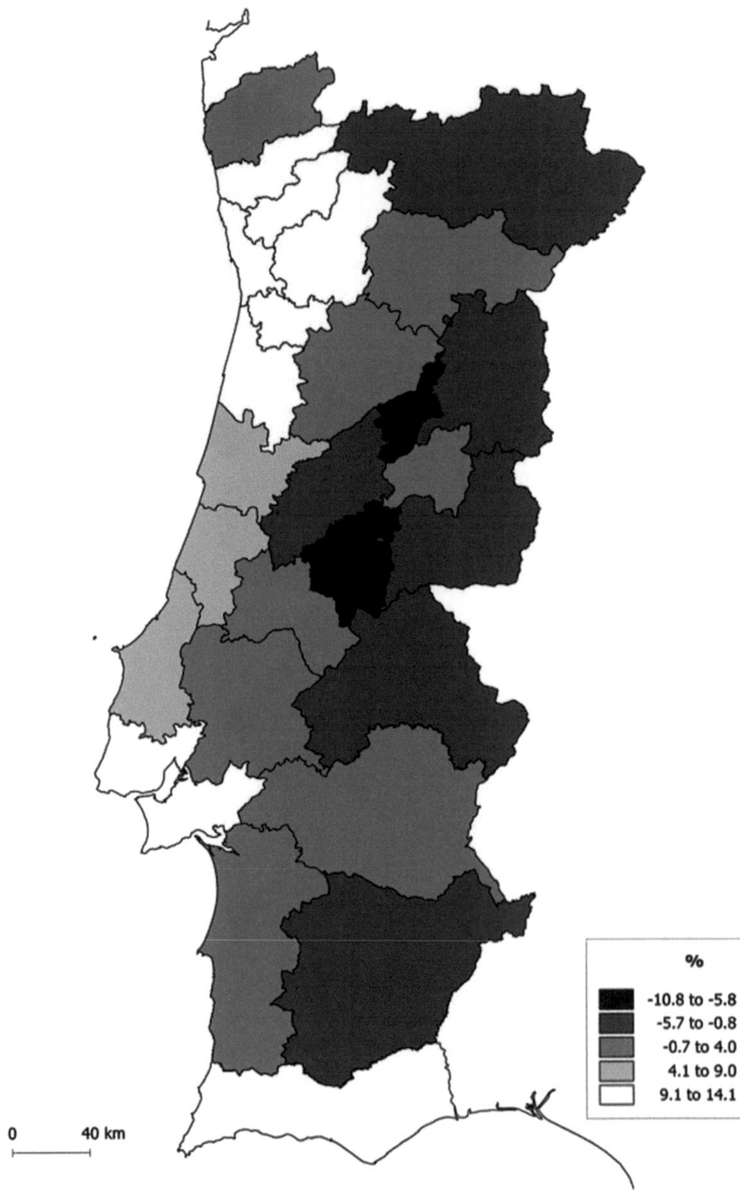

Fig. 12.11 Regional variation of the population, 2011–2051 (%): scenario F

Tâmega, Cávado, Ave and Entre Douro e Vouga) show population gains ranging from 9.1% to 14.1%.

According to scenario G, Portugal will see its population shrink by 22.3%. The regional population losses are the highest of the four scenarios for the 2011–2051

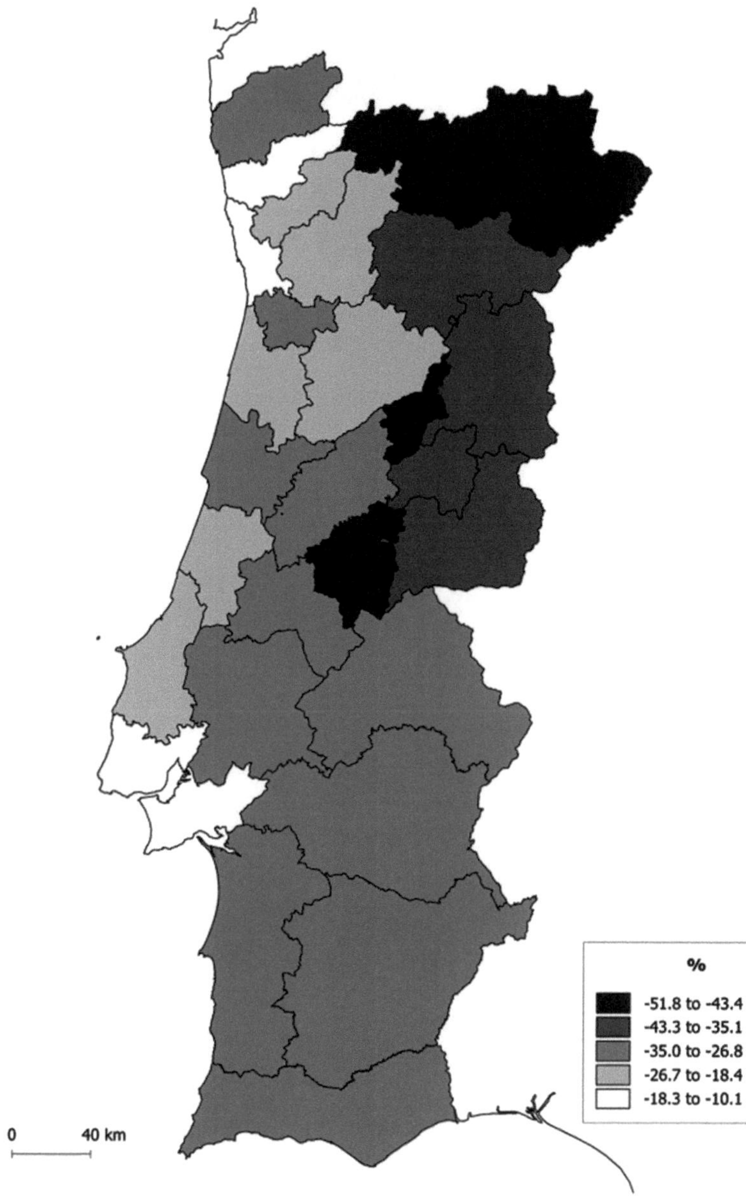

Fig. 12.12 Regional variation of the population, 2011–2051 (%): scenario G

period and all the 28 NUTS 3 have negative variations, ranging from 51.8% in Serra da Estrela to −10.1% in Cávado (Fig. 12.12).

Concerning the population aged 65 or older, its regional pattern of change ranges from a 2.7% increase in Pinhal Interior Sul, mostly due to the high proportion of

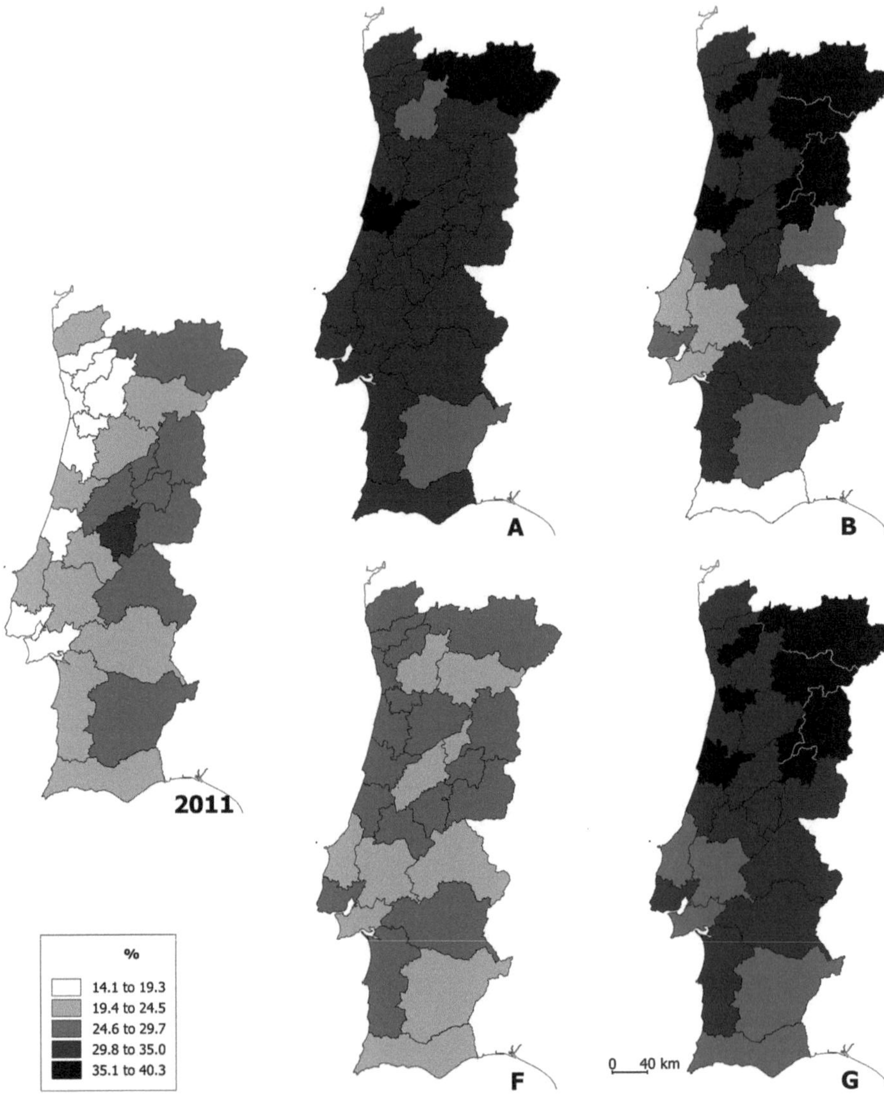

Fig. 12.13 Ageing population (aged 65 or more) in 2011, and according to the four scenarios of the MIGLF model in 2051 (%)

ageing people in 2011, to 121.4% in Cávado, more than the double of ageing citizens in 2011)—Fig. 12.13.

Comparing the figures for 2011 with the projections obtained in scenario G, the one including the effects of the structural crisis affecting the Portuguese economy today, it is possible to see that the relative weight aged 65 or older will grow from 19.3% in 2011 to 31.2% in 2051, meaning a 61.8% increase. From the regional point of view, the consequences are quite diverse in the set of NUTS 3 of mainland

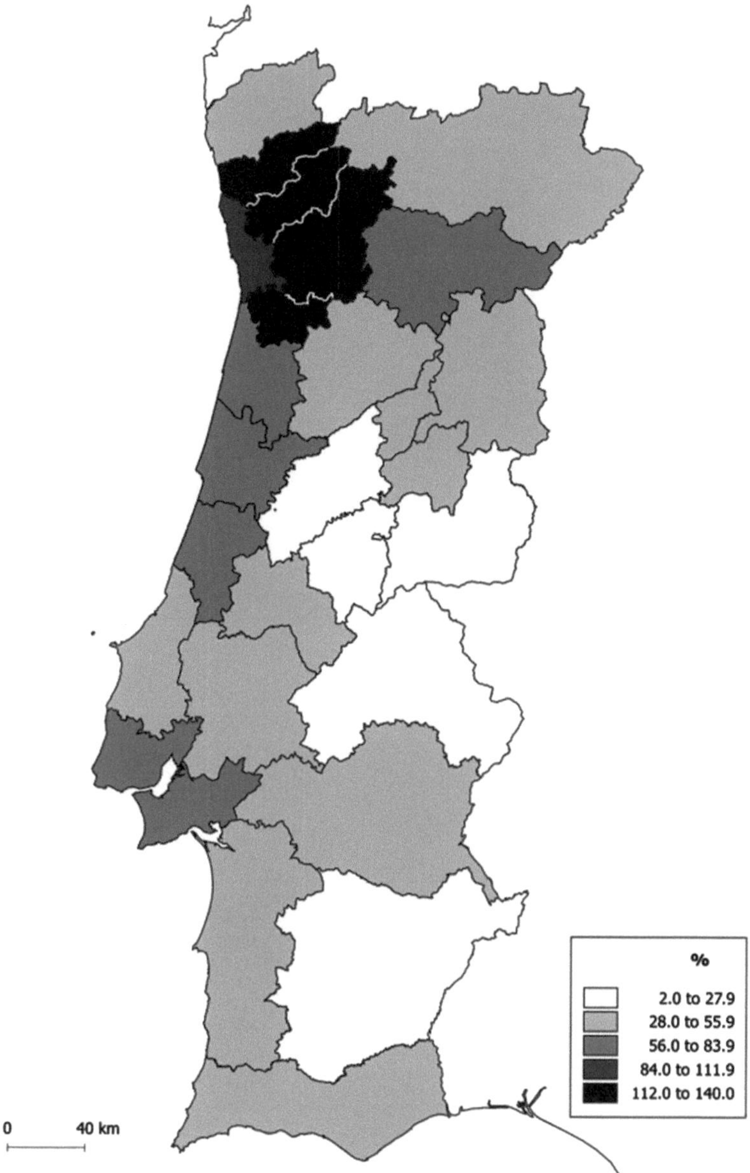

Fig. 12.14 Variation in the proportion of ageing people (aged 65 or more), 2011–2051—scenario G

Portugal, ranging from proportions higher than 100% in Ave (140.0%), Tâmega (135.0%), Entre Douro e Vouga (130.0%), Cávado (120.0%) and Grande Porto (100%), to almost stagnation with a very moderate growth in Pinhal Interior Sul

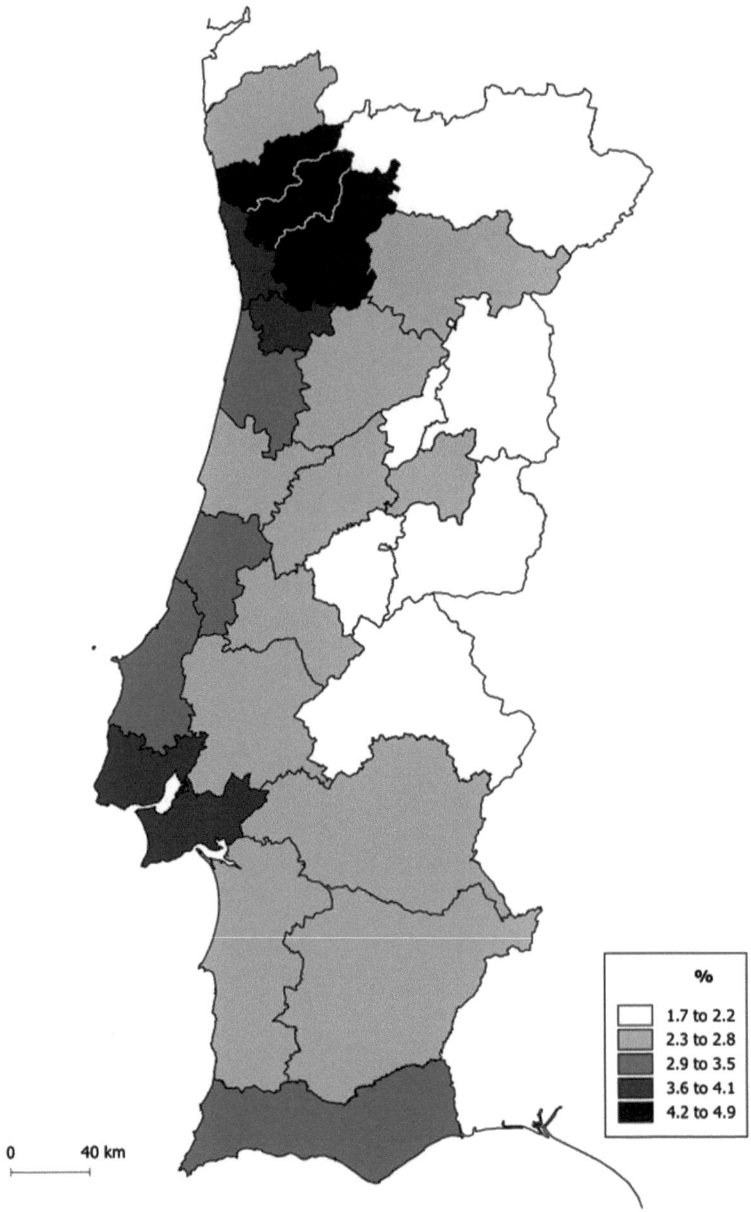

Fig. 12.15 Population support ratio in 2011, NUTS 3 (%)

(2.0%), and only 15.0% in Baixo Alentejo, and 18.0% in Alto Alentejo and in Beira Interior Sul (Figs. 12.13 and 12.14).

Both the remarkable growth and the fall can be explained: in the first case, these regions have a considerably young population today, whereas the NUTS 2 already has a very elderly population, whose majority will pass away before 2051. The typical evolution process of these interior regions has the following stages: first, there is a process of population ageing, which is followed by ageing with depopulation, and lastly a major population loss after the normal life period of the many ageing residents.

The population support ratio, an important indicator of economic sustainability, shows that in 2011 there were already strong regional differences among the NUTS 3 of mainland Portugal (Fig. 12.15).

Considering the higher probability of scenario G occurring, it is interesting to see the expected variation between 2011 and 2051 according to that scenario, although the analysis at the NUTS 3 level is less interesting because in Portugal the social security systems have a national, and not a regional, basis. Thus, for a global reduction of 47.4% of the PSR in mainland Portugal, the most notable changes will take place in the NUTS 3 of Ave and Entre Douro e Vouga (a reduction of 67.1% and 66.3%, respectively), whereas the smallest variations will occur in Pinhal Interior Sul (only −2.5%), in Baixo Alentejo and Alto Alentejo (−17.9 and 19.9%, respectively)—Fig. 12.16.

Concerning the younger generations, the map for 2011 shows major regional differences in mainland Portugal with regions like Tâmega and Cávado, in the Northwest part of the country, with the highest proportions of youth (17.2% and 16.4%, respectively), but also the Algarve, Grande Lisboa, Península de Setúbal and its neighbouring regions of Lezíria do Tejo, Oeste and Pinhal Litoral with proportions of people aged 14 or younger in the total population between 14.5% and 15.8% (Fig. 12.17). These NUTS 3 are in contrast with the interior of the country where proportions do not rise above 12% (e.g., Pinhal Interior Sul, Serra da Estrela, Beira Interior Norte, Beira Interior Sul). The differences are seen in the 2011–2051 variation for scenario G but with a clear north-south divide where the northern regions will have greater losses of young people and some southern regions like the Algarve will gain young residents (Fig. 12.18).

The issue of ageing of the Portuguese population is felt both at the top and at the base of the age pyramid and according to scenario G—the most likely to occur—the proportion of young people will decrease from 14.8% in 2011 to 12.7% in 2051. Conversely, the relative weight of ageing citizens will increase from 19.3% in 2011 to 31.2% in 2051 which will certainly be a challenge for the sustainability of the social security system (Fig. 12.19).

Due to this major issue of the Portuguese economy, governments, both from centre-right-wing and centre-left-wing parties have implemented changes in the rules of access to social benefits and retirement pensions establishing more restrictive pathways for beneficiaries and longer working lives for the active population (Mendes 2005; Leiria and Pereira 2000).

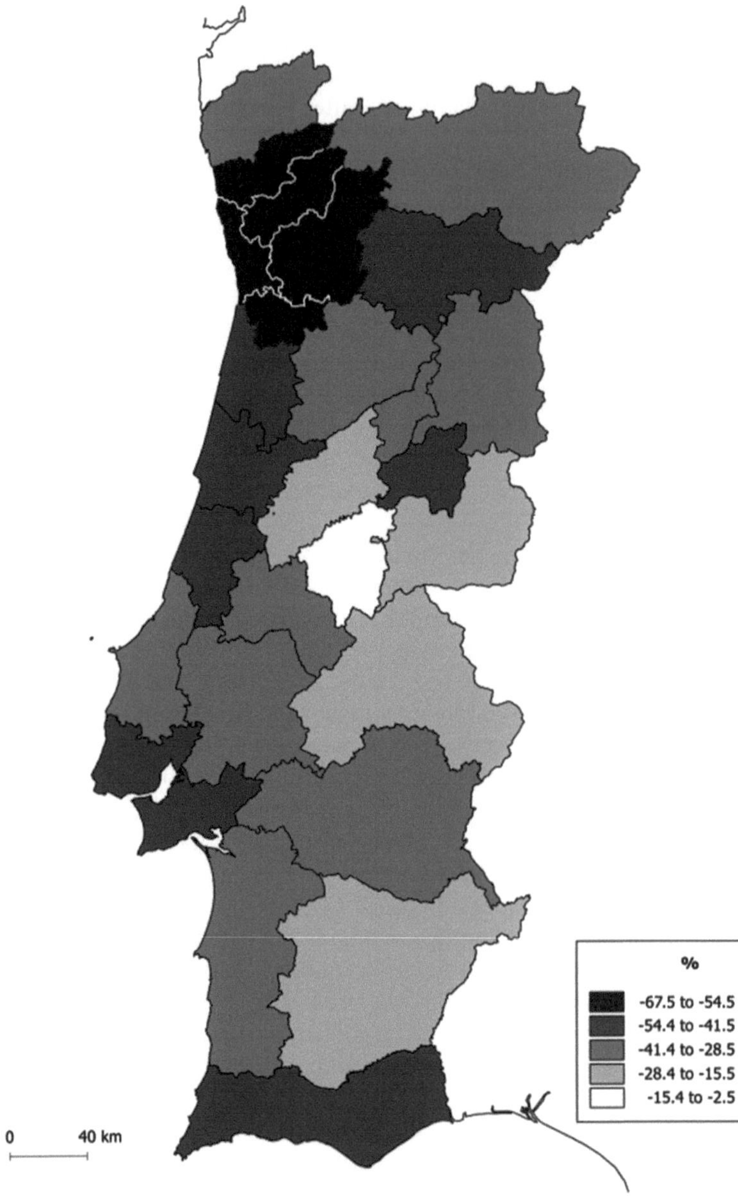

Fig. 12.16 Variation in the PSR 2011-2051 (%)—scenario G

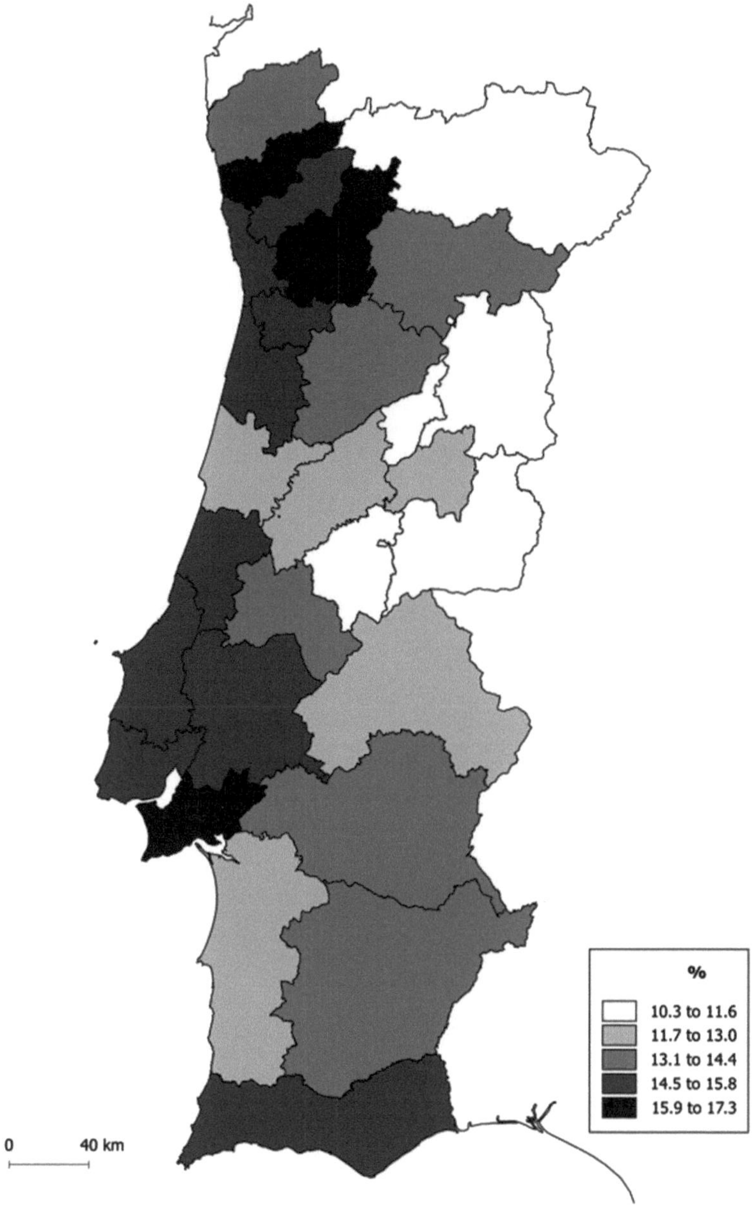

Fig. 12.17 Young people (aged <=14 years) in 2011, NUTS 3 (%)

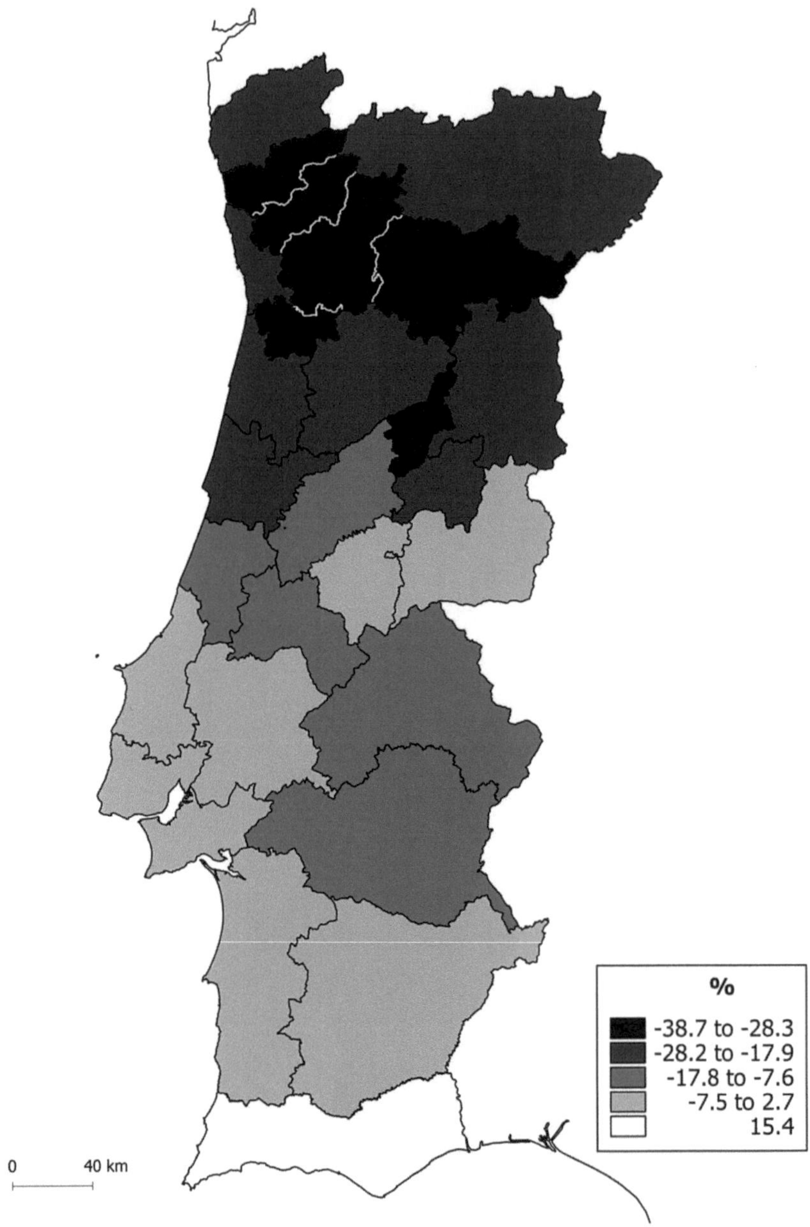

Fig. 12.18 Variation in the proportion of young people (aged <=14 years) between 2011 and 2051 for scenario G, NUTS 3

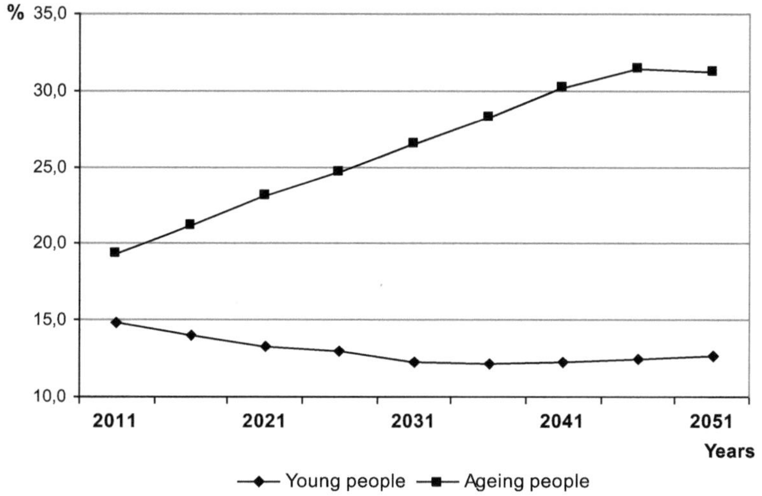

Fig. 12.19 Evolution of young and ageing people according to scenario G of the MIGLF model, 2011–2051 (%)

12.7 Concluding Remarks

The ageing of the Portuguese population is a long-term trend that has become more evident in recent years. Considering the small demographic change associated with natural growth, and even the negative net balance of the more recent years, the role of international migration is paramount in defining the evolution of the population residing in the country. This is not new but has acquired a major relevance in recent years.

Moreover, Portugal is a country with an uneven population distribution across its territory, with a major concentration in the coastal area between the NUTS 3 of Minho-Lima and Península de Setúbal and also in the NUTS 3 of Algarve. In fact, as previously mentioned, the disparities across regions are very striking and not all of them will have the same capacity for growth and attracting population.

This asymmetric distribution of the population goes side by side with profound regional disparities concerning income and wealth (Lewis and Williams 1986). According to the work of Duarte and Simões (2010), the economic inequality among Portuguese regions, assessed by the earnings of the employees working full time and using the Gini coefficient, has widened between 1995 and 2007. These asymmetries have not decreased, and in 2011, Portugal was the country with the 6th highest Gini coefficient among the 34 OECD countries (0.353), well above the OECD20 average (0.316) or the OECD34 average (0.314) (OECD 2011).

The NUTS 3 of Grande Lisbon, Grande Porto and Algarve have pulled national growth from the top and will probably continue to do so, concentrating economic activities and younger residents. Conversely, a large group of regions, mostly rural and in the interior, have less potential for development. Already struggling against rural exodus and an ageing population, their lack of human capital and economic activities will not attract younger residents in the future. Moreover, the closure of public services, like courts of law, hospitals, post offices, schools and tax offices, due to very low population thresholds reinforces territorial marginalization. Therefore, the population loss and ageing in the interior regions of the mainland still continues and is expected to become more serious in the future.

According to the most likely scenario of population projections for 2051, there will be a population loss together with a remarkable ageing, especially in the interior regions. The population support ratio (PSR) will reach extremely low figures (1.8) placing a huge pressure on the social security system. The relative weight of the ageing population will be particularly felt in the interior regions, of a more rural character, where it is expected to reach between 35% and 40% of the total population.

However, Portugal will only be able to attract foreign citizens, or Portuguese residing abroad, if its economy becomes more dynamic, creating jobs or favourable conditions for entrepreneurial migrants. Considering the present crisis of the sovereign debt and the small growth of the European economy, to which Portugal is hugely dependent on, this seems very unlikely to happen in the near future. According to scenario G of the model MIGLF, the most likely scenario to occur, the population living in Portugal will decrease until 2040 and there will be a sharp ageing.

Therefore, population ageing is unavoidable and cannot be compensated for by any population policy, immigration policy, or family policy. Immigration is essential to maintain the absolute numbers of active population. However, the performance of the Portuguese economy in the future will be the main drive of net migration and, consequently, of main demographic trends.

Appendix

See Fig. 12.20.

Fig. 12.20 NUTS 3 in mainland Portugal

References

Abreu D (2012) A geographic perspective on demographic evolution in Europe: the CEG participation in the ESPON 1.1.4 Project. In: Stimson R, Haynes KE (eds) Studies in applied geography and spatial analysis. *Addressing real world issues*. Cheltenham, Edward Elgar, pp 17–33

Abreu A, Peixoto J (2009) Demografia, mercado de trabalho e imigração de substituição: tendências, políticas e prospectiva no caso português. Análise Social XLIV(193):719–746. http://www.scielo.gpeari.mctes.pt/pdf/aso/n193/n193a04.pdf

Arroteia J (2011) A emigração portuguesa: breve retrospetiva. Cadernos Vianenses 45:37–47

Azevedo J (coord.) et al. (2014) Por um Portugal amigo das crianças, das famílias e da natalidade (2015–2035): remover os obstáculos à natalidade desejada. Lisboa, IFSC – Instituto Francisco Sá Carneiro. http://www.psd.pt/ficheiros/dossiers_politicos/dossier1405440683.pdf

Baganha MI, Ferrão J, Malheiros J (1999) Immigrants in the labour market: the Portuguese case. In: Metropolis International Workshop – Proceedings. Lisbon, Luso-American Development Foundation, pp 89–120

Baganha MI (1994) As correntes emigratórias portuguesas no século XX e o seu impacto na economia nacional. Análise Social XXIX(128): 959–980. http://analisesocial.ics.ul.pt/documentos/1223378081S4cET4df4Yh89IX7.pdf

Bijak J, Kupiszewska D, Kupiszewski M, Saczuk K (2013) Population ageing, population decline and replacement migration in Europe. In: Kupiszewski M (ed) International migration and the future of populations and labour force resources in Europe. Dordrecht, Springer, pp 243–265

Carvalho LX (2007) Os limites da formalidade e o trabalho imigrante em Portugal. Cadernos OI, Lisboa: ACIDI. http://www.oi.acidi.gov.pt/docs/CadernosOI/Caderno_1.pdf

Duarte A, Simões M (2010) Regional growth in Portugal: assessing the contribution of earnings and education inequality. Grupo de Estudos Monetários e Financeiros, no. 11. Coimbra, Faculdade de Economia da universidade de Coimbra. http://gemf.fe.uc.pt/workingpapers/pdf/2010/gemf_2010-11.pdf

EC (2009) Dealing with the impact of an ageing population in the EU (2009 Ageing Report). Commission Communication, COM (2009) 180/4, Brussels, 29.4.2009. file:///C:/Documents%20and%20Settings/Administrador/Os%20meus%20documentos/Downloads/Communication%20-%20Dealing%20with%20the%20impact%20of%20an%20ageing%20population_en.pdf

EC (2006) The demographic future of Europe – from challenge to opportunity. Commission Communication, COM (2006) 571 final, Brussels, 12.10.2006. http://eur-lex.europa.eu/LexUriServ/site/en/com/2006/com2006_0571en01.pdf

Fonseca ML, McGarrigle J (2014) Immigration and Policy: New Challenges after the Economic Crisis in Portugal. In: Levine E, Verea M (eds) Impacts of the Recent Economic Crisis (2008–2009) on International Migration. Universidad Nacional Autónoma de Mexico, Mexico City, pp 51–75

Fonseca ML (2005) The changing face of Portugal: immigration and ethnic pluralism. Canadian Diversity/Diversité Canadienne, 4.1, Winter 2005: 57–62

Fonseca ML, Caldeira MJ, Esteves A (2003) New forms of migration into the European South: challenges for citizenship and governance. The Portuguese case. Int J Popul Geogr 8 (2):135–152

Fonseca ML, Pereira S, Esteves A (2014) Migration of Ukrainian nationals to Portugal: changing flows and the critical role of social networks. Cent East Eur Migr Rev 3(1): 115–130. http://www.ceemr.uw.edu.pl/sites/default/files/CEEMR_Vol_3_No_1_Fonseca_Pereira_Esteves_Migration_of_Ukrainian_Nationals_to_Portugal.pdf

Fonseca ML, Esteves A, Malheiros J, McGarrigle J (2013) Habitação, imigração e integração sócio-territorial: notas e reflexões a partir do caso da Região do Algarve. In: Fonseca ML, Góis P, Marques JC, Peixoto J (orgs) Migrações na Europa e em Portugal. Ensaios de homenagem a Maria Ioannis Baganha. Edições Almedina, Coimbra, pp. 123–158

Fonseca ML, Malheiros J (2003) «Nouvelle» immigration, marché du travail et compétitivité des regions portugaises. Géographie, Économie, Société 5:161–181

Fonseca ML, Malheiros J, Esteves A, Caldeira MJ (2002) Immigrants in Lisbon. Routes of integration. EPRU, n° 56. Centro de Estudos Geográficos, Lisboa
Giannakouris K (2010) Regional population projections EUROPOP2008: most EU regions face older population profile in 2030, 1/2010. Eurostat, Publications Office of the European Union, Luxembourg. http://epp.eurostat.ec.europa.eu/cache/ITY_OFFPUB/KS-SF-10-001/EN/KS-SF-10-001-EN.PDF
Góis P, Marques JC (2007) Estudo prospectivo sobre imigrantes qualificados em Portugal. Colecção OI, 24. Lisboa, Observatório da Imigração, Alto Comissariado para a Imigração e Diálogo Intercultural (ACIDI). http://www.oi.acidi.gov.pt/docs/Estudos%20OI/Estudo_OI_24.pdf
INE (2014) Projeções de população residente 2012–2060, Destaque, 28 de Março de 2014. Instituto Nacional de Estatística, Lisboa. http://www.ine.pt/xportal/xmain?xpid=INE&xpgid=ine_destaques&DESTAQUESdest_boui=208819970&DESTAQUESmodo=2
INE/FFMS (2014) Fertility survey: final results. INE, Lisboa. http://www.ffms.pt/upload/docs/fertily-survey-2013_summary_english-version_RBh_n-8H7k-aSRPg9sUKsA.pdf
INE (2012) Censos 2011. Resultados definitivos – Portugal. INE, Lisboa
Lanzieri G (2011) Fewer, older and multicultural? Projections of the EU populations by foreign/national background. Eurostat, Publications Office of the European Union, Luxembourg. http://epp.eurostat.ec.europa.eu/cache/ITY_OFFPUB/KS-RA-11-019/EN/KS-RA-11-019-EN.PDF
Leiria P, Pereira PT (2000) Princípios de reforma do sistema de segurança social. In: Pereira PT (org) A reforma da segurança social. Contributos para reflexão. Celta Editora, Oeiras, pp 101–133
Lewis J, Williams A (1986) The economic impact of return migration in Central Portugal. In: King R (ed) Return migration and regional economic problems. Abingdon, Routledge, pp 100–128
Lutz W, Scherbov S (s/d) Can immigration compensate for Europe's low fertility?, European Demographic Research Papers. Vienna, Vienna Institute of Demography of the Austrian Academy of Sciences. http://www.oeaw.ac.at/vid/download/edrp_no1.pdf
Magalhães MG, Peixoto J (2008) O impacto de diferentes cenários migratórios no envelhecimento demográfico em Portugal, 2009–2060. Revista de Estudos Demográficos 2: 95–115. http://www.ine.pt/xportal/xmain?xpid=INE&xpgid=ine_estudos&ESTUDOSest_boui=56433784&ESTUDOSmodo=2
Malheiros J, Esteves A (coords) (2013) Diagnóstico da situação da população imigrante em Portugal: características, problemas e potencialidades, Colecção Portugal Imigrante. Lisboa, Alto Comissariado para a Imigração e Diálogo Intercultural (ACIDI). http://www.oi.acidi.gov.pt/docs/Col%20Portugal%20Imigrante/EstudoNacional_Web.pdf
Malheiros J (2011) Portugal 2010: o regresso do país de emigração? Notas e reflexões. Janus – anuário de relações exteriores 2(1): 133–142. http://janusonline.pt/popups2011_2012/2011_2012_3_3_9.pdf
Marques JC (2009) «E continuam a partir»: as migrações portuguesas contemporâneas. *Ler História* – especial Emigração/Imigração (56), 9–26. http://www.ces.uc.pt/cesfct/jcm/LH-JCMarques_Empre.pdf
Mendes FR (2005) Conspiração grisalha. Segurança social, competitividade e gerações. Oeiras, Celta Editora
Mota IA, Pinto M, Vasconcellos e Sá J, Soromenho Marques V, Félix Ribeiro J (2004) Estratégia Nacional para o Desenvolvimento Sustentável (ENDS) 2005–2015. Ministério das Cidades, Ordenamento do Território e Ambiente, Lisboa. https://infoeuropa.eurocid.pt/files/database/000015001-000020000/000019537.pdf
Muysken J (2008) Immigration can alleviate the ageing problem. EIPASCOPE 2008/3: 15–18. http://aei.pitt.edu/11030/1/20090203155203_SCOPE2008-3_2_JoanMuyken.pdf
OECD (2011) Divided we stand: why inequality keeps rising. OECD, Paris
Peixoto J (2012) A emigração portuguesa hoje: o que sabemos e o que não sabemos. SOCIUS Working Papers (5). ISEG, Universidade Técnica de Lisboa, Lisboa. http://www.repository.utl.pt/bitstream/10400.5/4892/1/WP_5_2012socius.pdf
Peixoto J (2008) Imigração e mercado de trabalho em Portugal: investigação e tendências recentes. Revista Migrações 2: 19–46. http://www.oi.acidi.gov.pt/docs/Revista_2/migracoes2_art1.pdf

Peixoto J (2004) País de emigração ou país de imigração? Mudanças e continuidade no regime migratório em Portugal. Socius Working Papers, n°2/2004. ISEG, Universidade Técnica de Lisboa, Lisboa. https://www.repository.utl.pt/bitstream/10400.5/2028/1/wp200402.pdf
Peixoto J (1993) A emigração portuguesa a partir de 1980: factos estatísticos e modalidades de evolução. Estudos Demográficos 31:35–74
Pires R Pena, Pereira C, Azevedo J, Ribeiro AC (2014) Emigração portuguesa. Relatório estatístico 2014. Lisboa, Observatório da Emigração and Rede Migra, Instituto Universitário de Lisboa (ISCTE-IUL), CIES-IUL, and DGACCP. http://www.observatorioemigracao.secomunidades.pt/np4/?newsId=3924&fileName=OEm_EmigracaoPortuguesa2014_RelatorioEst.pdf
Pires RP, Machado FL, Peixoto J, Vaz MJ (2010) Portugal. Atlas das Migrações Internacionais. Tinta da China e Fundação Calouste Gulbenkian, Lisboa
Reis J, Santos Pereira T, Tolda J, Serra N (2010) Imigrantes em Portugal. Economia, pessoas, qualificações e territórios. Coimbra, Almedina e Centro de Estudos Sociais da Universidade de Coimbra
Santos IS (2013) L'émigration au Portugal, avatar d'un pays "semi-périphérique", métropole postcoloniale. Hommes & Migrations (1302), 157–161. http://hommesmigrations.revues.org/2510?lang=en
SEF (2014) Relatório de imigração, fronteiras e asilo 2013. Serviço de Estrangeiros e Fronteiras, Oeiras. http://sefstat.sef.pt/Docs/Rifa_2013.pdf
SEF (2009) Relatório de imigração, fronteiras e asilo 2008. Serviço de Estrangeiros e Fronteiras, Oeiras. http://sefstat.sef.pt/Docs/Rifa_2008.pdf
Smith S, Tayman J, Swanson D (2001) State and local population projections: methodology and analysis. Springer, New York
Valente Rosa MJ, Seabra H, Santos T (2004) Contributos dos "imigrantes" na demografia portuguesa: o papel das populações de nacionalidade estrangeira. Colecção OI, 4. Observatório da Imigração, Alto Comissariado para a Imigração e Minorias Étnicas (ACIME), Lisboa. http://www.oi.acidi.gov.pt/docs/Estudos_OI/Estudos%20OI%204.pdf

Maria Lucinda Fonseca is Full Professor of Human Geography and Migration Studies and the Dean of the Institute of Geography and Spatial Planning, Universidade de Lisboa, Portugal, and Director of the PhD Programme on Migration studies and Coordinator of the research unit MIGRARE. She has worked extensively in the areas of migration studies and social and urban geography. She was the principal investigator for the project GEITONIES—Generating interethnic tolerance and neighbourhood integration in European urban spaces (funded by EU FP7) and the coordinator of the Portuguese team of the projects THEMIS—Theorising the Evolution of the European Migration Systems and Mobile Welfare—European Welfare Systems in Times of Mobility (both funded by NORFACE).

Diogo de Abreu is a Full Professor in the Institute of Geography and Spatial Planning, Universidade de Lisboa, Portugal, and former Scientific Director of the Centre for Geographical Studies of the same university. Professor Abreu conducts research in demographic modelling, population forecasting, economic geography, transportation and urban and regional development. He was a team member of the FP7-funded project SECOA—Solutions for Environmental Contrasts in Coastal Areas.

Alina Esteves is Assistant Professor of Human Geography at IGOT, Universidade de Lisboa, Portugal, and a researcher at the unit MIGRARE—Migration, Spaces and Societies at the Centre for Geographical Studies. She has worked in the areas of migration studies and social and urban geography. She coordinated the project CRISIMI (2014–2015) on the impact of the economic crisis on the living conditions and labour market incorporation of immigrants in Portugal (funded by the High Commission for Migrations) and was part of the Portuguese teams of the projects GEITONIES (funded by EU FP7), THEMIS and Mobile Welfare (both funded by NORFACE).

Chapter 13
Involving Universities in Regional Upgrading in the Periphery: Lessons from Northern Europe

Paul Benneworth and Rómulo Pinheiro

JEL Classification I23 • I25 • I28 • L38 • 010 • 030 • 043 • R11

13.1 Introduction

This volume is intimately concerned with understanding regional upgrading processes in southern Europe. Regional policy has latterly placed increasing emphasis on stimulating regional coalitions of innovations to engage in entrepreneurial discovery processes and developing what are called 'smart specialisation strategies' (McCann and Ortega Argiles 2013). This approach builds on a much longer tradition of supporting regional upgrading by encouraging regional partnerships to develop technology plans (Morgan 1992) and later, innovation strategies (Morgan and Nauwelaers 2002). Universities have become central to the arguments that are made about regional upgrading, as critical elements of regional innovation systems, generating knowledge within international networks that local actors are able to exploit, generating exports, raising productivity and competitiveness and ultimately social welfare (Cooke 2005).

P. Benneworth (✉)
School of Management and Governance, Center for Higher Education Policy Studies (CHEPS), University of Twente, P.O. Box 217, 7500, Enschede, The Netherlands

Agderforskning, Gimlemoen 19, 4630 Kristiansand S, Norway
e-mail: p.benneworth@utwente.nl

R. Pinheiro
Department of Political Science and Management, Faculty of Social Sciences, University of Agder, Post Box 422, 4604 Kristiansand, Norway

Agderforskning, Gimlemoen 19, 4630 Kristiansand S, Norway
e-mail: romulo.m.pinheiro@uia.no

M. Fonseca, U. Fratesi (eds.), *Regional Upgrading in Southern Europe*, Advances in Spatial Science, DOI 10.1007/978-3-319-49818-8_13

A huge amount of research has explored the ways in which universities work with their regions to help create these unique competitive advantages. This can be both directly in economic terms (*cf.* Hermannsson et al. 2013) but also indirectly, by contributing to social, environmental, and cultural development (Charles and Benneworth 2001; OECD 2007), social justice (Benneworth 2013) and regional governance (Gunasekara 2006). Their staff and their associated activities can help fill structural gaps in regional innovation systems, build social capital and unleash innovative potential (Hansson et al. 2004; Kallio et al. 2010). Universities can play leadership roles in these coalitions that develop regional innovation strategies (Sotarauta et al. 2012), and provide for a stewardship of place through their civic engagement building knowledge cities (Goddard and Vallance 2013). There has likewise been a flourishing of stories told about the vitality of universities to regional economic development, along with a set of recipes for what regions ought to do to engage with their regions based on a regional higher education partnership mapping the regional system and cleverly designing appropriate interventions (Goddard 2011).

In this chapter, we are concerned with understanding what universities can offer to regional development in the southern periphery, where the environments for regional engagement may be quite different from the contexts within which these more generalistic policy lessons are developed. Certainly, we are mindful here of the need to avoid making simplistic prescriptions and recipes for delivering regional upgrading that in reality involve inevitably fruitless attempts to mimic and chase after past successes (*cf.* Hospers 2006). However, we nevertheless argue that one area where southern universities and regions can learn from their 'northern neighbours' is in the internal university processes that are common across institutions and not dependent upon or inhibited by particularly munificent or sparse environments for regional innovation encouraging university behaviour.

The common conundrum for universities with which we are here concerned is the issue of 'situated learning', where universities attempt to develop courses relevant to and supportive of regional development trajectories. University knowledge is validated based on its generalisability and transferability. Developing and teaching context-specific, unique knowledge always raises a question of whether this is 'higher' education, or merely vocational training. This echoes a kind of *Bildung/Ausbildung* or Blue Skies vs Applied tension that recurs whenever universities engage with society. We argue that a common pressure on universities in the southern as well as northern periphery is to be globally excellent and pursue internal visibility. They may therefore regard regional engagement as being detrimental to this mission, and it is this tension—a tension facing universities as much on the southern as the northern periphery—with which this chapter is fundamentally concerned. In this chapter, we therefore pose the question of what lessons can southern Europe learn regarding improving university-regional engagement activity by better aligning universities' institutional interests with those of their host territories.

13.2 The Regional Conundrum: Tying Universities to Their Regions

To better understand how universities can contribute to regional development and work with regional actors across the public and private sectors, we argue that it is necessary to understand what universities are for and about the ways they are organised internally in/around their core activities of teaching and research. There is an overly simplistic elision between the observation that universities can under some circumstances work with regions in ways that are beneficial, and the normative statement that universities should work to contribute to regional upgrading. As Stefan Collini (2012) noted, if the key to being a successful societal institution was doing what funders immediately demanded, then technical colleges would be the model to which liberal arts universities aspired, and not vice versa. Universities as institutional forms have evolved over almost a millennium precisely because they have found ways to reinvent their societal usefulness whilst allowing them to retain a degree of resistance to such outside pressures (Bender 1988).

A key dimension of their resilience as institutions comes from the fact that they are highly flexible and adaptive (Karlsen and Pritchard 2013). This resilience and adaptive capacity derives, to a large degree, from the fact that they are formed from an overlapping kaleidoscope of different communities. These communities (e.g. staff in a department, students on a particular year of a course) all share the common characteristic of being interested in knowledge production and circulation, but each community will have their own interests and trajectories. The institution of university is formed from the aggregate of these communities that are held together in a way that may be regarded as being "loosely coupled" (Reponen 1999). Their core staff, academics, have evolved into distinctive disciplinary 'tribes' with their own approaches to creating, evaluating, judging, circulating and rejecting knowledge (Becher and Trowler 2001). Attempts to impose top-down, 'strategic' forms of management in the new public management vein (*cf.* Kickert 1995) have had to confront new problems in creating empowering environments for academics. A particular problem for top-down management are the deep-seated problems in developing fair metrics of university regional engagement that are capable of providing more than cursory insights into individual institutional performance improvement (van Vught and Westerheijden 2010; Charles and Wilson 2012).

There is huge variability in how seriously universities take the idea of a regional mission, not just between different kinds of institution (polytechnic versus university, technical vs broad, rural vs urban, pure vs applied disciplines), but also related to their specific history, culture and organisational structure. And, there is also a clear risk of portraying the university of loosely coupled communities as a single coherent institution where strategic-decision making is enough to encourage these diverse communities and tribes to follow a common direction of travel. What is common to those universities that take regional engagement seriously is that this (third) mission tends to fit with the interests, goals and desires of the various communities and 'tribes' within the university (*cf.* Pinheiro 2012b).

In this chapter, we therefore argue that understanding how universities can contribute to regional upgrading requires grasping how universities—and their various communities and tribes—can benefit from regional upgrading. For the university as a para-institution (i.e. the organisation is less significant as an institution than the sub-institutions, the communities of which it is composed), these effects come in terms of developing a more regional-engagement friendly set of formal structures as well as developing informal norms, practices, networks and institutions that support and facilitate regional engagement. For the region, this involves creating activities where there are more shared agendas, collaboration, clustering and evolution with regional partners, and the absence of strategic disagreement, competition, fragmentation and lock-in within other regional actors.

But at the same time, it is important to stress that universities do not have a single set of interests, logics or norms arising from their loosely coupled nature (Olsen 2007). Although the formal institution may have a single strategic vision, mission and goals, that can be at odds with a plurality of purposes and identities of different kinds of scholars and professionals derived from their 'tribes'. There are a set of material dependencies that universities face, as all universities are dependent on sponsors for survival, but at the same time need to ensure that sponsor financial dependency does not lead to a loss of their independence of inquiry upon which ultimately all their social benefits are created. Universities likewise need in some areas to take cohesive and united action, for example around estates development, to hold these tribes together, while at the same time ensuring that this does not stifle the individual autonomy upon which their creativity and utility is built. Universities as institutions may have a long set of histories and traditions upon which they are founded, but the fact that everyone in the university is engaged in progress means that managing institutional self-renewal becomes a critical task.

At the same time, in recognising the complexity of universities as institutions, it is important to acknowledge Lagendijk and Oinas's (2005) argument that regional economies are themselves complex, and co-ordinating activity between actors is a difficult process riven with tensions. Pinheiro et al. (2015) also point to four tensions within regions that affect universities' capacity to regionally engage. Firstly, regions are host to many actors with competing demands and interests—even municipalities may not all have a common 'regional' interest but seek preferential outcomes for their locality. Under such circumstances, engagement with some groups by a university may alienate and generate resistance from others.

Secondly, although the literature puts an emphasis on trust and social capital, innovation processes are commercially-laden processes where competition and secrecy can be critical, and firms may seek to limit the knowledge-overspill benefits that the region gets from them (Christopherson and Clark 2007). University efforts to profit from their knowledge often involve its privatisation and codification, which may reduce opportunities for regional collaboration and inhibit regional overspill effects.

Thirdly, firms may be more influenced by what is happening in their wider technological innovation system than in the local environment, particularly for emerging technologies (Bergek et al. 2008) and, as a result, construct multi-local valorisation systems where activities in other regions are more determining. It makes more sense for universities with particular technological specialities to engage with the key actors in that specific technological innovation system (outside the region) than trying to engage with regional actors lacking those underlying expertises are lacking.

Finally, and particularly important in the context of regional upgrading, are the tensions around breaking path-dependencies, which are associated with strong local networks that lock a region into old behaviours, and therefore resist upgrading (Hassink 2005). There can be a range of potential pathways to regional upgrading that involve universities stimulating these locked-in regional networks to identify and pursue new trajectories, but these can challenge the existence of some of the companies, and reduce the willingness of partners to co-operate around new technological areas.

Of course, the widespread fact that universities do work with regions in upgrading activities indicates that these barriers are not insurmountable. Our contribution in this chapter comes in identifying these processual steps that universities can take—whether in the north or south of Europe—to address these pressures that arise when engaging with regional partners. As these problems are less specific to regional context and more to the particular institutional form of universities, we argue they are more transferrable across national and regional contexts. Therefore, as a first step to develop some meaningful lessons for Southern Europe, we now develop a conceptual framework for understanding how universities—as complex actors—negotiate these tensions, and create formal structures and informal cultures that allow them to meaningfully contribute to and benefit from regional engagement activities.

13.3 The Logic of Universities' Regional Engagement & Upgrading Activities

Benneworth (2013) has argued that university engagement missions are at their most stable when they progress from being based on a sense of corporate responsibility, what he calls 'munificent beneficence', to being embedded in universities' core structures, routines and values. There is a dialectic element to this: universities have a series of tangible activities that have interdependencies with external communities, and the need to interact productively with external stakeholders influences the intangible norms and routines of universities' internal communities. Those intangible university elements, in turn, represent a form of social capital that contributes to the success of the regional element, also because they are not easily captured or appropriated by others. Earlier studies have identified three main types of communities with which universities typically engage; those that are geographically proximate to them ('regional communities'), ethically proximate to them (institutions with a religious background working with charities) or with a similar kind of mission (technology universities working with businesses) (Benneworth and Osborne 2014; CERI 1982). The interplay between these internal, intangible institutions and external, tangible activities, can act to transform the university into becoming an engaged institution (*cf.* Goddard and Vallance 2013 for how this happens with regional communities).

That being said, engagement is not a simple process that can be achieved simply by creating a regional higher education partnership or a strategic management interface within the university. Engagement happens when communities within the university develop connections with external communities, and these connections ultimately create a mutual interdependence between university and regional interests at a strategic level. The art of strategic management in this case is in creating synergies and a supportive environment for these various communities. But, at the same time, tensions can arise because what these different communities do not have is a shared corporate sense of interest; their shared interests are emergent and related to individual knowledge exchanges around core processes of teaching and research, involving the creation, circulation, fusion, progression and withdrawal of knowledge. By looking at these underlying processes, critical insights into how these mutual interdependencies can be built (and managed) is greatly assisted. As argued above, lessons to be learned are not context dependent, but applicable wherever there are universities who feel themselves caught between regional relevance and global excellence (Perry 2012).

We, therefore, look at the dynamics of these boundary spanning communities involving both universities and regional actors in knowledge processes. Above it was described that, in successful cases of engagement, university staff come together with external partners, work jointly on issues of common interest and develop shared norms (and sometimes a shared identity, e.g. in the form of a 'regional coalition'), and, ultimately, align their long-term strategic interests, creating social capital. The processes by which this takes place can be considered to be social and situated learning processes, and understood through frameworks such as communities or networks of practices (*cf.* Benner 2003; Amin and Roberts 2008). These social learning processes involve a group of core actors coming together into a social 'learning space' to exchange different kinds of knowledge; which may be a virtual environment (Roberts 2014). Through this activity, engaged actors create situated forms of knowledge within the local group. Through their participation in other knowledge communities, local and global, the 'situated knowledge' that was initially created within a given local context is able to flow through these networks to other partners who can then use it to solve their own (local) problems.

Gertner et al. (2011) provide a good example of this through an analysis of the 'Knowledge Transfer Partnership' (KTP) programme undertaken by Strathclyde University in the UK, a detailed knowledge exchange between university and firms involving individuals employed by the university but placed in the firm. They show how the programme operates through individuals who are 'boundary-spanners' with multi-memberships of university learning communities (Mutch 2003). The core of the learning community is the KTP(-s), and at the periphery stand the university academic and the firm R&D manager, who are at the core of their own communities of practices concerned with academic research and innovation,

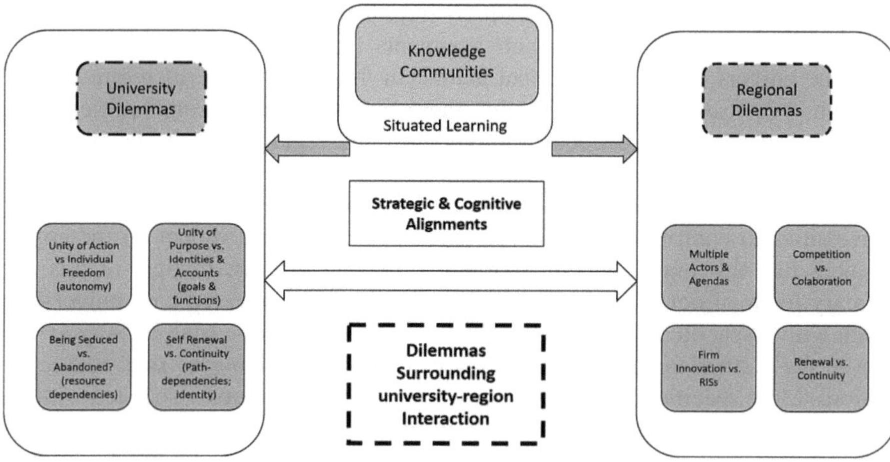

Fig. 13.1 Situated learning communities resolving institutional and regional tensions in university engagement

respectively. Knowledge circulates within these three communities around the pivot of the KTPs, with the effect that academic research and firm innovation are mutually enriched, hence creating a shared strategic interest between university and regional firm.

Notwithstanding, these individual learning communities are exposed to the various tensions outlined above. Academics participating in schemes such as the KTP must balance: commercial interests with academic autonomy; their scholarly needs with the university's commercial interests; consultancy time with teaching and research time; in addition to maintaining their place in university structures. Likewise, firms engaging with universities are situated within their own corporate hierarchies, being active in international innovation networks that may ultimately be more important to their decision-making. They often worry about 'leakage' of ideas to competitors via the university, and try to ensure that they can profit commercially from innovation expenditure. The existence of the scheme shows that these tensions can be overcome at a micro-scale, on a case-wise basis. But the more important issue here is how does this translate up from the micro-level (of individual interaction), to the meso-level (of university and region working together), creating situated knowledge that drives regional upgrading against the backdrop of given these prevailing meso-tensions within universities and regions. This process is depicted in Fig. 13.1.

13.4 Two Stories of Regional Upgrading

Our key concern here is on how these situated learning environments do two things, both anchoring engagement within the university (stimulating university success), but also creating situated knowledge communities that make new kinds of knowledge available for regional partners (regional upgrading). We focus not only on the individual situated learning environments, but also consider how these affect both the university and the regional actors. In this chapter, we therefore explore through two case studies: (i) how these micro-learning communities were institutionalised and embedded in universities and regions; (ii) the tensions they faced, and the barriers they overcame; and (iii) the effect that this ultimately had on regional upgrading. We thereby identify potential barriers regions may face in using universities to contribute to their economic upgrading, and reflect on the consequences that this may have for Southern European regions. In light of this, the primary focus of our analysis lies on the role played by selected case universities (each with a specific institutional profile) in Northern Europe (one in Norway and one in the Netherlands) in supporting the regional upgrading of their respective regions. More specifically, we investigate how academic groups associated with the field of medicine played a critical role in the establishment of 'situated learning communities' that were locally-embedded, yet globally connected to other centres of knowledge and expertise, thus providing a gateway to/from the region to the outside world. In this section, we set out the events that took place, and in Sect. 13.5, we explore these events more critically through the lens of universities as a loose coalition of loosely coupled communities. This enables us, in the concluding section, to draw a set of broad or universal institutional lessons independent of regional contextual specificities thereby having a greater relevance for universities throughout southern Europe.

13.5 Norway

13.5.1 The Regional Context

Northern Norway covers a geographic area of approximately 113 thousand square kilometres, a third of the total, and a combined population of about 460 thousand inhabitants (9.6% of the total). Historically, fishery and farming dominated the life of the region. In the last couple of decades substantial changes have occurred in the three Northern counties (Fig. 13.2). Nordland became a stronghold for industrial activity. Troms experienced the steady rise of a tertiary sector. Tourism and energy exploration have become important income sources for Finnmark. The region is characterised by its vast public sector infrastructure, the largest in the country in per capita figures. The regional economy is dominated by small, often family-owned, businesses of less than ten employees. No large corporations are headquartered in the region, with their presence being limit to local branches or subsidiaries for major domestic and international players across sectors like manufacturing, construction, energy/oil, etc.

One of the biggest economic challenges facing Northern Norway pertains to the structural changes that have occurred within the fishery industry in the last two

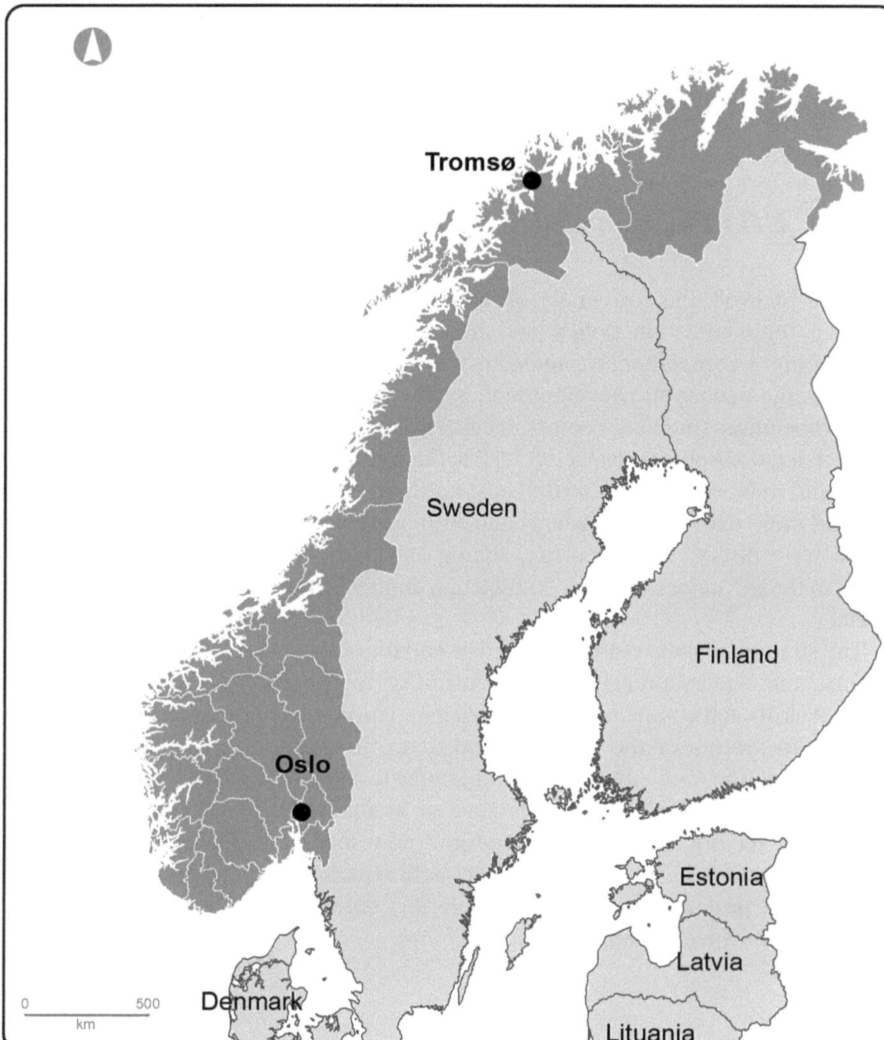

Fig. 13.2 Norway's NUTs3 regions

decades. Deregulation and the rise of a global fishery sector dominated by large scale, highly efficient fleet operators have had a catastrophic effect on both the size and competitiveness of small, local businesses. The recent global financial crisis has resulted in over-pricing and the lack of demand for local products. There is a gradual move from low skilled industries based on abundant natural resources like fish towards highly profitable knowledge-based sectors such as marine bio-prospecting. As far as regional development policy is concerned, the most significant event in recent years pertains to an ambitious government-led initiative (since 2006) targeting the region; the so-called "strategy for the High North", an area encompassing the Artic and Barents Sea. It involves a total of 14 Ministries and spans across a broad portfolio of strategic areas from foreign policy to knowledge generation and competence building to environment to indigenous people/ culture, etc. (Pinheiro 2012a).

13.5.2 UiT: The Knowledge Hub for the 'High North'

Founded in 1968, the University of Tromsø (UiT) was the result of the interface between regionalization policy and higher education policy. The rationale for establishing a comprehensive university above the Arctic Circle was the need to promote socio-economic development, by providing the region with adequate skills and competences (medical doctors, teachers, lawyers, etc.) as well as knowledge, to enhance local absorptive capacity. UiT is the fourth largest university (out of eight, all public) in Norway. It is also the most northern university in the world. In 2014, it enrolled more than 12,000 students and employed close to 3000 employees, 56% of whom were directly involved in teaching and research activities. UiT's strategy. refers to the the university as a "knowledge engine" (*Kunskapsmotor*) for the High-North.

The strategy makes reference to active collaborations with the public and private sectors, and underscores UiT's responsibility for producing graduates with the relevant skills and competencies for local and national labour markets. An emphasis is given to sectors of the economy linked to the provision of welfare services; health, education, and culture. When it comes to industrial growth and innovation, UiT's strategy highlights the importance of graduates across the *natural sciences* (oil/energy sectors, bio-tech), *technology* (new media, ICT), and *economics*. A special mention is made of UiT's willingness to collaborate with other knowledge-based institutions located in the region as to better address local demands and expectations.

13.5.3 Situated Learning: The Case of Community Medicine

In the light of its original vision of becoming a different—more responsive and innovative—university, medicine academics at UiT decided to embark on a number of innovative practices and structures, some of which have turned out to be rather successful over the years.[1] On the teaching front, these included: student internships

[1]UiT's first appointed rector, Peter F. Hjort, has been characterised as an 'enterprising rector' (Arbo and Eskelinen 2003). Before taking the job, Hjort, a respected professor of medicine from Oslo, demanded a guarantee from the government that it would back a rapid build-up of the university including a fully integrated medical school and a university hospital.

at hospitals located in rural areas, as an integral component of university education; and, joint teaching activities for future medical doctors and nurses. In the research realm, the field of *community medicine* was then identified as an area of potential benefit for both the region and UiT's scientific profile, nationally and internationally. When compared to other parts of the country, Northern Norway possessed a higher incidence of certain type of health-related problems such as cardio-vascular diseases.[2] Starting in the mid-70s, a group of health scholars decided to undertake a series of mostly quantitative studies on the topic, what became known as 'the Trømso study'.[3] The latter aimed at determining the reasons for the high mortality associated with cardiovascular disease and to develop ways of preventing heart attacks and strokes. The study was gradually expanded to include many other diseases—rheumatism, neurological and mental diseases, skin diseases, stomach and bowel-related diseases, cancer and osteoporosis, etc.—and repeated at regular intervals, involving a large proportion of the local population (Table 13.1).

Over the years, the study became an international reference within the field, catapulting the rather small academic milieu of community medicine at UiT to the forefront of scientific developments on a global scale. A particular strength of the Tromsø Study is that it has made it possible to regularly study the development of risk factors for diseases among the same group of individuals during a period of more than three decades. A key success ingredient has been the high levels of participation.

Somewhat remarkably, the studies occurred in the absence of a long-term publicly funded programme, by either the regional or national authorities, with UiT's academics being the ones responsible for initiating the process and securing its long-term financial sustainability. External dynamics did play a key role nonetheless. In the early 80s, professional bodies like the American Public Health Association, the Polar Research Board of the US National Academy of Science, together with a number of other international groups, participated in a series of

Table 13.1 'The Tromso heart' study (1974–2008)

Study year	Study's name	Number of participants	Response rate	Age group
1974	Tromsø 1	6595—men only	74%	20–49
1979–80	Tromsø 2	16,621—men & women	78%	20–54
1986–87	Tromsø 3	21,826—men & women	76%	dez/67
1994–95	Tromsø 4	27,158—men & women	73%	25–97
2001–02	Tromsø 5	8130 men and women	79%	30–89
2007–8	Tromsø 6	12,984 men and women	66%	30–87

Source: UiT

[2]In the mid-1970s, 20% of Norwegian men died of myocardial infarction before the age of 75, while the situation in Northern Norway was even bleaker.

[3]https://en.uit.no/prosjekter/prosjekt?p_document_id=80172

discussions on 'Arctic health research'. Today, the department of community-medicine employs more than 100 staff (37 professors and associate professors), half of whom are attached to externally-funded research projects, including about 40 PhDs. At the time of the inquiry (Spring 2014), the unit, one of seven departments at the faculty of health sciences, was structured around 5 sections or specialities, and hosted a number of high profile research units such as the *Centre for Sami Health Research* and the *National Centre of Rural Medicine*.

13.6 Twente, The Netherlands

13.6.1 The Regional Context[4]

The region of Twente is located on the eastern border of the Netherlands, within the province of Overijssel (Fig. 13.3). Covering a surface area of a little over 1500 km^2, and with around 620,000 residents, the region is comprised of 14 municipalities, with a clear distinction between core urban concentration around the cities of Enschede, Hengelo, and Almelo, and a rural hinterland. Located approximately 100 km to the north of the great rivers, the region is split by the Salland moraine hills. The very sandy and slightly rolling landscapes of Twente originally offered relatively unfertile lands for farming, and the region developed a farming economy from the Sixteenth century onwards with a high degree of interdependence between farmers, and economic diversification within households.

An important element of that diversification was in home weaving, and by the Nineteenth century, the region had developed a specialisation in farm-produced textiles. This was displaced by the rise of the textiles industry in Flanders and Tilburg. But following Belgian independence in 1830, and domestic political unrest in the west, the newly crown King William invested heavily in building up his domestic textiles industry in the remote isolation of Twente. Textiles provided the motor for regional growth until the 1960s when global competition forced regional companies into a steady and eventually terminal decline. Since the 1970s, the Twente region has faced a continual struggle to reindustrialise and build a new knowledge economy. Despite policy-makers' best efforts, Twente continues to underperform the national average in terms of key employment, unemployment and knowledge economy variables.

[4]This section draws extensively on the case study of the Twente region undertaken as part of the ESRC-funded project "Bringing Cambridge to Consett", and draws upon Benneworth and Hospers (2007a, b).

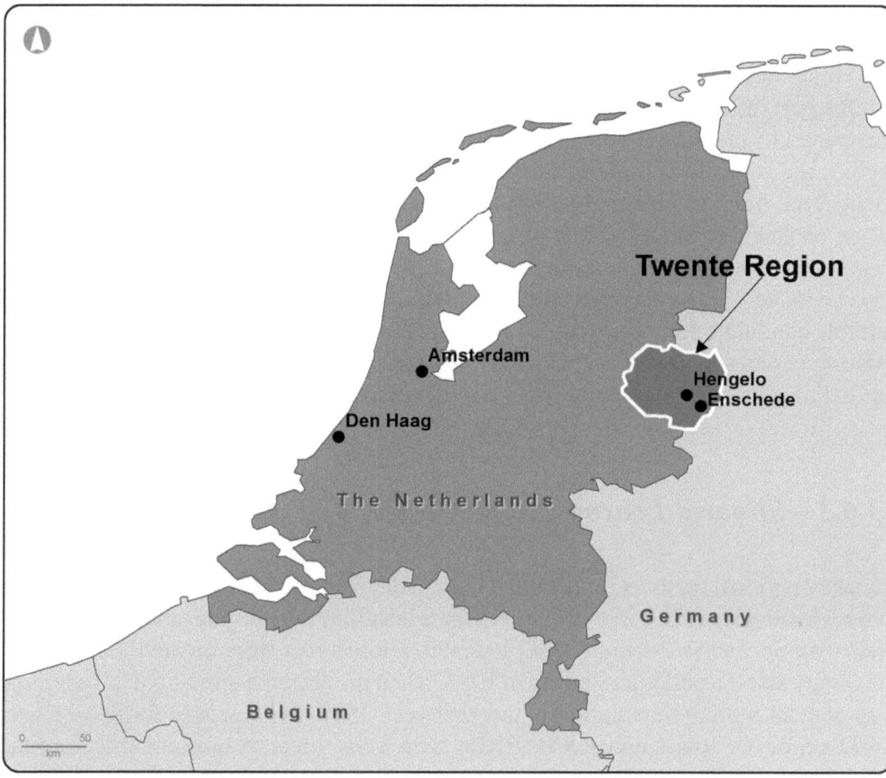

Fig. 13.3 The Twente region

13.6.2 The University of Twente as a Key Knowledge Economy Actor

An important element of policy-makers' response to the domestic economic crisis of Twente was the creation of a new university. From the post-war period, industrialists formed a Foundation 'for the promotion of technical higher education in the northern and eastern provinces of the Netherlands', to revitalise the region's declining industries. In the 1950s, this Foundation led a regional campaign for the newly announced third technical university for the Netherlands (after Delft and Eindhoven) to be located in Twente. Indeed Minister Cals announced in 1959 that the new Technische Hogeschool Twente (THT or Twente Technical College) would be located at Drienerlo, a country estate between the two main cities of Hengelo and Enschede. The university began its life in 1961 with the first students being admitted in 1964, but immediately entered a period of turmoil, with low student numbers and the steady decline of the industry it was supposed to support calling into question its continued viability. The university was established as an innovative and experimental institution that had to use an existing professoriat from the two technical universities in Delft and Eindhoven to create courses in entirely novel areas. The university survived largely by reinventing itself as a source of new growth for the region, working with regional policy-makers to develop new sectors and create new jobs, wealth and ultimately a new regional knowledge economy.

One part of its struggle for survival came in efforts to broaden its courses, and in particular, to create a medical faculty. Despite serious lobbying from within the region, the ninth Dutch medical faculty was awarded to the University of Maastricht. That institution was then in the process being created as part of a compensation package for the province of Limburg, at that time in crisis as a result of the closure of the nationalised mining industry. However, despite that initial failure, the University of Twente has placed considerable efforts into positioning itself to be a suitable candidate for a medical faculty. The university's strategy has been using its existing base as an university with several expertise in applied technology, drawing on its linkages with regional partners, to develop new specialisations.

13.6.3 Situated Learning: The Case of Technical Medicine

Two key regional partners for the university in developing this situated expertise were two regional hospitals, *'t Roessingh* specialist rehabilitation hospital and the generalist *Medische Spectrum Twente* (MST) hospital. Close links were created between the university and 't Roessingh starting in 1984, when the research director of 't Roessingh was granted a professorship at the university; in 1993, *'t Roessingh* formed its own R&D centre ('t Roessingh R&D, RRD) with close links to the university around rehabilitative medicine, complementing the university's expertise in device technology. Likewise, the university developed linkages with the MST Trust, with the perhaps overambitious hope to become a University Medical Centre Twente were it ever to be awarded medical degree-awarding powers. Its specialists were able to hold chairs at UT to carry out their medical research and develop their careers.

Those developments formed the basis for the launch of the Technical Medicine degree in 2003, approved by the Ministry of Education, technically split between two three year phases (bachelor-masters) but in practice handled as a single course (QANU 2011). The pedagogical basis for this course is in training medical technicians with higher-education based competencies to carry out a number of specific medical technological interventions and procedures. The higher education based nature of the course means that the student is trained as a research professional with the capacity to improve and innovate in those areas, and there is the opportunity to progress at the end of the Masters' course into Ph.D. positions. The course handbook describes itself as creating a new kind of professional, the Technical Physician, "a new academic professional who has the knowledge, skills and problem solving mind-set to design and safely apply improved diagnostics and therapeutics for the benefit of patients".[5] In 2011, the Dutch Quality Assurance Agency for

[5]http://www.utwente.nl/tg/index2/

Higher Education (QANU) accredited the Technical Medicine programme and found that it was satisfactory or good in every dimension of education quality. In 2013, the course was taken up in the national Individual Health Care Professionals act (Wet BIG), which means that its graduates have the rights reserved to physicians to treat patients independently and perform procedures.[6]

This new capacity draws heavily on the regional partnership built up since the 1980s and embedded within key university teaching and research activities. An important element underpinning the creation of this new course was its location within a rich research environment. This research environment—supervising students and Ph.D.s—is currently provided by the MIRA research institute (formerly the Biomedical Technology Institute, or BMTI). BMTI was created by the university in 1992 as one of its four (then) leading technological institutes, bringing together a range of research fields to better profile them. BMTI (later MIRA) provided an institutional framework to host clinical professors from MST and RRD, in return for providing them with career opportunities comparable to their colleagues in University Medical Centres. These attached professors in turn provided UT with the medical expertise to put together and ultimately win a bid for this new course, and all graduating students participate in research projects overseen by research professors within considerable clinical medical expertise.

As part of the wider collaboration between the university and regional medical institutions around technical medicine, UT opened in 2011 the Experimental Centre for Technical Medicine[7] (ECTM). Part of the rationale for ECTM was to createan on-campus training centre where students can learn how to use the various technologies necessary for their course. At the same time, those facilities were used by local hospitals in terms of the continuing professional development of their staff, for example in the use of new technological interventions in Intensive Care and Emergency Room settings. Finally, the ECTM offered a research infrastructure facility for the beta testing of new technological medical interventions by research companies as well as supporting the research activities of technical medical researchers attached to MIRA.

13.7 The Reality of Universities and Regional Upgrading in the Northern Periphery

In this chapter, we are interested in understanding how regions and universities can work together to steer university internal processes in order to better couple regional engagement activities—of whatever kind—to key university structures. Our two cases have illustrated that this coupling may happen when there is mutual

[6]http://www.utwente.nl/en/archive/2013/11/technical-physicians-of-the-university-of-twente-included-in-the-individual-health-care-professions-act/

[7]http://www.technischweekblad.nl/opereren-op-poppen.127605.lynkx

beneficiality for universities and their surrounding localities in the context of regional upgrading strategies. We contend that this finding is not strongly contextual dependent, and because it relates to the ways that universities function as self-governing and loosely-coupled communities, these lessons have a wider applicability beyond Norway and the Netherlands and in particular for the southern periphery, the topic of this volume. In order to explicate these lessons more clearly, we recall the three elements set out above, namely:

- how these micro-learning communities were institutionalised and embedded in universities and regions;
- the tensions they faced, and the barriers they overcame; and
- the effect that this ultimately had on regional upgrading.

13.7.1 Institutionalising Micro-learning Communities

The first issue relates to what universities can do to institutionalise and embed these new micro-learning communities. In both cases, what has proven important is in generating successes that are recognised as such by universities' wider stakeholder communities, and by which universities feel themselves to be validated by these regional activities. In both these cases there was a 'stickiness' to the region that held these coalitions together over long-term periods necessary to build up these courses, and to address the emerging problems and tensions.

In the case of UiT, community medicine was an important element of the university being able to demonstrate to the Ministry of Health and the Norwegian parliament that it was an 'excellent research university' and deserved the funding brought by that status. In turn, these accomplishments contributed to enhance UiT's internal and external legitimacies, securing needed moral and financial support by key internal (university and organizational field) and external (government and society) stakeholders. The legitimization process was not only as regards knowledge production per se, but in embedding the generated knowledge within a specific knowledge (community medicine) and local (Northern Norway) community. It is indeed the case that that knowledge community was, in turn, rooted in regional specificities, but, more importantly, and in line of our non-contextual sensitive argument exposed above, this knowledge community became actively engaged in creating and transferring fundamental (universal) knowledge. This legitimises the activity as more than applied or 'mode-2' knowledge production geared towards local relevance, and, instead, emphasises how, in essence, it was a regionally-contextualised, globally excellent activity (consult Perry and May 2006).

In Twente, the micro-institutionalisation of the learning community came by integrating a novel theme into the existing structure of the university. The failure to award the ninth medical faculty to Enschede was also a problem for regional medical institutions as they did not have a ready stream of new graduates to work in the emerging innovative fields, thereby threatening their own vitality. In the context of a university at the time searching for ways to validate itself as being both excellent and relevant, the presence of two other local knowledge institutions created an opportunity which was subsequently enthusiastically embraced. The presence of a regional critical mass around a particular theme—especially one which carried such a clear emotional resonance with some staff members—allowed the new activities to be constructed with limited internal resistance.

13.7.2 Overcoming Tensions and Barriers

The second issue in upgrading is addressing the tensions that arise when universities develop connections with their regions; effective university-region interaction requires that universities gain clear benefits for their core processes (e.g. teaching or research) from that engagement activity, whilst there are also clear value-added benefits for a wide set of regional stakeholders. Although the nature of the regional benefits will vary substantially with regional context, thereby inhibiting drawing sensible lessons for the southern periphery, it is clear there were similarities in the ways that the two universities were able to create obvious and demonstrable benefits through these regional learning community activities. The key issue has been in ensuring that the regional embedded learning continues to deliver benefits for the university over a long time period, as the nature of the activity evolves from being marginal to a more central part of the institution.

In Tromsø, tensions and dilemmas were largely associated with the lack of long term financial support for pursuing the academic agenda associated with the Tromsø study. These were, to a large degree, solved by the pro-active effort of (some) entrepreneurial academics that went to great lengths to secure vital internal and external financial support, thus guaranteeing the sustainability of the project. Another aspect relates to finding a balance between (global) scientific excellence and local relevance, accomplished in the form of efficient knowledge diffusion and direct participation in policy making process by some of the university actors. By clearly demonstrating the value of the knowledge generated in the Tromsø studies, for the university, the region, governmental authorities and for other knowledge production institutions as well (organisational field),, academics involved with community medicine were able to achieve vital internal and external support.

In UT the benefit was building a necessary critical mass around teaching and research to achieve accreditation and thereby allow a self-sustaining community to take root within the university. The solution taken was to first build up a university research strength in biomedicine as a natural iteration of existing strengths in technology fields (chemical engineering, sensors, telematics). The Biomedical Technological Institute provided a shared infrastructure for the diverse activities then spread across the existing faculties. This was also helped by a decision in 2000 by the University Board to give the 'spear point' research centres equivalence with faculties, allowing focus and investment to build up research excellence from which education later emerged, firstly as a speciality Biomedical Engineering masters, and latterly the accredited technical medicine course.

13.7.3 Net Effects on Regional Upgrading

The final important element of the model (Fig. 13.1). relates to regional upgrading, and not merely creating a locally embedded university community, but in how that local community experience benefits in terms of its wider innovativeness, competitiveness and quality of life.

In both our case universities, these embedded knowledge communities, rooted in regional particularities mediated through the university became important nodes within wider knowledge circulation and valorisation networks, and ultimately global value chains. This, in turn, legitimated the activities within the regions, by avoiding any potential criticisms that the universities were merely 'cathedrals in the desert'. In both cases, these shared knowledge communities have been acknowledged by key external stakeholders as being of national economic significance, and helping two peripheral regions to bring themselves to the attention of policy-makers.

UiT has had a number of effects around common areas of interests and developing knowledge relevant to the challenges of Arctic life, helping to raise regional productivity and the attractiveness of the region as a place of residence, as well as supportive policies and strategies in developing those strengths. Its international profile has helped other regional partners to have profiled themselves as being in a dynamic, rather than a backward, region, and therefore worthy of support for their knowledge and innovation activities. Additionally, health-related innovations have helped fuelled interest towards health-related issues like telemedicine. These efforts, combined with UiT's proven expertise within the natural sciences (fishery sciences included) have become the foundation for the rise of a set of regional knowledge-intensive marine biotechnology activities (Karlsen et al. 2011). The value for the region has, therefore, been in finding a way to see the university as helping to create future opportunities for the region, in revitalise a declining industry and enable future job and growth opportunities.

The regional upgrading effects of UT have formed part of a wider process in Twente involving the creation of a series of anchors for embedded knowledge communities supported by the university, local and regional governance structures and also business. These embedded knowledge communities are not merely located in and around the university, but have also become embedded in other regional actors, and influential in their own formal organisations and informal cultures. There is a strategic co-operation between the university, the local municipality and region ('Kennispark') that has been active in investment towards research activities of mutual interest; at the same time, Kennispark is visible as a public-private partnership to government investors as an ideal type of knowledge valorisation space. This is something that has been very important to local stakeholders in being able to legitimate UT's activities as being value to them, and ultimately has led to this partnership to adopt a target of creating 10,000 new high-technology jobs by 2020.

13.8 Lessons for University-Regional Engagement in Southern Europe

Regional upgrading processes (cf. Cooke and Piccaluga 2012) necessarily encompass a number of critical aspects far beyond this chapter's limited scope, although knowledge structures and university activities clearly contribute to regional upgrading by fostering regional collaboration and situated learning (Gertner et al. 2011). In this final section, we seek to draw some more general lessons that can be applied in the Southern European periphery in those circumstances where universities seeking to create and exploit contextualised knowledge are restricted in doing so by institutional counter-pressures, which we here refer to by the short-hand of being more 'globally excellent'. Under these circumstances, partners should be aware of the need to permit universities to book these successes as a necessary precondition of the parallel production of the contextualised knowledge.

The first is that knowledge exploitation process must also allow the university to legitimate itself in its own national political economy as a legitimate (research-intensive) university, and not find its role unnecessarily prescribed to being that as a regionally-relevant institution (Pinheiro et al. 2012). This transcends mere institutional pride—all knowledge is created somewhere, and universities that can achieve wider recognition and validation for their locally-created knowledge will *ceteris paribus* also have a greater local impact (Feldman and Desrochers 2003). Tromsø was able to position itself as a knowledge hub for the 'High North', but that in turn allowed it to demonstrate its significance to a government at times often blinkered towards seeing Oslo, Bergen and the National Technical University at Trondheim (NTNU) as the extent of the Norwegian university system. In Twente, the validity of commercial activities was partly related to the fact that they were research-intensive and were validated externally in different ways including national research evaluations, international peer reviewed publications and, in part due to their capacity to win excellence-based research funding (*cf.* Kwiek 2012).

A second element worth referring to is the role of certain academics who have been active in ensuring the structural changes necessary before contextual learning can be embraced within the university. We here distinguish three layers—firstly are those academics who are actively engaged with regional partners in creating new regionally-contextualised learning activities and thereby creating assets of value to the regional community, akin to what Shattock (2009) calls 'academic intrapreneurs'. But two other groups are also important within the university, and their scope for action and wider support dictates the extent to which they can fulfil this mission. The first are the university senior managers, who are critical in terms of depicting regional engagement activities as a core mission for the university, and at the same time being insistent upon their conformance with wider academic norms of excellence and universality. The second are academic peers, not themselves active within creating contextualised knowledge, but instead active within university teaching, research, promotions and resources committees: their willingness to lend these contextualised learning activities the imprimatur of legitimacy also helps to shape academic intrapreneurs' span of control.

We acknowledge that the case universities—both in Norway and the Netherlands—are embedded in national policy contexts where a privileged emphasis is placed on an active societal role for universities, conditions that are not necessarily present in southern peripheries (Benneworth and Hospers 2007a). In terms of drawing general lessons from our inquiry, we argue that universities' capacities to undertake societal activities is shaped by these national regulatory conditions; although in Twente, for example, the university was active as an entrepreneur university before the legal changes were made that 'permitted' that approach. To make it clear, we are not arguing that the national institutional frameworks per se (funding allocations included) dictate university activities, but where universities have an encouraging and institutionalised regulatory framework, as is the case of the Nordics and the Netherlands, they are freed from continually renegotiating their social missions and resource pools, thus ensuring them a certain degree of continuity and manoeuvrability (for the case of the Nordics consult Gornitzka and Maassen 2011). Even, or perhaps particularly, where these national conditions are not so supportive, as is the case of some Southern European countries (*cf.* Neave and Amaral 2011), then regional partners can support universities to create more contextualised knowledge activities and structures by appreciating that sometimes universities need to portray themselves in particular ways to central stakeholders that can lead them to appear regionally sensitive. If regional partners then accuse those institutions of being regional insensitivity, it further undermines the validity of external engagement, and therefore directly works counter to what those regional partners could otherwise potentially achieve.

References

Amin A, Roberts J (2008) Knowing in action: beyond communities of practice. Res Policy 37 (2):353–369

Arbo P, Eskelinen H (2003) The role of small, comprehensive universities in regional economic development: experiences from two Nordic case. Paper for the 43 rd ERSA Congress Jyväskylä, Finland

Becher T, Trowler PR (2001) Academic tribes and territories intellectual enquiry and the culture of disciplines. The Society for Research into Higher Education & Open University Press, Buckingham

Bender T (ed) (1988) The university and the city. from medieval origins to the present. Oxford University Press, New York

Benner C (2003) Learning communities in a learning region: the soft infrastructure of cross firm learning networks in silicon valley. Environ Plan A 35(10):1809–1830

Benneworth P (2013) The engaged university in practice? In: Benneworth P (ed) University engagement with socially excluded communities. Springer, Dordrecht, pp 329–343
Benneworth PS, Hospers G-J (2007a) Urban competitiveness in the knowledge economy: Universities as new planning animateurs. Prog plan 67(2):99–198
Benneworth PS, Hospers G-J (2007b) The new economic geography of old industrial regions: universities as global–local pipelines. Environ Plann C Govern Policy 25(6):779–802
Benneworth P, Osborne M (2014) Knowledge, engagement, and higher education in Europe. In: Tandon R, Hall B (eds) Higher education in the world 5: knowledge engagement and higher education: contributing to social change. Palgrave Macmillan, London, pp 219–231
Bergek A, Jacobsson S, Carlsson B, Lindmark S, Rickne A (2008) Analyzing the functional dynamics of technological innovation systems: a scheme of analysis. Res Policy 37(3):407–429
CERI (1982) The university and the community: the problems of changing relationships. OECD publishing, Paris
Charles DR, Benneworth P (2001) The regional contribution of higher education. HEFCE/Universities UK, London
Charles D, Wilson B (2012) Managing regional engagement: the role of benchmarking. In: Pinheiro R, Benneworth P, Jones GA (eds) Universities and regional development: a critical assessment of tensions and contradictions. Routledge, Milton Park, pp 219–238
Christopherson S, Clark J (2007) Power in firm networks: what it means for regional innovation systems. Reg Stud 41(9):1223–1236
Collini S (2012) What are universities for? Penguin, London
Cooke P (2005) Regionally asymmetric knowledge capabilities and open innovation: exploring 'Globalisation 2'—a new model of industry organisation. Res Policy 34:1128–1149
Cooke P, Piccaluga A (2012) Regional development in the knowledge economy. Routledge, Milton Park
Feldman M, Desrochers P (2003) Research universities and local economic development: lessons from the history of the johns hopkins university. Ind Innov 10(1):5–24
Gertner D, Roberts J, Charles D (2011) University-industry collaboration: a CoPs approach to KTPs. J Knowl Manag 15(4):625–647
Goddard J (2011) Connecting universities to regional growth: a practical guide. DG REGIO, Brussels
Goddard J, Vallance P (2013) The university and the city. Routledge, London
Gornitzka Å, Maassen P (2011) University governance reforms, global scripts and the "Nordic Model". Accounting for policy change? In: Schmid J, Amos K, Schrader ATJ (eds) Welten der Bildung? Vergleichende Analysen von Bildungspolitik und Bildungssystemen. Nomos Verlagsgesellschaft, Baden-Baden, pp 149–177
Gunasekara C (2006) The generative and developmental roles of universities in regional innovation systems. Sci Public Policy 33(2):137–150. doi:10.3152/147154306781779118
Hansson F, Husted K, Vestergaard J (2004) Rethinking science parks—from structural holes jockeys to social capital catalysts. Technovation 25(10):1039–1049
Hassink R (2005) How to unlock regional economies from path dependency? From learning region to learning cluster. Eur Plan Stud 13(4):521–535
Hermannsson K, Lisenkova K, McGregor P, Swales J (2013) The expenditure impacts of individual higher education institutions and their students on the Scottish economy under a regional government budget constraint: homogeneity or heterogeneity? Environ Plan A 45(3):710–727
Hospers G (2006) Silicon somewhere? Assessing the usefulness of best practices in regional policy. Policy Stud 27:1–15
Kallio A, Harmaakorpi V, Pihkala T (2010) Absorptive capacity and social capital in regional innovation systems: the case of the Lahti region in Finland. Urban Stud 47(2):303–319
Karlsen JE, Pritchard R (eds) (2013) Resilient universities: confronting changes in a challenging world. Peter Lang, Oxford
Karlsen J, Isaksen A, Spilling O (2011) The challenge of constructing regional advantages in peripheral areas: the case of marine biotechnology in Tromsø, Norway. Entrep Reg Dev 23 (3–4):235–257. doi:10.1080/08985620903233945

Kickert W (1995) Steering at a distance: a new paradigm of public governance in Dutch higher education. Governance 8(1):135–157

Kwiek M (2012) Changing higher education policies: from the deinstitutionalization to the reinstitutionalization of the research mission in Polish universities. Sci Public Policy 39 (5):641–654. doi:10.1093/scipol/scs042

Lagendijk A, Oinas P (2005) Proximity, distance and diversity, issues on economic interaction and local development. Ashgate, London

McCann P, Ortega-Argilés R (2013) Smart specialization, regional growth and applications to European union cohesion policy. Reg Stud 49(8):1291–1302

Morgan K (1992) Innovating by networking—new models of corporate and regional development. In: Dunford M, Kaflakas G (eds) Cities and regions in the New Europe. Belhaven, London, pp 150–169

Morgan K, Nauwelaers C (eds) (2002) Regional innovation strategies: the challenge for less-favoured regions. Routledge, London

Mutch A (2003) Communities of practice and habitus: a critique. Organ Stud 24(3):383–401

Neave G, Amaral A (2011) Higher education in Portugal 1974–2009: a nation, a generation. Springer, Dordrecht

OECD (2007) Higher education and regions: globally competitive, regionally engaged. OECD Publishing, Paris

Olsen JP (2007) The institutional dynamics of the European university. In: Maassen P, Olsen JP (eds) University dynamics and European integration. Springer, Dordrecht, pp 25–54

Perry B (2012) Excellence, relevance and the construction of regional science policy: science frictions and fictions in the North West of England. In: Pinheiro R, Benneworth P, Jones GA (eds) Universities and regional development: a critical assessment of tensions and contradictions. Routledge, Milton Park, pp 105–123

Perry B, May T (2006) Excellence, relevance and the university: the "missing middle" in socio-economic engagement. J High Educ Afr 4(3):69–92

Pinheiro R (2012a) Knowledge and the 'Europe of the regions': the case of the high north. In: Kwiek M, Maassen P (eds) National higher education reforms in a European context: comparative reflections on Poland and Norway. Peter Lang, Frankfurt, pp 179–208

Pinheiro R (2012b) University ambiguity and institutionalization: a tale of three regions. In: Pinheiro R, Benneworth P, Jones GA (eds) Universities and regional development: a critical assessment of tensions and contradictions. Routledge, Milton Park, pp 35–55

Pinheiro R, Benneworth P, Jones GA (2012) Understanding regions and the institutionalization of universities. In: Pinheiro R, Benneworth P, Jones GA (eds) Universities and regional development: an assessment of tensions and contradictions. Routledge, Milton Park, pp 11–32

Pinheiro R, Benneworth P, Jones GA (2015) Beyond the obvious: tensions and volitions surrounding the contributions of universities to regional developmen. In: Farinha L, Ferreira J, Lawton-Smith H, Bagchi-Sen S (eds) Handbook of research on global competitive advantage through innovation and entrepreneurship. IGI, Hershey, PA, pp 150–172

QANU (2011) Technical medicine: faculteit technische wetenschappen, Utrecht, QANU, May 2011. Available online at: https://search.nvao.net/files/4f182c7078ae6_rapport%20UTwente%20wo-ma%20Technical%20Medicine.pdf. Accessed 15 Sep 2015

Reponen T (1999) Is leadership possible at loosely coupled organizations such as universities? High Educ Pol 12(3):237–244

Roberts J (2014) Community and the dynamics of spatially distributed knowledge production: the case of wikipedia. In: Rutten R, Benneworth P, Irawati D, Boekema F (eds) The social dynamics of innovation networks. Routledge, London, pp 180–200

Shattock M (2009) Entrepreneurialism in universities and the knowledge economy: diversification and organizational change in European higher education. SRHE & Open University Press, London

Sotarauta M, Horlings I, Liddle J (eds) (2012) Leadership and change in sustainable regional development. Routledge, London

van Vught F, Westerheijden D (2010) Multidimensional ranking: a new transparency tool for higher education and research. High Educ Manag Policy 22(3):1–26

Paul Benneworth is a senior researcher at the Center for Higher Education Policy Studies, University of Twente, the Netherlands, and Agderforskning, Kristiansand, Norway. Paul's research focuses on the dynamics of innovation and regional development and in particular the ways in which cooperations and coalitions function in supporting regional innovation processes. He has been chief scientist of projects for a range of research funders including the European Framework Programme/ERA-NET, research councils in the UK, the Netherlands and Norway as well as a wide range of government and not-for-profit funders. He is the editor of 8 scientific works, including three in the RSA *Cities & Regions* series. He has published more than thirty peer-reviewed scientific articles in the last decade, serves as reviewer for a range of journals, research councils and funding agencies internationally and is currently acting as special scientific adviser to three research council funded projects in Norway, Austria and Belgium.

Rómulo Pinheiro is Professor of Public Policy and Administration at the University of Agder, Norway, where he heads the research group on Public Governance and Leadership. He is also a Senior Researcher at Agderforskning and the Centre for Advanced Studies in Regional Innovation Strategies (RIS), a Visiting Professor in Higher Education Policy & Management at the University of Tampere (Finland) and Affiliated Member of the ExCID (*Expert cultures and institutional dynamics: Studies in higher education and work)* research group based at the University of Oslo. Rómulo's research interests are located at the intersection of public policy and administration, organisational theory, economic geography, innovation and higher education studies. His work has been published in Public Administration Review, Science and Public Policy, Higher Education, Studies in Higher Education, European Journal of Higher Education, Cambridge Journal of Regions, Economy and Society, Tertiary Education and Management, City, Culture and Society, International Journal of Cultural Policy, etc.

Chapter 14
Higher Education, Human Capital, and Regional Dynamics in Southern Europe

Ricardo Biscaia, Pedro Teixeira, Vera Rocha, and Margarida Fonseca Cardoso

JEL Classification R12 • J24 • I23 • I25

14.1 Introduction

Despite the term "human capital" having remote historical roots, being already widespread in the writings of the founding fathers of economic analysis (Teixeira 2005), it was during the second half of the twentieth century that an increasing debate

R. Biscaia (✉)
Center for Research in Higher Education Policies, CIPES, Rua 1° de Dezembro, 399, 4450-227 Matosinhos, Portugal

Portucalense University Infante D.Henrique, Rua Dr. António Bernardino de Almeida, 541, 4200-072 Porto, Portugal
e-mail: Ricardo_Biscaia@hotmail.com

P. Teixeira
Center for Research in Higher Education Policies, CIPES, Rua 1° de Dezembro, 399, 4450-227 Matosinhos, Portugal

FEP – Faculty of Economics, University of Porto, Rua Dr. Roberto Frias, 4200-464 Porto, Portugal
e-mail: pedrotx@fep.up.pt

V. Rocha
Center for Research in Higher Education Policies, CIPES, Rua 1° de Dezembro, 399, 4450-227 Matosinhos, Portugal

Department of Innovation and Organizational Economics, Copenhagen Business School, Kilevej, Kilen 14A, 2000 Frederiksberg, Denmark
e-mail: vr.ino@cbs.dk

M.F. Cardoso
Center for Research in Higher Education Policies, CIPES, Rua 1° de Dezembro, 399, 4450-227 Matosinhos, Portugal

ICBAS – Instituto de Ciências Biomédicas Abel Salazar, Largo Prof. Abel Salazar, 2, 4099-003 Porto, Portugal
e-mail: mcard@icbas.up.pt

M. Fonseca, U. Fratesi (eds.), *Regional Upgrading in Southern Europe*, Advances in Spatial Science, DOI 10.1007/978-3-319-49818-8_14

around human capital emerged among scholars. New economic theories started suggesting that human capital in general—and education in particular—could work as an engine for the economic growth and development of nations (e.g., Romer 1990; Schultz 1993). The increasing relevance of human capital for economic growth was also associated with the role of technology and its impact in enhancing the demand for more and better qualified workers (e.g., Goldin and Katz 1998). At the same time, the returns on investment to human capital started to be expected to be higher in those contexts where productive learning opportunities existed or could be exploited. However, the capacity of societies to take advantage of those investments has been found to be more complex and uncertain than it was initially portrayed.

A more recent line of research started recognizing the potential role of human capital at the regional level also. Moreover, further developments in econometric methods—particularly in spatial econometrics, pioneered by Anselin (1988)—offered a new way to account for spatial correlation between different variables in regional growth studies, as well as potential spillover effects that can be dependent on the neighbouring relationships between countries and/or regions. Hence, in this chapter we aim to understand the role of human capital on regional convergence for Southern Europe countries, with particular emphasis on recent empirical studies. In the next section we discuss the role of human capital in the framework of growth convergence theories and the issue of human capital migration as a potential factor influencing regional disparities in Europe. In Sect 14.3 we focus on an important component of human capital formation—the role of higher education institutions at the regional level. Then, in Sect. 14.4 we review the empirical findings on these issues in the context of Southern Europe (Greece, Italy, Portugal, and Spain). Section 14.5 provides a brief exploratory analysis of the potential association between the education of the population and the GDP per capita at the regional-level for those four countries. We present some concluding reflections in Sect. 14.6.

14.2 Regional Disparities and Human Capital in Growth Theory

14.2.1 Education and Regional Convergence

The early assessment of growth disparities among nations relied on the concept of "convergence". Convergence studies have become highly influential since the early 1990s, not only due to the renewed interest in economic growth fuelled by endogenous growth theories (e.g., Romer 1990), but also owing to the emergence of reliable macroeconomic data (see Summers and Heston 1988). As a result, empirical works assessing whether or not countries starting with the same structural conditions (such as human and physical capital, unemployment rates or saving rates) converge to the same level of GDP per capita became abundant.[1]

Convergence analyses were then easily transposed to regional studies (Martin and Sunley 1998). As regional economies tend to diverge from each other due to the spatial unevenness of market forces, economies of scale and agglomeration effects typically result in a strong concentration of labour and capital in some regions, which subsequently lead to (self-reinforcing and persistent) growth disparities among regions. The increasing recognition of this growth heterogeneity within countries, along with the intensified debates about the role of human capital in regional growth and convergence, has thus motivated many studies about this subject.

Neven and Gouyette (1995) analysed 82 NUTS II regions of Northern Europe using school enrolment as a proxy for human capital. Similarly, to Mankiw et al. (1992), they concluded that regions with higher human capital had higher growth rates, and that β-convergence was higher whenever human capital differences were controlled for. Arena et al. (2000) studied 105 British counties and measured human capital through the proportion of the working age population with post compulsory education. They, instead, concluded that controlling for human capital did not significantly change the β-convergence parameter, which implied that human capital differences did not explain counties' growth disparities.

Some authors also attempted to explain regional disparities using endogenous growth model approaches. Rodriguez-Pose and Fratesi (2004) concluded that out of the structural funds of the European Union aimed at reducing regional inequalities, only the investment in human capital and education had a significant effect in achieving this goal, even though this type of investment only represented around one eighth of the aforementioned structural funds. Many studies further showed that the growth of European regions is spatially correlated among them (e.g., Fingleton and McCombie 1998; Lopéz-Bazo et al. 1999; Baumont et al. 2003; Badinger and Tondl 2003; Dall'erba 2005a, b; Digiacinto and Nuzzo 2006; Dall'erba and LeGallo 2008). Overall, they suggest that the geographical location and spillovers can matter more than other "traditional" macroeconomic factors (Quah 1996; Moreno and Trehan 1997). More recently, Basile (2008) concluded that, for a sample of 108 NUTS 2 regions in Europe, the role of human capital in the convergence was non-linear: an increase in the rate of schooling only increased growth rate when the level of investment was above the EU average. Moreover, regions having neighbouring regions with high levels of human capital benefited from externalities, which were materialized into larger rates of economic growth.

[1]This corresponds to the concept of "conditional convergence". Unconditional convergence, instead, occurs whenever all countries/regions converge to the same level of GDP per capita, independently of their initial structural conditions. Closer to the "conditional convergence" definition is that of "club convergence". It is associated with multiple equilibrium values of GDP per capita to which countries will converge, depending on their initial conditions.

14.2.2 Migration and Regional Convergence

The regional role of human capital is also closely linked to the "brain drain" phenomenon, which is defined as the process of migration of highly educated people, massively or individually, from one geographical location to another. Several factors explain these phenomena, though the main one seems to be the fact that "different societies and cultures tend to generate skills and talents in different proportions and to require talents and skills in different proportions" (Johnson 1965, p. 301). Therefore, some regions may not have the necessary "absorptive capacity" to retain the human capital that was generated in the region. If the region does not have sufficient demand for the high-skills that are created by the universities, it is expected that those high-skilled workers will migrate elsewhere, where they can benefit from better working conditions.

Several studies addressed the effects of human capital migration, both at national and regional levels. Similar to developed and developing countries, regions within a country also have different degrees of development. Consequently, more developed regions may be able to offer better working conditions for skilled workers, so highly educated workers have a greater incentive to migrate to these regions, within the same country. Accordingly, the existence of a dissimilar concentration of human capital may be a reason for significant growth disparities between regions of the same country, even if these regions may benefit from internal labour mobility.

Ritsila and Ovaskainen (2001) analysed the regional distribution of human capital in Finland, based on the argument that workers choose rationally where they want to be located in the country. They concluded that more educated individuals were more prone to migrate. Moreover, migration patterns seem to occur from remote regions to more populated ones. For the EU, Rodriguez-Pose and Vilalta-Bufi (2005) noticed that while the GDP per capita of EU countries might be converging, a closer look at the regional GDP reveals that the regional disparities have been stable or even increased since the 1990s. By analysing the human capital endowments of these regions, the authors argue that regional performance is closely related to human capital factors, namely the stock of human capital, the average level of education, the match between education and the labour market, and migration flows. In particular, they found that regions that were able to attract better-endowed workers were those that grew faster.[2] Later, Ramos et al. (2012) presented valuable extensions of this work, by expanding the dataset and introducing different variables regarding over-education. They concluded that overqualified workers still contribute to the growth of a region.

Also for EU NUTS II regions, Huber and Tondl (2012) studied the relation between GDP per capita and migration flows during 2000–2007. They concluded that migration flows did not accelerate convergence, as receiving regions—which

[2]Similar results about the importance of migration and human capital in generating regional inequalities are shown in Duranton and Monastiriotis (2002), Overman and Puga (2002) and Faggian and McCann (2009).

were already richer—increased their GDP per capita with the flows. Moreover, long-run effects of migration seemed to be more important than immediate effects, which suggested that increasing labour mobility may be a force operating against regional convergence.

14.3 The Effect of HEIs on Regional Development

One critical aspect in the debate about the potential role of human capital in regional economic dynamics concerns the role of higher education institutions (HEIs) in the formation of human capital. Thus, this section reviews prior results on the impact of HEIs on regional development.

It is often argued that HEIs contribute to the economic life of a region due to the direct expenditure-multiplier effects and the jobs provided to local economies (Faggian and McCann 2009). However, we are mainly interested in understanding, based on the existing evidence, whether and how the existence of HEIs in a given region promotes its growth through the increase of human capital levels, accumulation of knowledge and consequent increase of innovation capacity. All of these are important economic dimensions for the establishment of HEIs in a given region.

Universities are expected to enhance Regional Innovation Systems, which in turn play a more important role than ever in regional rates of innovation (Kitagawa 2004). Anselin et al. (1997)'s results pointed out that both high-technology innovative industries and private R&D seem to be positively affected by the presence of a university. Goldstein and Drucker (2006) also argued that knowledge-based university activities such as teaching and research, as well as the existence of spatial spillovers, were crucial to the growth of regions. Moreover, these effects were even more significant in smaller and medium regions, supporting the importance of universities in the reduction of regional inequalities. However, Huggins et al. (2008) underline that, while universities can be a key to regional innovation, their role alone is not sufficient in itself for the development of innovation. They defend that teaching and research activities should be coupled with a system of publicly funded research institutes and laboratories dedicated to applied research.

The formation of human capital is another channel through which HEIs may influence regional economic dynamics, even though subsequent migration may pose important challenges to the upgrading of the human capital of certain regions (see, for instance, Justman and Thisse 1997; Suedekum 2005; Franco et al. 2010; Abel and Deitz 2012). Actually, the existence of higher skill premiums in more developed regions, combined with the fact that migration is more likely to be a choice for the most educated individuals, can create significant barriers to human capital accumulation in less developed regions, regardless the presence of HEIs in these regions.

Even so, there are other positive effects associated with the presence of universities. By providing basic research and higher levels of human capital, HEIs can contribute positively to the likelihood of technologic innovation in a given region and also to an increase in the productivity of the private sector due to the existence of knowledge spillovers (Arrow 1962; Nelson 1959; Bartel and Lichtenberg 1987). Andersson et al. (2004), for instance, found that policies of spatial decentralization of universities in Sweden had a significant and positive effect on workers' productivity, and that these effects were higher in municipalities surrounded by newly created HEIs.

HEIs' presence may also promote new firm creation and their performance. Lindelof and Lofsten (2004) showed that new technology-based firms located in science parks with links to universities have a competitive advantage over other firms of the same type. Audretsch et al.'s (2005) results also indicate that new knowledge-based firms have a higher propensity to be located close to the universities, though this effect may be dependent on the type of spillover mechanism (human capital *versus* research) or the different types of knowledge spillovers (natural sciences *versus* social sciences), which calls for further research. Overall, the literature seems to agree that geographical proximity between HEIs and new firms seems to be a necessary condition for the "quality" of spillovers generated between different agents (Stahlecker and Koschatzky 2004), and that the role of universities tends to be especially important in structurally weak regions where the production of intellectual capital is lacking (Baptista et al. 2011).

Finally, a number of studies also provided evidence on the positive effects that HEIs may have on innovation activities. Fischer and Varga (2003) found that university research generated positive spillovers in Austria in terms of patent applications, while for Sweden, Andersson et al. (2009) found that the number of patents in different regions were significantly linked to the prior creation of new universities and the amount of investment in university research. However, both found that spillovers tend to decrease with the distance from the university. In this regard, Ponds et al. (2010) argue that university-industry links are less geographically bounded than other possible components of the university spillovers, such as labour or the creation of new firms, suggesting that the impact of academic research on regional innovation is not only mediated by geographical proximity, but also by networks stemming from university-industry collaboration.[3]

HEIs are also acknowledged to have different roles in promoting regional development and Regional Innovation Systems (Gunasekara 2006). After the emergence of the "Triple Helix" Model in 1997 (Etzkowitz and Leydesdorff 1997), in which universities, industry and government (the three helices of the model) should interact with each other in an overlapping manner—resembling the helix movements in helicopters—a different role, at least conceptually, has emerged for universities in an innovation system. A different perspective from the Triple Helix model in how this third role of universities should be interpreted is in the "Engaged University" Framework (Chatterton and Goddard 2000). While having some common features with the Triple Helix model, the Engaged University

[3]For recent reviews on the effects of Higher Education Institutions in the Industry, see Casper (2013) and Perkmann et al. (2013).

should involve itself with the Industry and Government beyond the academic entrepreneurialism, focusing on the lifelong learning and adaptation of contents and learning methods to the specificities of the region. According to Gunasekara, (2006), the roles that different universities should play are evaluated according to some of their characteristics, such as the university orientation to regional engagement or the previous history of university–region linkages.

The role of HEIs in promoting regional growth is also acknowledged by the governments and policy frameworks. HEIs are supposed to play a key role in Regional Innovation Systems as well as in the Research and Innovation Smart Specialization Strategies (RIS3). The RIS3 framework is the most recent proof (1301/2013 European Parliament Law) that the role of universities and higher education is still viewed by policymakers as one of the most important determinants for the success in innovation strategies, as stated by the EP Law: "Smart Specialisation Strategies shall be developed through involving national or regional managing authorities and stakeholders, such as universities and other higher education institutions, industry and social partners in an entrepreneurial discovery process".

14.4 Human Capital and Regional Growth in Southern Europe

Regional disparities are an important issue in the context of the European Union, since the rhythm of convergence within the EU has stagnated since the late 1970s and early 1980s (Lopéz-Bazo et al. 1999). The situation is complex, as a different behaviour is observed among the Northern and Southern countries of the EU (Baumont et al. (2003), and different rates of convergence are observed between different NUTS II regions within the same country (Bartkowska and Riedl 2012). Accordingly, in this section, we review the recent efforts developed to explain regional disparities based on the human capital theory, by looking at four Southern European countries: Greece, Italy, Portugal, and Spain.

14.4.1 Human Capital and Regional Convergence in Southern Europe

There is clearly a divide between the two largest and the two smaller countries regarding the amount of research so far available on these topics. For Greece and Portugal, we find a limited number of studies addressing the effects of the distribution or migration of human capital in both countries' regional inequalities. By contrast, there is far more empirical evidence on the two larger countries—Italy and Spain.

A thorough summary of the Greek experience is provided by Petrakos and Artelaris (2008). Evidence for 2004, based on data for NUTS III regions, reports that the richest regions were clustered in the centre of the country and around the capital city of Athens. In contrast, a clustering of the "poorer" regions did not seem to exist by then (p. 129). Regarding the evolution since the early 1980s, the variation of the GDP per capita of Greek regions was stable in the 1980s and the 1990s, however it rose significantly in the early twenty first century. Though the average GDP per capita of the 10 poorest and the 10 richest regions have been increasing steadily, a faster increase in the former group, however, led to an enlargement of the regional differences.

To the best of our knowledge, only a few articles explore how a different distribution of human capital, or how labour migration affects the regional (in) equality in Greece.[4] Petrakos and Saratsis (2000) evaluated the role of human capital—measured by the share of population with higher education—to the β-convergence between the regions, and showed that it positively affected regional growth. Additionally, after controlling for differences in regional endowments (human capital included), they found conditional convergence between the Greek regions during the period analysed. More recently, Benos and Karagiannis (2013), based on data for Greek NUTS II regions between 1981 and 2003, conclude that higher levels of tertiary education have a strong positive association with higher labour productivity, while secondary education has a negative effect, suggesting that increasing the levels of education in the poorer regions favours convergence.

Although many studies focus on the regional convergence in Italy—given that Italy is one of the best-examples in terms of persistent regional divide (e.g., Paci and Saba 1998; DiGiacinto and Nuzzo 2006; Maffezoli 2006)—not many authors focus on the effects of human capital. Regional disparities in terms of GDP per capita have been characterized by a divide between the northern (relatively richer) and the southern (relatively poorer) regions since the unification of the territory in 1861. Since the 1990s, the divide remained significant though there were some weak signs of improvement (Etzo 2011).

Ciccone (2004) suggested that human capital could be further used as a tool to promote regional equality, since there was evidence that it reduced the existing regional productivity differentials (differences in education accounted for 23–38% of the differences in regional productivity). Maffezzoli (2006) concluded that introducing human capital in their analysis of regional disparities significantly reduced the importance of technological progress, suggesting that these were correlated. Moreover, the introduction of human capital variables amplified the differences between the southern and northern regions, indicating that there were imbalances in the human capital distribution in Italy that favoured the existence of regional disparities. Finally, using long time-series covering data since 1891, Felice (2012) tested the role of human and social capital on the process of regional

[4]Some authors deal instead with the relationship between human capital and growth (e.g., Asteriou and Agiomirgianakis 2001; Tsamadias and Prontzas 2012).

convergence in Italy. The proxies used for human capital were the literacy rates, the gross enrolment rates and a composite index between the two in order to account for the different importance of each factor throughout time. He concluded that, for the entire period, human capital played a small role in the convergence process, though from 1951 on there were signs of convergence conditional on human capital.

Regarding the migration effects, Coniglio and Prota (2008) analysed the decisions of graduates from a peripheral region in Italy (Basilicata) that subsidized the population to complete their degrees. They conclude that more talented workers were more prone to move, as well as younger graduates, graduates in business and engineering, and individuals with previous migration experience. Etzo (2008) also analysed the role of internal migration in Italy, further distinguishing workers' quality. Migration rates seemed only to have an effect on convergence in the second decade (1993–2002). Controlling for the quality of migrants, only the net migration of "high" human capital seemed to affect regional growth. The fact that migration flows became more "educated" in this second decade explains why the first decade did not have much impact on growth. They also conducted more detailed analyses for the centre-north and the "Mezzogiorno" regions, and found that more advanced regions were more in need of better qualities of human capital comparatively to the least developed regions.

More recently, Capasso et al. (2012) added new evidence for Italy by analysing the effect of total (internal and external) migration flows on regional growth. They confirmed that the composition of the migration flows cannot be neglected, as important differences exist in the human capital levels of arriving/departing citizens, though the effects of migration do not seem to depend on regions' development. A similar study by Piras (2013) for the period 1970–2005 also provided evidence of brain drain from the southern to the northern Italian regions.

In Portugal, the regional divide in terms of GDP per capita is also visible—the closer to the coast, the richer the regions tend to be. Similar to Greece, there is a limited number of authors that deal with the Portuguese experience. The connection between human capital and regional growth disparities has been mainly addressed by Cardoso and Pentecost (2011a, b). The authors analysed the role of human capital in the regional growth and found conditional convergence in the Portuguese NUTS III regions. Moreover, all the several human capital measures considered (the proportion of secondary and tertiary graduates and the average years of schooling) were found to improve regional economic growth. In Cardoso and Pentecost (2011b), the authors introduced elements of spatial analysis in their empirical study and analysed both Portuguese and Spanish NUTS III regions. Their results showed that there were two "convergence clubs" in the peninsula and that those in the "periphery" were converging, while those in the "core" were not. In addition, human capital only seemed to have an effect on the economic growth of the core regions, suggesting that a minimum threshold of income and economic activity was necessary before human capital became relevant.

In the case of Spain there is also an identified pattern of regional disparities. The richest provinces are clustered in three different positions: the Basque Country; the provinces surrounding Barcelona; and the province of Madrid. The poorest regions are in the southern and southwest regions (Andalucía and Extremadura), as well as in the northwest (Galicia).

According to De la Fuente and Vives (1995), if the human capital differences in Spain were eliminated, the regional disparities would decrease by one sixth, confirming that imbalances in human capital endowments were favouring regional divergences. For the period of 1980–2007, Ramos et al. (2011) found that only the proportion of tertiary graduates helped convergence, while alternative human capital measures had no effect. Similarly, for the period 1960–1997, Manca (2012) concluded that Spanish regions that increased the share of workers with tertiary education were able to close the gap between the richest regions at a faster pace.

Regarding the effects of labour migration, Raymond and Garcia (1996) found that the convergence process observed in Spain since the 1960s slowed down and eventually stopped due to an increase in the internal migration rates from the poorest to the richest regions. A similar result was obtained by Maza (2006) for the period 1995–2002, who concluded that the internal migration trends have offset the regional convergence of GDP per capita. Focusing on the movements of the foreign-born, Hierro and Maza (2010) demonstrated that the movements of these individuals were significantly different from other migration flows and that foreign-born flows contributed positively to the regional convergence among Spanish regions, though at a reduced scale.

Summing up, our review identifies some significant trends, bearing in mind the aforementioned limitations regarding the amount of research on the two larger and on the two smaller countries under analysis. Although for both Greece and Portugal there is limited knowledge on the role that human capital has been playing in regional convergence, the existing evidence suggests a positive influence of human capital endowments and flows and documents the existence of convergence clubs. We have far more evidence regarding Italy and Spain. For Italy, available research suggests that the current distribution of human capital across the country does not seem to favour the convergence between regions. Regarding the migration flows, these do not seem to be balancing the differences in human capital endowments between the least and the most developed regions. Overall, the distribution and adjustments of human capital seem to be contributing to the divergence found among Italian regions. In the Spanish case, the current scenario also seems to favour divergence. The ability of regions to obtain higher levels of human capital is predicted to reduce the development gaps observed across the country. Similar to the Italian experience, the current internal migration rates seem to be blocking the convergence process among Spanish regions. In conclusion, although human capital seems to play a relevant role in regional dynamics, further research is needed in order to better understand the links between the formation of human capital and regional development in Southern European countries.

14.4.2 HEIs and Human Capital Growth Effects in Southern Europe

The analysis of the role of HEIs for regional growth is still largely unstudied in Southern Europe. Part of the explanation comes from the limited communication between higher education research and regional development studies (Pinheiro et al. 2012). Moreover, most of the work about the contribution of human capital has been done at the national level. Nevertheless, there are a few studies that may help us to build a preliminary picture on those interactions and their significance for Southern Europe.

Regarding the effects of HEIs in new firm creation and performance, Piergiovanni et al. (1997) investigated the source of innovative inputs for small Italian firms and concluded that while bigger firms benefited more from the presence of industrial R&D, smaller firms benefited more from university research. Similar evidence had also been found by Link and Rees for the United States (1990). More recently, Colombo et al. (2010) studied how new technology-based firms located close to Italian universities react to university research and they concluded that the quality of research undertaken by HEIs was important for the growth of academic based start-ups, but not for the growth of non-academic new technology-based firms.

For Spain, Barrio-Castro and Garcia-Quevedo (2005) showed that university research impacted positively on regional innovation output, in a context of regional expansion of the higher education system. Acosta et al. (2011) analysed the effect of three channels of spillovers on the location of new businesses: knowledge-based graduates, research activities, and technological knowledge. Their overall conclusion confirmed that the positive externalities that may arise from the proximity to HEIs—namely through the easier access to knowledge-based graduates—were crucial to the location decisions of new businesses. Though there is also limited evidence about Portugal, Baptista and Mendonça (2010) provided some results suggesting that a higher presence of universities in a municipality, as well as a larger number of students and graduates, had positive and significant effects on new knowledge-based firm creation at the regional-level.

Overall, and despite the limitations regarding the number of studies, the literature suggests a positive effect of university activities on regional dynamics in Southern Europe. Either by promoting the creation of new firms (more specifically, knowledge-based firms), or by enhancing worker productivity and inducing higher innovation rates, HEIs have been found to play a beneficial role to the regions where they are established.

14.5 Higher Education's Role in the Formation of Human Capital in Southern Europe: A Brief Look at the Regional Distribution of Enrolments

In an attempt to analyse in a very exploratory way the potential role of higher education as an engine for the production of human capital and, indirectly, for regional growth, we now provide some descriptive statistics for the NUTS II regions of the four countries covered in this book. We look at the proportion of enrolled students in higher education (in total regional population) and regional GDP per capita, in order to find whether (or not) any significant association exists between these indicators.

Our data comes from two sources. GDP per capita and population for each NUTS II regions were obtained from EUROSTAT. The number of enrolled students was collected from the EUMIDA project, which covers the academic year of 2008/2009. Since we are focusing on the potential role that public HEIs might have in the reduction of regional inequalities in terms of human capital, we only consider public HEIs in this analysis.[5]

We compared the association between the two variables—the proportion of enrolled students in the region and regional GDP per capita—for each of the four Southern European countries under study. Table 14.1 reports and compares these statistics for all NUTS II regions.

Given that it is hard to identify any patterns in the association between both variables from Table 14.1, we have calculated the correlation coefficients between those variables. Additionally, we present the respective scatterplots for each country, in an attempt to find any association between public HEIs' role as human capital generators and regional disparities inducers.

Some NUTS II regions could possibly be excluded from this exercise due to their special characteristics. In Spain, two regions (Ceuta and Melilla) are actually excluded, being two autonomous cities with small population and with no presence of HEIs. In Italy, we also exclude the regions of Valle d'Aosta and South-Tyrol given their small populations, lack of presence of HEIs, mountainous

[5]The EUMIDA Project (EUMIDA 2010) was carried out under the European Commission (Directorate General [DG] Research, DG Education and Culture, and EUROSTAT). Data collections were performed at the country level and included 1518 public and 931 private HEIs in the academic year of 2008/09. Data cover HEIs from 27 countries: the European Union member states (excluding Croatia, Denmark and France) plus Norway and Switzerland. The dataset includes information on the regions where each HEI is located. However, only the total number of enrolled students is provided, and this number is not divided by regions. Therefore, for institutions present in multiple regions, we cannot distinguish the actual number of enrolled students per region. For simplicity, we assume that the number of students is equally divided between the different regions, though we will bear in mind possible implications of this assumption. The weight of the private sectors varies significantly between the different countries in our analysis, being very small in Greece and much more significant in Portugal. Removing the private sector will result in a bias favoring the less developed regions, since it is documented that private institutions are usually located in the richest regions of the country (Teixeira et al. 2014).

Table 14.1 Proportion of enrolled students in the regional population and GDP per capita indexes in the NUTS II regions of the countries in analysis

Regions	Proportion of Enrolled (country = 100)	GDP per Capita (country = 100)	Regions	Proportion of Enrolled (country = 100)	GDP per Capita (country = 100)
Portugal			Lombardia	67.67	128.57
Norte	86.61	79.49	South Tyrol	0.81	137.14
Algarve	76.64	110.26	Veneto	80.86	115.24
Centro	105.30	82.05	Friuli-Venezia Giulia	100.55	113.33
Lisboa	129.96	139.74	Emilia-Romagna	N/A	N/A
Alentejo	83.29	91.03	Toscana	122.87	106.67
Açores	54.94	93.59	Umbria	133.51	93.33
Madeira	47.42	132.05	Marche	N/A	N/A
Spain			Lazio	140.73	114.29
Galicia	101.87	88.46	Abruzzo	159.20	82.86
Asturias	101.30	93.27	Molise	105.82	78.10
Cantabria	76.63	96.15	Campania	112.44	62.86
Basque Community	84.29	128.85	Puglia	87.87	64.76
Navarre	48.95	125.00	Basilicata	51.47	70.48
La Rioja	81.69	109.62	Calabria	99.56	63.81
Aragon	97.51	110.58	Sicilia	110.26	64.76
Madrid	131.86	128.85	Sardegna	108.43	75.24
Castille–Leon	121.12	94.23	*Greece*		
Castille-La Mancha	55.08	81.73	Anatoliki Makedonia	90.00	73.12
Extremadura	84.72	68.27	Kentriki Makedonia	122.56	79.57

(continued)

Table 14.1 (continued)

Regions	Proportion of Enrolled (country = 100)	GDP per Capita (country = 100)	Regions	Proportion of Enrolled (country = 100)	GDP per Capita (country = 100)
Catalonia	85.94	115.38	Dytiki Makedonia	147.07	91.40
Valencian Community	104.86	90.38	Thessalia	67.55	76.34
Balearic Islands	50.58	106.73	Ipeiros	149.64	68.82
Andalusia	114.57	76.92	Ionia Nisia	48.46	93.55
Region of Murcia	90.70	84.62	Dytiki Ellada	163.20	72.04
Canary Islands	87.93	85.58	Sterea Ellada	62.06	91.40
Ceuta	0.00	87.50	Peloponnisos	30.01	80.65
Melilla	0.00	81.73	Attiki	101.95	130.11
Italy			Voreio Aigaio	83.28	82.80
Piemonte	78.38	108.57	Notio Aigaio	1.32	122.58
Valle d'Aosta	0	126.67	Kriti	113.69	90.32
Liguria	76.41	105.71			

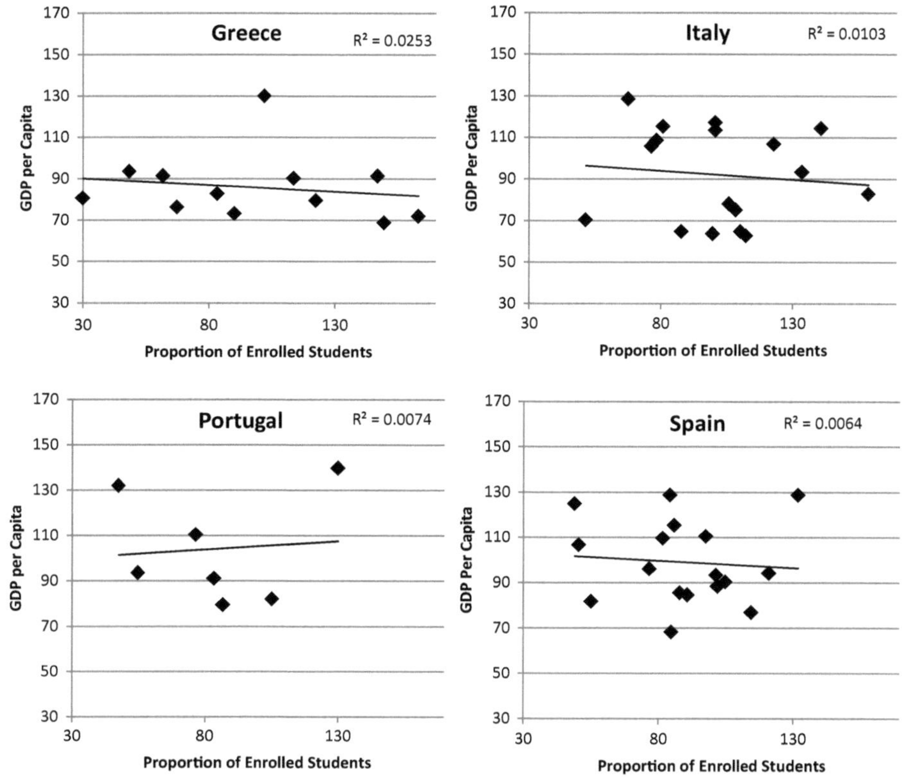

Fig. 14.1 Scatterplots between the proportion of enrolled students and GDP per capita indexes

characteristics, and huge bordering influences with the neighbouring countries. Emilia-Romagna and Marche are also excluded due to the lack of information from the EUROSTAT on their GDP per capita. For Greece, we exclude the region of Notio Aigaio because it is composed of a huge number of islands, which raises some challenges in the establishment of HEIs, resulting in a low number of enrolled students. The inclusion of these regions significantly affects the results, confirming that their inclusion could represent an important source of distortion due to these regions' characteristics.

From the scatterplots (Fig. 14.1), we clearly see that the correlation (measured by the R-Squared, which in this case coincides with the square of the correlation coefficient) between the potential human capital formation and current GDP per capita is weak and statistically irrelevant.[6,7] In other words, richer and poorer

[6]The global significance tests for the regression yielded $p = 0.748$ for Spain; $p = 0.611$ for Greece, $p = 0.695$ for Italy and $p = 0.855$ for Portugal.

[7]Table 14.2 in the Appendix shows the sensitivity of the results towards the presence of certain regions.

regions with public HEIs do not seem to have a significantly different proportion of enrolled students in tertiary education.

This result could signal a possible divide between policy aims and the results already well-established in the literature: whereas human capital may be an important force driving regions to economic growth and possibly reducing regional disparities, the attention every region is given regarding the proportion of their population currently acquiring higher education does not seem to be associated with its GDP per capita levels. This, combined with the potentially undesired effects of human capital migration, may point out that current efforts to reduce the human capital disparities within countries—and consequently, to reduce the existing GDP per capita differences—are not enough.

We must however highlight a number of limitations that may have a significant influence on the results obtained from this preliminary analysis. This exercise may be biased towards a convergent behaviour and therefore, the real results may be hiding that most developed regions are actually capturing most of the benefits from the overall human capital formation in the country. The first limitation concerns the data constraints. Equally dividing the students between regions where the HEIs are located favours the least developed regions in our study, because larger HEIs, which tend to be located in richer regions, usually open smaller establishments away from their region of origin. Therefore, the equal proportion of students we have allocated to the poorer regions may actually be favouring them in this example.

A second limitation is the exclusion of the private sector in our study. Private HEIs are usually located in richer regions, where they find a larger potential demand for higher education, which is an important driver of these for-profit institutions (Teixeira et al. 2014). Therefore, in countries where the private sector is relevant—as happens in Portugal, Spain and Italy—the actual weight of enrolled students is higher in richer regions than shown in our analysis.

Another limitation concerns the effect of post-graduation migration movements. The fact that a region generates human capital is not *per se* a condition for the human capital levels to increase in the region. Finally, there are particular specificities of NUTS II regions, which cannot be entirely captured by this preliminary analysis, such as their political setting, demographic and economic structure. The/A research agenda should thus try to cover these issues.

A final limitation of our exercise is the inability to disaggregate the enrolled students by field of study. The field of studies is naturally critical in determining the relative value of tertiary graduates to its region, given that there is an increasing pressure to have programs that are adapted to the regional context where the HEI is inserted. Unfortunately, our exercise does not capture these differences, leaving this question open for additional future research.

14.6 Concluding Remarks

In this chapter we reviewed prior evidence of the role that human capital formation and HEIs may play in regional convergence, focusing on four Southern European countries. Available results point out that universities and other HEIs have a relevant effect on some variables related to regional economic dynamics, by promoting human capital formation, new venture creation and productivity improvements. This was a first exploration into the complex relationship between higher education and regional economic dynamics, since there is an important set of factors that may change human capital patterns in a given region, and consequently its impact on regional economic growth and development. Nonetheless, despite some limitations, we believe that this preliminary analysis provides a snapshot of the regional disparities in human capital creation and development, identifying a number of issues that future research can consider in their empirical analyses.

Our main finding from this review underlines the influence that HEIs may play at the regional scale, especially if coupled with other favourable characteristics of the region. In particular, regions will only benefit with the presence of high human capital levels if there are the minimum conditions to absorb those high-skill individuals. Otherwise, most of the educated labour force may migrate, and most of the regional investments in human capital upgrading may end up favouring other regions (typically, the richer ones) and potentially reinforcing existing regional disparities. Policy incentives towards new firm formation, especially among recent graduates, may be part of the strategy aimed at reducing regional disparities and mitigating human capital imbalances caused by migration. The promotion of stronger university-industry links and funding support for new R&D projects based on specific regional industries may also be possible routes. Improving these conditions would directly and indirectly imply the creation of opportunities for graduates to work and stay in the given region, and for the benefits of the presence of high human capital to be internalized there.

The challenges and the complexities suggested by the analysis indicate that HEIs are a necessary but insufficient condition and that their presence needs to be articulated through a broader strategy which needs to be coordinated at a more aggregated level. It also highlights how intertwined higher education and regional policies are in this respect and the need to devise congruent policies for both dimensions, especially in more peripheral economic regions. Looking at the higher education side, without an efficient regional policy there is a risk that graduates will move elsewhere as the local economic dynamics will be insufficient to retain and take advantage of the human capital's potential. Looking at the regional policy, not coordinating it with the particular dynamics of HEIs also risks being ineffective, as they need to internalize those objectives in order to contribute to a successful growth path at the regional level. Thus, this points towards the need for greater interaction and coordination between leading actors in higher education and regional policies in order to promote more cohesive and effective economic policies through the qualification of human capital.

Appendix

Table 14.2 Sensitivity of correlation coefficients to the inclusion of specific regions

Spain		Italy		Greece	
All Regions	0.1534	All Regions	−0.4468	All Regions	−0.4135
Without Ceuta; Melilla	−0.0802	Without South Tyrol; Valle d'Aosta	−0.1016	Without Notio Aigaio	−0.1592

References

Abel J, Deitz R (2012) Do colleges and universities increase their region's human capital? J Econ Geogr 12:667–691

Acosta M, Coronado D, Flores E (2011) University spillovers and new business location in high-technology sectors: Spanish evidence. Small Bus Econ 36:365–376

Andersson R, Quigley J, Wilhelmsson M (2004) University decentralization as regional policy: the Swedish experiment. J Econ Geogr 4:371–388

Andersson R, Quigley J, Wilhelmsson M (2009) Urbanization productivity and innovation: evidence from investment in higher education. J Urban Econ 66:2–15

Anselin L (1988) Model validation in spatial econometrics: a review and evaluation of alternative approaches. Int Reg Sci Rev 11(3):279–316

Anselin L, Varga A, Acs Z (1997) Local geographic spillovers between university research and high technology innovations. J Urban Econ 42:422–448

Arena P, Button K, Lall S (2000) Do regional economies converge? Int Adv Econ Res 6(1):1–14

Arrow K (1962) Economic welfare and the allocation of resources for invention. In: Nelson R (ed) The rate and direction of inventive activity. Princeton University Press, Princeton

Asteriou D, Agiomirgianakis G (2001) Human capital and economic growth: time series evidence from Greece. J Policy Model 23:481–489

Audretsch D, Lehmann E, Warning S (2005) University spillovers and new firm location. Res Policy 34:1113–1122

Badinger H, Tondl G (2003) Trade, human capital, and innovation: the engines of European regional growth in the 90s. In: Fingleton B (ed) European regional growth: advances in spatial science. Springer, Berlin, pp 215–239

Baptista R, Mendonça J (2010) Proximity to knowledge sources and the location of knowledge-based start-ups. Ann Reg Sci 45:5–29

Baptista R, Lima F, Mendonça J (2011) Establishment of higher education institutions and new firm entry. Res Policy 40:751–760

Barrio-Castro T, García-Quevedo J (2005) Effects of university research on the geography of innovation. Reg Stud 39(9):1217–1229

Bartel A, Lichtenberg F (1987) The comparative advantage of educated workers in implementing new technology. Rev Econ Stat 69(1):1–11

Bartkowska M, Riedl A (2012) Regional convergence clubs in Europe: identification and conditioning factors. Econ Model 29:22–31

Basile R (2008) Regional economic growth in Europe: a semiparametric spatial dependence approach. Pap Reg Sci 87(4):527–544

Baumont C, Ertur C, Le Gallo G (2003) Spatial convergence clubs and the European growth process, 1980–1995. In: Fingleton B (ed) European regional growth: advances in spatial science. Springer, Berlin, pp 131–158

Benos K, Karagiannis S (2013) Do cross-section dependence and parameter heterogeneity matter? Evidence on human capital and productivity in Greece. MPRA Working Paper No. 53326

Capasso S, Carillo M, Siano R (2012) Migration flows, structural change and growth convergence: a panel data analysis of the Italian regions. Manch Sch 80(4):468–498
Cardoso C, Pentecost E (2011a) Regional growth and convergence: the role of human capital in the Portuguese regions. Loughborough University Department of Economics Discussion Paper Series 2011-03
Cardoso C, Pentecost E (2011b) Human capital and spatial heterogeneity in the Iberian countries' regional growth and convergence. Loughborough University Department of Economics Discussion Paper Series 2011-04
Casper S (2013) The spill-over theory reversed: the impact of regional economies on the commercialization of university science. Res Policy 42:1313–1324
Chatterton P, Goddard J (2000) The response of higher education institutions to regional needs. Eur J Educ 35(4):475–496
Ciccone A (2004) Human capital as a factor of growth and employment at the regional level: the case of Italy. Final Report, Universitat Pompeu Fabra and CEPR
Colombo M, D'Adda M, Piva E (2010) The contribution of university research to the growth of academic start-ups: an empirical analysis. J Technol Transfer 35:113–140
Coniglio N, Prota F (2008) Human capital accumulation and migration in a peripheral EU region: the case of Basilicata. Pap Reg Sci 87(1):78–95
Dall'erba S (2005a) Distribution of regional income and regional funds in Europe 1989–1999: an exploratory spatial data analysis. Ann Reg Sci 39:121–148
Dall'erba S (2005b) Productivity convergence and spatial dependence among Spanish regions. J Geogr Sys 7:207–227
Dall'erba S, Le Gallo J (2008) Regional convergence and the impact of European structural funds over 1989–1999: a spatial econometric analysis. Pap Reg Sci 87(2):219–244
De la Fuente A, Vives X (1995) Infrastructure and education as instruments of regional policy: evidence from Spain. Econ Policy 10(20):11–51
DiGiacinto V, Nuzzo G (2006) Explaining labour productivity differentials across Italian regions: the role of socio-economic structure and factor endowments. Pap Reg Sci 85(2):299–320
Duranton G, Monastiriotis V (2002) Mind the gaps: the evolution of regional earnings inequalities in the U.K., 1982–1997. J Reg Sci 42(2):219–256
Etzkowitz H, Leydesdorff L (1997) Introduction: universities in the global knowledge economy. In: Etzkowitz H, Leydesdorff L (eds) Universities and the global knowledge economy: a triple helix of university-industry-government relations. Pinter, London, pp 1–8
Etzo I (2008) Internal migration and growth in Italy. MPRA Working Paper No. 8642
Etzo I (2011) The determinants of the recent interregional migration flows in Italy: a panel data analysis. J Reg Sci 51(5):948–966
EUMIDA (2010) Final study report. Available at http://ec.europa.eu/research/era/docs/en/eumida-final-report.pdf. Accessed 23 Oct 2013
Faggian A, McCann P (2009) Human capital graduate migration and innovation in British regions. Camb J Econ 33:317–333
Felice E (2012) Regional convergence in Italy, 1891–2001: testing human and social capital. Cliometrica 6:267–306
Fingleton B, McCombie J (1998) Increasing returns and economic growth: some evidence for manufacturing from the European union regions. Oxf Econ Pap 50:89–105
Fischer M, Varga A (2003) Spatial knowledge spillovers and university research: evidence from Austria. Ann Reg Sci 37:303–322
Franco M, Haase H, Lautenschlager A (2010) Do universities impact regional employment? A cross-regional comparison of migration effects. Actual Probl Econ 7(109):301–312
Goldin C, Katz L (1998) The origins of state-level differences in the public provision of higher education: 1890–1940. Am Econ Rev 88(2):303–308
Goldstein H, Drucker G (2006) The economic development impacts of universities on regions: do size and distance matter? Econ Dev Q 20(1):22–43
Gunasekara C (2006) The generative and developmental roles of universities in regional innovation systems. Sci Public Policy 33(2):137–150

Hierro M, Maza A (2010) Per capita income convergence and internal migration in Spain: are foreign-born migrants playing an important role? Pap Reg Sci 89(1):90–107
Huber P, Tondl G (2012) Migration and regional convergence in the European union. Empirica 39:439–460
Huggins R, Johnston A, Steffenson R (2008) Universities, knowledge networks and regional policy. Camb J Reg Econ Soc 1:321–340
Johnson H (1965) The economics of the "brain drain": the Canadian case. Minerva 3(3):299–311
Justman M, Thisse J (1997) Implications of the mobility of skilled labor for local public funding of higher education. Econ Lett 55:409–412
Kitagawa F (2004) Universities and regional advantage: higher education and innovation policies in English regions. Eur Plan Stud 12(6):835–852
Lindelof P, Lofsten H (2004) Proximity as a resource base for competitive advantage: university-industry links for technology transfer. J Technol Transfer 29:311–326
Link A, Rees J (1990) Firm size, university based research and returns to R&D. Small Bus Econ 2:25–32
Lopéz-Bazo E, Vaya E, Mora A, Suriñach J (1999) Regional economic dynamics and convergence in the European union. Ann Reg Sci 33:343–370
Maffezzoli M (2006) Convergence across Italian regions and role of technological catch-up. Top Macroecon 6(1), Article 15
Manca F (2012) Human capital composition and economic growth at the regional level. Reg Stud 46(10):1367–1388
Mankiw G, Romer D, Weil D (1992) A contribution to the empirics of economic growth. Q J Econ 107(2):407–437
Martin R, Sunley P (1998) Slow convergence? The new endogenous growth theory and regional development. Econ Geogr 74(3):201–227
Maza A (2006) Migrations and regional convergence: the case of Spain. Jahrbuch fur Regionalwissenschaft 26:191–202
Moreno R, Theran B (1997) Location and the growth of nations. J Econ Growth 2:399–418
Nelson R (1959) The simple economics of basic scientific research. J Polit Econ 67:297–306
Neven D, Gouyette C (1995) Regional Convergence in the European Community. J Common Mark Stud 33(1):47–65
Overman H, Puga D (2002) Unemployment clusters across Europe's regions and countries. Econ Policy 17(34):115–148
Paci R, Saba A (1998) The empirics of regional economic growth in Italy: 1951–1993. CRENos Working Paper
Perkmann M, Tartari V, McKelvey M, Autio E, Brostrom A, D'Este P, Fini R, Geuna A, Grimaldi R, Hughes A, Krabel S, Kitson M, Llerena P, Lissoni F, Salter A, Sobrero M (2013) Academic engagement and commercialisation: a review of the literature on university–industry relations. Res Policy 42:423–442
Petrakos G, Artelaris G (2008) Regional inequalities in Greece. In: Coccossis H, Psycharis Y (eds) Regional analysis and policy: the Greek experience. Springer, Heidelberg, pp 121–140
Petrakos G, Saratsis Y (2000) Regional inequalities in Greece. Pap Reg Sci 79:57–74
Piergiovanni R, Santarelli E, Vivarelli M (1997) From which source do small firms derive their innovative inputs? Some evidence from Italian industry. Rev Ind Organ 12:243–258
Pinheiro R, Benneworth P, Jones GA (eds) (2012) Universities and regional development: a critical assessment of tensions and contradictions. Routledge, Milton Park
Piras R (2013) Can the augmented solow model with migration explain the Italian internal brain drain? Labour 27(2):140–163
Ponds R, van Oort R, Frenken K (2010) Innovation, spillovers and university-industry collaboration: an extended knowledge production function approach. J Econ Geogr 10:231–255
Quah D (1996) Regional convergence clusters around Europe. Eur Econ Rev 40:951–958
Ramos R, Surinach J, Artis M (2011) Human capital spillovers, productivity and regional convergence in Spain. Pap Reg Sci 89(2):436–447

Ramos R, Surinach J, Artis M (2012) Regional economic growth and human capital: the role of over-education. Reg Stud 46(10):1389–1400
Raymond J, Garcia B (1996) Distribución regional de la renta y movimientos migratorios. Papeles de Economía Española 67:185–201
Ritsila J, Ovaskainen M (2001) Migration and regional centralization of human capital. Appl Econ 33(3):317–325
Rodriguez-Pose A, Fratesi U (2004) Between development and social policies: the impact of European structural funds in objective 1 regions. Reg Stud 38(1):97–113
Rodriguez-Pose A, Vilalta-Bufi M (2005) Education, migration, and job satisfaction: the regional returns of human capital in the EU. J Econ Geogr 5:545–566
Romer P (1990) Endogenous technological change. J Polit Econ 98(5):S71–S102
Schultz T (1993) The economic importance of human capital in modernization. Educ Econ 1 (1):13–19
Stahlecker T, Koschatzky K (2004) On the significance of geographical proximity for the structure and development of newly founded knowledge intensive business service firms. Working Papers Firms and Regions, No. R2/2004. Fraunhofer Institute
Suedekum J (2005) The pitfalls of regional education policy. FinaznzArchiv 61(3):327–352
Summers R, Heston A (1988) A new set of international comparisons of real product and price level estimates for 130 countries, 1950–1985. Rev Income Wealth 34(1):1–25
Teixeira P (2005) The human capital revolution in economics. Hist Econ Ideas 13(2):129–148
Teixeira P, Rocha V, Biscaia R, Cardoso M (2014) Policy changes, marketisation trends and spatial dispersion in European higher education: comparing public and private sectors. Camb J Reg Econ Soc 7(2):271–288
Tsamadias C, Prontzas P (2012) The effect of education on economic growth in Greece over the 1960–2000 period. Educ Econ 20(5):522–537

Ricardo Biscaia is an assistant professor at Universidade Portucalense Infante D. Henrique and an associate researcher at CIPES. He holds a PhD in Economics since January 2014, with a thesis on Location Theory. His main research interests are in the fields of Industrial Economics, Regional and Urban Economics and Higher Education Policies, the latter being focused on Higher Education funding and bibliometrics. Some of his work has been published in several Journals, such as Public Administration Review, Papers in Regional Science, Applied Economics, Higher Education, Studies in Higher Education or Cambridge Journal of Economics.

Pedro Teixeira is Associate Professor in Economics and Vice Rector for Academic Affairs at the University of Porto and Director of CIPES—Centre of Research on Higher Education Policy. He is Secretary General of CHER—Consortium of Higher Education Researchers (since 2013) and member of the Scientific Board of RESUP. He is the Advisor on Higher Education and Science to the President of Portugal (since April 2016). He is a member of the Board of the Bial Foundation (since 2015) and a member of the Education Council of the Foundation Francisco Manuel dos Santos (since 2013). His research focuses on the economics of higher education and the history of economic thought, and his work has been published in leading scientific Journals including European Journal of History of Economic Thought, Higher Education, Higher Education Quarterly, Journal of Economic Methodology, Public Administration Review, Research Policy and Studies in Higher Education.

Vera Rocha is a Postdoc in Economics of Entrepreneurship at Copenhagen Business School (Department of Innovation and Organizational Economics). Her main research interests are related to higher education (HE funding, competition and diversification), industrial organisation (firm and industry dynamics, new venture creation) and labour economics (wage differentials, human capital and occupational choice), with focus on entrepreneurial careers and entrepreneurship dynamics.

Margarida F. Cardoso is Assistant Professor in the Biomedical School of University of Porto, Portugal: ICBAS—Instituto de Ciências Biomédicas Abel Salazar, in the scientific areas of biostatistics and epidemiology. Her research interests include Epidemiology, Public Health and Education. She is co-author of several publications in the area of higher education as a result of her collaboration with CIPES and has also publications in the biomedical area.

Part IV
Postscript

Chapter 15
Implications for European Economic Integration After the Brexit

Alberto Amaral

15.1 Europe or the Triumph of Failed Ideas

Paul Krugman (2010) in his New York Times column writes about the "strange triumph of failed ideas" referring to the increasing domination of free-market fundamentalists despite being wrong about everything. This is also the title of a book *"A triumph of failed ideas. European models of capitalism in the crisis"*, edited by Steffen Lehndorff (2012). In the introduction of the book, Lehndorff argues:

> The EU single market project in general and EMU in particular are fatally flawed due to their unbalanced focus on free markets without adequate countervailing social and labour standards, and on price stability and austerity without adequate reference to sustainable economic development, employment and social equity (Lehndorff 2012, pp. 23)

Indeed, the European Union has been facing a number of significant problems, namely in terms of high unemployment levels (unacceptably high among the young population), and slow economic growth. Even before the crisis the Eurozone was characterised by a very low growth rate compared to the rest of the world (Cafruny and Ryner 2007; Sapir 2003). In 2000 the European Council proudly announced the Lisbon strategy aimed at making the European Union "the most competitive and dynamic knowledge-based economy in the world, capable of sustainable economic growth with more and better jobs and greater social cohesion" (European Council 2000).

Dehousse (2002) considers that the Lisbon strategy has come to life as left of centre governments, elected in the mid-1990s, had concerns with social problems and tried to compensate for the effects of building the European Monetary Union (EMU) and, as Scharpf formulated later, an internal market that favoured

A. Amaral (✉)
University of Porto, Porto, Portugal
e-mail: aamaral@cipes.up.pt

M. Fonseca, U. Fratesi (eds.), *Regional Upgrading in Southern Europe*, Advances in Spatial Science, DOI 10.1007/978-3-319-49818-8_15

liberalisation and competition rules over social protection rules (Scharpf 2006). The Lisbon strategy also proposes to modernise the European social model by increasing employment, protecting an ageing population and fighting against social exclusion.

For a number of more sceptical authors, that proposed virtuous combination of economic, social and environmental measures which at the same time allow a nation/region "to attain growth, productivity, social inclusion and sustainable development... looks like the quintessential contemporary utopia: the end of political trade-offs" (Creel et al. 2005) or, as others already had argued before, simultaneously offering employment, income equality and fiscal restraint was just impossible (Iversen and Wren 1998).

Unfortunately, those sceptics were right and the Lisbon strategy proved to be a failure, as demonstrated by the present high employment levels in Europe and the extremely slow growth capacity of its economy. Progressively, Europe has reinforced its neo-liberal political stance, giving priority to the development of internal markets at any cost, to the detriment of socially friendly policies. It is interesting to note that the European Court of Justice systematically upholds the position of the European Commission, as recognised by the Norwegian Confederation of Trade Unions—*Fagforbundet*:

> From the start, the ECJ has regarded it as its supreme duty to realise the fundamental principles of the EU Treaty on the free movement of goods, services, capital and persons. Whatever the politicians cannot—or dare not—clarify, is clarified by the judges in the ECJ (Fagforbundet 2008, p. 4).

To promote the development of a knowledge society, the Lisbon strategy needed a well-educated work force, which made the inclusion of a human capital development component necessary. This led to its appropriation of the Bologna process and the Bologna Declaration (1999) had already proposed the concept of a 'Europe of Knowledge' as an 'irreplaceable factor of social and human growth'. However, the implementation of an internal European market once more took precedence over social problems. The replacement of 'employment' with 'employability', one of the buzzwords of the Bologna Process, has contributed to the individualisation of social problems (Streckeisen 2009) by making unemployment or poverty the responsibility of individual misconduct. Under the Lisbon Strategy, social problems derive from deficient knowledge, education and (occupational) training, being the responsibility of each individual to invest in lifelong education in order to remain employable (Sin et al. 2016).

Creel et al. (2005) argue that the incapacity of the EU to design an economic union capable of sustaining the monetary union may be the result of the incapacity of the EU "to develop the coherent economic policy institutions able to foster its potential growth" and consider that "implementing 'structural reforms' of the kind needed by the EU-25... without a coherent growth-friendly macroeconomic governance is almost an impossible task" (Creel et al. 2005, p. 4). The use of the Open Method of Coordination and the resource of naming and shaming mechanisms is a very poor tool for the difficult task of building an economic union. And those authors add in a rather provocative way:

> . . .a global strategy for the EU can not have for principle to reward the virtuous and blame the vicious. This method of "governance by morality" has proven a failure many times in the EU history: The powerful instruments at EU disposal should not be used (and wasted) to divide and rank member states by order of merit, but to unite them in a mutually beneficial strategy (Creel et al. 2005, p. 21)

The sovereign debt crisis has exacerbated the problems and made evident the inadequacy of the policies implemented at the EU level. Ball et al. (2011, p. 20), based on large scale analyses published by the IMF, argue that "slamming on the brakes too quickly will hurt the recovery and worsen job prospects" and that "fiscal consolidations typically have the short-run effect of reducing incomes and raising unemployment. . . are contractionary, with no evidence of any surge of consumption or investment. . . and add to the pain of those who are likely to be already suffering the most—the long-term unemployed" (p. 22). Therefore, quoting Christine Lagarde (2011), they propose a "slower pace of consolidation combined with policies to support growth". However, in the cases of Greece and Portugal, the imposed rate of consolidation was too fast and produced unacceptable and unforeseen GDP losses.

At present, many European citizens are feeling that the European dream was transformed into a nightmare. The interventions of the Commission lack the support of democratic principles and more and more there is the sensation that European citizens no longer have control over their life conditions and choices. By showing total incapacity to deal in an efficient and timely way with problems such as those of immigration, the Community has fostered a resurgence of nationalisms, which has already found concrete expression in the decision of the UK to quit. In many countries the conditions of life have deteriorated, the Commission and the Council have shown incapacity in dealing with the sluggish growth rate of the EU economy by using austerity policies, there are unacceptable unemployment levels, employment is becoming increasingly volatile and there is a growing feeling of unfair competition from immigrants.

15.2 Regional Convergence

Convergence has been an important theme in the process of European economic integration. New accession countries had the hope that membership in the European Union would allow them to "catch up with EU living standards" (Bongardt and Torres 2013), which implied that they needed "to grow faster in a sustainable way to catch up with the EU average" (*ibid*). For instance, Pérez et al. consider that Spain has placed too much trust in the short-term benefits derived from the arrival of the Euro (Pérez et al. 2011) and Faiña et al. (Chap. 5) argue that looking at "Spain's economic policy in the last few decades would highlight excessive trust in economic integration in the EU, as today it is clear that integration in European markets and the short-term financial benefits of the Euro are not sufficient in order to face up to the challenges of the new economy and intensified competition on a global scale". There is no doubt that accession countries saw integration in the EU as becoming members of a rich club that would allow for the development of their economies and the improvement of their life conditions.

The EU has implanted a regional policy aimed at bringing about "concrete results, furthering economic and social cohesion to reduce the gap between the development levels of the various regions... The idea is to create potential so that the regions can fully contribute to achieving greater growth and competitiveness and, at the same time, to exchange ideas and best practices" (European Commission 2016). The EMU had been expected not only to provide for more macroeconomic stability in cohesion countries but also to intensify economic competition and to promote patterns of specialization.

However, there were indications that, despite European regional policies, convergence was far from being a reality and regional disparities at the country level were in some cases even increasing (Fonseca and Fratesi Chap. 1). The sovereign debt crisis has put the lack of convergence (once more) at the top of the European agenda. The former cohesion countries—Greece, Ireland, Portugal and Spain (but also Italy)—began to diverge with respect to the Eurozone core countries in terms of real GDP growth.

15.3 Convergence and the Southern European Countries

The publication of this new book is therefore very timely to understand the difficulties of the Southern European countries and their regions. Why has the European regional policy failed? Are there structural problems or governance problems? Is it a question of lack of human capital? Is their slow growth an important factor in their negative risk assessment by financial markets? Are the present austerity policies adequate to solve those problems?

Fratesi (Chap. 3) refers to Affuso et al. to define three possible successful strategies to deal with the problems of countries with globalization: "increasing productivity through innovation, reconverting to higher phases in the production process and reconverting the regional sectoral structure" (Affuso et al. 2011). Fratesi lists a number of characteristics affecting the growth of the economies of Southern European countries:

> Low level infrastructure, inability to attract FDI [Foreign Direct Investment], difficult innovative patterns, politics and institutions, and to a large extent to weak human capital and especially to the inability to use it, all coupled with ineffective public policies, not directly targeting the upgrading of the economic structure but rather the infrastructure upon which the economy is built on, or the set-up of new businesses.

Fratesi argues that Southern European countries, in the period before the sovereign debt crisis, were following growth patterns compatible with the lower production phases and were never able to raise to higher functions despite investments in human capital development. The private sector economy was weak, relying on the creation of self-employment in small-businesses with low growth prospects, set-up by individuals to compensate for the lack of job opportunities.

Capello and Lenzi (Chap. 4) show that in Southern Europe "there are no regions in the most knowledge- and innovation-intensive group specialized in general-purpose technologies and with a more original and general knowledge base (i.e., the European science-based area)". They argue that all Southern European countries "share an innovation profile characterized by low R&D and patent intensity and somewhat lag behind the European average in terms of more traditional indicators of knowledge creation and innovation". However, "the four countries [Greece, Italy, Portugal and Spain] are ahead of the European average in terms of intensity of informal knowledge and process innovation" and Kalogeresis (Chap. 8) states that Southern European countries "are still focused on producing medium to low tech products and constitute an area of low competitiveness". Faiña et al. (Chap. 5), a propos of Spain, consider that "the specialisation of production has not strengthened the presence of innovative activities and those with a high technological content as would be expected from an advanced economy, but instead in traditional and highly cyclical sectors such as construction. Low productivity levels have affected nearly all of the country's activities".

Attracting Foreign Direct Investment (FDI) is another problem for Southern European countries. It is true that the Southern European countries were able to attract a number of foreign firms looking for low labour costs and public incentives resulting from the European Structural Funds. This represented a substantial contribution from foreign investment, although conditioned by low labour costs and the production of goods, which did not need very sophisticated technology. Unfortunately, the integration of the new Eastern European member states as a result of the European eastern enlargement has resulted in the relocation of many of those firms in search of even lower salaries and new public incentives. As mentioned by Fonseca and Fratesi (Chap. 1) those firms fled at a high speed, leaving behind unemployment and lower incomes, meaning that "regional upgrading in the lagging regions of Southern European countries has hence been interrupted before being achieved, and a trend to downgrading seems to be emerging, with the weakest regions risking being considered as liabilities to their own countries". Another important factor is the quality of national and regional governance (Resmini Chap. 6) (Rodriguez-Posé and Di Cataldo 2015). Charron et al. (2010) have defined an EU regional quality governance index, which can be related to the attractiveness of regions. Again Southern European countries show very poor levels of governance, both at regional and national levels.

Coniglio and Prota (Chap. 11) argue that "inducing changes in local firms which have a structural low demand of qualified workers might be more difficult than attracting new players and/or boosting the creation of new innovative firms". Investing in educating new scientists and engineers for attracting firms that make use of this scarce factor of production would probably be better "incentives rather than transitory financial support that are the cornerstone of investment attraction policies in the EU periphery".

15.4 The Human Capital Factor

Some chapters have tried to analyse the relations between human capital, employment (or population) and growth (Fonseca; Tselios et al.; Enrique López-Bazo; Coniglio and Prota; Biscaia et al.). López-Bazo et al. (Chap. 10) formulates the hypothesis that "the regional distribution of individuals' education would be a key driver of disparities in labour market outcomes and in regional responses to the crisis, and that the impact that education has on unemployment and wages varies depending on the region".

Figure 15.1 shows the education level of Portuguese and Spanish employers and workers against the European average. It makes evident why it is difficult for these countries to move to higher phases of the production process or why it is difficult to take advantage of upgraded human capital due to the very low qualification level of employers.

From the different chapters it is possible to conclude that human capital or education is a necessary but not sufficient ingredient for economic growth. Rodríguez-Pose and Vilalta-Bufi (2005) have identified differences in human capital development as barriers to convergence in the European Union and Tselios et al. (Chap. 7) have identified human capital as one of the major forces that

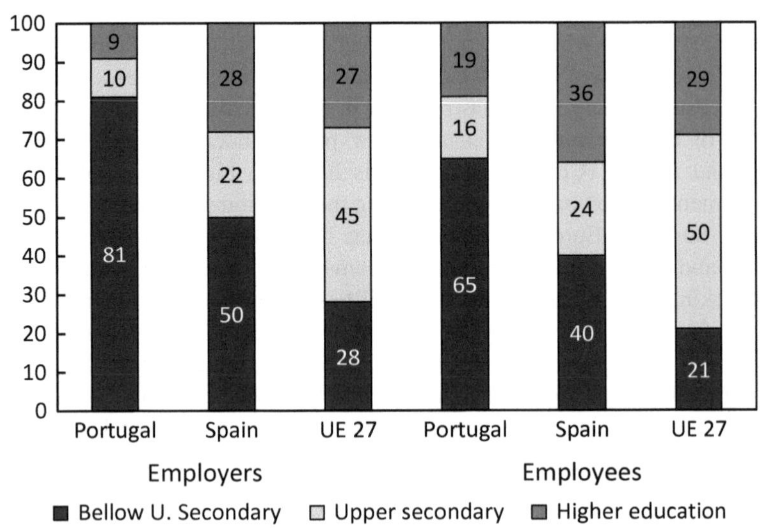

Fig. 15.1 Education level of workers and employers 2008, adapted from Instituto Nacional de Estatística (2010)

determine educational development. They have concluded that in the case of Greece the correlation between economic wealth and educational level seems to be very high. On the contrary, Basile (2008) concluded that the role of human capital in the convergence was non-linear. Coniglio and Prota (Chap. 11) also show that there is no clear correlation between economic performance of regions and their human capital endowment. These authors find that the higher the individual competences (measured by holding a PhD degree), the higher the likelihood of not using these skills in the current job or of being unemployed or employed in highly precarious occupations. There is also some anecdotal evidence that in Portugal, candidates for employment frequently hide holding a PhD to improve their chances of being hired.

The mismatch between education and the labour market is a most relevant problem of the Southern European countries as mentioned by several authors in this book (Coniglio and Prota, Lopez-Bazo and Bisacaia et al.). Well-educated people have a higher tendency to migrate if they do not find employment compatible with their qualifications in the area where they live (Fonseca; Coniglio and Prota; Biscaia et al.).

The low qualification level of many employers and the incapacity of moving into higher levels in the production process create a situation where there is an apparent inability to sufficiently utilise the educational endowment available to each region (Lopez-Bazo et al. Chap. 10). People with a university degree may find difficulty in obtaining employment compatible with their qualifications, which may lead to internal migrations to more developed regions or even to immigration, thus wasting most of the regional investments in human capital upgrading and destroying its contribution to regional economic growth. This explains some of the empirical findings, for instance that "the attention every region is given regarding the proportion of their population currently acquiring higher education does not seem to be associated with its GDP per capita levels" (Biscaia et al. Chap. 14) or the dysfunctional character of some labour markets where "even with a substantial rise in unemployment, as shown earlier, education continues to be non-influential in sorting individuals between employment and unemployment" (Lopez-Bazo et al. Chap. 10).

A final problem results from the minimum threshold levels of human capital, economic activity and investment in research and development activities before they can produce positive results. As argued by Biscaia et al. (Chap. 14) "human capital only seemed to have an effect on the economic growth of the core regions, suggesting that a minimum threshold of income and economic activity was necessary before human capital became relevant". The same argument is presented by Fonseca (Chap. 2): "The effects of the investment in research and development on the innovative potential of a region however, are conditioned by several factors including a minimum threshold of prior knowledge or human capital (Meusburger 2013; Rodriguez-Posé 2001; Charlot et al. 2015)".

15.5 Can the Problems Be Solved?

The book is not only an endless unfolding of the cruel reality that seems to emerge from the different chapters. There are also some suggestions about strategies and policies to improve the present situation. Capello and Lenzi (Chap. 4) mention that smaller firms and more traditional sectors "rely more on technologies embodied in machinery and equipment and on informal knowledge embedded in professionals rather than on formal knowledge (Conte and Vivarelli 2005; Piergiovanni et al. 1997). Therefore, they caution against the "one size fits all" policy suggested in the Europe 2020 agenda to increase R&D investments over GDP to improve European competitiveness. Investing in R&D without being able to reach the necessary minimum investment threshold may be just a waste of resources.

Capello and Lenzi (Chap. 4) suggest the implementation of smart innovation policies (Camagni and Capello 2013) "to increase the innovation capability of an area and to enhance local expertise in knowledge production and use". Such policies might include an R&D support policy, incentives for co-invented applications, promoting the upgrading of present specializations or shifting from old to new uses, and "adaptation of already existing innovations in order to reach particular market niches or specific territories".

Coniglio and Prota (Chap. 11) ask the question: "Are human capital promotion policies in the EU periphery predestined to be ineffective in terms of upgrading the productive system?" This raises the problem of the capacity of regional labour for absorption of well-qualified people who otherwise may move away through outmigration. They suggest that human capital upgrading policies must be coordinated with 'moving' qualified job opportunities into the periphery. Biscaia et al. (Chap. 14) propose creating "policy incentives towards new firm formation, especially among recent graduates," and the "promotion of stronger university-industry links and funding support for new R&D projects based on specific regional industries may also be possible routes".

Faiña et al. (Chap. 5) recommend that "in the future, it will be necessary to insist on greater rigour in the selection of investments, in order to guarantee a cost effectiveness and productivity in line with the capital resources" and several authors refer to the need to improve governance, both at the national and regional levels.

However, those suggestions are like trying to cure cancer by using aspirin while some more aggressive surgery will be necessary to save the patient. It is our opinion that improving the present situation requires a change in European policies to make them friendlier to economic growth.

To present our arguments we maintain that the varieties of the capitalism approach (Hall and Soskice 2001) contend that each state has its own model of capitalism, shaped by culture, history, mentality and economic-political system. National cases can be grouped under different models of market economies. Each model is characterised by particular macro-economic policies, market coordination models, institutional configurations and interactions among economic actors, approaches to skills development, work organisation, and welfare.

Lehndorff (2012) argues that instead of "varieties of capitalism", today Europe has "varieties of vulnerability" as "the predominance of neoliberalism is promoting the destabilization of national models of capitalism" (Lehndorff 2012, p. 10). "Core elements of the EU single market strategy had contributed to destabilise existing models ('negative integration'), given the weakness of countervailing powers aimed at social institution building at both national and EU levels" (ibid p. 9). He quotes Becker and Jäger (2011) who portray the crisis in terms of "unfolding contradictions between different national capitalisms, characterised by [broadly] financialised or by neo-mercantilist regimes of accumulation": in other words, a monetary union between an export-focused and surplus-oriented core and a periphery that is dependent on imports and capital inflow has proven to be "fatally flawed and unsustainable" (Lehndorff 2012, p. 23).

The sovereign debt crisis could be seen as an opportunity "to introduce corrections to the previous growth model, in which rising inequality was a prominent feature" (Leschke et al. 2011, p. 276). However, this was not to be so. "In the aftermath of the 'great recession', austerity policy dominates the scene. The obsession with cutting public expenditure is undermining or even blocking the road to recovery and the revitalisation of socio-economic models" (Lehndorff 2012, p. 16).

Becker and Jäger (2011: 17) argue that "the main political forces seek to restore as much as possible of the pre-crisis accumulation models, to radicalise neo-liberal policies and to weaken trade unions and other progressive forces" and Lehndorff cautions that the upcoming institutional design for a so-called economic government "must be blocked to give countries more room to breathe and, not least, for the sake of democratic legitimacy" (Lehndorff 2012, p. 23). Indeed, ongoing changes of the EU economic governance aim to entrench neo-liberal rule-based policy making mechanisms and increase the difficulty of implementing progressive policy changes. What is necessary is a reform of the European treaties to "establish the long-needed rebalancing of economic and social rights in order to put more emphasis on the reduction of inequality and to pave the way for more sustainable models of socio-economic development" (Lehndorff 2012, p. 24).

Becker and Jäger (2011) proposed this same idea of inevitable crisis. They argue that European economic integration was based on a division of labour between primarily financialised economies (importing goods and capital) and primarily export-oriented economies (exporting goods and providing credits). Easily accessible credit and low interest rates fuelled the escalating current account deficits. "The establishment of the Eurozone cemented uneven economic development trajectories in Europe and facilitated debt driven growth and the emergence of enormous unbalances in the EU. The crisis of European economies is the expression of a structural crisis of European integration" (Becker and Jäger 2011, p. 17).

However, the European crisis is not only a financial and political crisis, it is also an identity crisis. Ntampoudi (2014: 1) considers that the present diverse economic crises (global, sovereign debt and Eurozone) "pose considerable challenges on

European unity and solidarity by giving rise to nationalist movements, popular discontent and resistance towards the EU (Garton Ash 2012; Laquer 2012; Serricchio et al. 2013)". This was not unexpected and some even described it as "the chronicle of a crisis foretold" (Garton Ash 2012). Ntampoudi argues (2014, p. 3) this was the inevitable result of:

> . . . joining extremely different economies with disparate growth and exporting capacities, as well as deficits and debt rates, under a single currency with no fiscal union, lack of sufficient supervision and absence of substantial stabilising mechanisms (Baimbridge et al. 2012; Garton Ash 2012; Hadjimichalis 2011; Knedlik and von Schweinitz 2012; Lucarelli 2012; Müller 2012).

Ntampoudi (2014) believes there are four different identity areas: An international identity associated with the image of EU as a champion of peace, welfare, democracy and prosperity, an image profoundly tarnished by the Eurozone crisis; an economic and social identity, the celebrated European social model which Delors contrasted against the US pure market capitalism and is now being questioned due to diminishing labour rights and welfare responses; the crisis of diverse identity torn between a European character based on economic values such as efficiency, industriousness, work ethic and honesty or based on political values such as cosmopolitanism and solidarity which resulted in diminished perceptions of European belongingness; and finally, a united identity "related to the internal consistency of the Union understood as citizens support for continuous and further integration legitimised through the notions of unity and solidarity" which is confronted with disintegrating tendencies in the EU and suggestions of splits and exits, which have already come true in Brexit.

If nothing is made to reverse the present policies, disintegrating tendencies will increase and it is possible that in Southern Europe we will see voices calling for other exits growing louder. Can European politicians understand this possibility or will Commission officials continue to show their traditional arrogance and servility to capital and the markets?

References

Affuso A, Capello R, Fratesi U (2011) Globalization and competitive strategies in European vulnerable regions. Reg Stud 45(5):657–675

Baimbridge M, Burkitt B, Whyman PB (2012) The eurozone as a flawed currency area. Polit Q 83 (1):96–107

Ball L, Leigh D, Loungani P (2011) Painful medicine. Finance Dev 48(3):20–23

Basile R (2008) Regional economic growth in Europe: a semi-parametric spatial dependence approach. Pap Reg Sci 87(4):527–544

Becker J, Jäger J (2011) European integration in crisis: the centre-periphery divide, Paper presented at the 17th EuroMemo Workshop on Alternative Economic Policy, Vienna, 16–18 September 2011

Bologna Declaration (1999) The Bologna Declaration of 19 June 1999. Joint declaration of the European Ministers of Education, Bologna

Bongardt A, Torres F (2013) Forging sustainable growth: the issues of convergence of preferences and institutions in EMU. Intereconomics 48(2):72–92
Cafruny AW, Ryner JM (2007) Europe at Bay: in the shadow of US Hegemony. Lynne Rienner Publishers, Boulder
Camagni R, Capello R (2013) Regional innovation strategies and the EU regional policy reform: towards smart innovation policies. Growth Chang 44(2):355–389
Charlot S, Crescenzi R, Musolesi A (2015) Econometric modelling of the regional knowledge production function in Europe. J Econ Geogr 15:1227–1259
Charron N, Dijkstra L, Lapuente V (2010) Mapping quality of government in the European union: a study of national and sub-national variation, QoG Working Paper Series 2010:22
Conte A, Vivarelli M (2005) One or many knowledge production functions? Mapping innovative activity using microdata, IZA Discussion Papers 1878
Creel J, Laurent E, Le Cacheux J (2005) Delegation in inconsistency: the Lisbon strategy record as an Institutional Failure, Department d´études de l' OFCE, Sciences Po, https://hal-sciencespo.archives-ouvertes.fr/hal-00972772/document. Accessed 25 Feb 2015
Dehousse R (2002) The open method of coordination: a new policy paradigm? Paper presented at the First Pan-European Conference on European Union Politics, The Politics of European Integration: Academic Acquis and Future Challenges, Bordeaux, 26–28 September 2002
European Commission (2016) Why do we need regional policy? Regional Policy—Inforegio, http://ec.europa.eu/regional_policy/archive/policy/why/index_en.htm. Accessed 25 June 2016
European Council (2000) Lisbon European Council. 23 and 24 March 2000. Presidency Conclusions. (Lisbon Strategy), http://www.europarl.europa.eu/summits/lis1_en.htm
Fagforbundet (2008) The EU services directive and the public services—a Norwegian perspective. Fagforbundet, Oslo
Garton Ash T (2012) The crisis of Europe. Foreign Aff 91(5):2–15
Hadjimichalis C (2011) Uneven geographical development and socio-spatial justice and solidarity: European regions after the 2009 financial crisis. Eur Urban Reg Stud 18(3):254–274
Hall PA, Soskice D (2001) An introduction to varieties of capitalism. In: Hall PH, Soskice D (eds) Varieties of capitalism: the institutional foundations of comparative advantage. Oxford University Press, Oxford, pp 1–68
Instituto Nacional de Estatística (2010). Destaque. Informação à Comunicação Social, 01 April 2010
Iversen T, Wren A (1998) Equality, employment and budgetary restraint: the trilemma of the service economy. World Politics 50(4):507–546
Knedlik T, Von Schweinitz G (2012) Macroeconomic imbalances as indicators for debt crises in Europe. J Common Mark Stud 50(5):726–745
Krugman P (2010) When zombies win. New York Times, December 19, 2010
Lagarde C (2011) Don't let fiscal brakes stall global recovery, The Financial Times, August 15
Laquer W (2012) The Weimar union: Europe, back to the 30s, The New Republic, August 2, 2012, pp. 15–17
Lehndorff S (ed) (2012) A triumph of failed ideas. European models of capitalism in the crisis. European Trade Union Institute (ETUI), Brussels
Leschke J, Theodoropoulou S, Watt A (2011) How do economic governance reforms and austerity measures affect inclusive growth as formulated in the Europe 2020 strategy? In: Lehndorff S (ed) A triumph of failed ideas. European models of capitalism in the crisis. Brussels, European Trade Union Institute (ETUI), pp 244–281
Lucarelli B (2012) German neomercantilism and the European sovereign debt crisis. J Post Keynesian Econ 34(2):205–224
Meusburger P (2013) Relations between knowledge and economic development: some methodological considerations. In: Meusburger P, Glueckler J, Meskioui M (eds) Knowledge and the economy. Springer, Dordrecht, pp 15–42
Müller J-W (2012) Europe's perfect storm: the political and economic consequences of the eurocrisis. Dissent 59(4):47–53

Ntampoudi I (2014) The eurozone crisis and the European union's multiple identity crisis, Paper presented at the UACES Student Forum conference, New Horizons in European Studies, Aston University, Birmingham, 24–25 April 2014
Pérez F, Mas M, Maudos J, Quesada J, Serrano L, Chorén P, Cucarella V, Hernández L, Robledo JC, Solaz M, Soler A (2011) Crecimiento y competitividad, Trajetoria y perspectivas de la economia espanõla. Fondación BBVA, Madrid
Piergiovanni R, Santarelli E, Vivarelli M (1997) From which source do small firm derive their innovative inputs? Some evidence from Italian provinces. Rev Ind Organ 12:243–258
Rodríguez-Pose A (2001) Is R&D investment in lagging areas of Europe worthwhile? Theory and empirical evidence. Pap Reg Sci 80:275–295. doi:10.1007/PL00013631
Rodríguez-Pose A, Di Cataldo M (2015) Quality of government and innovative performance in the regions of Europe. J Econ Geogr 15:673–706
Rodríguez-Pose A, Vilalta-Bufi M (2005) Education, migration and job satisfaction: the regional returns of human capital in the EU. J Econ Geogr 5(5):545–566
Sapir A (2003) An agenda for a growing Europe. Making the EU economic system deliver. Report of an Independent High-Level Study Group established on the initiative of the President of the European Commission. Brussels, European Commission (The Sapir Report)
Scharpf FW (2006) Problem solving effectiveness and democratic accountability in the EU, IHS political science series, vol 107. Institute for Advanced Studies, Vienna
Serricchio F, Tsakatika M, Quaglia L (2013) Euroscepticism and the global financial crisis. J Common Mark Stud 51(1):51–64
Sin C, Veiga A, Amaral A (2016) Analysing European policy implementation: the Bologna process. Palgrave McMillan, London
Streckeisen P (2009) Knowledge society—or contemporary capitalism's fanciest dress. Analyse & Kritik 1:181–197

Alberto Amaral holds a doctorate from Cambridge and is a professor at the University of Porto and a researcher at CIPES—Centre for Research on Higher Education Policies. He was the rector of Porto University from 1985 to 1998, former member of the Executive Board of the Conference of European Rectors, former chair of the Consortium of Higher Education Researchers, former member of IMHE (OECD) and life member of the International Association of University Presidents. At present, he is the chair of the administrative council of the Portuguese Agency for Assessment and Accreditation of Higher Education. Recent books include European Integration and Governance of Higher Education and Research (Springer), Higher Education in Portugal 1974–2009. A Nation, a Generation. (Springer), Quality Assurance in Higher Education. Contemporary Debates (Palgrave), Cross-Border Higher Education and Quality Assurance: Commerce, The Service Directive and Governing Higher Education (Palgrave) and Analysing European Policy Implementation: The Bologna Process (Palgrave).

MIX
Papier aus verantwortungsvollen Quellen
Paper from responsible sources
FSC® C105338

FSC
www.fsc.org

If you have any concerns about our products,
you can contact us on
ProductSafety@springernature.com

In case Publisher is established outside the EU,
the EU authorized representative is:
Springer Nature Customer Service Center GmbH
Europaplatz 3, 69115 Heidelberg, Germany

Printed by Libri Plureos GmbH
in Hamburg, Germany